HEART AFLAME

Foreword by Sinclair B. Ferguson

JOHN
CALVIN

HEART AFLAME

Daily Readings

from Calvin

on the Psalms

P&R
PUBLISHING
P.O. BOX 817 • PHILLIPSBURG • NEW JERSEY 08865-0817

Unless marked by an asterisk, italic Scripture excerpts *preceding* Calvin's exposition are
from the HOLY BIBLE, NEW INTERNATIONAL VERSION®. NIV®. Copyright ©
1973, 1978, 1984 by International Bible Society. Used by permission of Zondervan
Publishing House. All rights reserved. Phrases of Scripture *within* Calvin's exposition
are based on an unidentified older translation, or in rare instances modified to conform
to the NIV excerpts preceding Calvin's exposition.

Page design by Tobias Design
Typesetting by Michelle Feaster

Printed in the United States of America

Library of Congress Cataloging-in-Publication Data

Calvin, Jean, 1509–1564.
    [Commentarius in librum Psalmorum. English. Selections. 1999]
    Heart aflame : daily readings from Calvin on the Psalms / John Calvin ;
foreword by Sinclair B. Ferguson.
       p. cm.
    ISBN 0-87552-458-3 (pbk.)
    1. Bible. O.T. Psalms—Commentaries. 2. Bible. O.T. Psalms—Devotional
literature. 3. Devotional calendars. I. Title.
BS1430.4.C33213 1999
223'.207—dc21   98-50430

FOREWORD

Sinclair B. Ferguson

You may have mixed feelings about a book of daily readings from John Calvin's writings. His name is not the first that comes to the minds of most Christians as the ideal companion to give the wisdom, encouragement, and direction that most of us are looking for each day. We use books like this one to "prime the pump" spiritually, and Calvin's name is not often associated with giving people a "quick start"! Was he not a towering genius, intimidating in his theological acumen, rather than the kind of person whose daily company we might naturally seek?

If those questions are in your mind, I suspect you will experience a delightful surprise as you read through these well-chosen daily meditations. For your companion for the year was not only a man who found the Psalms a mineral-rich quarry of theology, but someone who discovered his own experience mirrored in them. You will find him to be a sure-footed and wise guide, and I suspect you will come to love him—as well as the Psalms—better before the year is ended.

Calvin vividly described the Psalms as "an anatomy of all the parts of the soul." The description is a very apt one, since every experience, every emotion, all the heights and depths, all the joys and sorrows, all the mysteries of human life, are here.

To the reading of the Psalms (and to the rest of Scripture, for that matter), Calvin brought a remarkable gift. He possessed a skill in biblical understanding and spiritual intelligence akin to that of a brilliant medical diagnostician: an uncanny knack of seeing the real issue—an unlearnable combination of understanding, logic, sensitivity, and illumination.

In fact, as Calvin tells us in rare autobiographical comment in the introduction to his *Commentary on the Psalms* (from which this material is drawn), shortly after his own conversion people were flocking to him asking him to explain the message of the Scriptures:

Before a year had passed, all who had a desire for purer doctrine were continually coming to me to learn—although I myself was just a mere novice and tyro!

In later life, as pastor-theologian in Geneva, Calvin was preaching and lecturing so many times each week, and maintaining such a huge correspondence as well as a strenuous personal ministry, that it is clear his preparation time must have been minimal. Yet, his tremendous knowledge of the Scriptures, his gift of illumination, and the depth of his personal experience combined—as in this material on the Psalms—to enable him to give his people (and now us) rich treasures of biblical exposition.

So, at least in my own view, in these pages you will find the Spirit-inspired biblical anatomy of the Psalms and the hands of an outstanding physician and surgeon of the spirit. Reading them on a daily basis can hardly fail to bring you spiritual health and strength.

There are several reasons why this devotional book deserves an enthusiastic welcome.

First of all, these select comments from Calvin's much larger work will take you through the book of Psalms in an orderly fashion. The Psalter used to be the basic diet of Christians. In many churches for centuries the Psalms were the only items of praise. Believers would sing them daily at home around the table. Almost without thinking about what they were doing, they were hiding God's Word in their hearts and learning not to sin against him; it was a lamp to their feet, a light to their path (Ps. 119:11, 105). That kind of knowledge of Scripture is now unusual among God's people, and we are weaker and poorer for it. If all this book did were to encourage us to read the Psalms on a daily basis, it would be worth its weight in gold.

Second, Calvin's own exposition of the Psalms is remarkable in the way in which he follows the flow of the text, seems to catch the developments in it, and leads us with deceptive simplicity from statement to statement. He does not leap from the text into a story or an illustration; rather, he takes a deep breath and holds it until the truth of a passage, and its application, have been grasped. In our short attention-span age, surrounded by influences that create mental flightiness and an inability to concentrate and meditate, we badly need instructors who will help us to do this.

Third, Calvin knew what he was talking about. In much that is written today by Christian scholars—valuable in the contribution it makes—one gets all too little a sense that they know what the psalmist actually experienced. Literary genres, brilliance of linguistic use, weaving in of earlier biblical material, tracing of patterns—these elements of literary analysis in which contemporary commentators shine fascinate and engage the intellect. But Calvin offers us much more. He spoke of substance more than form and style, for he had sat where David sat, and had experienced hurt where David had hurt.

There is something even more striking about Calvin's exposition. Modern scholars and preachers endeavor to expound the message of the Bible, and preach *on* or *about* the Bible. But Calvin seems to come to us *from within the Bible*, from inside the reality described in the text. He had learned the meaning of the command to love God "with all your mind." The result was that God's Word had begun to dwell in him richly (Col. 3:16), and he learned to live his life from within it.

Fourth, Calvin's way of reading the Bible was deeply influenced by Luke's marvelous account of the disciples on the road to Emmaus (Luke 24:13–35). He was gripped by the idea that the whole Bible was somehow related to Christ ("Christ is the scope of all the Scriptures" was how he expressed it). He had meditated long and hard on this, and the fruit of it shows in the natural way in which he brings us to see Christ in all the Scriptures, including the Psalms (cf. Luke 24:44–45).

Shortly before his death in May 1564, and conscious that it could not be long in coming, Calvin dictated a brief letter to William Farel, the long-time colleague and friend who had been instrumental in first bringing him to minister in Geneva. Reflecting the words of Paul in Philippians 1:21, Calvin movingly expressed the deepest longing of his own heart: "It is enough that I live and die for Christ, who is to all his followers a gain both in life and death." A little over three weeks later he breathed his last, leaving his colleague and successor Theodore Beza to write by way of epitaph, "It has pleased God to show us in the life of a single man of our time how to live and how to die."

That is the kind of Christian faith these readings will encourage.

St George's-Tron Church
Glasgow, Scotland

COMPILER'S PREFACE

This book of daily readings contains key portions of John Calvin's *Commentary on the Psalms*. Calvin wrote commentaries on most of the books of the Bible. The Rev. James Anderson, who translated into English the volumes on the Psalms, said of these volumes in June 1845,

> Such is the acuteness of judgment, and success in discovering the mind of the Spirit which distinguish these prelections, that they are not superseded by any modern Commentary on the same subject: and though it is nearly three centuries since they were written, there are few separate works on The Psalms from which the student of the present day, who wishes critically to examine them, will derive more important assistance.

Such volumes are most often found in the libraries of pastors and theological scholars. They are used for in-depth study and exegesis of each psalm or for quick reference.

This book of daily readings, however, makes Calvin's exposition more accessible to the average Christian reader, thereby sharing more widely the varied and splendid riches contained in this treasury of inspired poetry called the Psalms. It offers a faithful rendering of Calvin with only the slightest emendation in order to weave excerpts from larger passages into seamless, concise meditations. The style and language of Anderson's faithful translation of Calvin has been faithfully retained, his English not really too ancient or cumbersome for most readers today.

It did seem a good idea, however, rather than to use the old translation of the Psalms that appears in Calvin's commentary, to use instead the NIV rendering in most cases, with which today's readers are more familiar. In a few instances, marked by an asterisk or brackets, the older Scripture version is retained when Calvin's argument requires that wording, or when the original is more consistent with his tone and sentiment. In such cases a modern translation may have distracted from the clearest sense or departed from Calvin's own way of expressing and illustrating ideas.

Care has been taken not to effect the slightest change in the exact meaning of Calvin's teachings. Therefore alterations in wording, spelling, or punctuation have been kept to the barest minimum, and then only for syntactical purposes. For the most part his commentary has been copied verbatim, with an eye toward extracting only the lessons in Christian faith, doctrinal remarks, and evangelical sentiment from the larger, more technical discussions. Omitted here are discussions such as Calvin's comparing a variety of probable interpretations of the text; or his commenting on the precise grammatical and literal sense and use of certain words and expressions in the Hebrew text; or his giving details of history, customs, and philosophy; or other profound criticisms. Thus the parts left out are mainly those which serve scholars who do critical analysis of the Psalms. As these make up the greater part of the commentary, it seemed best not to clutter the book with ellipsis points to indicate where sentences or passages have been omitted as excerpts have been woven together.

Calvin's own devotion to the Psalms finds expression in the following excerpt from his July 1557 preface to his commentary:

> I have been accustomed to call this book, I think not inappropriately, "An Anatomy of all the Parts of the Soul;" for there is not an emotion of which any one can be conscious that is not here represented as in a mirror. Or rather, the Holy Spirit has here drawn to the life all the griefs, sorrows, fears, doubts, hopes, cares, perplexities, in short, all the distracting emotions with which the minds of men are wont to be agitated. The other parts of Scripture contain the commandments which God enjoined his servants to announce to us. But here the prophets themselves, seeing they are exhibited to us as speaking to God, and laying open all their inmost thoughts and affections, call, or rather draw, each of us to the examination of himself in particular, in order than none of the many infirmities to which we are subject, and of the many vices with which we abound, may remain concealed. . . . We see on the one hand, the flesh manifesting its infirmity; and on the other, faith putting forth its power; and if it is not so valiant and courageous as might be desired, it is at least prepared to fight until by degrees it acquire

perfect strength. But as those things which serve to teach us the true method of praying aright will be found scattered through the whole of this Commentary, I will not now stop to treat of topics which it will be necessary afterwards to repeat, nor detain my readers from proceeding to the work itself. Only it appeared to me to be requisite to show in passing, that this book makes known to us this privilege, which is desirable above all others— that not only is there opened up to us familiar access to God, but also that we have permission and freedom granted to us to lay open before him our infirmities, which we would be ashamed to confess before men. Besides, there is also here prescribed to us an infallible rule for directing us with respect to the right manner of offering to God the sacrifices of praise, which he declares to be most precious in his sight, and of the sweetest odour. There is no other book in which there is to be found more express and magnificent commendations, both of the unparalleled liberality of God towards his Church, and of all his works; there is no other book in which there is recorded so many deliverances, nor one in which the evidences and experiences of the fatherly providence and solicitude which God exercises towards us, are celebrated with such splendour of diction, and yet with the strictest adherence to truth; in short, there is no other book in which we are more perfectly taught the right manner of praising God, or in which we are more powerfully stirred up to the performance of this religious exercise. Moreover, although The Psalms are replete with all the precepts which serve to frame our life to every part of holiness, piety, and righteousness, yet they will principally teach and train us to bear the cross; and the bearing of the cross is a genuine proof of our obedience, since by doing this, we renounce the guidance of our own affections, and submit ourselves entirely to God, leaving him to govern us, and to dispose of our life according to his will, so that the affections which are the bitterest and most severe to our nature, become sweet to us, because they proceed from him. In one word, not only will we here find general commendations of the goodness of God, which may teach men to repose themselves in him alone, and to seek all their happiness solely in him; and which are intended to teach true believers with their whole hearts confidently to look to him for help in all their necessities; but we will also find that the free remission of sins, which alone reconciles God towards us, and procures for us settled peace with him, is so set forth and magnified, as that here there is nothing wanting which relates to the knowledge of eternal salvation.

Day 1 J A N U A R Y 1

Blessed is the man. The meaning of the Psalmist is that it shall be always well with God's devout servants, whose constant endeavour it is to make progress in the study of his law. He teaches us how impossible it is for anyone to apply his mind to meditation upon God's law, who has not first withdrawn and separated himself from the society of the ungodly. It is necessary to remember that the world is fraught with deadly corruption, and that the first step to living well is to renounce the company of the ungodly, otherwise it is sure to infect us with its own pollution.

Who does not walk in the counsel of the wicked, or stand in the way of sinners, or sit in the seat of mockers. Here the Psalmist shows how, little by little, men are ordinarily induced to turn aside from the right path. When a person willingly *walks* after the gratification of his corrupt lusts, the practice of sinning so infatuates him, that, forgetful of himself, he grows hardened in wickedness; and this the prophet terms *standing in the way of sinners.* Then at length follows a desperate obstinacy, which he expresses by the figure of *sitting.*

But his delight is in the law of the LORD. The Psalmist does not simply pronounce those happy who fear God, but designates godliness by the *study of the law,* teaching us that God is only rightly served when his law is obeyed. It is not left to every man to frame a system of religion according to his own judgment, but the standard of godliness is to be taken from the Word of God. From his characterising the godly as *delighting* in the law of the Lord, we may learn that forced or servile obedience is not at all acceptable to God, and that those only are worthy students of the law who come to it with a cheerful mind, and are so delighted with its instructions, as to account nothing more desirable or delicious than to make progress therein. From this love of the law proceeds constant *meditation* on it.

PSALM 1:3-6

The Psalmist shows in what respect those who fear God are to be accounted happy, namely, not because they enjoy an evanescent and empty gladness, but because they are in a desirable condition. It is the blessing of God alone which preserves any in a prosperous condition.

He is like a tree planted by streams of water, which yields its fruit in season and whose leaf does not wither. Whatever he does prospers. With the figure of the faithful *bringing forth their fruit in season*, the Psalmist meant that the children of God constantly flourish. They are always watered with the secret influences of divine grace, so that whatever may happen to them is conducive to their salvation. On the other hand, the ungodly are carried away by the sudden tempest or consumed by the scorching heat. He expresses the full maturity of the fruit produced, whereas, although the ungodly may present the appearance of precocious fruitfulness, yet they produce nothing that comes to perfection.

Not so the wicked! They are like chaff that the wind blows away. The Psalmist's mind is seriously pondering on the destruction which awaits the ungodly, and will at length overtake them. The meaning, therefore, is, although the ungodly now live prosperously, yet by and by they shall be like chaff; for when the Lord has brought them low, he shall scatter them with the blast of his wrath.

For the LORD watches over the way of the righteous, but the way of the wicked will perish. The prophet teaches that a happy life depends on a good conscience. We now see how the Psalmist pronounces the ungodly to be miserable because happiness is the inward blessing of a good conscience. God is the Judge of the world. Granting this, it follows that it cannot but be well with the upright and the just, while, on the other hand, the most terrible destruction must impend over the ungodly. Instead, therefore, of allowing ourselves to be deceived with their imaginary felicity, let us, in circumstances of distress, have ever before our eyes the providence of God, to whom it belongs to settle the affairs of the world, and to bring order out of confusion.

Day 3

Why do the nations conspire and the peoples plot in vain?
We know how many conspired against David, and endeavoured to prevent his coming to the throne, but David was thoroughly persuaded that he had been made king by divine appointment. He encouraged himself by strong confidence in God against the whole world as he nobly poured contempt both on kings and their armies, because they waged war, not against mortal man, but against God himself. The ground of such confidence was that he only followed the call of God. From this he concluded that in his person, God was assailed; and God could not but show himself the defender of the kingdom of which he was the founder. God principally proves his faithfulness in this, that he does not forsake the work of his own hands, but continually defends those whom he has once received into his favour.

By honouring himself with the title of the Anointed, David declares that he reigned only by the authority and command of God. That he prophesied concerning Christ, is clearly manifest from this, that he knew his own kingdom to be merely a shadow. Those things which David testified concerning his own kingdom are properly applicable to Christ.

Let this, therefore, be held as a settled point, that all who do not submit themselves to the authority of Christ make war against God. Since it seems good to God to rule by the hand of his own Son, those who refuse to obey Christ himself deny the authority of God, and it is vain for them to profess otherwise.

Wicked men may now conduct themselves as wickedly as they please, but they shall at length feel what it is to make war against heaven. God is so far exalted above the men of this world, that the whole mass of them could not possibly obscure his glory in the least degree. As often, then, as the power of man appears formidable to us, let us remember how much it is transcended by the power of God. In these words there is set before us the unchangeable and eternal purpose of God effectually to defend the kingdom of his Son, of which he is the founder; and this may well support our faith amid the troublous storms of the world. Whatever plots, therefore, men may form against it, let this one consideration be sufficient to satisfy us, that they cannot render ineffectual the anointing of God.

PSALM 2:7

He said to me, "You are my Son; today I have become your Father." David, indeed, could with propriety be called the son of God, on account of his royal dignity, just as we know that princes, because they are elevated above others, are called both gods and the sons of God. But here God, by the singularly high title with which he honours David, exalts him not only above all mortal men, but even above the angels. This the apostle (Heb. 1:5) wisely and diligently considers, when he tells us this language was never used with respect to any of the angels. David, individually considered, was inferior to the angles, but in so far as he represented the person of Christ, he is with very good reason preferred far above them. By the Son of God in this place we are therefore not to understand one son among many, but his only begotten Son, Christ Jesus, that he alone should have pre-eminence both in heaven and on earth.

When God says, *I have become your Father* or *I have begotten you*, it ought to be understood as referring to men's understanding or knowledge of it; for David was begotten by God when the choice of him to be king was clearly manifested. The same explanation is to be given of the words as applied to Christ. He is not said to be begotten in any other sense than as the Father bore testimony to him as being his own Son. It is not implied that he then began to be the Son of God, but that his being so was then made manifest to the world.

Finally, this begetting ought not to be understood of the mutual love which exists between the Father and the Son; it only signifies that he who had been hidden from the beginning in the sacred bosom of the Father, and who afterwards had been obscurely shadowed forth under the law, was known to be the Son of God from the time when he came forth with authentic and evident marks of Sonship, according to what is said in John 1:14, "We have seen his glory, as of the only begotten of the Father."

Ask of me, and I will make the nations your inheritance, the ends of the earth your possession. The Father will deny nothing to his Son which relates to the extension of his kingdom to the uttermost ends of the earth. Christ collects the dispersed remnants of his people from all quarters and keeps them joined together by the sacred bond of faith, so that not one corner only, but the whole world, is subjected to his authority.

PSALM 2:8-12

Therefore, you kings, be wise; be warned you rulers of the earth. David does not even spare kings or rulers themselves, who seem unrestrained by laws, and exempted from ordinary rules. Much more does his exhortation apply to the common class of men, in order that all, from the highest to the lowest, may humble themselves before God. A speedy repentance is necessary, since they will not always be favoured with the like opportunity. David says *be wise.* The beginning of true wisdom is when a man lays aside his pride, and submits himself to the authority of Christ and serves him with fear. This service is not grievous, but pleasant and desirable, since it furnishes matter of true gladness. The only true and salutary joy is that which arises from resting in the fear and reverence of God.

Kiss the Son, lest he be angry and you be destroyed in your way. Since it is the will of God to reign by the hand of his Son, and since he has engraven on his person the marks and insignia of his own glory, the proper proof of our obedience and piety towards him is reverently to embrace his Son, whom he has appointed king over us. The term *kiss* refers to the solemn token or sign of honour which subjects were accustomed to yield to their sovereigns.

God is defrauded of his honour if he is not served in Christ. The ungodly is warned that the wrath of God will cut them off when they think themselves to be only in the middle of their race. But David, in the end encourages God's faithful and devout servants to entertain good hope, by setting forth the sweetness of his grace. As believers might have applied the severity of which he makes mention, he opens to them a sanctuary of hope, where they may flee, in order not to be overwhelmed by the terror of God's wrath.

PSALM 3

O LORD, *how many are my foes!* How bitter David's sorrow was under the conspiracy of his own household against him, which arose from the treachery of his own son, it is easy for every one of us to conjecture from the feelings of nature. And when, in addition to this, he knew that this disaster was brought upon him by God for his own fault in having defiled another man's wife, and for shedding innocent blood, he might have sunk into despair, and been overwhelmed with anguish, if he had not been encouraged by the promise of God, and thus hoped for life even in death.

From his making no allusion here to his sins, we are led to infer that only one part of his prayers is comprised in this psalm. Since God punished him expressly on account of his adultery, and his wicked treachery towards Uriah, there can be no doubt that he was at first distressed with grievous and dreadful torments of mind. But after he had humbled himself before God, he took courage; and being well assured of having obtained forgiveness, he was fully persuaded that God was on his side, and knew that he would always preside over his kingdom, and show himself its protector.

If at any time God makes use of wicked and mischievous men, as scourges to chastise us, it becomes us first diligently to consider the cause, namely, that we suffer nothing which we have not deserved, in order that this reflection may lead us to repentance. But if our enemies, in persecuting us, rather fight against God than against us, let the consideration of their doing so be immediately followed by the confident persuasion of our safety under the protection of him, whose grace, which he has promised to us, they despise and trample under foot. As the power of God is infinite, it shall be invincible against all assaults, outrages, preparations, and forces of the whole world. And, indeed, unless we ascribe this honour to God, our courage shall be always failing us.

From the LORD *comes deliverance.* Salvation or deliverance is only in the hands of God. The Church shall always be delivered from the calamities which befall her, because God, who is able to save her, will never withdraw his grace and blessing from her.

PSALM 4

How long, O men, will you turn my glory into shame? While nothing is more painful to us than to be falsely condemned, and to endure, at one and the same time, wrongful violence and slander; yet to be ill spoken of for doing well, is an affliction which daily befalls the saints. When a man not only keeps himself from revenging the injuries which he has received, but endeavours to overcome evil by doing good, he manifests one of the graces of a renewed and sanctified nature and in this way proves himself to be one of the children of God; for such meekness proceeds only from the Spirit of adoption. If at any time our uprightness is not seen and acknowledged by the world, we ought not on that account to despond, inasmuch as we have one in heaven to vindicate our cause. If, therefore, we cannot find justice anywhere in the world, the only support of our patience is to look to God, and to rest contented with the equity of his judgment.

Commune with your heart upon your bed, and be still.* Here we learn that, in solitude we can give to any subject a closer attention. David, therefore, exhorts his enemies to withdraw and to be alone, that they may examine themselves more truthfully and honestly. There is nothing to which men are more prone than to deceive one another with empty applause, until each man enter into himself, and commune alone with his own heart.

You have filled my heart with greater joy than when their grain and new wine abound. The faithful, forming a low estimate of present good things, rest in God alone, and account nothing of more value than to know from experience that they are interested in his favour. Those only can be truly and perfectly happy who are interested in the favour of God, and they ought to live as strangers and pilgrims in the world, in order through hope and patience to obtain, in due time, a better life. Although the faithful also desire and seek after their worldly comforts, yet they do not pursue them with immoderate and irregular ardour; but can patiently bear to be deprived of them, provided they know themselves to be objects of the divine care. David justly prefers the joy produced by the light of God's fatherly love before all other objects.

PSALM 5

In the morning, O LORD, you hear my voice; in the morning I lay my request before you and wait in expectation. David says, that after he had unburdened his cares into the bosom of God, he would, with an anxious mind, look out, as it were, like a sentinel, until it should appear, that indeed God had heard him. No doubt, in the exercise of longing, there is always implied some degree of uneasiness; but he who is looking out for the grace of God with anxious desire, will patiently wait for it. Here we see the uselessness of those prayers to which there is not added that hope which may be said to elevate the minds of the petitioners into a watch-tower.

But I, by your great mercy, will come into your house. David encourages himself in the assured hope of preservation from the mercy of God; but at the same time he shows, that upon obtaining deliverance, he will be grateful to God for it, and keep it in remembrance. It is only through the goodness of God that we have access to him; and that no man prays aright but he who, having experienced his grace, believes and is fully persuaded that he will be merciful to him.

But let all who take refuge in you be glad; let them ever sing for joy. We are ungrateful to God if we do not take encouragement and comfort from whatever blessings he confers upon our neighbours, since by these he testifies that he will always be ready to bestow his goodness upon all the godly in common. The remembrance of God must be sweet to us, and fill our hearts with joy, or rather ravish us with love to him after he has caused us to taste of his goodness.

For surely, O LORD, you bless the righteous. The word, *to bless*, signifies, as the act of God, the same thing as to prosper a man, or to enrich him abundantly with all good things; for since the favour of God is efficacious, his blessing of itself produces an abundance of every good thing. Those who are called righteous in Scripture, are not so called on account of the merit of their works, but because they aspire after righteousness; for after God has received them into his favour, by not imputing their sins to them, he accepts their upright endeavours for perfect righteousness.

O LORD, do not rebuke me in your anger or discipline me in your wrath. Men, when they are compelled to feel that God is angry with them, often indulge in complaints full of impiety, rather than find fault with themselves and their own sins. It is to be particularly noticed that David does not simply ascribe to God the afflictions under which he is now suffering, but acknowledges them to be the just recompense of his sins. He does not take God to task as if he had been an enemy, treating him with cruelty without any just cause; but yielding to him the right of rebuking and chastening. He desires and prays only that bounds may be set to the punishment inflicted on him. By this he declares God to be a just Judge, in taking vengeance on the sins of men. As often, then, as we are pressed down by adversity, let us learn, from the example of David, to have recourse to this remedy, that we may be brought into a state of peace with God; for it is not to be expected that it can be well or prosperous with us if we are not interested in his favour. Whence it follows, that we shall never be without a load of evils, until he forgives our sins.

How long, O LORD, how long? God, in his compassion towards us, permits us to pray to him to make haste to succour us; but when we have freely complained of his long delay, that our prayers or sorrow on this account may not pass beyond bounds, we must submit our case entirely to his will, and not wish him to make greater haste than shall seem good to him.

The LORD has heard my cry for mercy. The grace of God is the only light of life to the godly; and, as soon as he has manifested some token of his anger, they are not only greatly afraid, but also, as it were, plunged into the darkness of death; while, on the other hand, as soon as they discover anew that God is merciful to them, they are immediately restored to life. There is nothing in the whole world, whatever it may be, and whatever opposition it may make to us, which we may not despise, if we are fully persuaded of our being beloved by God; and by this also we understand what his fatherly love can do for us.

O LORD my God, I take refuge in you; save and deliver me from all who pursue me. David constantly entertained confidence in God in his afflictions. This is a genuine and an undoubted proof of our faith, when, being visited with adversity, we, notwithstanding, persevere in cherishing and exercising hope in God. The gate of mercy is shut against our prayers if the key of faith do not open it for us.

If I have done this and there is guilt on my hands. David, by entreating God to succour him upon no other condition than this, that his integrity should upon trial be found to be untarnished, teaches us by his example, that as often as we have recourse to God, we must make it our first care to be well assured in our own consciences with respect to the righteousness of our cause; for we do him great wrong if we wish to engage him as the advocate and defender of a bad cause. Since God is no respecter of persons, we cannot expect him to be on our side, and to favour us, if our cause is not good.

Awake, my God; decree justice. We should in everything conform our requests to the divine will. We can never pray in faith unless we attend to what God commands, that our minds may not rashly and at random start aside in desiring more than we are permitted to desire and pray for. David, therefore, in order to pray aright, reposes himself on the word and promise of God.

His violence comes down on his own head. However skilled in craft our enemies may be, and whatever means of doing mischief they may have, we must nevertheless look for the issue which God here promises, that they shall fall by their own sword. And this is not a thing which happens by chance; but God, by the secret direction of his own hand, causes the evil which they intend to bring upon the innocent to return upon their own heads.

I will give thanks to the LORD because of his righteousness. God does not shut up or conceal his righteousness from our view in the secret recesses of his own mind, but manifests it for our advantage when he defends us against all wrongful violence, delivers us from oppression, and preserves us in safety, although wicked men make war upon us and persecute us.

Day 11 JANUARY 11

O Lord, our Lord, how majestic is your name in all the earth! David sets before his eyes the wonderful power and glory of God in the creation and government of the material universe. There is presented to us in the whole order of nature, the most abundant matter for sharing forth the glory of God, but, as we are unquestionably more powerfully affected with what we ourselves experience, David here, with great propriety, expressly celebrates the special favour which God manifests towards mankind; for this, of all the subjects which come under our contemplation, is the brightest mirror in which we can behold his glory. David, when reflecting on the incomprehensible goodness which God has been graciously pleased to bestow on the human race, and feeling all his thoughts and senses swallowed up, and overwhelmed in the contemplation, exclaims that it is a subject worthy of admiration, because it cannot be set forth in words.

PSALM 8:1-2

From the lips of children and infants you have ordained praise. David declares that the providence of God, in order to make itself known to mankind, does not wait till men arrive at the age of maturity, but even from the very dawn of infancy shines forth so brightly as is sufficient to confute all the ungodly, who, through their profane contempt of God, would wish to extinguish his very name. He says that babes and sucklings are advocates sufficiently powerful to vindicate the providence of God. Whence is it that nourishment is ready for them as soon as they are born, but because God wonderfully changes blood into milk? Whence, also, have they the skill to suck, but because the same God has, by a mysterious instinct, fitted their tongues for doing so? David, therefore, has the best reason for declaring, that although the tongues of all, who have arrived at the age of manhood, should become silent, the speechless mouth of infants is sufficiently able to celebrate the praise of God. And when he not only introduces babes as witnesses and preachers of God's glory, but also attributes *mature strength* to their mouth, the expression is very emphatic. In other words, so early as the generation or birth of man, the splendour of Divine Providence is so apparent, that even infants, who hang upon their mothers' breasts, can bring down to the ground the fury of the enemies of God.

PSALM 8:3-5

What is man that you are mindful of him, the son of man that you care for him? God's wonderful goodness is displayed the more brightly in that so glorious a Creator, whose majesty shines resplendently in the heavens, graciously condescends to adorn a creature so miserable and vile as man is with the greatest glory, and to enrich him with numberless blessings. Whoever, therefore, is not astonished and deeply affected at this miracle, is more than ungrateful and stupid. When it is said, God is *mindful of man*, it signifies the same thing as that he bears towards him a fatherly love, defends and cherishes him, and extends his providence towards him.

You made him a little lower than the heavenly beings and crowned him with glory and honor. The Psalmist represents man as adorned with so many honours as to render their condition not far inferior to divine and celestial glory. He, no doubt, intends the distinguished endowments which clearly manifest that men were formed after the image of God, and created to the hope of a blessed and immortal life. The reason with which they are endued, and by which they can distinguish between good and evil; the principle of religion which is planted in them; their intercourse with each other, which is preserved from being broken up by certain sacred bonds; the regard to what is becoming, and the sense of shame which guilt awakens in them, as well as their continuing to be governed by laws; all these things are clear indications of pre-eminent and celestial wisdom. What David here relates belongs properly to the beginning of the creation, when man's nature was perfect. But we know that, by the fall of Adam, all mankind fell from their primeval state of integrity, for by this the image of God was almost entirely effaced from us. From a state of the highest excellence, we were reduced to a condition of wretched and shameful destitution. But as the heavenly Father has bestowed upon his Son an immeasurable fullness of all blessings, that all of us may draw from this fountain, it follows that whatever God bestows on us by him belongs of right to him in the highest degree; yea, he himself is the living image of God, according to which we must be renewed, upon which depends our participation of the invaluable blessings which are here spoken of. These gifts proceed from the free grace of God.

Day 13 JANUARY 13

You made him ruler over the works of your hands. From the dominion over all things which God has conferred upon men, it is evident how great is the love which he has borne towards them, and how much account he has made of them. As he does not stand in need of any thing himself, he has destined all the riches, both of heaven and earth, for their use. It is certainly a singular honour and one which cannot be sufficiently estimated, that mortal man, as the representative of God, has dominion over the world, as if it pertained to him by right, and that to whatever quarter he turns his eyes, he sees nothing wanting which may contribute to the convenience and happiness of his life. Now, there is no doubt, that if there is any thing in heaven or on earth which is opposed to men, the beautiful order which God had established in the world at the beginning is now thrown into confusion. The consequence of this is, that mankind, after they were ruined by the fall of Adam, were not only deprived of so distinguished and honourable an estate, and dispossessed of their former dominion, but are also held captive under a degrading and ignominious bondage. Christ, it is true, is the lawful heir of heaven and earth, by whom the faithful recover what they had lost in Adam; but he has not as yet actually entered upon the full possession of his empire and dominion. What is here said by David will not be perfectly accomplished until death be abolished. There remains the hope of a better state than the present.

All flocks and herds, and the beasts of the field. It is by the wonderful providence of God that horses and oxen yield their service to men,—that sheep produce wool to clothe them,—and that all sorts of animals supply them with food for their nourishment and support, even from their own flesh. And the more that this dominion is apparent, the more ought we to be affected with a sense of the goodness and grace of our God as often as we either eat food, or enjoy any of the other comforts of life.

PSALM 9:1

I will praise you, O LORD, with all my heart. As God continues his favour towards his own people without intermission, all the good he has hitherto done to us should serve to inspire us with confidence and hope, that he will be gracious and merciful to us in the time to come. There is, indeed, in these words a profession of gratitude for the favours which David has received from God; but, in remembering his past mercies, he encourages himself to expect succour and aid in future emergencies; and by this means he opens the gate of prayer. *The whole heart* is taken for an upright or sincere heart, which is opposed to a double heart. Thus he distinguishes himself not only from gross hypocrites, who praise God only with their lips outwardly, without having their hearts in any way affected, but also acknowledges that whatever he had hitherto done which was commendable, proceeded entirely from the pure grace of God. Even irreligious men, when they have obtained some memorable victory, are ashamed to defraud God of the praise which is due to him; but we see that as soon as they have uttered a single expression in acknowledgement of the assistance God has afforded them, they immediately begin to boast loudly, and to sing triumphs in honour of their own valour, as if they were under no obligations whatever to God. In short, it is a piece of pure mockery when they profess that their exploits have been done by the help of God; for, after having made oblation to him they sacrifice to their own counsels, skill, courage, and resources. David affirms that he is unlike the children of this world, whose hypocrisy or fraud is discovered by the wicked and dishonest distribution which they make between God and themselves, arrogating to themselves the greater part of the praise which they pretended to ascribe to God. He praised God with his whole heart, which they did not; for certainly it is not praising God with the whole heart when a mortal man dares to appropriate the smallest portion of the glory which God claims for himself. God cannot bear with seeing his glory appropriated by the creature in even the smallest degree, so intolerable to him is the sacrilegious arrogance of those who, by praising themselves, obscure his glory as far as they can.

PSALM
9:1-2

I will tell of all your wonders. David applies the term *won-ders* not to all the benefits which he had received from God, but to those more signal and memorable deliverances in which was exhibited a bright and striking manifestation of the divine power. God would have us to acknowledge him as the author of all our blessings; but on some of his gifts he has engraven more evident marks in order the more effectually to awaken our senses, which are otherwise as if asleep or dead. David's language, therefore, is an acknowledgement that he was preserved of God, not by ordinary means, but by the spe-cial power of God, which was conspicuously displayed in this matter; inasmuch as he had stretched forth his hand in a miraculous manner, and above the common and usual way.

I will be glad and rejoice in you. Observe how the faithful praise God sincerely and without hypocrisy, when they do not rest on themselves for happiness, and are not intoxicated with foolish and carnal presumption, but rejoice in God alone; which is nothing else than to seek the matter of their joy from the favour of God, and from no other source, since in it perfect happiness consists. We ought to consider how great is the differ-ence and opposition between the character of the joy which men endeavour to find in themselves, and the character of the joy which they seek in God. David, the more forcibly to express how he renounces every thing which may keep hold of or occupy him with vain delight, adds the word *exult,* by which he means that he finds in God a full and an over-flowing abundance of joy, so that he is not under the necessity of seeking even the smallest drop in any other quarter. Moreover, it is of importance to remember that David sets before himself the testimonies of the divine goodness which he had formerly experienced, in order to encourage him-self with the more alacrity to lay open his heart to God, and to present his prayers before him. He who begins his prayer by affirming that God is the great source and object of his joy, fortifies himself before-hand with the strongest confidence, in presenting his supplications to the hearer of prayer.

PSALM 93-5

My enemies turn back: they fall down and are put to flight at your presence.* In these words he assigns the reason why he undertakes to sing the praises of God, namely, because he acknowledges that his frequent victories had been achieved, not by his own power, nor by the power of his soldiers, but by the free favour of God. David acted wisely, when, upon seeing his enemies turn their backs, he lifted up the eyes of his mind to God, in order to perceive that victory flowed to him from no other source than from the secret and incomprehensible aid of God. And, doubtless, it is he only who guides the simple by the spirit of wisdom, while he inflicts madness on the crafty, and strikes them with amazement,—who inspires with courage the faint and timid, while he causes the boldest to tremble with fear,—who restores to the feeble their strength, while he reduces the strong to weakness,—who upholds the fainthearted by his power, while he makes the sword to fall from the hands of the valiant;—and, finally, who brings the battle to a prosperous or disastrous issue, just as he pleases. When, therefore, we see our enemies overthrown, we must beware of limiting our view to what is visible to the eye of sense, like ungodly men, who, while they see with their bodily eyes, are yet blind; but let us instantly call to our remembrance this truth, that when our enemies turn back, they are put to flight by the presence of the Lord.

You have blotted out their name for ever and ever. This may be understood as meaning, that they were destroyed without any hope of ever being able to rise again, and devoted to everlasting shame. We could not otherwise discern how God buries the name of the ungodly with themselves, did we not hear him declare that the memory of the righteous shall be for ever blessed (Prov. 10:7).

PSALM 9:6-9

He has established his throne for judgment. As often as nothing but destruction presents itself to our view, to whatever side we may turn, let us remember to lift up our eyes to the heavenly throne, whence God beholds all that is done here below. In the world our affairs may have been brought to such an extremity, that there is no longer hope in regard to them; but the shield with which we ought to repel all the temptations by which we are assailed is this, that God, nevertheless, sits Judge in heaven. Yea, when he seems to take no notice of us, and does not immediately remedy the evils which we suffer, it becomes us to realise by faith his secret providence. The Psalmist says, in the first place, *God sits forever*, by which he means, that however high the violence of men may be carried, and although their fury may burst forth without measure, they can never drag God from his seat. He farther means by this expression, that it is impossible for God to abdicate the office and authority of judge.

The LORD is a refuge for the oppressed. God delays his aid, and to outward appearance forsakes his faithful ones, in order at length to succour them at a more convenient season, according to the greatness of their necessity and affliction. From this it follows, that he by no means ceases from the exercise of his office, although he suffer the good and the innocent to be reduced to extreme poverty, and although he exercise them with weeping and lamentations; for by doing this he lights up a lamp to enable them to see his judgments the more clearly.

A stronghold in times of trouble. From this we are taught the duty of giving his providence time to make itself at length manifest in the season of need. And if protection by the power of God, and the experience of his fatherly favour, is the greatest blessing which we can receive, let us not feel so uneasy at being accounted poor and miserable before the world, but let this consolatory consideration assuage our grief, that God is not far from us, seeing our afflictions call upon him to come to our aid.

Those who know your name will trust in you. When the Lord delivers the righteous, the fruit which results from it is, that they themselves, and all the rest of the righteous, acquire increasing confidence in his grace; for, unless we are fully persuaded that God exercises a care about men and human affairs, we must necessarily be troubled with constant disquietude.

Where there is no godliness, there is no sense of the works of God. David attributes to the faithful *the knowledge of God.* Many take the *name of God* simply for God himself; but something more is expressed by this term. As God's essence is hidden and incomprehensible, his name just means his character, as far as he has been pleased to make it known to us.

Sing praises to the LORD. It is not enough for persons to honour and reverence some deity indiscriminately or at random; they must distinctly yield to the only living and true God the worship which belongs to him, and which he commands. Let us be fully persuaded, that wherever the faithful, who worship him purely and in due form, according to the appointment of his word, are assembled together to engage in the solemn acts of religious worship, he is graciously present, and presides in the midst of them.

For he who avenges blood remembers; he does not ignore the cry of the afflicted. There is here a repetition of what the Psalmist had said a little before, that we ought especially to consider God's power, as it is manifested in the mercy which he exercises towards his servants, who are unrighteously persecuted by wicked men. From the numerous works of God, he selects one which he commends as especially worthy of being remembered, namely, his work in delivering the poor from death. God sometimes leaves them in his holy providence to be persecuted by men; but at length he takes vengeance for the wrongs inflicted upon them. God requires innocent blood and remembers the cry of his people. If we measure the help of God according to our senses, our courage will ever and anon fail us, and in the end our hope will be entirely extinguished, and will give place to despondency and despair.

Let this consolatory consideration, however, sustain us, that he will at length actually show how precious our blood was in his sight.

PSALM
9:17-20

The wicked return to the grave, all the nations that forget God. Here is described to us the sudden and unexpected change, by which God, when he pleases, restores to order things which were in confusion. When, therefore, we see the wicked flying aloft devoid of all fear, let us, by the eyes of faith, behold the grave which is prepared for them; and rest assured that the hand of God, although it is unseen, is very near, which can turn them back in the midst of their course in which they aim at reaching heaven, and make them tumble into hell in a moment.

But the needy will not always be forgotten, nor the hope of the afflicted ever perish. The faithful, also, it is true, descend into the grave, but not with such fearful violence as plunges them into it without hope of coming out again. So far is this from being the case, that even when shut up in the grave, they dwell already in heaven by hope. David speaks expressly of *hope* or *expectation,* thereby to encourage us to prayer. The reason why God seems to take no notice of our afflictions is, because he would have us to awaken him by means of our prayers; for when he hears our requests, (as if he began but then to be mindful of us,) he stretches forth his powerful hand to help us. David again repeats that this is not done immediately, in order that we may persevere in hoping well, even although our expectations may not be instantly gratified.

Strike them with terror, O LORD; let the nations know they are but men. God commonly subdues even his chosen ones to obedience by means of fear. But as he moderates his rigour towards them, and, at the same time, softens their stony hearts, so that they willingly and quietly submit themselves to him, he cannot be properly said to compel them by fear. With respect to the reprobate, he takes a different way of dealing. As their obduracy is inflexible, so that it is easier to break than to bend them, he subdues their desperate obstinacy by force; not, indeed, that they are reformed, but, whether they will or not, an acknowledgement of their own weakness is extorted from them. Augustine has well and wisely said, that the whole humility of man consists in the knowledge of himself.

PSALM 10:1-4

Why, O LORD, do you stand far off? Although David here complains that God kept himself afar off, he was, notwithstanding, fully persuaded of his presence with him, otherwise it would have been in vain to have called upon him for aid.

In his arrogance the wicked man hunts down the weak. Pride is the mother of all wrongs; for if a man did not through pride magnify himself above his neighbours, and through an overweening conceit of himself despise them, even common humanity would teach us with what humility and justice we ought to conduct ourselves towards each other. Let everyone, therefore, who desires to live justly and unblameably with his brethren, beware of indulging or taking pleasure in treating others disdainfully; and let him endeavour, above all things, to have his mind freed from the disease of pride.

In his pride the wicked does not seek him; in all his thoughts there is no room for God. David teaches that the cause of the careless indulgence of the ungodly in the gratification of their lusts, is their base contempt of God. He who duly reflects that God will be his judge, is so much alarmed by this reflection, that he dares not bless his soul while his conscience accuses him of guilt and of being given to the practice of sin. The ungodly, without examination, permit themselves to do any thing, or do not distinguish between what is lawful and unlawful, because their own lust is their law, yea, rather, as if superior to all laws, they fancy that it is lawful for them to do whatever they please. The beginning of well-doing in a man's life is inquiry; in other words, we can only begin to do well when we keep ourselves from following, without choice and discrimination, the dictates of our own fancy, and from being carried away by the wayward propensities of our flesh. But the exercise of inquiring proceeds from humility, when we assign to God, as is reasonable, the place of judge and ruler over us.

Whoever refuses to admit that the world is subject to the providence of God, or do not believe that his hand is stretched forth from on high to govern it, do as much as in them lies to put an end to the existence of God. It is not, however, enough to have some cold and unimpressive knowledge of him in the head; it is only the true and heartfelt conviction of his providence which makes us reverence him, and which keeps us in subjection to him.

His ways are always prosperous; he is haughty and your laws are far from him. As the wicked enjoy a continued course of prosperity, they dream that God is bound or plighted to them, and hence they put his judgments far from them; and if any man oppose them, they are confident they can immediately put him down, or dash him to pieces with a puff or breath. Now, we understand the simple meaning of the prophet to be, that the ungodly mock God, taking encouragement from his forbearance; as that base tyrant, Dionysius, because he had a prosperous voyage, after having plundered the temple of Proserpine, boasted that God favoured the sacrilegious. Hence it is, that they put far from them the judgments of God.

Presuming upon the great distance of God from them, they promise themselves not only at truce with death during their whole life, but also an everlasting covenant with it. We see how, by procrastinating the evil day, they harden themselves, and become more and more obstinate in evil; yes, persuading themselves that God is shut up in heaven, as if they had nothing to do with him, they strengthen themselves in the hope of escaping unpunished.

He says to himself, "Nothing shall shake me; I'll always be happy and never have trouble." There is a very great difference between a despiser of God who, enjoying prosperity today, is so forgetful of the condition of man in this world, as through a distempered imagination to build his nest above the clouds, and who persuades himself that he shall always enjoy comfort and repose, —there is a very great difference between him and the godly man, who, knowing that his life hangs only by a thread, and is encompassed by a thousand deaths, and who, ready to endure any kind of afflictions which shall be sent upon him, and living in the world as if he were sailing upon a tempestuous and dangerous sea, nevertheless, bears patiently all his troubles and sorrows, and comforts himself in his afflictions, because he leans wholly upon the grace of God, and entirely confides in it. The ungodly man thinks himself sufficiently strong and powerful to bear up against all the assaults which shall be made upon him. The faithful man says that although he may even fall and sink into the lowest depths, his fall will not be fatal, for God will put his hand under him to sustain him.

PSALM 10:11-18

He says to himself, "God has forgotten; he covers his face and never sees." The ungodly, when all things happen to them according to their wishes, form such a judgment of their prosperity as to persuade themselves that God is in a manner bound or obliged to them. Whence it comes to pass, that they live in a state of constant security, because they do not reflect, that after God has long exercised patience towards them, they will undergo a solemn reckoning, and that their condemnation will be the more terrible, the greater the long-suffering of God.

Why does the wicked man revile God? It is, indeed, superfluous to bring arguments before God, for the purpose of persuading him to grant us what we ask; but still he permits us to make use of them, and to speak to him in prayer, as familiarly as a son speaks to an earthly father. It should always be observed, that the use of praying is, that God may be the witness of all our affections; not that they would otherwise be hidden from him, but when we pour out our hearts before him, our cares are hereby greatly lightened, and our confidence of obtaining our requests increases. Since it is the peculiar province of God to take cognisance of all wrongs, David says that it is impossible for God to shut his eyes when the ungodly are wrecklessly and without restraint committing their outrages.

The LORD *is King for ever and ever.* By the title of *King*, David vindicates God's claim to the government of the world, and when he describes him as *King for ever and ever*, this shows how absurd it is to think to shut him up within the narrow limits of time. As the course of human life is short, even those who sway the sceptre over the greatest empires, being but mortal men, very often disappoint the expectations of their servants, as we are taught in Psalm 146:3–4, "Put not your trust in princes, nor in the son of man, in whom there is no help. His breath goes forth, he returns to his earth; in that very day his thoughts perish." We ought to entertain more exalted and honourable conceptions of our heavenly King; for although he does not immediately execute his judgments, yet he has always the full and the perfect power of doing so. He reigns not for himself in particular; it is for us that he reigns for ever and ever.

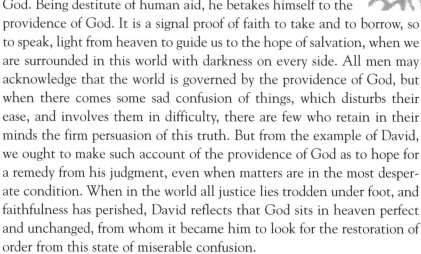

PSALM
11:1-4

In the LORD *I take refuge.* However much the world may hate and persecute us, we ought nevertheless to continue stedfast at our post, that we may not deprive ourselves of a right to lay claim to the promises of God, or that these may not slip away from us; and, however much and however long we may be harassed, we ought always to continue firm and unwavering in the faith of our having the call of God.

The LORD *is in his holy temple; the* LORD *is on his heavenly throne.* The Psalmist glories in the assurance of the favour of God. Being destitute of human aid, he betakes himself to the providence of God. It is a signal proof of faith to take and to borrow, so to speak, light from heaven to guide us to the hope of salvation, when we are surrounded in this world with darkness on every side. All men may acknowledge that the world is governed by the providence of God, but when there comes some sad confusion of things, which disturbs their ease, and involves them in difficulty, there are few who retain in their minds the firm persuasion of this truth. But from the example of David, we ought to make such account of the providence of God as to hope for a remedy from his judgment, even when matters are in the most desperate condition. When in the world all justice lies trodden under foot, and faithfulness has perished, David reflects that God sits in heaven perfect and unchanged, from whom it became him to look for the restoration of order from this state of miserable confusion.

He does not simply say that God dwells in heaven; but that he reigns there, as it were, in a royal palace, and has his throne of judgment there. Nor do we indeed render to him the honour which is his due, unless we are fully persuaded that his judgment-seat is a sacred sanctuary for all who are in affliction and unrighteously oppressed. When, therefore, deceit, craft, treachery, cruelty, violence, and extortion reign in the world; in short, when all things are thrown into disorder and darkness by injustice and wickedness, let faith serve as a lamp to enable us to behold God's heavenly throne, and let that sight suffice to make us wait in patience for the restoration of things to a better state.

PSALM 11:4-7

He observes the sons of men; his eyes examine them. Nothing is hidden from God, and, therefore, men will be obliged to render up to him an account of all that they have done. If God reigns in heaven, and if his throne is erected there, it follows that he must necessarily attend to the affairs of men, in order one day to sit in judgment upon them. Epicurus, and such like him as would persuade themselves that God is idle, and indulges in repose in heaven, may be said rather to spread for him a couch on which to sleep, than to erect for him a throne of judgment. But it is the glory of our faith that God, the Creator of the world, does not disregard or abandon the order which he himself at first established. And when he suspends his judgment for a time, it becomes us to lean upon this one truth—that he beholds from heaven; just as we now see David contenting himself with this consolatory consideration alone, that God rules over mankind, and observes whatever is transacted in the world, although his knowledge, and the exercise of his jurisdiction, are not at first sight apparent.

*He approves the righteous, but hates the wicked.** God so inquires into the cause of every man as to distinguish between the righteous and the unrighteous, and in such a way as shows that he is not an idle spectator. God hates those who are set upon the infliction of injuries, and upon doing mischief. As he has ordained mutual intercourse between men, so he would have us to maintain it inviolable. In order, therefore, to preserve this his own sacred and appointed order, he must be the enemy of the wicked, who wrong and are troublesome to others. There is also here contrasted God's hatred of the wicked, and wicked men's *love of iniquity*, to teach us that those who please and flatter themselves in their mischievous practices gain nothing by such flatteries, and only deceive themselves.

For the LORD is righteous, he loves justice. God graciously exercises a special care over the upright and the sincere, takes them under his protection, and keeps them in perfect safety. All those who, depending upon the grace of God, sincerely follow after righteousness, shall be safe under his protection.

PSALM 12

*Every man speaks deceit.** As those who are resolved to act truthfully in their intercourse with their neighbours, freely and ingenuously lay open their whole heart; so treacherous and deceitful persons keep a part of their feeling hidden within their own breast, and cover it with the varnish of hypocrisy and a fair outside; so that from their speech we cannot gather any thing certain with respect to their intention. Our speech, therefore, must be sincere in order that it may be as it were a mirror, in which the uprightness of our heart may be beheld.

*The words of God are pure words, purified seven times.** God promises nothing in vain, or for the purpose of disappointing man. God is not deceitful, he does not delude or beguile us with empty words, and he does not magnify beyond all measure either his power or his goodness, but whatever he promises in word he will perform in deed. There is no man, it is true, who will not frankly confess that he entertains the same conviction which David here records, *that the words of God are pure;* but those who while lying in the shade and living at their ease liberally extol by their praises the truth of God's word, when they come to struggle with adversity in good earnest, although they may not venture openly to pour forth blasphemies against God, often charge him with not keeping his word. Whenever he delays his assistance, we call in question his fidelity to his promises and murmur just as if he had deceived us. There is no truth which is more generally received among men than that God is true; but there are a few who frankly give him credit for this when they are in adversity. It is, therefore, highly necessary for us to cut off the occasion of our distrust; and whenever any doubt respecting the faithfulness of God's promises steal in upon us, we ought immediately to lift up against it this shield, that the words of the Lord are pure.

PSALM 13

To enlighten the eyes* signifies the same thing in the Hebrew language as to give the breath of life, for the vigour of life appears chiefly in the eyes. When Jonathan fainted for hunger, the sacred history relates that his eyes were overcast with dimness; and again, that when he had tasted of the honeycomb, his eyes were enlightened (1 Sam. 14:27). David confesses, that unless God cause the light of life to shine upon him, he will be immediately overwhelmed with the darkness of death, and that he is already as a man without life, unless God breathe into him new vigour. And certainly our confidence of life depends on this, that although the world may threaten us with a thousand deaths, yet God is possessed of numberless means of restoring us to life.

But I trust in your unfailing love. The Psalmist does not as yet feel how much he has profited by praying; but depending upon the hope of deliverance, which the faithful promise of God enabled him to entertain, he makes use of this hope as a shield to repel those temptations with the terror of which he might be greatly distressed. Although, therefore, he is severely afflicted, and a multiplicity of cares urge him to despair, he, notwithstanding, declares it to be his resolution to continue firm in his reliance upon the grace of God, and in the hope of salvation. With the very same confidence ought all the godly to be furnished and sustained, that they may duly persevere in prayer. It is by faith that we apprehend the grace of God, which is hidden from and unknown to the understanding of the flesh.

I will sing to the LORD. Surely it becomes us to engage in prayer in such a frame of mind as at the same time to be ready to sing the praises of God; a thing which is impossible, unless we are fully persuaded that our prayers will not be ineffectual. We may not be wholly free from sorrow, but it is nevertheless necessary that this cheerfulness of faith rise above it, and put into our mouth a song on account of the joy which is reserved for us in the future, although not as yet experienced by us; just as we see David here preparing himself to celebrate in songs the grace of God, before he perceives the issue of his troubles.

The fool says in his heart, "There is no God." All profane persons who have cast off all fear of God and abandoned themselves to iniquity, are convicted of madness. David does not bring against his enemies the charge of common foolishness, but rather inveighs against the folly and insane hardihood of those whom the world accounts eminent for their wisdom. We commonly see that those who, in the estimation both of themselves and of others, highly excel in sagacity and wisdom, employ their cunning in laying snares, and exercise the ingenuity of their minds in despising and mocking God. It is therefore important for us, in the first place, to know, that however much the world applauds these crafty and scoffing characters, who allow themselves to indulge to any extent in wickedness, yet the Holy Spirit condemns them as being fools; for there is no stupidity more brutish than forgetfulness of God.

We ought, however, at the same time, carefully to mark the evidence on which the Psalmist comes to the conclusion that they have cast off all sense of religion, and it is this: that they have overthrown all order, so that they no longer make any distinction between right and wrong, and have no regard for honesty, nor love of humanity. David, therefore, does not speak of the hidden affection of the heart of the wicked, except in so far as they discover themselves by their external actions. The import of his language is, How does it come to pass, that these men indulge themselves in their lusts so boldly and so outrageously, that they pay no regard to righteousness or equity; in short, that they madly rush into every kind of wickedness, if it is not because they have shaken off all sense of religion, and extinguished, as far as they can, all rememberance of God from their minds? When persons retain in their heart any sense of religion, they must necessarily have some modesty, and be in some measure restrained and prevented from entirely disregarding the dictates of their conscience. From this it follows, that when the ungodly allow themselves to follow their own inclinations, so obstinately and audaciously as they are here represented as doing, without any sense of shame, it is an evidence that they have cast off all fear of God.

PSALM 14:2

The LORD looks down from heaven. God himself is here introduced as speaking on the subject of human depravity, and this renders the discourse of David more emphatic than if he had pronounced the sentence in his own person. When God is exhibited to us as sitting on his throne to take cognisance of the conduct of men, unless we are stupefied in an extraordinary degree, his majesty must strike us with terror.

The effect of the habit of sinning is, that men grow hardened in their sins, and discern nothing, as if they were enveloped in thick darkness. David, therefore, to teach them that they gain nothing by flattering and deceiving themselves as they do, when wickedness reigns in the world with impunity, testifies that God looks down from heaven, and casts his eye on all sides, for the purpose of knowing what is done among men. God, it is true, has no need to make inquisition or search; but when he compares himself to an earthly judge, it is in adaptation to our limited capacity, and to enable us gradually to form some apprehension of his secret providence, which our reason cannot all at once comprehend.

If only this manner of speaking had the effect of teaching us to summon ourselves before his tribunal; and that, while the world are flattering themselves, and the reprobate are trying to bury their sins in forgetfulness by their want of thought, hypocrisy, or shamelessness, and are blinded in their obstinacy as if they were intoxicated, we might be led to shake off all indifference and stupidity by reflecting on this truth, that God, notwithstanding, looks down from his high throne in heaven, and beholds what is going on here below!

To see if there are any who understand. As the whole economy of a good and righteous life depends upon our being governed and directed by the light of understanding, David has justly taught us in the beginning of the psalm, that folly is the root of all wickedness. And in this clause he also very justly declares, that the commencement of integrity and uprightness of life consists in an enlightened and sound mind. But as the greater part misapply their intellectual powers to deceitful purposes, David immediately after defines, in one word, what true understanding is, namely, that it consists *in seeking God;* by which he means, that unless men devote themselves wholly to God, their life cannot be well ordered.

Day 29 JANUARY 29

PSALM 14:3-6

All have turned aside. David here not only censures a portion of the people, but pronounces them all to be equally involved in the same condemnation. It is against the carnal and degenerate body of the Israelitish nation that he here inveighs, and the small number constituting the seed which God had set apart for himself is not included among them. When David places himself and a small remnant of the godly on one side, and puts on the other the body of the people, in general, this implies that there is a manifest difference between the children of God who are created anew by his Spirit, and all the posterity of Adam, in whom corruption and depravity exercise dominion. Whence it follows, that all of us, when we are born, bring with us from our mother's womb this folly and filthiness manifested in the whole life, which David here describes, and that we continue such until God make us new creatures by his mysterious grace.

You evildoers frustrate the plans of the poor, but the LORD *is their refuge.* David inveighs against those giants who mock at the faithful for their simplicity, in calmly expecting, in their distresses, that God will show himself to be their deliverer. And, certainly, nothing seems more irrational to the flesh than to betake ourselves to God when yet he does not relieve us from our calamities; and the reason is, because the flesh judges of God only according to what it presently beholds of his grace. Whenever, therefore, unbelievers see the children of God overwhelmed with calamities, they reproach them for their groundless confidence, as it appears to them to be, and with sarcastic jeers laugh at the assured hope with which they rely upon God, from whom, notwithstanding, they receive no sensible aid. David, therefore, defies and derides this insolence of the wicked, and threatens that their mockery of the poor and the wretched, and their charging them with folly in depending upon the protection of God, and not sinking under their calamities, will be the cause of their destruction. At the same time, he teaches them that there is no resolution to which we can come which is better advised than the resolution to depend upon God, and that to repose on his salvation, and on the assistance which he has promised us, even although we may be surrounded with calamities, is the highest wisdom.

*Who shall give salvation to Israel out of Zion?** David, after having laid down the doctrine of consolation, again returns to prayers and groanings. By this he teaches us, that although God may leave us for a long time to languish, yet we ought not to weary, or lose courage, but should always glory in him; and, again, that while our troubles continue, the most effectual solace we can have is often to return to the exercise of prayer.

By the word *Zion*, which he adds, he testifies that his hope is fixed on God; for Zion was the holy place from which God had promised to hear the prayers of his servants; and it was the dwelling-place of the ark of the covenant, which was an external pledge and symbol of the presence of God. He does not, therefore, doubt who would be the author of his salvation; but he asks, with a sorrowful heart, when at length that salvation will come forth which is to be expected from no other source than from God alone.

By expressing his desire for the deliverance of Israel, we are taught that he was chiefly anxious about the welfare of the whole body of the Church, and that his thoughts were more occupied about this than about himself individually. While our attention is engrossed with our own particular sorrows, we are in danger of almost entirely neglecting the welfare of our brethren. And yet the particular afflictions with which God visits each of us are intended to admonish us to direct our attention and care to the whole body of the Church, and to think of its necessities, just as we see David here including Israel with himself.

David concludes that God will not suffer the faithful to languish under continual sorrow (Ps. 126:5), "They that sow in tears shall reap in joy." He doubtless aims at confirming and encouraging himself and all the godly to hope for the promised deliverance.

*The captivity,** of which he makes mention here refers to an oppression at home, when the wicked exercise dominion like tyrants in the Church. We are, therefore, taught by these words, that when such furious enemies waste and destroy the flock of God, or proudly tread it under foot, we ought to have recourse to God, whose peculiar office it is to gather together his Israel from all places whither they have been dispersed.

Day 31 JANUARY 31

LORD, *who may dwell in your sanctuary?* As nothing is more common in the world than falsely to assume the name of God, or to pretend to be his people, and as a great part of men allow themselves to do this without any apprehension of the danger it involves, David, without stopping to speak to men, addresses himself to God, which he considers the better course; and he intimates, that if men assume the title of the people of God, without being so in deed and in truth, they gain nothing by their self-delusion, for God continues always like himself, and as he is faithful himself, so will he have us to keep faith with him in return. No doubt, he adopted Abraham freely, but, at the same time, he stipulated with him that he should live a holy and an upright life, and this is the general rule of the covenant which God has, from the beginning, made with his Church.

The sum is, that hypocrites, who occupy a place in the temple of God, in vain pretend to be his people, for he acknowledges none as such but those who follow after justice and uprightness during the whole course of their life. David saw the temple crowded with a great multitude of men who all made a profession of the same religion, and presented themselves before God as to the outward ceremony; and, therefore, assuming the person of one wondering at the spectacle, he directs his discourse to God, who, in such a confusion and medley of characters, could easily distinguish his own people from strangers.

If we really wish to be reckoned among the number of the children of God, the Holy Ghost teaches us, that we must show ourselves to be such by a holy and an upright life; for it is not enough to serve God by outward ceremonies, unless we also live uprightly, and without doing wrong to our neighbours.

David makes mention of *the tabernacle*, because the temple was not yet built.

The meaning of his discourse, to express it in a few words, is this, that those only have access to God who are his genuine servants, and who live a holy life.

PSALM 15:1

Who may live on your holy hill? As we too often see the Church of God defaced by much impurity, to prevent us from stumbling at what appears so offensive, a distinction is made between those who are permanent citizens of the Church, and strangers who are mingled among them only for a time. This is undoubtedly a warning highly necessary, in order that when the temple of God happens to be tainted by many impurities, we may not contract such disgust and chagrin as will make us withdraw from it. By impurities we understand the vices of a corrupt and polluted life. Provided religion continue pure as to doctrine and worship, we must not be so much stumbled at the faults and sins which men commit, as on that account to rend the unity of the Church. Yet the experience of all ages teaches us how dangerous a temptation it is when we behold the church of God, which ought to be free from all polluting stains, and to shine in uncorrupted purity, cherishing in her bosom many ungodly hypocrites, or wicked persons. From this the Catharists, Novatians, and Donatists, took occasion in former times to separate themselves from the fellowship of the godly. The Anabaptists, at the present day, renew the same schisms, because it does not seem to them that a church in which vices are tolerated can be a true church. But Christ, in Matthew 25:32 justly claims it as his own peculiar office to separate the sheep from the goats; and thereby admonishes us, that we must bear with evils which it is not in our power to correct, until all things become ripe, and the proper season of purging the Church arrive.

At the same time, the faithful are here enjoined, each in his own sphere, to use their endeavours that the Church of God may be purified from the corruptions which still exist within her. God's sacred barn-floor will not be perfectly cleansed before the last day, when Christ at his coming will cast out the chaff; but he has already begun to do this by the doctrine of his gospel, which on this account he terms a fan. We must, therefore, by no means be indifferent about this matter; on the contrary, we ought rather to exert ourselves in good earnest, that all who profess themselves Christians may lead a holy and an unspotted life. But above all, what God here declares with respect to all the unrighteousness should be deeply imprinted on our memory; namely, that he prohibits them from coming to his sanctuary, and condemns their impious presumption, in irreverently thrusting themselves into the society of the godly.

He whose walk is blameless and who does what is righteous, who speaks the truth from his heart. Here is an implied contrast between the vain boasting of those who are only the people of God in name or who make only a bare profession of being so, which consists in outward observances, and this indubitable and genuine evidence of true godliness which David commends. But it might be asked, As the service of God takes precedence of the duties of charity towards our neighbours, why is there no mention here made of faith and prayer; for, certainly, these are the marks by which the genuine children of God ought to have been distinguished from hypocrites? The answer is easy: David does not intend to exclude faith and prayer, and other spiritual sacrifices; but as hypocrites, in order to promote their own interests, are not sparing in their attention to a multiplicity of external religious observances, while their ungodliness, notwithstanding, is manifested outwardly in the life, seeing they are full of pride, cruelty, violence, and are given to deceitfulness and extortion,—the Psalmist, for the purpose of discovering and drawing forth into the light all who are of such a character, takes the marks and evidence of true and sincere faith from the second table of the law. According to the care which every man takes to practise righteousness and equity towards his neighbours, so does he actually show that he fears God.

David, then, is not here to be understood as resting satisfied with political or social justice, as if it were enough to render to our fellow-men what is their own, while we may lawfully defraud God of his right; but he describes the approved servants of God, as distinguished and known by the fruits of righteousness which they produce. In the first place, he requires *sincerity*; in other words, that men should conduct themselves in all their affairs with singleness of heart, and without sinful craft or cunning. Secondly, he requires *justice*; that is to say, that they should study to do good to their neighbours, hurt nobody, and abstain form all wrong. Thirdly, he requires *truth* in their speech, so that they may speak nothing falsely or deceitfully.

PSALM 15:3

And has no slander on his tongue. David, after having briefly set forth the virtues with which all who desire to have a place in the Church ought to be endued, now enumerates certain vices from which they ought to be free. In the first place, he tells them they must not be *slanderers,* or *detractors;* secondly, that they must restrain themselves from doing any thing mischievous and injurious to their neighbours; and, thirdly, that they must not aid in giving currency to calumnies and false reports.

David, then, sets down calumny and detraction as the first point of injustice by which our neighbours are injured. If a good name is a treasure, more precious than all the riches of the world (Prov. 22:1), no greater injury can be inflicted upon men than to wound their reputation. It is not, however, every injurious word which is here condemned; but the disease and lust of detraction, which stirs up malicious persons to spread abroad calumnies. At the same time, it cannot be doubted that the design of the Holy Spirit is to condemn all false and wicked accusations.

Who does his neighbor no wrong. By the word *neighbour,* the Psalmist means not only those with whom we enjoy familiar intercourse, and live on terms of intimate friendship, but all men, to whom we are bound by the ties of humanity and a common nature. He employs these terms to show more clearly the odiousness of what he condemns, and that the saints may have the greater abhorrence of all wrong dealing, since every man who hurts his neighbour violates the fundamental law of human society.

There is also here rebuked the vice of undue credulity, which, when any evil reports are spread against our neighbours, leads us either eagerly to listen to them, or at least, to receive them without sufficient reason; whereas we ought rather to use all means to suppress and trample them under foot. When any one is the bearer of invented falsehoods, those who reject them leave them, as it were, to fall to the ground; on the contrary, those who propagate and publish them from one person to another, are by an expressive form of speech, said to raise them up.

Who despises a vile man. The children of God despise the ungodly, and form that low and contemptuous estimate of them which their character deserves. The godly, it is true, although living a praiseworthy and virtuous life, are not inflated with presumption, but, on the contrary, are rather dissatisfied with themselves, because they feel how far short they are as yet of the perfection which is required. The Psalmist commends a free and upright judgment of human character, by which the wicked, on the one hand, are not spared, while virtue, on the other, receives the honour which belongs to it; for flattery, which nourishes vices by covering them, is an evil not less pernicious than it is common.

If the wicked are in authority, we ought not to carry our contempt of them the length of refusing to obey them in so far as a regard to our duty will permit; but, at the same time, we must beware of flattery and of accommodating ourselves to them, which would be to involve us in the same condemnation with them. He who not only seems to regard their wicked actions with indifference, but also honours them, shows that he approves of them as much as it is in his power. Paul therefore teaches us (Eph. 5:2) that it is a species of fellowship with the unfruitful works of darkness when we do not reprove them.

But honors those who fear the LORD. To *honour* the righteous and *those who fear God,* is no mean virtue. The greater part of mankind refuse the friendship of good men, and leave them to be despised, which cannot be done without grievous and heinous injury to God. Let us learn then not to value men by their estate or their money, or their transitory honours, but to hold in estimation godliness, or the fear of God. And certainly no man will ever truly apply his mind to the study of godliness who does not, at the same time, reverence the servants of God; as, on the other hand, the love we bear them incites us to imitate them in sanctity of life.

PSALM 15:4

Who keeps his oath even when it hurts. The faithful will rather submit to suffer loss than to break their word. When a man keeps his promises, in as far as he sees it to be for his own advantage, there is in this no argument to prove his uprightness and faithfulness. But when men make a promise to each other, there is nothing more common than from some slight loss which the performance of it would occasion, to endeavour to find a pretext for breaking their engagements. Every one considers with himself what is for his own advantage, and if it puts him to inconvenience or trouble to stand to his promises, he is ingenious enough to imagine that he will incur a far greater loss than there is any reason to apprehend. It seems, indeed, a fair excuse when a man complains that, if he does not depart from his engagement, he will suffer great loss. Hence it is, that we generally see so much unfaithfulness among men, that they do not consider themselves bound to perform the promises which they have made, except in so far as it will promote their own personal interest. David, therefore, condemning this inconstancy, requires the children of God to exhibit the greatest stedfastness in the fulfilment of their promises. Here the question might be asked, If a man, having fallen into the hands of a highwayman, promise him a sum of money to save his life, and if, in consequence of this, he is let to go, should he in that case keep his promise? Again, if a man has been basely deceived, in entering into a contract, is it lawful for him to break the oath which he shall have made in such an engagement? With respect to the highwayman, he who confers upon him money falls into another fault, for he supports at his own expense a common enemy of mankind to the detriment of the public welfare. David does not impose upon the faithful such an alternative as this, but only enjoins them to show greater regard to their promises than to their own personal interests, and to do this especially when their promises have been confirmed by an oath. As to the other case, namely, when a person has sworn, from being deceived and imposed upon by wicked artifice, he ought certainly to hold the holy name of God in such veneration, as rather patiently to submit to loss than violate his oath. Yet it is perfectly lawful for him to discover or reveal the fraud which has been practised upon him, provided he is not led to do so by a regard to his own personal interest; and there is, besides, nothing to hinder him from peaceably endeavouring to compromise the matter with his adversary.

Day 37 F E B R U A R Y 6

Who lends his money without usury and does not accept a bribe against the innocent. In this verse David enjoins the godly neither to oppress their neighbours by usury, nor to suffer themselves to be corrupted with bribes to favour unrighteous causes. David seems to condemn all kinds of usury in general, so that the very name has been everywhere held in detestation. But crafty men have invented specious names under which to conceal the vice; and thinking by this artifice to escape, they have plundered with greater excess than if they had lent on usury avowedly and openly. God, however, will not be dealt with and imposed upon by sophistry and false pretences. He looks upon the thing as it really is. There is no worse species of usury than an unjust way of making bargains, where equity is disregarded on both sides. Let us then remember that all bargains in which the one party unrighteously strives to make gain by the loss of the other party, whatever name may be given to them, are condemned.

PSALM 15:5

With respect to usury, it is scarcely possible to find in the world a usurer who is not at the same time an extortioner, and addicted to unlawful and dishonourable gain. Accordingly, Cato of old justly placed the practice of usury and the killing of men in the same rank of criminality, for the object of this class of people is to suck the blood of other men. It is also a very strange and shameful thing, that, while all other men obtain the means of their subsistence with much toil, while husbandmen fatigue themselves by their daily occupations, and artisans serve the community by the sweat of their brow, and merchants not only employ themselves in labours, but also depose themselves to many inconveniences and dangers,—moneymongers should sit at their ease without doing any thing, and receive tribute from the labour of all other people.

We should keep ourselves from plundering and devouring the poor who are in distress and want.

The gain which he who lends his money upon interest acquires, without doing injury to any one, is not to be included under the head of unlawful usury.

PSALM 16:1-2

Keep me safe, O God, for in you I take refuge. This is a prayer in which David commits himself to the protection of God. God is ready to succour all of us, provided we rely upon him with a sure and stedfast faith; and that he takes under his protection none but those who commit themselves to him with their whole heart.

You are my Lord, my well-doing cannot extend to you.* David begins by stating that he can bestow nothing upon God, not only because God stands in no need of anything, but also because mortal man cannot merit the favour of God by any service which he can perform to him. At the same time, however, he takes courage, and, as God accepts our devotion, and the service which we yield to him, David protests that he will be one of his servants.

Two things are distinctly laid down in this verse. The first is, that God has a right to require of us whatever he pleases, seeing we are fully bound to him as our rightful proprietor and Lord. David, by ascribing to him the power and the dominion of *Lord,* declares that both himself and all he possessed are the property of God.

Let men strive ever so much to lay themselves out for God, yet they can bring no advantage to him. Our goodness extends not to him, not only because, having in himself alone an all-sufficiency, he stands in need of nothing, but also because we are empty and destitute of all good things, and have nothing with which to show ourselves liberal towards him.

It is impossible for men, by any merits of their own, to bring God under obligation to them, so as to make him their debtor. The sum of the discourse is, that when we come before God, we must lay aside all presumption. When we imagine that there is any good thing in us, we need not wonder if he reject us, as we thus take away from him a principal part of the honour which is his due. On the contrary, if we acknowledge that all the services which we can yield to him are in themselves things of nought, and undeserving of any recompense, this humility is as a perfume of a sweet odour, which will procure for them acceptance with God.

PSALM
16:3

As for the saints who are in the land, they are the glorious ones in whom is all my delight. The only way of serving God aright is to endeavour to do good to his holy servants. And the truth is, that God, as our good deeds cannot extend to him, substitutes the saints in his place, towards whom we are to exercise our charity. When men, therefore, mutually exert themselves in doing good to one another, this is to yield to God right and acceptable service.

David intimates that he will unite himself with the devout worshippers of God, and be their associate or companion; even as all the children of God ought to be joined together by the bond of fraternal unity, that they may all serve and call upon their common Father with the same affection and zeal. We thus see that David, after having confessed that he can find nothing in himself to bring to God, seeing he is indebted to him for every thing which he has, sets his affection upon the saints, because it is the will of God that, in this world, he should be magnified and exalted in the assembly of the just, whom he has adopted into his family for this end, that they may live together with one accord under his authority, and under the guidance of his Holy Spirit. This passage, therefore, teaches us that there is no sacrifice more acceptable to God than when we sincerely and heartily connect ourselves with the society of the righteous, and being knit together by the sacred bond of godliness, cultivate and maintain with them brotherly goodwill. In this consists the communion of saints which separates them from the degrading pollutions of the world, that they may be the holy and peculiar people of God.

The faithful bear the image of God, that, by their example, we may be stirred up to meditation upon the heavenly life. For the same reason, the Psalmist calls them *excellent,* or honourable, because there is nothing which ought to be more precious to us than righteousness and holiness, in which the brightness of God's Spirit shines forth. We ought, therefore, highly to value and esteem the true and devoted servants of God, and to regard nothing as of greater importance than to connect ourselves with their society; and this we will actually do if we wisely reflect in what true excellence and dignity consist, and do not allow the vain splendour of the world and its deceitful pomps to dazzle our eyes.

PSALM 16:4-5

I will not pour out their libations of blood or take up their names on my lips. The Psalmist now describes the true way of maintaining brotherly concord with the saints, by declaring that he will have nothing to do with unbelievers and the superstitious. We cannot be united into the one body of the Church under God, if we do not break off all the bonds of impiety, separate ourselves from idolaters, and keep ourselves pure and at a distance from all the pollutions which corrupt and vitiate the holy service of God.

The earth is filled with an immense accumulation of superstitions in every possible variety, and idolaters are lavish beyond all bounds in ornamenting their idols; but the good and the holy will ever regard all their superstitious inventions with abhorrence.

LORD, *you have assigned me my portion and my cup, you have made my lot secure.* David rests in the only true God as his portion. All who have not their foundation and trust in God must necessarily be often in a state of irresolution and uncertainty; and those who do not hold the true faith in such a manner as to be guided and governed by it, must be often carried away by the overflowing floods of errors which prevail in the world. None are taught aright in true godliness but those who reckon God alone sufficient for their happiness.

David says that he is so fully satisfied with God alone, as neither to covet any thing besides him, nor to be excited by any depraved desires. Let us therefore learn, when God offers himself to us, to embrace him with the whole heart, and to seek in him only all the ingredients and the fullness of our happiness.

We do not actually possess him unless "he is the portion of our inheritance"; in other words, unless we are wholly devoted to him, so as no longer to have any desire unfaithfully to depart from him. For this reason, God, when he upbraids the Jews who had wandered from him as apostates, with having run about after idols, addresses them thus, "Let them be your inheritance, and your portion." By these words he shows, that if we do not reckon him alone an all-sufficient portion for us, and if we will have idols along with him, he gives place entirely to them, and lets them have the full possession of our hearts.

PSALM
16:6-7

The boundary lines have fallen for me in pleasant places; surely I have a delightful inheritance. The Psalmist so glories in God as nobly to despise all that the world imagines to be excellent and desirable without him. By magnifying God in such honourable and exalted strains, he gives us to understand that he does not desire anything more as his portion and felicity. This doctrine may be profitable to us in many ways. It ought to draw us away not only from all the perverse inventions of superstition, but also from all the allurements of the flesh and of the world. Whenever, therefore, those things present themselves to us which would lead us away from resting in God alone, let us make use of this sentiment as an antidote against them, that we have sufficient cause for being contented, since he who has in himself an absolute fullness of all good, has given himself to be enjoyed by us. In this way we will experience our condition to be always pleasant and comfortable; for he who has God as his portion is destitute of nothing which is requisite to constitute a happy life.

I will praise the LORD, who counsels me; even at night my heart instructs me. David confesses that it was entirely owing to the pure grace of God that he had come to possess so great a good, and that he had been made a partaker of it by faith. It would be of no advantage to us for God to offer himself freely and graciously to us, if we did not receive him by faith, seeing he invites to himself both the reprobate and the elect in common; but the former, by their ingratitude, defraud themselves of this inestimable blessing. Let us, therefore, know that both these things proceed from the free liberality of God; first, his being our inheritance, and next, our coming to the possession of him by faith. The *counsel* of which David makes mention is the inward illumination of the Holy Spirit, by which we are prevented from rejecting the salvation to which he calls us, which we would otherwise certainly do, considering the blindness of our flesh. Whence we gather, that those who attribute to the free will of man the choice of accepting or rejecting the grace of God basely mangle that grace, and show as much ignorance as impiety.

PSALM 16:8-9

I have set the LORD always before me. Because he is at my right hand, I will not be shaken. To set God before us is nothing else than to keep all our senses bound and captive, that they may not run out and go astray after any other object. We must look to him with other eyes than those of the flesh, for we shall seldom be able to perceive him unless we elevate our minds above the world; and faith prevents us from turning our back upon him. David kept his mind so intently fixed upon the providence of God, as to be fully persuaded, that whenever any difficulty or distress should befall him, God would be always at hand to assist him.

We ought so to depend upon God as to continue to be fully persuaded of his being near to us, even when he seems to be removed to the greatest distance from us. When we shall have thus turned our eyes towards him, the masks and the vain illusions of this world will no longer deceive us.

Therefore my heart is glad and my tongue rejoices; my body also will rest secure. Here the Psalmist commends the inestimable fruit of faith, of which Scripture every where makes mention, in that, by placing us under the protection of God, it makes us not only to live in the enjoyment of mental tranquillity, but, what is more, to live joyful and cheerful. The principal, the essential part of a happy life, as we know, is to possess tranquillity of conscience and of mind; as, on the contrary, there is no greater infelicity than to be tossed amidst a multiplicity of care and fears.

Calmly to rejoice is the lot of no man but of him who has learned to place his confidence in God alone, and to commit his life and safety to his protection. When, therefore, encompassed with innumerable troubles on all sides, let us be persuaded, that the only remedy is to direct our eyes towards God; and if we do this, faith will not only tranquillise our minds, but also replenish them with fullness of joy. True believers not only have this spiritual joy in the secret affection of their heart, but also manifest it by the tongue, inasmuch as they glory in God as he who protects them and secures their salvation.

*You will not leave my soul in the grave.** The Psalmist declares that, as he is not afraid of death, there is nothing wanting which is requisite to the completion of his joy. Whence it follows, that no one truly trusts in God but he who takes such hold of the salvation which God has promised him as to despise death. Moreover, it is to be observed, that David's language is not to be limited to some particular kind of deliverance, but he entertains the undoubted assurance of eternal salvation, which freed him from all anxiety and fear.

You have made known to me the path of life; you will fill me with joy in your presence, with eternal pleasures at your right hand. The Psalmist explains the way in which God will exempt him from the bondage of death, namely by conducting and bringing him at length safely to the possession of eternal life.

This passage touches upon the difference which there is between true believers and aliens, or reprobates, with respect to their everlasting state. It is a mere cavil to say, that when David here speaks of *the path of life* being shown to him, it means the prolongation of his natural life. It is to form a very low estimate, indeed, of the grace of God to speak of him as a guide to his people in the path of life only for a very few years in this world. In this case, they would differ nothing from the reprobate, who enjoy the light of the sun in common with them. If, therefore, it is the special grace of God which he communicates to none but his own children, that David here magnifies and exalts, the showing of the way of life, of which he speaks, must undoubtedly be viewed as extending to a blessed immortality; and, indeed, he only knows the way of life who is so united to God that he lives in God, and cannot live without him.

David next adds, that when God is reconciled to us, we have all things which are necessary to perfect happiness. True and solid joy in which the minds of men may rest will never be found any where else but in God; and therefore, none but the faithful, who are contented with his grace alone, can be truly and perfectly happy.

PSALM 17:1

*Hear, O L*ORD*, my righteous plea; listen to my cry. Give ear to my prayer—it does not rise from deceitful lips.* David, confiding in his own integrity, interposes God as a Judge between himself and his enemies, to cognise or determine in his cause. When we have to deal with wicked men, we may warrantably protest our innocence before God. As, however, it would not be enough for the faithful to have the approving testimony of a good conscience, David adds to his protestation earnest prayer. Even irreligious persons may often be able justly to boast of having a good cause; but as they do not acknowledge that the world is governed by the providence of God, they content themselves with enjoying the approbation of their own conscience, as they speak, and, gnawing the bit, bear the injuries which are done to them rather obstinately than stedfastly, seeing they do not seek for any consolation in faith and prayer. But the faithful not only depend upon the goodness of their cause, they also commit it to God that he may defend and maintain it; and whenever any adversity befalls them, they betake themselves to him for help.

This, therefore, is the meaning of the passage; it is a prayer that God, who knew David to have done justly, and to have performed his duty without giving occasion to any to blame him, and, therefore, to be unrighteously molested by his enemies, would graciously look upon him; and that he would do this especially, since, confiding in his aid, he entertained good hope, and, at the same time, prays to him with a sincere heart. By this form of prayer the Holy Spirit teaches us, that we ought diligently to endeavour to live an upright and innocent life, so that, if there are any who give us trouble, we may be able to boast that we are blamed and persecuted wrongfully. Again, whenever the wicked assault us, the same Spirit calls upon us to engage in prayer; and if any man, trusting to the testimony of a good conscience which he enjoys, neglects the exercise of prayer, he defrauds God of the honour which belongs to him, in not referring his cause to him, and in not leaving him to judge and determine in it. Let us learn, also, that when we present ourselves before God in prayer, it is not to be done with the ornaments of an artificial eloquence, for the finest rhetoric and the best grace which we can have before him consist in pure simplicity.

Day 45 F E B R U A R Y 1 4

Though you probe my heart and examine me at night, though you test me, you will find nothing; I have resolved that my mouth will not sin. These words may be suitably explained in this way: You, Lord, who understands all the secret affections and thoughts of my heart, even as it is your peculiar prerogative to try men, knows very well that I am not a double man, and do not cherish any deceit within. David subjects himself to an impartial examination, seeing God, whose prerogative it is to search the secret recesses of the heart, cannot be deceived by the external appearance.

The time when he declares God to have visited him is during *the night,* because, when a man is withdrawn from the presence of his fellow creatures, he sees more clearly his sins, which otherwise would be hidden from his view; just as, on the contrary, the sight of men affects us with shame, and this is, as it were, a veil before our eyes, which prevents us from deliberately examining our faults. It is, therefore, as if David had said, O Lord, since the darkness of the night discovers the conscience more fully, all coverings being then taken away, and since, at that season, the affections, either good or bad, according to men's inclinations, manifest themselves more freely, when there is no person present to witness and pronounce judgment upon them; if you then examine me, there will be found neither disguise nor deceit in my heart.

As for the deeds of men—by the word of your lips I have kept myself from the ways of the violent. If we would have a good rule for governing ourselves, when our enemies, by their mischievous actions, provoke us to treat them in a similar manner, let us learn, after the example of David, to meditate upon the word of God, and to keep our eyes fixed upon it. By this means our minds will be preserved from ever being blinded, and we shall always avoid the paths of wickedness, seeing God will not only keep our affections under restraint by his commandments, but will also train them to patience by his promises. He withholds us from doing evil to our neighbours, not only by forbidding us, but by declaring, at the same time, that he will take into his own hand the execution of vengeance on those who injure us, he admonishes us to "give place unto wrath" (Rom. 12:19).

PSALM 17:4-15

Show the wonder of your great love, you who save by your right hand those who take refuge in you from their foes. David, perceiving that he could only be delivered from the perilous circumstances in which he was placed by singular and extraordinary means, betakes himself to the wonderful or miraculous power of God. Whenever we approach God, let the first thought impressed on our minds be, that as he is not in vain called the preserver of those who trust in him, we have no reason whatever to be afraid of his not being ready to succour us, provided our faith continue firmly to rely upon his grace. And if every way of deliverance is shut up, let us also at the same time remember that he is possessed of wonderful and inconceivable means of succouring us, which serve so much the more conspicuously to magnify and manifest his power.

Keep me as the apple of your eye; hide me in the shadow of your wings. God, to express the great care which he has of his own people, compares himself to a hen and other fowls, which spread out their wings to cherish and cover their young, and declares them to be no less dear to him than the apple of the eye, which is the tenderest part of the body. It follows that whenever men rise up to molest and injure the righteous, war is waged against God.

We have here presented to our contemplation a singular and astonishing proof of the goodness of God, in humbling himself so far, and in a manner so to speak, transforming himself, in order to lift up our faith above the conceptions of the flesh.

Deliver my soul . . . from men . . . whose portion is in life.* These men have their portion in life; they are exempted from all troubles, and abound in pleasures; in short, they do not experience the common condition of other men. David, therefore, intimates, that it is not a reasonable thing that the ungodly should be permitted to gad about in joy and gaiety without having any fear of death, and to claim for themselves, as if by hereditary right, a peaceful and happy life. The object of David's complaint is, that God would make haste to execute vengeance, seeing they have so long abused his liberality and gentle treatment.

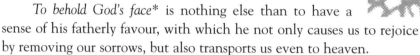

*But as for me, I shall see your face in righteousness.** There is here a tacit comparison between the well regulated state of things which will be seen when God by his judgment shall restore to order these things which are now embroiled and confused, and the deep and distressing darkness which is in the world, when God keeps silence, and hides his face. David, in order to enjoy supreme happiness, desires nothing more than to have always the taste and experience of this great blessing that God is reconciled to him.

*To behold God's face** is nothing else than to have a sense of his fatherly favour, with which he not only causes us to rejoice by removing our sorrows, but also transports us even to heaven.

By the word *righteousness*, David means that he will not be disappointed of the reward of a good conscience. As long as God humbles his people under manifold afflictions, the world insolently mocks at their simplicity, as if they deceived themselves, and lost their pains in devoting themselves to the cultivation and practice of purity and innocence. Against such kind of mockery and derision David is here struggling, and in opposition to it he assures himself that there is a recompense laid up for his godliness and uprightness, provided he continue to persevere in his obedience to the holy law of God; as Isaiah, in like manner (3:10), exhorts the faithful to support themselves from this consideration, that "it shall be well with the righteous: for they shall eat the fruit of their doings." We ought not, however, from this to think that he represents works as the cause of his salvation. It is not his purpose to treat of what constitutes the meritorious ground upon which he is to be received into the favour of God. He only lays it down as a principle, that they who serve God do not lose their labour, for although he may hide his face from them for a time, he causes them again in due season to behold his bright countenance and compassionate eye beaming upon them.

PSALM 17:15b

When I awake, I will be satisfied with seeing your likeness. This satisfaction of which David speaks will not in all respects be perfect before the last coming of Christ; but as the saints, when God causes some rays of the knowledge of his love to enter into their hearts, find great enjoyment in the light thus communicated, David justly calls this peace or joy of the Holy Spirit *satisfaction*.

The ungodly may be at their ease, and have abundance of good things, even to bursting, but as their desire is insatiable, or as they feed upon wind, in other words, upon earthly things, without tasting spiritual things, in which there is substance, or being so stupefied through the pungent remorse of conscience with which they are tormented, as not to enjoy the good things which they possess, they never have composed and tranquil minds, but are kept unhappy by the inward passions with which they are perplexed and agitated. It is therefore the grace of God alone which can give us contentment, and prevent us from being distracted by irregular desires. David, then, has here an allusion to the empty joys of the world, which only famish the soul, while they sharpen and increase the appetite the more, in order to show that those only are partakers of true and substantial happiness who seek their felicity in the enjoyment of God alone.

*In awaking by your face.** (Here we can view the word *awake* as meaning to obtain respite from sorrow.) The saints do not sustain and repel all the assaults which are made upon them so courageously as not, by reason of the weakness of their flesh, to feel languid and feeble for a time, or to be terrified, as if they were enveloped in darkness (David compares this perturbation of mind to a sleep). But when the favour of God shall again have arisen and shone brightly upon him, he declares that then he will recover spiritual strength and enjoy tranquillity of mind. It is true, indeed, as Paul declares, that so long as we continue in this state of earthly pilgrimage, "we walk by faith, not by sight"; but as we nevertheless behold the image of God not only in the glass of the gospel, but also in the numerous evidence of his grace which he daily exhibits to us, let each of us awaken himself from his lethargy, that we may now be satisfied with spiritual felicity, until God, in due time, bring us to his own immediate presence, and cause us to enjoy him face to face.

David the servant of the LORD. David, when his affairs were brought to a state of peace and prosperity, was not intoxicated with extravagant joy like irreligious men, who, when they have obtained deliverance from their calamities, shake off from their minds the rememberance of God's benefits, and plunge themselves into gross and degrading pleasures, or erect their crests, and obscure the glory of God by their proud and vain boasting. David, as the sacred history relates (2 Sam. 22), sung this song to the Lord, when he was now almost spent with age, and when, being delivered from all his troubles, he enjoyed tranquillity.

Amidst the many storms which he had to encounter, it was a support highly necessary to be well assured in his own mind of having undertaken nothing but by the appointment of God; or rather, this was to him a peaceful haven, and a secure retreat in the midst of so many broils and strange calamities. There is not a more wretched object than man in adversity, when he has brought himself into distress by acting according to the mere impulse of his own mind, and not by acting in obedience to the call of God. David, therefore, had a good reason for wishing it to be known that it was not ambition which impelled him to enter into those contests which were so painful and difficult for him to bear, and that he had not attempted any thing unlawful or by wicked means, but had always kept steadily in view the will of God, which served as a light to guide him in his path. This is a point which it is highly useful for us to know, in order that we may not expect to be exempted from all trouble, when we follow the call of God, but may rather prepare ourselves for a condition of warfare painful and disagreeable to our flesh.

We ought particularly to notice the humility of David, who, although distinguished by so many victories, and the conqueror of so many nations, and possessed of so great dignity and wealth, honours himself with no other title than this, *the servant of God;* as if he meant to show that he accounted it more honourable to have faithfully performed the duties of the office with which God had invested him, than to possess all the honours and excellence of the world.

PSALM 18:1-2

I love you, O LORD, my strength. It is to be observed, that love to God is here laid down as constituting the principal part of true godliness; for there is no better way of serving God than to love him. No doubt, the service which we owe him is better expressed by the word *reverence,* that thus his majesty may prominently stand forth to our view in its infinite greatness. But as he requires nothing so expressly as to possess all the affections of our heart, and to have them going towards him, so there is no sacrifice which he values more than when we are bound fast to him by the claim of a free and spontaneous love; and, on the other hand, there is nothing in which his glory shines forth more conspicuously than in his free and sovereign goodness. Moses, therefore (Deut. 10:12), when he meant to give a summary of the law, says, "And now, Israel, what does the Lord your God require of you but to love him?" In speaking thus, David, at the same time, intended to show that his thoughts and affections were not so intently fixed upon the benefits of God as to be ungrateful to him who was the author of them, a sin which has been too common in all ages. Even at this day we see how the greater part of mankind enjoy wholly at their ease the gifts of God without paying any regard to him, or, if they think of him at all, it is only to despise him. David, to prevent himself from falling into this ingratitude, in these words makes as it were a solemn vow, Lord, as you are my strength, I will continue united and devoted to you by unfeigned love.

The LORD is my rock, my fortress and my deliverer; my God is my rock, in whom I take refuge. He is my shield and the horn of my salvation, my stronghold. When David thus heaps together many titles by which to honour God, it is no useless or unnecessary accumulation of words. We know how difficult it is for men to keep their minds and hearts stayed in God. They either imagine that it is not enough to have God for them, and, consequently, are always seeking after support and succour elsewhere, or, at the first temptation which assails them, fall from the confidence which they placed in him. David, therefore, by attributing to God various methods of saving his people, protests that, provided he has God for his protector and defender, he is effectually fortified against all peril and assault.

PSALM 18:7–19

The earth trembled and quaked, and the foundations of the mountains shook; they trembled because he was angry. David, convinced that the aid of God, which he had experienced, was of such a character that it was impossible for him to extol it sufficiently and as it deserved, set forth an image of it in the sky and the earth, as if he had said, It has been as visible as the changes which give different appearances to the sky and the earth. If natural things always flowed in an even and uniform course, the power of God would not be so perceptible. But when he changes the face of the sky by sudden rain, or by loud thunder, or by dreadful tempests, those who before were, as it were, asleep and insensible, must necessarily be awakened, and be tremblingly conscious of the existence of a presiding God. Such sudden and unforeseen changes manifest more clearly the presence of the great Author of nature. No doubt, when the sky is unclouded and tranquil, we see in it sufficient evidence of the majesty of God, but as men will not stir up their minds to reflect upon that majesty, until it come nearer to them, David, the more powerfully to affect us, recounts the sudden changes by which we are usually moved and dismayed.

In short, the object of the Psalmist is to show that the God who, as often as he pleases, causes all parts of the world to tremble by his power, when he intended to manifest himself as the deliverer of David, was known as openly and by signs as evident as if he had displayed his power in all the creatures both above and beneath.

David does not here relate this as a piece of history, or as what had actually taken place, but he employs these similitudes for the purpose of removing all doubt, and for the greater confirmation of faith as to the power and providence of God; because men, from their slowness of understanding, cannot apprehend God except by means of external signs.

PSALM 18:20

The LORD has dealt with me according to my righteousness; according to the cleanness of my hands he has rewarded me. We ought to view the Holy Spirit as intending by the mouth of David to teach us the profitable doctrine, that the aid of God will never fail us, provided we follow our calling, keep ourselves within the limits which it prescribes, and undertake nothing without the command or warrant of God. At the same time, let this truth be deeply fixed in our minds, that we can only begin an upright course of life when God of his good pleasure adopts us into his family, and in effectually calling, anticipates us by his grace, without which neither we nor any creature would give him an opportunity of bestowing this blessing upon us.

When the Scripture uses the word *reward* or *recompense*, it is not to show that God owes us any thing, and it is therefore a groundless and false conclusion to infer from this that there is any merit or worth in works. God, as a just judge, rewards every man according to his works, but he does it in such a manner, as to show that all men are indebted to him, while he himself is under obligation to no one. The reason is not only that which St Augustine has assigned, namely, that God finds no righteousness in us to recompense, except what he himself has freely given us, but also because, forgiving the blemishes and imperfections which cleave to our works, he imputes to us for righteousness that which he might justly reject. If, therefore, none of our works please God, unless the sin which mingles with them is pardoned, it follows, that the recompense which he bestows on account of them proceeds not from our merit, but from his free and undeserved grace. We ought, however, to attend to the special reason why David here speaks of God rewarding him according to his righteousness. He does not presumptuously thrust himself into the presence of God, trusting to or depending upon his own obedience to the law as the ground of his justification; but knowing that God approved the affection of his heart, and wishing to defend and acquit himself from the false and wicked calumnies of his enemies, he makes God himself the judge of his cause.

For I have kept the ways of the LORD; I have not done evil by turning from my God. David, it is true, sometimes fell into sin through the weakness of the flesh, but he never desisted from following after godliness, nor deserted the service to which God had called him. Let us endeavour above all things to have a good conscience, and let us have the magnanimity to despise the false judgments of men, and to look up to heaven for the vindicator of our character and cause.

PSALM 18:21-24

All his laws are before me; I have not turned away from his decrees. David shows how he came to possess that unbending rectitude of character, by which he was enabled to act uprightly amidst so many and so grievous temptations, namely, because he always applied his mind to the study of the law of God. Whoever, therefore, would desire to persevere in uprightness and integrity of life, let them learn to exercise themselves daily in the study of the word of God; for, whenever a man despises or neglects instruction, he easily falls into carelessness and stupidity, and all fear of God vanishes from his mind.

According to the cleanness of my hands in his sight. In these words there is evidently a contrast between the eyes of God and blinded or malignant eyes of the world. The integrity which David attributes to himself is not perfection but sincerity, which is opposed to dissimulation and hypocrisy. This may be gathered from the clause where he says *I have kept myself from my iniquity.* In thus speaking, he tacitly acknowledges that he had not been so pure and free from sinful affections as that the malignity of his enemies did not frequently excite indignation within him, and gall him to the heart. He had therefore to fight in his own mind against many temptations, for as he was a man, he must have felt in the flesh on many occasions the stirrings of vexation and anger. But this was the proof of his virtue, that he imposed a restraint upon himself, and refrained from whatever he knew to be contrary to the word of God. A man will never persevere in the practice of uprightness and of godliness, unless he carefully keep himself from his iniquity.

PSALM 18.25-39

To the faithful you show yourself faithful, to the blameless you show yourself blameless. We ought to mark well this difference between the ungodly and the faithful, namely, that the former, intoxicated with prosperity, unblushingly boast of being acceptable to God, while yet they disregard him, and rather sacrifice to Fortune, and make it their God; whereas the latter in their prosperity magnify the grace of God, from the deep sense of his grace with which their consciences are affected.

God, in so often delivering an innocent man from death, when it was near him, showed, indeed, that he is merciful towards the merciful, and pure towards the pure. God never disappoints his servants, but always at length deals graciously with them, provided they wait for his aid with meekness and patience. To this purpose Jacob said, in Genesis 30:33, "God will make my righteousness to return upon me." The scope of the discourse is, that the people of God should entertain good hope, and encourage themselves to practise uprightness and integrity, since every man shall reap the fruit of his own righteousness.

As for God, his way is perfect; the word of the LORD is flawless. The phrase, *the way of God,* is not here taken for his revealed will, but for his method of dealing towards his people. The meaning, therefore, is, that God never disappoints or deceives his servants, nor forsakes them in the time of need, (as may be the case with men who do not aid their dependants, except in so far as it contributes to their own particular advantage,) but faithfully defends and maintains those whom he has once taken under his protection. But we will never have any nearness to God, unless he first come near to us by his word; and, for this reason, David, after having asserted that God aids his people in good earnest, adds, at the same time, that *his word is purified.* Let us, therefore, rest assured that God will actually show himself upright towards us, seeing he has promised to be the guardian and protector of our welfare, and his promise is certain and infallible truth.

PSALM 18:40-45

You have delivered me from the attacks of the people; you have made me the head of nations. As the kingdom of David was a type under which the Holy Spirit intended to shadow forth to us the kingdom of Christ, let us remember that, both in erecting and preserving it, it is necessary for God not only to stretch forth his arm and fight against avowed enemies, who from without rise up against him, but also to repress the tumults and strifes which may take place within the Church. This was clearly shown in the person of Christ from the beginning. In the first place, he met with much opposition from the infatuated obstinacy of those of his own nation. In the next place, the experience of all ages shows that the dissensions and strifes with which hypocrites rend and mangle the Church, are not less hurtful in undermining the kingdom of Christ, (if God do not interpose his hand to prevent their injurious effects,) than the violent efforts of his enemies. Accordingly, God to advance and maintain the kingdom of his own Son, not only overthrows before him external enemies, but also delivers him from domestic contentions; that is to say, from those within his kingdom, which is the Church.

People I did not know are subject to me. The conquests of David and the submission of the people to him, were only an obscure figure in which God has exhibited to us some faint representation of the boundless dominion of his own Son, whose kingdom extends "from the rising of the sun, even unto the going down of the same" (Mal. 1:11), and comprehends the whole world.

As soon as they hear me, they obey me. This applies more truly to the person of Christ, who, by means of his word, subdues the world to himself, and, at the simple hearing of his name, makes those obedient to him who before had been rebels against him. In like manner, David had acquired to himself so great a name by arms and warlike powers, that many of his enemies, subdued by fear, submitted themselves to him. And in this God exhibited a type of the conquest which Christ would make of the Gentiles, who, by the preaching of the Gospel alone, were subdued, and brought voluntarily to submit to his dominion; for the obedience of faith in which the dominion of Christ is founded "comes by hearing" (Rom. 10:17).

PSALM
18:46-50

The LORD lives! Praise be to my Rock! The life which David attributes to God is not to be restricted to the being or essence of God, but is rather to be understood of the evidence of it deducible from his works, which manifest to us that he lives. Whenever he withdraws the working of his power from before our eyes, the sense and cognisance of the truth, "God lives," also vanishes from our minds. He is, therefore, said *to live,* inasmuch as he shows, by evident proofs of his power, that it is he who preserves and upholds the world. And as David had known, by experience, this life of God, he celebrates it with praises and thanksgiving. God does not simply live in himself, and in his secret place, but displays his vital energy in the government of the whole world.

He is the God who avenges me, who subdues nations under me. If a man, upon receiving injury, breaks forth to avenge himself, he usurps the office of God; and, therefore, it is rash and impious for private individuals to retaliate the injuries which have been inflicted upon them. With respect to kings and magistrates, God, who declares the vengeance belongs to him, in arming them with the sword, constitutes them the ministers and executioners of his vengeance. David, therefore, has put the word *vengeance* for the just punishments which it was lawful for him to inflict by the commandment of God, provided he was led under the influence of a zeal duly regulated by the Holy Spirit, and not under the influence of the impetuosity of the flesh.

The Church militant, which is under the standard of Christ, has no permission to execute vengeance, except against those who obstinately refuse to be reclaimed. We are commanded to endeavour to overcome our enemies by doing them good, and to pray for their salvation. It becomes us, therefore, at the same time, to desire that they may be brought to repentance, and to a right state of mind, until it appear beyond all doubt that they are irrecoverably and hopelessly depraved. In the meantime, in regard to vengeance, it must be left to God, that we may not be carried headlong to execute it before the time.

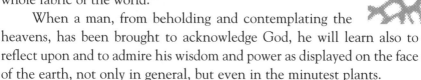

The heavens declare the glory of God; the skies proclaim the work of his hands. This psalm consists of two parts, in the first of which David celebrates the glory of God as manifested in his works; and, in the other, exalts and magnifies the knowledge of God which shines forth more clearly in his word. He only makes mention of the heavens; but, under this part of creation, which is the noblest, and the excellency of which is more conspicuous, he doubtless includes by synecdoche the whole fabric of the world.

When a man, from beholding and contemplating the heavens, has been brought to acknowledge God, he will learn also to reflect upon and to admire his wisdom and power as displayed on the face of the earth, not only in general, but even in the minutest plants.

It is indeed a great thing, that in the splendour of the heavens there is presented to our view a lively image of God; but, as the living voice has a greater effect in exciting our attention, or at least teaches us more surely and with greater profit than simple beholding, to which no oral instruction is added, we ought to mark the force of the figure which the Psalmist uses when he says, that the heavens by their preaching declare the glory of God.

David shows how it is that the heavens proclaim to us the glory of God, namely, by openly bearing testimony that they have not been put together by chance, but were wonderfully created by the supreme Architect. When we behold the heavens, we cannot but be elevated, by the contemplation of them, to him who is their great Creator; and the beautiful arrangement and wonderful variety which distinguish the courses and station of the heavenly bodies, together with the beauty and splendour which are manifest in them, cannot but furnish us with an evident proof of his providence. Scripture, indeed, makes known to us the time and manner of the creation; but the heavens themselves, although God should say nothing on the subject, proclaim loudly and distinctly enough that they have been fashioned by his hands: and this of itself abundantly suffices to bear testimony to men of his glory. As soon as we acknowledge God to be the supreme Architect, who has erected the beauteous fabric of the universe, our minds must necessarily be ravished with wonder at his infinite goodness, wisdom, and power.

PSALM 19:2-6

Day after day they pour forth speech; night after night they display knowledge. Philosophers, who have more penetration into those matters than others, understand how the stars are arranged in such beautiful order, that notwithstanding their immense number there is no confusion; but to the ignorant and unlettered, the continual succession of days is a more undoubted proof of the providence of God. David, therefore, having spoken of the heavens, does not here descend from them to other parts of the world; but, from an effect more sensible and nearer our apprehension, he confirms what he has just now said, namely, that the glory of God not only shines, but also resounds in the heavens.

David here teaches, from the established alternations of days and nights, that the course and revolutions of the sun, and moon, and stars, are regulated by the marvellous wisdom of God. If, indeed, we were as attentive as we ought to be, even one day would suffice to bear testimony to us of the glory of God, and even one night would be sufficient to perform to us the same office. But when we see the sun and the moon performing their daily revolutions,—the sun by day appearing over our heads, and the moon succeeding in its turn,—the sun ascending by degrees, while at the same time he approaches nearer us,—and afterwards bending his course so as to depart from us by little and little;—and when we see that by this means the length of the days and nights is regulated, and that the variation of their length is arranged according to a law so uniform, as invariably to recur at the same points of time in every successive year, we have in this a much brighter testimony to the glory of God. David, therefore, with the highest reason, declares, that although God should not speak a single word to men, yet the orderly and useful succession of days and nights eloquently proclaims the glory of God, and that there is now left to men no pretext for ignorance; for, since the days and nights perform towards us so well and so carefully the office of teachers, we may acquire, if we are duly attentive, a sufficient amount of knowledge under their tuition.

There is no speech or language where their voice is not heard. Different nations differ from each other as to language; but the heavens have a common language to teach all men without distinction.

The law of the LORD. While the heavens bear witness concerning God, their testimony does not lead men so far as that thereby they learn truly to fear him, and acquire a well-grounded knowledge of him; it serves only to render them inexcusable. It is doubtless true, that if we were not very dull and stupid, the signatures and proofs of Deity which are to be found on the theatre of the world, are abundant enough, to incite us to acknowledge and reverence God; but as, although surrounded with so clear a light, we are nevertheless blind. This splendid representation of the glory of God, without the aid of the word, would profit us nothing, although it should be to us as a loud and distinct proclamation sounding in our ears. Accordingly, God vouchsafes to those whom he has determined to call to salvation, special grace, just as in ancient times, while he gave to all men without exception evidences of his existence in his works, he communicated to the children of Abraham alone his Law, thereby to furnish them with a more certain and intimate knowledge of his majesty. Whence it follows, that the Jews are bound by a double tie to serve God. As the Gentiles, to whom God has spoken only by the dumb creatures, have no excuse for their ignorance, how much less is their stupidity to be endured who neglect to hear the voice which proceeds from his own sacred mouth? The end, therefore, which David here has in view, is to excite the Jews, whom God had bound to himself by a more sacred bond, to yield obedience to him with a more prompt and cheerful affection.

Further, under the term *law*, he not only means the rule of living righteously, or the Ten Commandments, but he also comprehends the covenant by which God had distinguished that people from the rest of the world, and the whole doctrine of Moses, the parts of which he afterwards enumerates under the terms *testimonies, statutes*, and other names. These titles and commendations by which he exalts the dignity and excellence of the Law would not agree with the Ten Commandments alone, unless there were, at the same time, joined to them a free adoption and the promises which depend upon it; and, in short, the whole body of doctrine of which true religion consists.

PSALM 19:7

The law of the LORD is perfect, reviving the soul. By the word *perfect* David means, that if a man is duly instructed in the law of God, he lacks nothing which is requisite to perfect wisdom. In the writings of heathen authors there are no doubt to be found true and useful sentences scattered here and there; and it is also true, that God has put into the minds of men some knowledge of justice and uprightness; but in consequence of the corruption of our nature, the true light of truth is not to be found among men where revelation is not enjoyed, but only certain mutilated principles which are involved in much obscurity and doubt.

As the soul gives vigour and strength to the body, so the law in like manner is the life of the soul. In saying that the soul is restored, he has an allusion to the miserable state in which we are all born. There, no doubt, still survive in us some small remains of the first creation; but as no part of our constitution is free from defilement and impurity, the condition of the soul thus corrupted and depraved differs little from death, and tends altogether to death. It is, therefore, necessary that God should employ the law as a remedy for restoring us to purity; not that the letter of the law can do this of itself, but because God employs his word as an instrument for restoring our souls.

The statutes of the LORD are trustworthy, making wise the simple. *Making wise* seems here to be added as the commencement of the restoration of the soul. Understanding is the most excellent endowment of the soul; and David teaches us that it is to be derived from the law, for we are naturally destitute of it. By the words *the simple*, he is not to be understood as meaning any particular class of persons, as if others were sufficiently wise of themselves; but by it he teaches us, in the first place, that none are endued with right understanding until they have made progress in the study of the law. In the second place, he shows by it what kind of scholars God requires, namely those who are fools in their own estimation (1 Cor. 3:18), and who come down to the rank of children, that the loftiness of their own understanding may not prevent them from giving themselves up, with a spirit of entire docility, to the teaching of the word of God.

The precepts of the LORD *are right, giving joy to the heart. The commands of the* LORD *are radiant, giving light to the eyes.* We know how much every man is wedded to himself, and how difficult it is to eradicate from our minds the vain confidence of our own wisdom. It is therefore of great importance to be well convinced of this truth, that a man's life cannot be ordered aright unless it is framed according to the law of God, and that without this he can only wander in labyrinths and crooked bypaths.

PSALM 19:8

David adds, *that God's precepts give joy to the heart.* This implies that there is no other joy true and solid but that which proceeds from a good conscience; and of this we become partakers when we are certainly persuaded that our life is pleasing and acceptable to God. No doubt, the source from which true peace of conscience proceeds is faith, which freely reconciles us to God. But to the saints who serve God with true affection of heart there arises unspeakable joy also, from the knowledge that they do not labour in his service in vain, or without hope of recompense, since they have God as the judge and approver of their life. In short, this joy is put in opposition to all the corrupt enticements and pleasures of the world, which are a deadly bait, luring wretched souls to their everlasting destruction. The import of the Psalmist's language is, Those who take delight in committing sin procure for themselves abundant matter of sorrow; but the observance of the law of God, on the contrary, brings to man true joy.

In the end of the verse, the Psalmist teaches that *the commands of the* LORD *are radiant, giving light to the eyes.* By this he gives us tacitly to understand that it is only in the commandments of God that we find the difference between good and evil laid down, and that it is in vain to seek it elsewhere, since whatever men devise of themselves is mere filth and refuse, corrupting the purity of the life. He farther intimates that men, with all their acuteness, are blind, and always wander in darkness, until they turn their eyes to the light of heavenly doctrine. Whence it follows, that none are truly wise but those who take God for their conductor and guide, following the path which he points to them, and who are diligently seeking after the peace which he offers and presents by his word.

The commands of the LORD *are radiant, giving light to the eyes.* Here a question of no small difficulty arises; for Paul seems entirely to overthrow these commendations of the law which David here recites. How can these things agree together: that the law restores the souls of men, while yet it is a dead and deadly letter? that it rejoices men's hearts, and yet, by bringing in the spirit of bondage, strikes them with terror? that it enlightens the eyes, and yet, by casting a veil before our minds, excludes the light which ought to penetrate within? But, in the first place, we must remember that David does not speak simply of precepts of the Moral Law, but comprehends the whole covenant by which God had adopted the descendants of Abraham to be his peculiar people; and, therefore, to the Moral Law—the rule of living well—he joins the free promises of salvation, or rather Christ himself, in whom and upon whom this adoption was founded. But Paul, who had to deal with persons who perverted and abused the law, and separated it from the grace and the Spirit of Christ, refers to the ministry of Moses viewed merely by itself, and according to the letter. It is certain, that if the Spirit of Christ does not quicken the law, the law is not only unprofitable, but also deadly to its disciples. Without Christ, there is in the law nothing but inexorable rigour, which adjudges all mankind to the wrath and curse of God. And farther, without Christ, there remains within us a rebelliousness of the flesh, which kindles in our hearts a hatred of God and of his law, and from this proceeds the distressing bondage and awful terror of which the Apostle speaks.

These different ways in which the law may be viewed, easily show us the manner of reconciling these passages of Paul and David, which seem at first view to be at variance. The design of Paul is to show what the law can do for us, taken by itself; that is to say, what it can do for us when, without the promise of grace, it strictly and rigorously exacts from us the duty which we owe to God; but David, in praising it as he here does, speaks of the whole doctrine of the law, which includes also the gospel, and, therefore, under the law he comprehends Christ.

Day 63   MARCH 3

The fear of the LORD is pure, enduring forever. The ordinances of the LORD are sure and altogether righteous. By *the fear of the LORD* we are here to understand the way in which God is to be served; and therefore it is taken in an active sense for the doctrine which prescribes to us the manner in which we ought to fear God. The way in which men generally manifest their fear of God, is by inventing false religions and a vitiated worship; in doing which they only so much more provoke his wrath. David, therefore, here indirectly condemns these corrupt inventions, about which men torment themselves in vain, and which often sanction impurity; and in opposition to them he justly affirms, that in the keeping of the law there is an exemption from every thing which defiles. He adds, that *it endures for ever;* as if he had said, This is the treasure of everlasting happiness. We see how mankind, without well thinking what they are doing, pursue, with impetuous and ardent affections, the transitory things of this world; but, in thus catching at the empty shadow of a happy life, they lose true happiness itself.

In the second clause, by calling the commandments of God *sure,* David shows that whatever men undertake to do at the mere suggesting of their own minds, without having a regard to the law of God as a rule, is error and falsehood. And, indeed, he could not have more effectually stirred us up to love, and zealously to live according to the law, than by giving us this warning, that all those who order their life, without having any respect to the law of God, deceive themselves, and follow after mere delusions.

When he says, *they are altogether righteous,* the meaning is, They are all righteous from the greatest to the least, without a single exception. By this commendation he distinguishes the law of God from all the doctrine of men, for no blemish or fault can be found in it, but it is in all points absolutely perfect.

PSALM 19:11

By them is your servant warned; in keeping them there is great reward. No man will ever speak truly and in good earnest of heavenly truth, but he who has it deeply fixed in his own heart. David therefore acknowledges, that whatever prudence he had for regulating and framing his life aright, he was indebted for it to the law of God. Although, however, it is properly of himself that he speaks, yet by his own example he sets forth a general rule, namely, that if persons wish to have a proper method for governing their life well, the law of God alone is perfectly sufficient for this purpose; but that, on the contrary, as soon as persons depart from it, they are liable to fall into numerous errors and sins. It is to be observed that David, by all at once turning his discourse to God, appeals to him as a witness of what he had said, the more effectually to convince men that he speaks sincerely and from the bottom of his heart.

In keeping them there is great reward. It is no mean commendation of the law when it is said, that in it God enters into covenant with us, and, so to speak, brings himself under obligation to recompense our obedience. In requiring from us whatever is contained in the law, he demands nothing but what he has a right to; yet such is his free and undeserved liberality, that he promises to his servants a reward, which, in point of justice, he does not owe them. The promises of the law, it is true, are made of no effect; but it is through our fault: for even he who is most perfect amongst us comes far short of full and complete righteousness; and men cannot expect any reward for their works until they have perfectly and to the full satisfied the requirements of the law. Thus these two doctrines completely harmonise: first, that eternal life shall be given as the reward of works to him who fulfils the law in all points; and, secondly, that the law notwithstanding denounces a curse against all men, because the whole human family are destitute of the righteousness of works. What God promises in the law to those who perfectly obey it, true believers obtain by his gracious liberality and fatherly goodness, inasmuch as he accepts for perfect righteousness their holy desires and earnest endeavours to obey.

Who can discern his errors? Forgive my hidden faults. Every man should examine his own life and compare not only his actions, but also his thoughts, with that perfect rule of righteousness which is laid down in the law. Thus it will come to pass, that all, from the least to the greatest, seeing themselves cut off from all hope of reward from the law, will be constrained to flee for refuge to the mercy of God.

PSALM 19:12

We should remember that we are not guilty of one offence only, but are overwhelmed with an immense mass of impurities. The more diligently any one examines himself, the more readily will he acknowledge with David, that if God should discover our secret faults, there would be found in us an abyss of sins so great as to have neither bottom nor shore, as we say; for no man can comprehend in how many ways he is guilty before God. From this also it appears, that the Papists are bewitched, and chargeable with the grossest hypocrisy, when they pretend that they can easily and speedily gather all their sins once a year into a bundle. The decree of the Lateran Council commands every one to confess all his sins once every year, and at the same time declares that there is no hope of pardon but in complying with that decree. Accordingly, the blinded Papist, by going to the confessional, to mutter his sins into the ear of the priest, thinks he has done all that is required, as if he could count upon his fingers all the sins which he has committed during the course of the whole year; whereas, even the saints, by strictly examining themselves, can scarcely come to the knowledge of the hundredth part of their sins, and, therefore, with one voice unite with David in saying, *Who can discern his errors?* Nor will it do to allege that it is enough if each performs the duty of reckoning up his sins to the utmost of his ability. This does not diminish, in any degree, the absurdity of this famous decree. As it is impossible for us to do what the law requires, all whose hearts are really and deeply imbued with the principle of the fear of God must necessarily be overwhelmed with despair, so long as they think themselves bound to enumerate all their sins, in order to their being pardoned; and those who imagine they can disburden themselves of their sins in this way must be persons altogether stupid.

PSALM 19.13-14

Keep your servant also from willful sins; may they not rule over me. Then will I be blameless, innocent of great transgression. By *willful sins* David means known and evident transgressions, accompanied with proud contempt and obstinacy. By the words *keep from*, he intimates, that such is the natural propensity of the flesh to sin, that even the saints themselves would immediately break forth or rush headlong into it, did not God, by his own guardianship and protection, keep them back. It is to be observed, that while he calls himself *the servant of God*, he nevertheless acknowledges that he had need of the bridle, lest he should arrogantly and rebelliously break forth in transgressing the law of God. Being regenerated by the Spirit of God, he groaned, it is true, under the burden of his sins; but he knew, on the other hand, how great is the rebellion of the flesh, and how much we are inclined to forgetfulness of God, from which proceed contempt of his majesty and all impiety.

All mankind are naturally enslaved to sin, and the faithful themselves would become the bond-slaves of sin also, if God did not unceasingly watch over them to guide them in the path of holiness, and to strengthen them for persevering in it. We ought never to pray for pardon, without, at the same time, asking to be strengthened and fortified by the power of God for the time to come, that temptations, in future, may not gain advantage over us. The remedy to which we should have recourse is to pray to God to restrain us.

May the words of my mouth and the meditation of my heart be pleasing in your sight, O LORD, my Rock and my Redeemer. David asks still more expressly to be fortified by the grace of God, and thus enabled to live an upright and holy life. We know how difficult it is, even for the most perfect, so to bridle their words and thoughts, as that nothing may pass through their heart or mouth which is contrary to the will of God; and yet this inward purity is what the law chiefly requires of us. Now, the rarer this virtue—the rarer this strict control of the heart and of the tongue is, let us learn so much the more the necessity of our being governed by the Holy Spirit, in order to regulate our life uprightly and honestly.

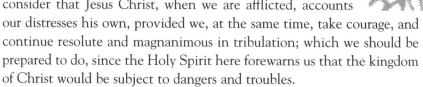

This is a prayer that God, by blessing the king, would show himself the Saviour of the whole people.

May the LORD answer you when you are in distress; may the name of the God of Jacob protect you. Since Christ, our King, being an everlasting priest, never ceases to make intercession with God, the whole body of the Church should unite in prayer with him; and further, we can have no hope of being heard except if he goes before us, and conduct us to God. And it serves in no small degree to assuage our sorrows to consider that Jesus Christ, when we are afflicted, accounts our distresses his own, provided we, at the same time, take courage, and continue resolute and magnanimous in tribulation; which we should be prepared to do, since the Holy Spirit here forewarns us that the kingdom of Christ would be subject to dangers and troubles.

May he remember all your sacrifices; and accept your burnt offerings. Selah. We know that whenever the fathers prayed under the law, their hope of obtaining what they asked was founded upon their sacrifices; and, in like manner, at this day our prayers are acceptable to God only insofar as Christ sprinkles and sanctifies them with the perfume of his own sacrifice.

Some trust in chariots and some in horses; but we trust in the name of the LORD our God. We see how natural it is to almost all men to be the more courageous and confident the more they possess of riches, power and military forces.

The people of God, therefore, here protest that they do not place their hope, as is the usual way with men, in their military forces and warlike apparatus, but only in the aid of God. As the Holy Spirit sets the assistance of God in opposition to human strength, it ought to be particularly noticed, that whenever our minds come to be occupied by carnal confidence, they fall at the same time into a forgetfulness of God. The inspired writer, therefore, uses the word *remember,* to show, that when the saints betake themselves to God, they must cast off every thing which would hinder them from placing an exclusive trust in him. This rememberance of God serves two important purposes to the faithful. In the first place, however much power and resources they may possess, it nevertheless withdraws them from all vain confidence, so that they do not expect any success except from the pure grace of God. In the second place, if they are bereft and utterly destitute of all succour, it notwithstanding so strengthens and encourages them, that they call upon God both with confidence and constancy.

PSALM 21

This psalm contains a public and solemn thanksgiving for the prosperous and happy condition of the king. It is shown that the safety and prosperity of the king ought to produce public and general rejoicing through the whole realm, inasmuch as God by this means intended to preserve the whole body in safety.

You will destroy their descendants from the earth, their posterity from mankind. David amplifies the greatness of God's wrath, from the circumstance that it shall extend even to the children of the wicked. It is a doctrine common enough in Scripture, that God not only inflicts punishment upon the first originators of wickedness, but makes it even to overflow into the bosom of their children. And yet when he thus pursues his vengeance to the third and fourth generation, he cannot be said indiscriminately to involve the innocent with the guilty. As the seed of the ungodly, whom he has deprived of his grace, are accursed, and as all are by nature children of wrath, devoted to everlasting destruction, he is no less just in exercising his severity towards the children than towards the fathers. Who can lay any thing to his charge, if he withhold from those who are unworthy of it the grace which he communicates to his own children? In both ways he shows how dear and precious to him is the kingdom of Christ; first, in extending his mercy to the children of the righteous even to a thousand generations; and, secondly, in causing his wrath to rest upon the reprobate, even to the third and fourth generation.

Be exalted, O LORD, in your strength. The psalm is at length concluded with a prayer, which again confirms that the kingdom which is spoken of is so connected with the glory of God, that his power is reflected from it. This was no doubt true with respect to the kingdom of David; for God in old time displayed his power in exalting him to the throne. But what is here stated was only fully accomplished in Christ, who was appointed by the heavenly Father to be King over us, and who is at the same time God manifest in the flesh. As his divine power ought justly to strike terror into the wicked, so it is described as full of the sweetest consolation to us, which ought to inspire us with joy, and incite us to celebrate it with songs of praise and thanksgiving.

My God, my God, why have you forsaken me? Why are you so far from saving me, so far from the words of my groaning? As our Saviour Jesus Christ, when hanging on the cross, and when ready to yield up his soul into the hands of God his Father, made use of these very words of David, who represented a type of Christ (Matt. 27:46), we must consider how these two things can agree, that Christ was the only begotten Son of God, and that yet he was so penetrated with grief, seized with so great mental trouble, as to cry out that God his Father had forsaken him. As Peter, in Acts 2:24, clearly testifies that, "it was not possible that he should be holden of the pains of death," it follows that he was not altogether exempted from them. And as he became our representative, and took upon him our sins, it was certainly necessary that he should appear before the judgment-seat of God as a sinner. From this proceeded the terror and dread which constrained him to pray for deliverance from death; not that it was so grievous to him merely to depart from this life; but because there was before his eyes the curse of God, to which all who are sinners are exposed. Now, if during his first conflict "his sweat was as it were great drops of blood," and he needed an angel to comfort him (Luke 22:43), it is not wonderful if, in his last sufferings on the cross, he uttered a complaint which indicated the deepest sorrow. Christ, although subject to human passions and affections, never fell into sin through the weakness of the flesh; for the perfection of his nature preserved him from all excess. He could therefore overcome all the temptations with which Satan assailed him, without receiving any wound in the conflict which might afterwards constrain him to halt.

But I am a worm and not a man, scorned by men and despised by the people. If God so severely exercised his most eminent servant David, and abased him so far that he had not a place even among the most despised of men, let us not take it ill, if, after his example, we are brought low. We ought, however, principally to call to our rememberance the Son of God, in whose person we know this also was fulfilled, as Isaiah had predicted (53:3), "He is despised and rejected of men; a man of sorrows, and acquainted with grief: and we hid as it were our faces from him; he was despised, and we esteemed him not."

PSALM 22:8-10

From birth I was cast upon you; from my mother's womb you have been my God. In acknowledging that he was *taken from the womb* by the hand of God, and that *from my mother's womb you have been my God,* the meaning is, that although it is by the operation of natural causes that infants come into the world, and are nourished with their mother's milk, yet therein the wonderful providence of God brightly shines forth. This miracle, it is true, because of its ordinary occurrence, is made less account of by us. But if ingratitude did not put upon our eyes the veil of stupidity, we would be ravished with admiration at every childbirth in the world. What prevents the child from perishing, as it might, a hundred times in its own corruption, before the time for bringing it forth arrives, but that God, by his secret and incomprehensible power, keeps it alive in its grave? And after it is brought into the world, seeing it is subject to so many miseries, and cannot stir a finger to help itself, how could it live even for a single day, did not God take it up into his fatherly bosom to nourish and protect it? It is, therefore, with good reason said, that the infant *is cast upon him;* for, unless he fed the tender little babes, and watched over all the offices of the nurse, even at the very time of their being brought forth, they are exposed to hundred deaths by which they would be suffocated in an instant.

Finally, David concludes that God was *his God.* God, it is true, to all appearances, shows the like goodness which is here celebrated even to the brute creation; but it is only to mankind that he shows himself to be father in a special manner. And although he does not immediately endue babes with the knowledge of himself, yet he is said *to give them confidence,* because, by showing in fact that he takes care of their life, he in a manner allures them to himself; as it is said in another place, "He gives the beast his food, and to the young ravens which cry" (Ps. 147:9). Since God anticipates in this manner, by his grace, little infants before they have yet the use of reason, it is certain that he will never disappoint the hope of his servants when they petition and call upon him. This is the argument by which David struggled with, and endeavoured to overcome temptation.

Day 71   M A R C H   1 1

I am poured out like water, and all my bones are out of joint. My heart has turned to wax; it has melted away within me. These sufferings are also applicable to Christ. Being a real man, he was truly subject to the infirmities of our flesh, only without the taint of sin. The perfect purity of his nature did not extinguish the human affection; it only regulated them, that they might not become sinful through excess. The greatness of his griefs, therefore could not so weaken him as to prevent him, even in the midst of his most excruciating sufferings, from submitting himself to the will of God, with a composed and peaceful mind.

My strength is dried up like a potsherd, and my tongue sticks to the roof of my mouth; you lay me in the dust of death. By this he intimates, that all hope of life was taken from him; and in this sense Paul also says (2 Cor. 1:9) that "he had received the sentence of death in himself." But David here speaks of himself in hyberbolical language, and he does this in order to lead us beyond himself to Christ. The dreadful encounter of our Redeemer with death, by which there was forced from his body blood instead of sweat; his descent into hell, by which he tasted of the wrath of God which was due to sinners; and, in short, his emptying himself, could not be adequately expressed by any of the ordinary forms of speech. Moreover, David speaks of death as those who are in trouble are accustomed to speak of it, who, struck with fear, can think of nothing but of their being reduced to dust and to destruction.

I will declare your name to my brothers; in the congregation I will praise you. In this psalm we saw that, under the figure of David, Christ has been here shadowed forth to us. By the name of *brothers*, the right of fraternal alliance with Christ has been confirmed to us. This, no doubt, to a certain extent, belongs to all mankind, but the true enjoyment thereof belongs properly to genuine believers alone. For this reason Christ himself, with his own mouth, limits this title to his disciples, saying, "Go to my brethren, and say unto them, I ascend unto my Father and your Father, and to my God and your God" (John 20:17).

The LORD *is my shepherd.* This psalm is neither intermingled with prayers, nor does it complain of miseries for the purpose of obtaining relief; but it contains simply a thanksgiving, from which it appears that it was composed when David had obtained peaceable possession of the kingdom, and lived in prosperity and in the enjoyment of all he could desire.

Although God, by his benefits, gently allures us to himself, as it were by a taste of his fatherly sweetness, yet there is nothing into which we more easily fall than into forgetfulness of him, when we are in the enjoyment of peace and comfort. Yea, prosperity not only so intoxicates many, as to carry them beyond all bounds in their mirth, but it also engenders insolence, which makes them proudly rise up and break forth against God. Accordingly, there is scarcely a hundredth part of those who enjoy in abundance the good things of God, who keep themselves in his fear, and live in the exercise of humility and temperance, which would be so becoming. For this reason, we ought the more carefully to mark the example which is here set before us by David, who, elevated to the dignity of sovereign power, surrounded with the splendour of riches and honours, possessed of the greatest abundance of temporal good things, and in the midst of princely pleasures, not only testifies that he is mindful of God, but calling to rememberance the benefits which God had conferred upon him, makes them ladders by which he may ascend nearer to him. By this means he not only bridles the wantonness of his flesh, but also excites himself with the greater earnestness of gratitude, and the other exercises of godliness, as appears from the concluding sentence of the psalm, where he says, "I shall dwell in the house of Jehovah for a length of days." In like manner, in the 18th psalm, which was composed at a period in his life when he was applauded on every side, by calling himself the servant of God, he showed the humility and simplicity of heart to which he had attained, and, at the same time, openly testified his gratitude, by applying himself to the celebration of the praises of God.

The LORD is my shepherd, I shall not be in want. Under the similitude of a shepherd, he commends the care which God, in his providence, had exercised towards him. His language implies that God had no less care of him than a shepherd has of the sheep who are committed to his charge. God, in the Scripture, frequently takes to himself the name, and puts on the character of a shepherd, and this is no mean token of his tender love towards us. As this is a lowly and homely manner of speaking, he who does not disdain to stoop so low for our sake, must bear a singularly strong affection towards us. It is therefore wonderful, that when he invites us to himself with such gentleness and familiarity, we are not drawn or allured to him, that we may rest in safety and peace under his guardianship.

But it should be observed, that God is a shepherd only to those who, touched with a sense of their own weakness and poverty, feel their need of his protection, and who willingly abide in his sheepfold, and surrender themselves to be governed by him. David, who excelled both in power and riches, nevertheless frankly confessed himself to be a poor sheep, that he might have God for his shepherd. Who is there, then, amongst us, who would exempt himself from this necessity, seeing our own weakness sufficiently shows that we are more than miserable if we do not live under the protection of this shepherd? We ought to bear in mind, that our happiness consists in this, that his hand is stretched forth to govern us, that we live under his shadow, and that his providence keeps watch and ward over our welfare. Although, therefore, we have abundance of all temporal good things, yet let us be assured that we cannot be truly happy unless God vouchsafe to reckon us among the number of his flock. Besides, we then only attribute to God the office of a Shepherd with due and rightful honour, when we are persuaded that his providence alone is sufficient to supply all our necessities. As those who enjoy the greatest abundance of outward good things are empty and famished if God is not their shepherd; so it is beyond all doubt that those whom he has taken under his charge shall not want a full abundance of all good things. David, therefore, declares that he is not afraid of wanting any thing, because God is his Shepherd.

PSALM 23:2-3

He makes me lie down in green pastures, he leads me beside quiet waters. David relates how abundantly God had provided for all his necessities. The heavenly Shepherd had omitted nothing which might contribute to make him live happily under his care. He, therefore, compares the great abundance of all things requisite for the purposes of the present life which he enjoyed, to meadows richly covered with grass, and to gently flowing streams of water; or he compares the benefit or advantage of such things to sheep-cots; for it would not have been enough to have been fed and satisfied in rich pasture, had there not also been provided waters to drink, and the shadow of the sheep-cot to cool and refresh him.

He restores my soul. He guides me in paths of righteousness for his name's sake. As is the duty of a good shepherd to cherish his sheep, and when they are diseased or weak to nurse and support them, David declares that this was the manner in which he was treated by God. *The restoring of the soul,* or *the conversion of the soul,* as it is, literally rendered, is of the same import as *to make anew,* or *to recover.*

By *the paths of righteousness,* David means easy and plain paths.

God is in no respect wanting to his people, seeing he sustains them by his power, invigorates and quickens them, and averts from them whatever is hurtful, and they may walk at ease in plain and straight paths. That, however, he may not ascribe any thing to his own worth or merit, David represents the goodness of God as the cause of so great liberality, declaring that God bestows all these things upon him *for his own name's sake.* And certainly his choosing us to be his sheep, and his performing towards us all the offices of a shepherd, is a blessing which proceeds entirely from his free and sovereign goodness.

Day 75

Even though I walk through the valley of the shadow of death, I will fear no evil, for you are with me; your rod and your staff, they comfort me. True believers, although they dwell safely under the protection of God, are, notwithstanding, exposed to many dangers, or rather they are liable to all the afflictions which befall mankind in common, that they may the better feel how much they need the protection of God. David, therefore, here expressly declares, that if any adversity should befall him, he would lean upon the providence of God. Thus he does not promise himself continual pleasures; but he fortifies himself by the help of God courageously to endure the various calamities with which he might be visited.

PSALM 23.4

When David speaks of *the shadow of death*, he makes an allusion to the dark recesses or dens of wild beasts, to which, when an individual approaches, he is suddenly seized at his first entrance with an apprehension and fear of death. Now, since God, in the person of his only begotten Son, has exhibited himself to us as our shepherd, much more clearly than he did in old time to the fathers who lived under the Law, we do not render sufficient honour to his protecting care, if we do not lift our eyes to behold it, and keeping them fixed upon it, tread all fears and terrors under our feet.

We thus see how, in his prosperity, he never forgot that he was a man, but even then seasonably meditated on the adversities which afterwards might come upon him. And certainly, the reason why we are so terrified, when it pleases God to exercise us with the cross, is, because every man, that he may sleep soundly and undisturbed, wraps himself up in carnal security. But there is a great difference between this sleep of stupidity and the repose which faith produces. Since God tries faith by adversity, it follows that no one truly confides in God, but he who is armed with invincible constancy for resisting all the fears with which he may be assailed. Yet David did not mean to say that he was devoid of all fear, but only that he would surmount it so as to go without fear wherever his shepherd should lead him.

PSALM 23:5

You prepare a table before me in the presence of my enemies. You anoint my head with oil. These words, which are put in the future tense, here denote a continued act. David, therefore, now repeats, without a figure, what he has hitherto declared, concerning the beneficence of God, under the similitude of a shepherd. He tells us that by his liberality he is supplied with all that is necessary for the maintenance of this life. When he says, *You prepare a table*, he means that God furnished him with sustenance without trouble or difficulty on his part, just as if a father should stretch forth his hand to give food to his child. He enhances this benefit from the additional consideration, that although many malicious persons envy his happiness, and desire his ruin, yea, endeavour to defraud him of the blessing of God; yet God does not desist from showing himself liberal towards him, and from doing him good.

What he subjoins concerning *oil*, has a reference to a custom which then prevailed. We know that in old time, ointments were used at the more magnificent feasts, and no man thought he had honourably received his guests if he had not perfumed them therewith. Now, this exuberant store of *oil*, and also this overflowing *cup*, ought to be explained as denoting the abundance which goes beyond the mere supply of the common necessaries of life; for it is spoken in commendation of the royal wealth with which, as the sacred historian records, David had been amply furnished. All men, it is true, are not treated with the same liberality with which David was treated; but there is not an individual who is not under the obligation to God by the benefits which God has conferred upon him, so that we are constrained to acknowledge that he is a kind and liberal Father to all his people.

In the meantime, let each of us stir himself up to gratitude to God for his benefits, and the more abundantly these have been bestowed upon us, our gratitude ought to be the greater. If he is ungrateful who, having only a coarse loaf, does not acknowledge in that the fatherly providence of God, how much less can the stupidity of those be tolerated, who glut themselves with the great abundance of the good things of God which they possess, without having any sense or taste of his goodness towards them?

PSALM
23:5

My cup overflows. David, by his own example, admonishes the rich of their duty, that they may be the more ardent in the expression of their gratitude to God, the more delicately he feeds them. Farther, let us remember, that those who have greater abundance than others are bound to observe moderation not less than if they had only as much of the food things of this life as would serve for their limited and temperate enjoyment. We are too much inclined by nature to excess; and, therefore, when God is, in respect of worldly things, bountiful to his people, it is not to stir up and nourish in them this disease. All men ought to attend to the rule of Paul, which is laid down in Philippians 4:12, that they "may know both how to be abased, and how to abound." That want may not sink us into despondency, we need to be sustained by patient endurance; and, on the other hand, that too great abundance may not elate us above measure, we need to be restrained by the bridle of temperance. Accordingly, the Lord, when he enriches his own people, restrains, at the same time, the licentious desire of the flesh by the spirit of continence, so that, of their own accord, they prescribe to themselves rules of temperance. Not that it is unlawful for rich men to enjoy more freely the abundance which they possess than if God had given them a smaller portion; but all men ought to beware, (and much more kings,) lest they should be dissolved in voluptuous pleasure. David, no doubt, as was perfectly lawful, allowed himself larger scope than if he had been only one of the common people, or than if he had still dwelt in his father's cottage, but he so regulated himself in the midst of his delicacies, as not at all to take pleasure in stuffing and fattening the body. He knew well how to distinguish between the table which God had prepared for him and a trough for swine. It is also worthy of particular notice, that although David lived upon his own lands, the tribute money and other revenues of the kingdom, he gave thanks to God just as if God had daily given him his food with his own hand. From this we conclude that he was not blinded with his riches, but always looked upon God as his householder, who brought forth meat and drink from his own store, and distributed it to him at the proper season.

PSALM 23:6

Surely goodness and love will follow me all the days of my life, and I will dwell in the house of the LORD forever. Having recounted the blessings which God had bestowed upon him, he now expresses his undoubted persuasion of the continuance of them to the end of his life. Although experience led him to hope well, yet it was principally on the promise by which God confirms his people with respect to the future that he depended. If it is objected that it is presumption for a man to promise himself a continued course of prosperity in this uncertain and changeable world, the answer is, that David did not speak in this manner with the view of imposing on God a law; but he hoped for such exercise of God's beneficence towards him as the condition of this world permits, with which he would be contented.

I will dwell in the house of the LORD. By this concluding sentence he manifestly shows that he does not confine his thoughts to earthly pleasures or comforts; but that the mark at which he aims is fixed in heaven, and to reach this was his great object in all things. It is as if he had said, I do not live for the mere purpose of living, but rather to exercise myself in the fear and service of God, and to make progress daily in all the branches of true godliness. And not only so, but he also intimates that to live to God is, in his estimation, of so great importance, that he valued all the comforts of the flesh only in proportion as they served to enable him to live to God. He plainly affirms, that the end which he contemplated in all the benefits which God had conferred upon him was, that he might dwell in the house of the Lord. Whence it follows, that when deprived of the enjoyment of this blessing, he made no account of all other things; as if he had said, I would take no pleasure in earthly comforts, unless I, at the same time, belonged to the flock of God, as he also writes in another place, "Happy are those whose God is the Lord" (Ps. 144:15). Why did he desire so greatly to frequent the temple, but to offer sacrifices there along with his fellow-worshippers, and to improve by the other exercises of religion in meditation upon the celestial life? It is, therefore, certain that the mind of David, by the aid of the temporal prosperity which he enjoyed, was elevated to the hope of the everlasting inheritance.

PSALM 24:1

The earth is the LORD's, *and everything in it, the world, and all who live in it.* We will find in many other places the children of Abraham compared with all the rest of mankind, that the free goodness of God, in selecting them from all other nations, and in embracing them with his favour, may shine forth the more conspicuously. The object of the beginning of the psalm is to show that the Jews had nothing of themselves which could entitle them to approach nearer or more familiarly to God than the Gentiles. As God by his providence preserves the world, the power of his government is alike extended to all, so that he ought to be worshipped by all, even as he also shows to all men, without exception, the fatherly care he has about them. But since he preferred the Jews to all other nations, it was indispensably necessary that there should be some sacred bond of connection between him and them, which might distinguish them from the heathen nations. By this argument David invites and exhorts them to holiness. He tells them that it was reasonable that those whom God had adopted as his children, should bear certain marks peculiar to themselves, and not be altogether like strangers, Not that he incites them to endeavour to prejudice God against others, in order to gain his exclusive favour; but he teaches them, from the end or design of their election, that they shall then have secured to them the firm and peaceful possession of the honour which God had conferred upon them above other nations, when they devote themselves to an upright and holy life. In vain would they have been collected together into a distinct body, as the peculiar people of God, if they did not apply themselves to the cultivation of holiness.

In short, the Psalmist pronounces God to be the King of the whole world, to let all men know that, even by the law of nature, they are bound to serve him.

With respect to the word *everything,* under it all the riches with which the earth is adorned are comprehended, as well as men themselves, who are the most illustrious ornament and glory of the earth. If they should fail, the earth would exhibit a scene of desolation and solitude, not less hideous than if God should despoil it of all its other riches.

PSALM
24:2

For he founded it upon the seas and established it upon the waters. The Psalmist here confirms the truth, that men are rightfully under the authority and power of God, so that in all places and countries they ought to acknowledge him as King. And he confirms it from the very order manifested in the creation; for the wonderful providence of God is clearly reflected in the whole face of the earth. The proof of it is most evident. How is it that the earth appears above the water, but because God purposely intended to prepare a habitation for men? Philosophers themselves admit, that as the element of the water is higher than the earth, it is contrary to the nature of the two elements, for any part of the earth to continue uncovered with the waters, and habitable. Accordingly, Job (28:11, 25) extols, in magnificent terms, that signal miracle by which God restrains the violent and tempestuous ragings of the sea, that it may not overwhelm the earth, which, if not thus restrained, it would immediately do, and produce horrible confusion. Nor does Moses forget to mention this in the history of creation. After having narrated that the waters were spread abroad so as to cover the whole earth, he adds, that by an express command of God they retired into one place, in order to leave empty space for the living creatures which were afterwards to be created (Gen. 1:9).

From that passage we learn that God had a care about men before they existed, inasmuch as he prepared for them a dwelling-place and other conveniences; and that he did not regard them as entire strangers, seeing he provided for their necessities, not less liberally than the father of a family does for his own children.

Who may ascend the hill of the LORD? Who may stand in his holy place? It being very well known that it was of pure grace the God erected his sanctuary, and chose for himself a dwelling-place among the Jews, David makes only a tacit reference to this subject. He insists principally on distinguishing true Israelites from the false and bastards. He takes the argument by which he exhorts the Jews to lead a holy and righteous life from this, that God had separated them from the rest of the world, to be his peculiar inheritance. The rest of mankind, it is true, seeing they were created by him, belong to his empire; but he who occupies a place in the church is more nearly related to him. All those, therefore, whom God receives into his flock he calls to holiness; and he lays them under obligations to follow it by his adoption. Moreover, by these words David indirectly rebukes hypocrites, who scrupled not falsely to take to themselves the holy name of God, as we know that they are usually lifted up with pride, because of the titles which they take without having the excellencies which these titles imply, contenting themselves with bearing only outside distinctions; yea, rather he purposely magnifies this singular grace of God, that every man may learn for himself, that he has no right of entrance or access to the sanctuary, unless he sanctify himself in order to serve God in purity. The ungodly and wicked, it is true, were in the habit of resorting to the tabernacle; and, therefore, God, by the prophet Isaiah (1:12), reproaches them for coming unworthily into his courts, and wearing the pavement thereof. But David here treats of those who may lawfully enter into God's sanctuary. The house of God being holy, if any rashly, and without right, rush into it, their corruption and abuse are nothing else but polluting it. As therefore they do not go up thither lawfully, David makes no account of their going up; yea, rather, under these words there is included a severe rebuke, of the conduct of wicked and profane men, in daring to go up into the sanctuary, and to pollute it with their impurity.

PSALM 24:4

He who has clean hands and a pure heart, who does not lift up his soul to an idol or swear by what is false. Under the purity of the hands and of the heart, and the reverence of God's name, David comprehends all religion, and denotes a well-ordered life. True purity, no doubt, has its seat in the heart, but it manifests its fruits in the works of the hands. The Psalmist, therefore, very properly joins to a pure heart the purity of the whole life; for that man acts a ridiculous part who boasts of having a sound heart, if he does not show by his fruits that the root is good. On the other hand, it will not suffice to frame the hands, feet, and eyes, according to the rule of righteousness, unless purity of heart precede outward continence. If any man should think it absurd that the first place is given to the hands, and not the heart, we answer without hesitation, that effects are often named before their causes, not that they precede them in order, but because it is sometimes advantageous to begin with things which are best known. David, then, would have the Jews to bring into the presence of God pure hands, and these along with an unfeigned heart.

A question may here be asked:—it may be asked, why David does not say so much as one word concerning faith and calling upon God. The reason of this is easily explained. As it seldom happens that a man behaves himself uprightly and innocently towards his brethren, unless he is so endued with the true fear of God as to walk circumspectly before him, David very justly forms his estimate of the piety of men towards God by the character of their conduct towards their fellow-men. For the same reason, Christ (Matt. 23:23) represents "judgment, mercy, and faith," as the principal points of the law; and Paul calls "charity" at one time "the end of the law" (1 Tim. 1:5), and at another "the bond of perfection" (Col. 3:14).

PSALM 24:5-6

He will receive blessing from the LORD and vindication from God his Savior. The more effectually to move the minds of the Israelites, David declares that nothing is more desirable than to be numbered among the flock of God, and to be members of the church. We must here consider that there is an implied contrast between true Israelites and those of them who were degenerate and bastards. The more license the wicked give themselves, the more presumptuous are they in pretending to the name of God, as if he were under obligation to them, because they are adorned with the same outward symbols of badges as true believers.

And when he speaks of *blessing,* he intimates that it is not those who boast of being the servants of God, while they have only the name, who shall be partakers of the promised blessing, but those only who answer to their calling with their whole heart, and without hypocrisy. It is, as we have already observed, a very powerful inducement to godliness and an upright life, when the faithful are assured that they do not lose their labour in following righteousness, since God has in reserve for them a blessing which cannot fail them.

He intends to show on the one hand, that it is not to be expected that the fruit or reward of righteousness will be bestowed on those who unrighteously profane God's sacred worship; and on the other hand, that it is impossible for God to disappoint his true worshippers; for it is his peculiar office to give evidence of his righteousness by doing them good.

Such is the generation of those who seek him, who seek your face, O God of Jacob. Selah. The Psalmist has limited the name of holy generation to the true observers of the law; as if he had said, All who have sprung from Abraham, according to the flesh, are not, on that account, his legitimate children. It is as if David had said here, Although circumcision distinguishes all the seed of Jacob according to the flesh from the Gentiles, yet we can only distinguish the chosen people by the fear and reverence of God, as Christ said, "Behold an Israelite indeed, in whom is no guile!" (John 1:47).

PSALM
24:7, 9

Lift up your heads, O you gates; be lifted up, you ancient doors, that the King of glory may come in. The magnificent and splendid structure of the temple, in which there was no more outward majesty than in the tabernacle, not being yet erected, David here speaks of the future building of it. By doing this, he encourages the pious Israelites to employ themselves more willingly, and with greater confidence, in the ceremonial observances of the law. It was no ordinary token of the goodness of God that he condescended to dwell in the midst of them by a visible symbol of his presence, and was willing that his heavenly dwelling-place should be seen upon earth.

This doctrine ought to be of use to us at this day; for it is an instance of the inestimable grace of God, that so far as the infirmity of our flesh will permit, we are lifted up even to God by the exercise of religion. What is the design of the preaching of the word, the sacraments, the holy assemblies, and the whole external government of the church, but that we may be united to God? It is not, therefore, without good reason that David extols so highly the service of God appointed in the law, seeing God exhibited himself to his saints in the ark of the covenant, and thereby gave them a certain pledge of speedy succour whenever they should invoke him for aid. God, it is true, "dwells not in temples made with hands," nor does he take delight in outward pomp; but as it was useful, as it was also the pleasure of God, that his ancient people, who were rude, and still in their infancy, should be lifted up to him by earthly elements, David does not here hesitate to set forth to them, for the confirmation of their faith, the sumptuous building of the temple, to assure them that it was not a useless theatre; but that when they rightly worshipped God in it, according to the appointment of his word, they stood as it were in his presence, and would actually experience that he was near them.

As David himself burned with intense desire for the erection of the temple, so he wished to inflame the hearts of all the godly with the same ardent desire, that, aided by the rudiments of the law, they might make more and more progress in the fear of God.

You ancient doors! David terms the *gates, ancient,* because the promise of God secured their continual stability. The temple excelled in materials and in workmanship, but its chief excellence consisted in this, that the promise of God was engraven upon it, as we shall see in Psalm 132:14, "This is my rest for ever." In terming the gates *everlasting,* the Psalmist, at the same time, makes a tacit contrast between the tabernacle and the temple. The tabernacle never had any certain abiding place, but being from time to time transported from one place to another, was like a wayfaring man. When, however, mount Zion was chosen, and the temple built, God then began to have there a certain and fixed place of abode. By the coming of Christ, that visible shadow vanished, and it is therefore not wonderful that the temple is no longer to be seen upon mount Zion, seeing it is now so great as to occupy the whole world. If it is objected, that at the time of the Babylonish captivity the gates which Solomon built were demolished, the answer is, God's decree stood fast, notwithstanding that temporary overthrow; and by virtue of it, the temple was soon after rebuilt; which was the same as if it had always continued entire.

PSALM 24:7b

PSALM 24:8, 10

Who is this King of glory? The LORD strong and mighty. . . . he is the King of glory. When God is spoken of as dwelling in the temple, it is not to be understood as if his infinite and incomprehensible essence had been shut up or confined within it; but that he was present there by his power and grace, as is implied in the promise which he made to Moses, "In all places where I record my name, I will come unto you, and I will bless you" (Ex. 20:24). That this was no vain and empty promise, but that God truly dwelt in the midst of the people, is what the faithful experienced who sought him not superstitiously, as if he had been fixed to the temple, but made use of the temple and of the service which was performed in it for elevating their hearts to heaven.

The amount of what is stated is, that whenever the people should call upon God in the temple, it would manifestly appear, from the effect which would follow, that the ark of the covenant was not a vain and illusory symbol of the presence of God, because he would always stretch forth his omnipotent arm for the defence and protection of his people. The repetition teaches us that true believers cannot be too constant and diligent in meditation on this subject. The son of God, clothed with our flesh, has now shown himself to be *king of glory* and LORD *strong and mighty,* and he is not entered into his temple only by shadows and figures, but really and in very deed, that he may dwell in the midst of us. There is, therefore, nothing to hinder us from boasting that we shall be invincible by his power.

Mount Zion, it is true, is not at this day the place appointed for the sanctuary, and the ark of the covenant is no longer the image or representation of God dwelling between the cherubim; but as we have this privilege in common with the fathers, that, by the preaching of the word and the sacraments, we may be united to God, it becomes us to use these helps with reverence; for if we despise them by a detestable pride, God cannot but at length utterly withdraw himself from us.

PSALM 25:1-3

To you, O LORD, I lift up my soul. The Psalmist declares at the very outset, that he is not driven here and there, after the manner of the ungodly, but that he directs all his desires and prayers to God alone. Nothing is more inconsistent with true and sincere prayer to God, than to waver and gaze about as the heathen do, for some help from the world; and at the same time to forsake God, or not to betake ourselves directly to his guardianship and protection. In order to strengthen the hope of obtaining his request, he declares, what is of the greatest importance in prayer, that he had his hope fixed in God, and that he was not ensnared by the allurements of the world, or prevented from lifting up his soul fully and unfeignedly to God. In order, therefore, that we may pray aright to God, let us be directed by this rule: not to distract our minds by various and uncertain hopes, nor to depend on worldly aid, but to yield to God the honour of lifting up our hearts to him in sincere and earnest prayer.

In you I trust, O my God. Do not let me be put to shame, nor let my enemies triumph over me. By the word *trust* David confirms that faith and hope are added as the cause of such an effect, namely, the lifting up of the soul. And, indeed, these are the wings by which our souls, rising above this world, are lifted up to God. David, then, was carried upwards to God with the whole desire of his heart, because, trusting to his promises, he thereby hoped for sure salvation. When he asks *that God would not let him be put to shame,* he offers up a prayer, which is taken from the ordinary doctrine of Scripture, namely, that they who trust in God shall never be ashamed. The reason which is added, is that he might not be exposed to the derision of his enemies, whose pride is no less hurtful to the feelings of the godly than it is displeasing to God.

No one whose hope is in you will ever be put to shame, but they will be put to shame who are treacherous without excuse. David declares that when he is delivered he will not enjoy exclusively the benefit of it; but that its fruit shall extend to all true believers; just as on the other hand, the faith of many would be shaken if he had been forsaken by God.

Day 88

PSALM 25:4-5

Show me your ways, O LORD, teach me your paths. The prayer which David offers up here, is to this effect: Lord, keep your servant in the firm persuasion of your promises, and do not let him turn aside to the right hand or to the left. When our minds are thus composed to patience, we undertake nothing rashly or by improper means, but depend wholly upon the providence of God. Accordingly, in this place David desires not merely to be directed by the Spirit of God, lest he should err from the right way, but also that God would clearly manifest to him his truth and faithfulness in the promises of his word, that he might live in peace before him, and be free from all impatience.

In the language of the Psalmist there is an allusion to those sudden and irregular emotions which arise in our minds when we are tossed by adversity, and by which we are precipitated into the devious and deceitful paths of error, till they are in due time subdued or allayed by the word of God. Although he frequently repeats the same thing, asking that God would make him to know his ways, and teach him in them, and lead him in his truth, there is no redundancy in these forms of speech. Our adversities are often like mists which darken the eyes; and every one knows from his own experience how difficult a thing it is, while these clouds of darkness continue, to discern in what way we ought to walk. But if David, so distinguished a prophet and endued with so much wisdom, stood in need of divine instruction, what shall become of us if, in our affliction, God dispel not from our minds those clouds of darkness which prevent us from seeing his light? As often, then, as any temptation may assail us, we ought always to pray that God would make the light of his truth to shine upon us, lest by having recourse to sinful devices, we should go astray, and wander into devious and forbidden paths.

For you are the God of my salvation. * By calling God *the God of his salvation,* he does so in order to strengthen his hope in God for the future, from a consideration of the benefits which he had already received from him; and then he repeats the testimony of his confidence towards God.

PSALM 25:6-7

Remember not the sins of my youth and my rebellious ways; according to your love remember me, for you are good, O LORD. As our sins are like a wall between us and God, which prevents him from hearing our prayers, or stretching forth his hand to help us, David now removes this obstruction. It is indeed true, in general, that men pray in a wrong way, and in vain, unless they begin by seeking the forgiveness of their sins. There is no hope of obtaining any favour from God unless he is reconciled to us. How shall he love us unless he first freely reconcile us to himself? The right and proper order of prayer therefore is, to ask, at the very outset, that God would pardon our sins. David here acknowledges, in explicit terms, that he cannot in any other way become a partaker of the grace of God than by having his sins blotted out. In order, therefore, that God may be mindful of his mercy towards us, it is necessary that he forget our sins, the very sight of which turns away his favour from us.

The Psalmist confirms by this that, although the wicked acted towards him with cruelty, and persecuted him unjustly, yet he ascribed to his own sins all the misery which he endured. For why should he ask the forgiveness of his sins, by having recourse to the mercy of God, but because he acknowledged, that by the cruel treatment he received from his enemies, he only suffered the punishment which he justly merited? He has, therefore, acted wisely in turning his thoughts to the first cause of his misery, that he may find out the true remedy; and thus he teaches us by his example, that when any outward affliction presses upon us, we must entreat God not only to deliver us from it, but also to blot out our sins, by which we have provoked his displeasure, and subjected ourselves to his chastening rod.

In order to express more fully that he supplicates a free pardon, he pleads before God only on the ground of his mere good pleasure; and therefore he says, *according to your love remember me.* When God casts our sins into oblivion, this leads him to behold us with fatherly regard. David can discover no other cause by which to account for this paternal regard of God, but that he is good, and hence it follows that there is nothing to induce God to receive us into his favour but his own good pleasure.

PSALM 25:8

Good and upright is the LORD; therefore he instructs sinners in his ways. Pausing for a little, as it were in the prosecution of his prayer, David exercises his thoughts in meditation upon the goodness of God, that he may return with renewed ardour to prayer. The faithful feel that their hearts soon languish in prayer, unless they are constantly stirring themselves up to it by new incitements; so rare and difficult a thing is it to persevere stedfastly and unweariedly in this duty. And, indeed, as one must frequently lay on fuel in order to preserve a fire, so the exercise of prayer requires the aid of such helps, that it may not languish, and at length be entirely extinguished. David, therefore, desirous to encourage himself to perseverance, speaks to himself, and affirms that God is *good and upright,* that, gathering new strength by meditating on this truth, he may return with the more alacrity to prayer. But we must observe this consequence—that God is good and upright, he stretches forth his hand *to sinners* to bring them back again into *the way.* To attribute to God an uprightness which he may exercise only towards the worthy and the meritorious, is a cold view of his character, and of little advantage to sinners, and yet the world commonly apprehends that God is good in no other sense. How comes it to pass that scarcely one in a hundred applies to himself the mercy of God, if it is not because men limit it to those who are worthy of it?

Now, on the contrary, it is here said, that God gives proof of his uprightness when he shows to transgressors the way; and this is of the same import as to call them to repentance, and to teach them to live uprightly. And, indeed, if the goodness of God did not penetrate even to hell, no man would ever become a partaker of it. David, therefore, here commends this preventing grace, as it is called, which is manifested either when God in calling us at first renews, by the Spirit of regeneration, our corrupt nature, or when he brings us back again into the right way, after we have gone astray from him by our sins. For since even those whom God receives for his disciples are here called sinners, it follows that he renews them by his Holy Spirit, that they may become docile and obedient.

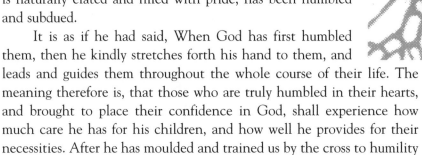

He guides the humble in what is right and teaches them his way. The Psalmist here specifies the second manifestation of his grace which God makes towards those who, being subdued by his power, and bought under his yoke, bear it willingly, and submit themselves to his government. But never will this docility be found in any man, until the heart, which is naturally elated and filled with pride, has been humbled and subdued.

It is as if he had said, When God has first humbled them, then he kindly stretches forth his hand to them, and leads and guides them throughout the whole course of their life. The meaning therefore is, that those who are truly humbled in their hearts, and brought to place their confidence in God, shall experience how much care he has for his children, and how well he provides for their necessities. After he has moulded and trained us by the cross to humility and meekness, he still shows himself to be a wise and provident father in guiding us through life.

For the sake of your name, O LORD. In order to show more distinctly that he depends entirely upon the free grace of God, David expressly says, *for the sake of your name;* meaning that God, as often as he vouchsafes to pardon his people, does so from no other cause than his own good pleasure. He was also constrained, by a consideration of the magnitude of his offence, to call upon the name of God: for he immediately adds, by the way of confession, *for my iniquity is great,* or *manifold,* as if he had said, My sins are, indeed, like a heavy burden which overwhelms me, so that the multitude or enormity of them might well deprive me of all hope of pardon; but, Lord, the infinite glory of your name will not suffer you to cast me off.

He will spend his days in prosperity, and his descendants will inherit the land. If the supreme felicity of man consists in undertaking or attempting nothing except by the warrant of God, it follows that it is also a high and incomparable benefit to have him for our conductor and guide through life, that we may never go astray. But, in addition to this, an earthly blessing is here promised, in which the fruit of the preceding grace is distinctly shown, as Paul also teaches (1 Tim.4:8), "Godliness is profitable unto all things, having promise of the life that now is, and of that which is to come."

PSALM 25:14

The LORD confides in those who fear him; he makes his covenant known to them. The Psalmist here confirms what he had just said in a preceding verse, namely, that God will faithfully discharge the office of a teacher and master to all the godly. The *covenant of God* is nothing else than his *secret counsel.* By the use of the term *secret,* he means to magnify and extol the excellency of the doctrine which is revealed to us in the law of God. However much worldly men, through the pride and haughtiness of their hearts, despise Moses and the prophets, the faithful nevertheless acknowledge, that in the doctrine which they contain, the secrets of heaven, which far surpass the comprehension of man, are revealed and unfolded. Whoever, therefore, desires to derive instruction from the law, let him regard with reverence and esteem the doctrine which it contains.

We are, further, by this place admonished to cultivate the graces of meekness and humility, lest, in reliance upon our own wisdom, or trusting to our own understanding, we should attempt, by our own efforts, to comprehend those mysteries and secrets, the knowledge of which David here declares to be the prerogative of God alone. Again, since the fear of the Lord is said to be the beginning, and as it were the way that leads to a right understanding of his will (Ps. 111:10), according as any one desires to increase in faith, so also let him endeavour to advance in the fear of the Lord. It is indeed true, that the covenant of God is a secret which far exceeds human comprehension; but as we know that he does not in vain enjoin us to seek him, we may rest assured that all those who endeavour to serve him with an upright desire will be brought, by the teaching of the Holy Spirit, to the knowledge of the heavenly wisdom which is appointed for their salvation. God, it is true, addresses his word indiscriminately to the righteous and the wicked; but men do not comprehend it, unless they have sincere piety; just as Isaiah 29:11 says, that as regards the ungodly, the law is like "a book that is sealed." And, therefore, it is no wonder that there is here made a distinction between those who truly serve God, and to whom he makes known his secret, and the wicked and hypocrites.

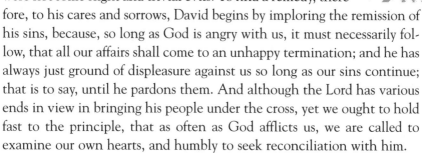

PSALM
25:15-22

My eyes are ever on the LORD. David shows to others, by his own example, the right manner of prayer, telling them that they should endeavour to keep their thoughts fixed upon God. As the sense of sight is very quick, and exercises an entire influence over the whole frame, it is no uncommon thing to find all the affections denoted by the term *eyes.*

Look upon my affliction and my distress and take away all my sins. By repeating these complaints so frequently, David plainly shows that the calamities with which he was assailed were not some slight and trivial evils. To find a remedy, therefore, to his cares and sorrows, David begins by imploring the remission of his sins, because, so long as God is angry with us, it must necessarily follow, that all our affairs shall come to an unhappy termination; and he has always just ground of displeasure against us so long as our sins continue; that is to say, until he pardons them. And although the Lord has various ends in view in bringing his people under the cross, yet we ought to hold fast to the principle, that as often as God afflicts us, we are called to examine our own hearts, and humbly to seek reconciliation with him.

May integrity and uprightness protect me. In order that God may become the protector and defender of our innocence, let us first conduct ourselves uprightly and innocently towards our enemies, and then commit ourselves entirely to his protection.

Redeem Israel, O God, from all their troubles! David shows that he has respect not merely to his own benefit, but that he comprehends in his prayer the state of the whole realm, just as the mutual communion and connection which subsist among the saints require that every individual, deeply affected by a sense of the public calamities which befall the Church at large, should unite with all the others in lamentation before God. This contributed in no small degree to confirm the faith of David, when, regarding himself as in all things connected with the whole body of the faithful, he considered that all the afflictions and wrongs which he endured were common to himself with them. And we ought to regard it as of the greatest importance, that in accordance with this rule, every one of us, in bewailing his private miseries and trials, should extend his desires and prayers to the whole Church.

PSALM 26

I do not sit with deceitful men, nor do I consort with hypocrites. David denies that he had any intercourse with vain and deceitful men. And certainly the best remedy to recall and save us from the assembly of the wicked is to fix our eyes upon God's goodness; for he who walks in the confidence of God's protection, committing all events to his providence, will never imitate their deceitfulness.

Do not take away my soul along with sinners, my life with bloodthirsty men. Having now affirmed his innocence, David has recourse again to prayer, and call upon God to defend him. At first sight, indeed, it appears strange to pray that God would not involve a righteous man in the same destruction with the wicked; but God, with paternal indulgence, allows this freedom in prayer, that his people may themselves in this way correct their anxieties, and overcome the fears with which they are tempted. David, when he conceived this supplication, in order to free himself from anxiety and fear, placed before his eyes the righteous judgment of God, to whom nothing is more abhorrent than to mingle good and bad together without distinction. This was the objection stated by Abraham (Gen. 18:25), "That be far from you to do after this manner, to slay the righteous with the wicked: and that the righteous should be as the wicked, that be far from you." Let us remember, therefore, that these forms of prayer are dictated by the Holy Spirit, in order that the faithful may unhesitatingly assure themselves that God still sits in inquisition upon every man's case, in order to give righteous judgment at last.

My feet stand on level ground; in the great assembly I will praise the LORD. As David knew that it was the hand of God alone which enabled him to stand, he therefore addresses himself to the exercise of praise and thanksgiving. Nor does he merely say, that he will acknowledge in private the goodness of God bestowed upon him, but in public also, that the assemblies of God's people may be witnesses of it. It is highly necessary that every one should publicly celebrate his experience of the grace of God, as an example to others to confide in him.

The LORD is my light and my salvation—whom shall I fear? The LORD is the stronghold of my life—of whom shall I be afraid? Certainly we find that all our fears arise from this source, that we are too anxious about life, while we acknowledge not that God is its preserver. We can have no tranquillity, therefore, until we attain the persuasion that our life is sufficiently guarded, because it is protected by his omnipotent power. The interrogation, too, shows how highly David esteemed the Divine protection, as he thus bodily exults all his enemies and dangers. Nor assuredly do we ascribe due homage to God, unless, trusting to his promised aid, we dare to boast of the certainty of our safety. Weighing, as it were, in scales the whole power of earth and hell, David accounts it all lighter than a feather, and considers God alone as far outweighing the whole.

Let us learn, therefore, to put such a value on God's power to protect us as to put to flight all our fears. Not that the minds of the faithful can, by reason of the infirmity of the flesh, be at all times entirely devoid of fear; but immediately recovering courage, let us, from the high tower of our confidence, look down upon all our dangers with contempt. Moreover, we must extend this confidence still further, in order to banish all fears from our consciences, like Paul, who, when speaking of his eternal salvation, boldly exclaims, "If God be for us, who can be against us?" (Rom. 8:34).

One thing I ask of the LORD, this is what I seek: that I may dwell in the house of the LORD all the days of my life, to gaze upon the beauty of the LORD and to seek him in his temple. Although David was banished from his country, despoiled of his wife, bereft of his kinsfolk; and, finally, dispossessed of his substance, yet he was not so desirous for the recovery of these, as he was grieved and afflicted for his banishment from God's sanctuary, and the loss of his sacred privileges. Under the word *one*, there is an implied antithesis, in which David, disregarding all other interests, displays his intense affection for the service of God; so that it was bitterer to him to be an exile from the sanctuary, than to be denied access to his own house.

PSALM
27:5-14

My heart says of you, "Seek his face!" It is indeed true that we are far from God so long as we abide in this world, because faith is far removed from sight; but it is equally true, that we now see God as in a mirror, and darkly (1 Cor. 13:12), until he shall openly show himself to us at the last day. Under this word *face,* are represented to us those helps by which God raises us to his presence, descending from his inconceivable glory to us, and furnishing us on earth with vision of his heavenly glory. But as it is according to his own sovereign pleasure that God vouchsafes us to look upon him, (as he does in Word and sacraments,) it becomes us steadily to fix our eyes on this view, that it may not be with us as with the Papists, who, by means of the wildest inventions, wickedly transform God into whatever shapes please their fancy, or their brains have conceived.

Though my father and mother forsake me, the LORD *will receive me.* Whatever benevolence, love, zeal, attention, or service, might be found among men, they are far inferior to the paternal mercy with which God encircles his people. The highest degree of love among men, it is true, is to be found in parents who love their children as their own bowels. But God advances us higher, declaring, by the prophet Isaiah, that although a mother may forget the child of her womb, he would always be mindful of us (Isa. 49:15). In this degree does David place him, so that he who is the source of all goodness far surpasses all mortals, who are naturally malevolent and niggardly. It is, however, an imperfect mode of speech, like that in Isaiah 63:16, "Doubtless, you are our Father, though Abraham be ignorant of us, and Israel acknowledge us not."

The sum of the whole is this: However inclined by nature earthly parents are to help their children, nay, though they should endeavour to cherish them with the greatest ardour of affection, yet should affection be wholly extinguished in the earth, God would fulfil the duty of both father and mother to his people. From which it follows, that we basely undervalue the grace of God, if our faith rise not above all the affections of nature; for sooner shall the laws of nature be overturned a hundred times, than God shall fail his people.

Repay them for their deeds and for their evil work. Here occurs the difficult question about praying for vengeance. It is unquestionable, that if the flesh move us to seek revenge, the desire is wicked in the sight of God. We must observe this general rule, that we cordially desire and labour for the welfare of the whole human race. Thus it will come to pass, that we shall not only give way to the exercise of God's mercy, but shall also wish the conversion of those who seem obstinately to rush upon their own destruction. In short, David, being free from every evil passion, and likewise endued with the spirit of discretion and judgment, pleads here not so much his own cause as the cause of God. And by this prayer, he further reminds both himself and the faithful, that although the wicked may give themselves loose reins in the commission of every species of vice with impunity for a time, they must at length stand before the judgment-seat of God.

Save your people and bless your inheritance; be their shepherd and carry them forever. In this verse David shows that it was not so much his own welfare as the welfare of the whole Church which was the object of his concern, and that he neither lived nor reigned for himself, but for the common good of the people. He well knew that he was appointed king for no other end. In this he declares himself to be a type of the Son of God, of whom, when Zechariah (9:9) predicts that he would come "having salvation," there is no doubt that he promises nothing to him apart from his members, but that the effects of this salvation would diffuse themselves throughout the whole body.

By this example, accordingly, he prescribes a rule to earthly kings, that, devoting themselves to the public good, they should only desire to be preserved for the sake of their people.

Let us therefore remember that David is like a mirror, in which God sets before us the continual course of his grace. Only we must be careful, that the obedience of our faith may correspond to his fatherly love, that he may acknowledge us for his people and inheritance. The Scriptures often designate David by the name of a shepherd; but he himself assigns that office to God, thus confessing that he is altogether unfit for it, save only in as far as he is God's minister.

The voice of the LORD is over the waters. We see how the prophet, in order to subdue the stubbornness of men, shows, by every word, that God is terrible. He also seems to rebuke, in passing, the madness of the proud, and of those who swell with vain presumption, because they hearken not to the voice of God in his thunders, rending the air with his lightning, shaking the lofty mountains, prostrating and overthrowing the loftiest trees. What a momentous thing is it, that while all the irrational portion of the creation tremble before God, men alone, who are endued with sense and reason, are not moved! Moreover, though they possess genius and learning, they employ enchantments to shut their ears against God's voice, however powerful, lest it should reach their hearts. Philosophers think not that they have reasoned skilfully enough about inferior causes, unless they separate God very far from his works. It is a diabolical science, however, which fixes our contemplations on the works of nature, and turns them away from God. If any one who wished to know a man and should take no notice of his face, but should fix his eyes only on the points of his nails, his folly might justly be derided. But far greater is the folly of those philosophers, who, out of mediate and proximate causes, weave themselves veils, lest they should be compelled to acknowledge the hand of God, which manifestly displays itself in his works.

Aristotle, in his book on Meteors, reasons very shrewdly about these things, in so far as relates to proximate causes, only that he omits the chief point. The investigation of these would, indeed, be both a profitable and pleasant exercise, were we led by it, as we ought, to the Author of Nature himself. But nothing is more preposterous than, when we meet with mediate causes, however many, to be stopped and retarded by them, as by so many obstacles, from approaching God; for this is the same as if a man were to remain at the very rudiments of things during his whole life, without going further. In short, this is to learn in such a manner that you can never know any thing. That shrewdness alone, therefore, is worthy of praise, which elevates us by these means even to heaven, in order that not a confused noise may strike our ears, but that the voice of the Lord may penetrate our hearts, and teach us to pray and serve God.

Day 99   A P R I L   8

And in his temple all cry, "Glory!" God's voice fills the whole world, and spreads itself to its furthest limits; but the prophet declares that his glory is celebrated only in his church, because God not only speaks intelligibly and distinctly there, but also there gently allures the faithful to himself. As men profit not so much in the common school of Nature as to submit themselves to God, David wisely says especially that the faithful sing the praises of God in his temple, because, being familiarly instructed there by his fatherly voice, they devote and consecrate themselves wholly to his service.

It is the doctrine of salvation alone, therefore, which cheers our hearts and opens our mouths in his praises, by clearly revealing to us his grace, and the whole of his will. It is from thence that we must learn how we ought to praise him. We may also unquestionably see that at that time there was nothing of the light of godliness in the whole world, except in Judea. Even philosophers, who appeared to approach nearest to the knowledge of God, contributed nothing whatever that might truly glorify him. All that they say concerning religion is not only frigid, but for the most part insipid. It is therefore in his word alone that there shines forth the truth which may lead us to true piety, and to fear and serve God aright.

The LORD *gives strength to his people; the* LORD *blesses his people with peace.* Although God exhibits his visible power to the view of the whole world indiscriminately, yet he exerts it in a peculiar manner in behalf of his elect people. He does this not as one who overwhelms with fear and dread those to whom he speaks, but as one who upholds, cherishes, and strengthens them. Everything necessary to the preservation of the life of the godly depends entirely upon the grace of God. God is said to *bless with peace* those whom he trusts, liberally and kindly, so that nothing is awanting to the prosperous course of their life, and to their complete happiness. From this we may learn that we ought to stand in awe of the majesty of God, in such a manner as to hope from him all that is necessary to our prosperity; and let us be assuredly persuaded, that since his power is infinite, we are defended by an invincible fortress.

PSALM 30:1-5

For his anger lasts only a moment, but his favor lasts a life-time. Our own fretfulness and impatience under affliction makes every minute an age; while, on the other hand, our repining and ingratitude lead us to imagine that God's favour, however long it may be exercised towards us, is but for a moment. It is our own perversity, therefore, in reality, which hinders us from perceiving that God's anger is but of short duration, while his favour is continued towards us during the whole course of our life. Nor does God in vain so often declare that he is merciful and gracious to a thousand generations, long-suffering, slow to anger, and ready to forgive. And as what he says by the prophet Isaiah has a special reference to the kingdom of Christ, it must be daily fulfilled, "For a small moment have I afflicted you but with everlasting mercies will I gather you" (Isa. 54:7).

However much God may terrify and humble his faithful servants, with manifold signs of his displeasure, he always besprinkles them with the sweetness of his favour to moderate and assuage their grief. If they weigh, therefore, his *anger* and his *favour* in an equal balance, they will always find it verified, that while the former is but for a moment, the latter continues to the end of life; no, it goes beyond it, for it were a grievous mistake to confine the favour of God within the boundaries of this transitory life. And it is unquestionably certain, that none but those whose minds have been raised above the world by a taste of heavenly life really experience this perpetual and uninterrupted manifestation of the divine favour, which enables them to bear their chastisements with cheerfulness. Paul, accordingly, that he may inspire us with invincible patience, refers to this in 2 Corinthians 4:17, "For our light affliction, which is but for a moment, work for us a far more exceeding and eternal weight of glory, while we look not at the things which are seen, but at the things which are not seen." In the meantime, it is to be observed that God never inflicts such heavy and continued chastisements on his people, without frequently mitigating them, and sweetening their bitterness with some consolation. Whoever, therefore, directs his mind to meditation upon the heavenly life, will never faint under his afflictions, however long continued; and, comparing them with the exceeding great and manifold favours of God towards him, he will put such honour on the latter as to judge that God's goodness, in his estimation, outweighs his displeasure a hundred fold.

When I felt secure, I said, "I will never be shaken." It is here as if David had said, When fortune smiled upon me on every side, and no danger appeared to occasion fear, my mind sunk as it were into a deep sleep, and I flattered myself that my happy condition would always continue, and that things would always go on in the same course.

This carnal confidence frequently creeps upon the saints when they indulge themselves in their prosperity, and so to speak, wallow upon their dunghill. Hence Jeremiah (31:18) compares himself to a wild bullock before the Lord tamed him and accustomed him to the yoke. This may at first sight appear to be but a small crime, yet we may gather from its punishment how much it is displeasing to God. As deaths innumerable hover before our eyes, and as there are so many examples of change to awaken us to fear and caution, those must be bewitched with devilish pride who persuade themselves that their life is privileged above the common lot of the world. They see the whole earth jumbled together in undistinguishing variety, and its individual parts in a manner tossed hither and thither; and yet, as if they did not belong to the human race, they imagine that they shall always continue stable and liable to no changes. Hence that wantonness of the flesh, with which they so licentiously indulge their lusts; hence their pride and cruelty, and neglect of prayer. How indeed should those flee to God, who have no sense of their need to instigate or move them to that?

What occurred to David, also occurred to the pious King Hezekiah, who, although lately afflicted with a sore disease, as soon as all was well and according to his wish, was hurried by the vanity of the flesh to pride and vain boasting. So by this we are taught to be on our guard when in prosperity, that Satan may not bewitch us with his flatteries. The more bountifully God deals with any one, the more carefully ought he to watch against such snares. It is not, indeed, probable that David had become so hardened as to despise God and defy all misfortunes, like many of the great men in this world, who, when immersed among their luxuries and sufferings, insolently scoff at all God's judgments; but an effeminate listlessness having come over his mind, he became more lukewarm in prayer, nor did he depend on the favour of God; in short he put too much confidence in his uncertain and transitory prosperity.

PSALM 30:7-12

To you, O LORD, I called; to the LORD I cried for mercy. Now follows the fruit of David's chastisement. He had been previously sleeping profoundly, and fostering his indolence by forgetfulness; but being now awakened all of a sudden with fear and terror, he begins to cry to God. And this is the chief advantage of afflictions, that while they make us sensible of our wretchedness, they stimulate us again to supplicate the favour of God.

You have turned my mourning into dancing; you have put off my sackcloth and girded me with gladness. David affirms that it was by the help and blessing of God that he had escaped safe, and then adds, that the final object of his escape was, that he might employ the rest of his life in celebrating the praises of God. Moreover, he shows us that he was not insensible or obdurate under his afflictions, but mourned in heaviness and sorrow, and he also shows that his very mourning had been the means of leading him to pray to God to deprecate his wrath. Both these points are most worthy of our observation, in order, first, that we may not suppose that the saints are guilty of stoical insensibility, depriving them of all feeling of grief; and, secondly, that we may perceive that in their mourning they were exercised to repentance. This latter he denotes by the term sackcloth. It was a common practice among the ancients to clothe themselves with sackcloth when mourning, for no other reason, indeed, than that like guilty criminals, they might approach their heavenly Judge, imploring his forgiveness with all humility, and testifying by this clothing their humiliation and dissatisfaction with themselves. We know also that the orientals were addicted beyond all others to ceremonies. We perceive, therefore, that David, although he patiently submitted himself to God, was not free from grief. We also see that his sorrow was "after a godly sort," as Paul speaks (2 Cor. 7:10); for to testify his penitence he clothed himself with sackcloth. By the term dancing, he does not mean any wanton or profane leaping, but a sober and holy exhibition of joy like that which sacred Scripture mentions when David conveyed the ark of the covenant to its place (2 Sam. 6:15).

Day 103 APRIL 12

Into your hands I commit my spirit; redeem me, O Lord, the God of truth. Whoever relies not on the providence of God, so as to commit his life to its faithful guardianship, has not yet learned aright what it is to live. On the other hand, he who shall entrust the keeping of his life to God's care, will not doubt of its safety even in the midst of death. We must therefore put our life into God's hand, not only that he may keep it safely in this world, but also that he may preserve it from destruction in death itself, as Christ's own example has taught us. As David wished to have his life prolonged amidst the dangers of death, so Christ passed out of this transitory life that his soul might be saved in death.

PSALM 31:1-5

We ought further to assure ourselves, that we are not forsaken of God either in life or in death; for those whom God brings safely by his power to the end of their course, he at last receives to himself at their death.

This is one of the principal places of Scripture which are most suitable for correcting distrust. It teaches us, first, that the faithful ought not to torment themselves above measure with unhappy cares and anxieties; and, secondly, that they should not be so distracted with fear as to cease from performing their duty, nor decline and faint in such a manner as to grasp at vain hopes and deceitful helps, nor give way to fears and alarms; and, finally, that they should not be afraid of death, which, though it destroys the body, cannot extinguish the soul. This, indeed, ought to be our principal argument for overcoming all temptations, that Christ, when commending his soul to his Father, undertook the guardianship of the souls of all his people. Stephen, therefore, calls upon him to be his keeper, saying, "Lord Jesus, receive my spirit," (Acts 7:59). As the soul is the seat of life, it is on this account, as is well known, used to signify life.

What David here declares concerning his temporal life, Paul transfers to eternal salvation. "I know," says he, "whom I have believed, and am persuaded that he is able to keep that which I have committed to him," (2 Tim. 1:12). And surely, if David derived so much confidence from temporal deliverance, it is more than wicked and ungrateful on our part, if the redemption purchased by the blood of Christ does not furnish us with invincible courage against all the devices of Satan.

PSALM 31:6-24

Let your face shine on your servant; save me in your unfailing love. This form of speech is taken from the common apprehension of men, who think that God regards them not, unless he really show his care of them by its effects. According to the judgment of sense, afflictions hide his countenance, just as clouds obscure the brightness of the sun. David therefore supplicates that God, by affording him immediate assistance, would make it evident to him that he enjoyed his grace and favour, which it is not very easy to discern amidst the darkness of afflictions. Now, God is said to lift the light of his countenance upon us in two ways; either when he opens his eyes to take care of our affairs, or when he shows to us his favour. These two things are indeed inseparable, or rather, the one depends upon the other. But by the first mode of speech, we, according to our carnal conceptions, attribute to God a mutability which, properly speaking, does not belong to him: whereas the second form of speech indicates, that our own eyes, rather than the eyes of God, are shut or heavy when he seems to have no regard to our afflictions.

How great is your goodness, which you have stored up for those who fear you, which you bestow in the sight of men on those who take refuge in you. The Psalmist here speaks of the protection and other blessings which belong to the preservation of the present life; which he declares to be so manifest that even the ungodly themselves are forced to become eye-witnesses of them. The world passes over all the works of God with its eyes shut, and is especially ignorant of his fatherly care of the saints; still it is certain that there shines forth such daily proofs of it, that even the reprobate cannot but see them, except in so far as they willingly shut their eyes against the light. David, therefore, speaks according to truth, when he declares that God gives evidences of his goodness to his people before the sons of men, that it may be clearly seen that they do not serve him unadvisedly or in vain.

Be of good courage, and he shall strengthen your heart,* all you who hope in the LORD. As no man is able of himself to sustain his daily conflicts, David urges us to hope for and ask the spirit of fortitude from God.

Blessed is he whose transgressions are forgiven, whose sins are covered. The remission of sins which is here treated of does not agree with satisfactions. God, in lifting off or taking away sins, and likewise in covering and not imputing them, freely pardons them. On this account the Papists, by thrusting in their satisfactions and works of supererogation as they call them, bereave themselves of this blessedness. Besides, David applies these words to complete forgiveness. The distinction, therefore which the Papists here make between the remission of the punishment and of the fault, by which they make only half a pardon, is not at all to the purpose. Now, it is necessary to consider to whom this happiness belongs, which may be easily gathered from the circumstance of the time. When David was taught that he was blessed through the mercy of God alone, he was not an alien from the church of God; on the contrary, he had profited above many in the fear and service of God, and in holiness of life, and had exercised himself in all the duties of godliness. and even after making these advances in religion, God so exercised him, that he placed the alpha and omega of his salvation in his gratuitous reconciliation to God. Nor is it without reason that Zacharias, in his song, represents " the knowledge of salvation" as consisting in knowing "the remission of sins" (Luke 1:77).

The more eminently that anyone excels in holiness, the further he feels himself from perfect righteousness, and the more clearly he perceives that he can trust in nothing but the mercy of God alone. Hence it appears, that those are grossly mistaken who conceive that the pardon of sin is necessary only to the beginning of righteousness. As believers are every day involved in many faults, it will profit them nothing that they have once entered the way of righteousness, unless the same grace which brought them into it accompany them to the last step of their life. Does anyone object, that they are elsewhere said to be blessed "who fear the Lord," "who walk in his ways," "who are upright in heart," etc.? The answer is easy, namely, that as the perfect fear of the Lord, the perfect observance of his law, and perfect uprightness of heart, are nowhere to be found, all that the Scripture anywhere says, concerning blessedness, is founded upon the free favour of God, by which he reconciles us to himself.

Therefore let everyone who is godly pray to you while you may be found. Here the Psalmist expressly states that whatever he has hitherto set forth in his own person, belongs in common to all the children of God. And this is to be carefully observed, because, from our native unbelief, the greater part of us are slow and reluctant to appropriate the grace of God. We may also learn from this, that David obtained forgiveness, not by the mere act of confession, as some speak, but by faith and prayer. Here he directs believers to the same means of obtaining it, bidding them to betake themselves to prayer, which is the true sacrifice of faith.

While he may be found, refers to that place in Isaiah (55:6) where it is said, "Seek you the Lord while he may be found, call you upon him while he is near." It is never out of season, indeed, to seek God, for every moment we need his grace, and he is always willing to meet us. But as slothfulness or dullness hinders us from seeking him, David here particularly intimates the critical seasons when believers are stimulated by a sense of their own need to have recourse to God.

You are my hiding place; you will protect me from trouble and surround me with songs of deliverance. The Psalmist, in the first place, denies that there is any other haven of safety but in God himself. Secondly, he assures himself that God will be his faithful keeper hereafter; and lastly, whatever adversity may befall him, he is persuaded that God will be his deliverer.

Rejoice in the LORD and be glad, you righteous; sing, all you who are upright in heart! After teaching how ready and accessible true happiness is to all the godly, David, with much reason, exhorts them to gladness. He commands them to rejoice in the Lord, as if he had said, There is nothing to prevent them from assuring themselves of God's favour, seeing he so liberally and so kindly offers to be reconciled to them. In the meantime, we may observe that this is the incomparable fruit of faith which Paul likewise commends, namely, when the consciences of the godly being quiet and cheerful, enjoy peace and spiritual joy. Wherever faith is lively, this holy rejoicing will follow.

Day 107   A P R I L   1 6

Praise the LORD *with the harp; make music to him on the ten-stringed lyre.* It is evident that the Psalmist here expresses the vehement and ardent affection which the faithful ought to have in praising God, when he enjoins musical instruments to be employed for this purpose. He would have nothing omitted by believers which tends to animate the minds and feelings of men in singing God's praises. The name of God, no doubt, can, properly speaking, be celebrated only by the articulate voice; but it is not without reason that David adds to this those aids by which believers were wont to stim-ulate themselves the more to this exercise; especially considering that he was speaking to God's ancient people. There is a distinction, however, to observe here, that we may not indiscriminately consider as applicable to ourselves, every thing which was formerly enjoined upon the Jews. No doubt, playing upon cymbals, touching the harp and the violin, and all that kind of music, which is so frequently mentioned in the Psalms, was a part of their education; that is to say, the puerile instruction of the law: that is of the stated service of the temple. For even now, if believers choose to cheer themselves with musical instruments, they should make it their object not to dissever their cheerfulness from the praises of God. But when they frequent their sacred assemblies, musical instruments in celebrating the praises of God would be no more suitable than the burn-ing of incense, the lighting up of lamps, and the restoration of the other shadows of the law. The Papists, therefore, have foolishly borrowed this, as well as many other things, from the Jews. Men who are fond of out-ward pomp may delight in that noise; but the simplicity which God rec-ommends to us by the apostle is far more pleasing to him. What shall we then say of chanting, which fills the ears with nothing but an empty sound? Does anyone object that music is very useful for awakening the minds of men and moving their hearts? Certainly, but we should always take care that no corruption creep in, which might both defile the pure worship of God and involve men in superstition. Moreover, since the Holy Spirit expressly warns us of this danger by the mouth of Paul, to pro-ceed beyond what we are there warranted by him is not only unadvised zeal, but wicked and perverse obstinacy.

PSALM
33:1-3

By the word of the LORD were the heavens made, their starry host by the breath of his mouth. That he may stir us up to think more closely of God's works, the Psalmist brings before us the creation of the world itself; for until God be acknowledged as the Creator and Framer of the world, who will believe that he attends to the affairs of men, and that the state of the world is controlled by his wisdom and power? But the creation of the world leads us by direct consequence to the providence of God. Not that all men reason so justly, or are endued with so sound a judgment, as to conclude that the world is at this day maintained by the same divine power which was once put forth in creating it: on the contrary, the great majority imagine that he is an idle spectator in heaven of whatever is transacted on earth. But no man truly believes that the world was created by God unless he is also firmly persuaded that it is maintained and preserved by him. Wisely and properly, therefore, does the prophet carry us back to the very origin of the world, in order to fix in our minds the certainty of God's providence in the continual order of nature.

The breath of his mouth is used figuratively for the very utterance of speech; as if it had been said, As soon as God uttered the breath of his mouth, or proclaimed in word what he wished to be done, the heavens were instantly brought into existence, and were furnished, too, with an inconceivable number and variety of stars. It is indeed true that this similitude is borrowed from men; but the Scriptures often teach in other places, that the world was created by that Eternal Word, who, being the only begotten Son of God, appeared afterwards in the flesh.

From heaven the LORD looks down and sees all mankind. The Psalmist still proceeds with the same doctrine, namely, that human affairs are not tossed here and there fortuitously, but that God secretly guides and directs all that we see taking place. Now he here commends God's inspection of all things, that we on our part may learn to behold, and to contemplate with the eye of faith, his invisible providence. There are, no doubt, evident proofs of it continually before our eyes; but the great majority of men, in their blindness, imagine that all things are under the conduct of a blind fortune.

Day 109   A P R I L   1 8

PSALM 34:1-7

I will extol the LORD at all times; his praise will always be on my lips. David here extols the greatness of God, promising to keep in remembrance during his whole life the goodness which he had bestowed upon him. God assists his people daily, that they may continually employ themselves in praising him; yet it is certain that the blessing which is said to be worthy of everlasting remembrance is distinguished by this mark from other benefits which are ordinary and common. This, therefore, is a rule which should be observed by the saints: they should often call into remembrance whatever good has been bestowed upon them by God; but if at any time he should display his power more illustriously in preserving them from some danger, so much the more does it become them earnestly to testify their gratitude. Now if by one benefit alone God lays us under obligation to himself all our life, so that we may never lawfully cease from setting forth his praises, how much more when he heaps upon us innumerable benefits?

Glorify the LORD with me; let us exalt his name together. The Psalmist calls upon the godly to unite with him in this exercise, inviting and exhorting them heartily and with one consent to extol the Lord. Let us therefore learn, from the many instances in which God may have given help to any of his people, to abound in hope; and when each recites the personal benefits which he has received, let all be animated unitedly and in a public manner to give praise to God.

The angel of the LORD encamps around those who fear him, and he delivers them. David here says that those whom God would preserve in safety he defends by the power and ministration of angels. The power of God alone would indeed be sufficient of itself to perform this; but in mercy to our infirmity he vouchsafes to employ angels as his ministers. It serves not a little for the confirmation of our faith to know that God has innumerable legions of angels who are always ready for his service as often as he is pleased to aid us; nay, more, that the angels too, who are called principalities and powers, are ever intent upon the preservation of our life, because they know that this duty is intrusted to them.

PSALM 34:8-22

Taste and see that the LORD *is good.* David calls upon men to stir up their senses, and to bring a palate endued with some capacity of tasting, that God's goodness may become known to them. His meaning, therefore, is that there is nothing on the part of God to prevent the godly, to whom he particularly speaks in this place, from arriving at the knowledge of his goodness by actual experience. From this it follows, that they also are infected with the common malady of dullness. This doctrine is confirmed by the promise immediately added, Blessed is the man who trusts in him; for God never disappoints the expectations of those who seek his favour. Our own unbelief is the only impediment which prevents him from satisfying us largely and bountifully with abundance of all good things.

Fear the LORD, *you his saints.* David here implies that men, laying aside all wilfulness of spirit, and having subdued the ardour and impetuosity of their minds, should become docile and meek. He has put the fear of the Lord for the rule of a pious and holy life: as if he had said, While virtue and righteousness are in every man's mouth, there are few who lead a holy life, and live as they ought; because they know not what it is to serve God.

Seek peace and pursue it. In our own personal affairs we should be meek and condescending, and endeavour, as far as it depends on us, to maintain peace, though its maintenance should prove to us a source of much trouble and inconvenience.

The eyes of the LORD *are on the righteous.* The best support of our patience is a firm persuasion that God regards us, and that according as every man perseveres in a course of uprightness and equity, so shall he be preserved in peace and safety under his protection. In order, therefore, that the faithful may not think that they are exposed to the caprice of the world, while they are endeavouring to keep themselves innocent, and that they may not, under the influence of this fear, go astray from the right path, David exhorts them to reflect upon the providence of God, and to rest assured that they are safe under his wings. He says, then, that the eyes of the Lord are upon the righteous, to preserve them, in order that the good and simple may persevere the more cheerfully in their uprightness. At the same time, he encourages them to supplication and prayer, if at any time the world should unjustly persecute them.

Take up shield and buckler; arise and come to my aid. When troubles and dangers arise, when terrors assail us on every side, when even death presents itself to our view, it is difficult to realise the secret and invisible power of God, which is able to deliver us from all anxiety and fear; for our understandings, which are gross and earthly, tend downward to the earth. That our faith, therefore, may ascend by degrees to the heavenly power of God, he is here introduced armed, after the manner of men, with sword and shield. In the same way, also, when he is in another place termed "a man of war," it is doubtless in adaptation to the imperfection of our present state, because our minds, from their limited capacity, could in no other way comprehend the extent of that infinite power, which contains in itself every form of help, and has no need of aid from any other quarter. This, therefore, is a prayer that God, by the exercise of his secret and intrinsic power, would show that he alone is able to encounter the whole strength and forces of the ungodly.

Say to my soul, "I am your salvation." David desires to have it thoroughly fixed in his mind, and to be fully persuaded that God is the author of his salvation. This he was unable, from the present aspect of things, to ascertain and determine; for such is the insensibility and dullness of our natures, that God often delivers us whilst we sleep and are ignorant of it. Accordingly, he makes use of a very forcible manner of expression, in praying that God would grant him a lively sense of his favour, so that being armed with this buckler, he might sustain every conflict, and surmount every opposing obstacle; as if he had said, Lord, whatever may arise to discourage me, confirm me in this persuasion, that my salvation is assuredly in you; and although temptations drive me hither and thither, recall my thoughts to you in such a manner, as that my hope of salvation may rise superior to all the dangers to which I shall be exposed; nay, more, that I may become as infallibly certain as if you had said it, that through your favour I shall be saved.

PSALM 36

There is no fear of God before his eyes. There is contained in these verses a contrast between the ungodly and the people of God. The former deceive themselves by flattery; the latter exercise over themselves a strict control, and examine themselves with a rigid scrutiny: the former, throwing loose the reins, rush headlong into evil; the latter are restrained by the fear of God: the former cloak or disguise their offences by sophistry, and turn light into darkness; the latter willingly acknowledge their guilt, and by a candid confession are brought to repentance: the former reject all sound judgment; the latter always desire to vindicate themselves by coming to the open light of day: the former upon their bed invent various ways of doing evil; the latter are sedulously on their guard that they may not devise or stir up within themselves any sinful desire: the former indulge a deep and fixed contempt of God; the latter willingly cherish a constant displeasure at their sins.

Your love, O LORD, *reaches to the heavens.* The meaning here is, Although we may see among men sad and frightful confusion, which, like a great gulf, would swallow up the minds of the godly, David, nevertheless, maintains that the world is full of the goodness and righteousness of God, and that he governs heaven and earth on the strictest principles of equity.

For with you is the fountain of life. The ungodly do not acknowledge that it is in God they live, move, and have their being, but rather imagine that they are sustained by their own power; and, accordingly, David, on the contrary, here affirms from the experience of the godly, and as it were in their name, that the fountain of life is in God. By this he means, that there is not a drop of life to be found without him, or which flows not from his grace.

Continue your love to those who know you. We learn from this that true godliness springs from the knowledge of God, and again, that the light of faith must necessarily dispose us to uprightness of heart. At the same time, we ought always to bear in mind, that we only know God aright when we render to him the honour to which he is entitled; that is, when we place entire confidence in him.

Day 113 APRIL 22

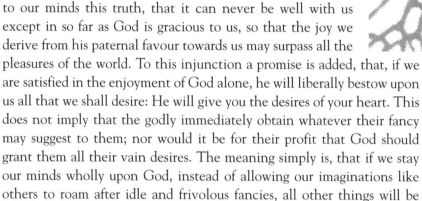

PSALM 37:1-15

Trust in the LORD and do good. It is not without good reason that the Psalmist begins with the doctrine of faith, or trust in God; for there is nothing more difficult for men to preserve their minds in a state of peace and tranquillity, undisturbed by any disquieting fears, whilst they are in this world, which is subject to so many changes.

Delight yourself in the LORD. We must constantly recall to our minds this truth, that it can never be well with us except in so far as God is gracious to us, so that the joy we derive from his paternal favour towards us may surpass all the pleasures of the world. To this injunction a promise is added, that, if we are satisfied in the enjoyment of God alone, he will liberally bestow upon us all that we shall desire: He will give you the desires of your heart. This does not imply that the godly immediately obtain whatever their fancy may suggest to them; nor would it be for their profit that God should grant them all their vain desires. The meaning simply is, that if we stay our minds wholly upon God, instead of allowing our imaginations like others to roam after idle and frivolous fancies, all other things will be bestowed upon us in due season.

But the meek will inherit the land and enjoy great peace. The Psalmist means the godly shall live in such a manner as that the blessing of God shall follow them, even to the grave. The possession of the earth is not always realised to the children of God, because it is the will of the Lord that they should live as strangers and pilgrims in it; neither does he permit them to have any fixed abode in it, but rather tries them with frequent troubles, that they may desire with greater alacrity the everlasting dwelling-place of heaven. The flesh is always seeking to build its nest for ever here; and were we not tossed hither and thither, and not suffered to rest, we would by and by forget heaven and the everlasting inheritance. Yet, in the midst of this disquietude, the possession of the earth, of which David here speaks, is not taken away from the children of God; for they know most certainly that they are the rightful heirs of the world. Hence it is that they eat their bread with a quiet conscience, and although they suffer want, yet God provides for their necessities in due season.

PSALM 37:16-40

Better the little that the righteous have than the wealth of many wicked. There is nothing stable in the world except it be sustained by the power of God; but we are plainly told that the righteous only are upheld by him, and that the power of the ungodly shall be broken. Here again we see, that in order to form a right and proper estimate of true felicity, we must look forward to the future, or contemplate by the eye of faith the secret grace of God, and his hidden judgments. Unless we are persuaded by faith that God cherishes us in his bosom as a father does his children, our poverty will always be a source of trouble to us; and, on the other hand, unless we bear in mind what is here said concerning the wicked, that their arms shall be broken, we will make too great account of their present condition. But if this doctrine be deeply fixed in the heart of the faithful, as soon as they shall have learned to rely upon the divine blessing, the delight and joy which they will experience from their little store shall be equal to the magnanimity with which they shall look down, as it were from an eminence, upon the vast treasures in which the ungodly glory.

But the righteous give generously. Whatever we need for the preservation and maintenance of life, and for the exercise of humanity towards others, comes to us neither from the heavens nor from the earth, but only from the favour and blessing of God; and that if he once withdraw his grace, the abundance of the whole world would not satisfy us.

The mouth of the righteous man utters wisdom, and his tongue speaks what is just. The meaning is, first, that the righteous speak honourably and reverently of the righteousness of God, that they may cherish in themselves and others, to a large extent, the knowledge and the fear of God; secondly, that both in their own affairs and those of others, they approve, without disguise or deceit, of what is just and reasonable, and are not given to justify what is wrong under the colour and varnish of sophistry; and, finally, that they never depart from the truth. The source whence this integrity of heart proceed is, that the Law of God has its seat in the heart; and it is it alone which prescribes the best rule of life and imbues the minds of men with the love of righteousness.

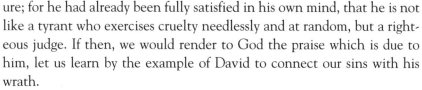

PSALM 38

For your arrows have pierced me. David shows that he was constrained by dire necessity to ask an alleviation of his misery; for he was crushed under the weight of the burden which he sustained. This rule is always to be observed in our prayers—to keep God's promises present to our view. God has promised that he will chastise his servants, not according to what they deserve, but as they are able to bear.

There is no health in my body . . . because of my sin. David, as soon as he recognised his affliction as coming from God, turns to his own sin as the cause of the Divine displeasure; for he had already been fully satisfied in his own mind, that he is not like a tyrant who exercises cruelty needlessly and at random, but a righteous judge. If then, we would render to God the praise which is due to him, let us learn by the example of David to connect our sins with his wrath.

I am bowed down and brought very low. The Apostle Peter (1 Peter 5:6) exhorts all the godly to "humble themselves under the mighty hand of God." There is no other way by which we can obtain consolation under our afflictions, than by laying aside all stubbornness and pride, and humbly submitting to the chastisement of God.

I wait for you, O Lord; you will answer. Certainly, the mind of man will never be framed to gentleness and meekness, nor will he be able to subdue his passions, until he has learned never to give up hope. The Psalmists says that he cherished his hope by constant meditation, lest he should yield to despair. And this is the only means of our perseverance, when, on the ground of his own promises, with which we are furnished, we appeal to him yea, rather when setting before our view his fidelity and his constancy in fulfilling what he has promised, we are sureties to ourselves for him.

Come quickly to help me, O Lord my Savior. Waiting was wearisome to David according to the flesh, yet in one word he plainly shows that he did not pray in uncertainty when he calls God *his salvation.* David rather sets this up as a wall of defence against all the devices by which, as we have seen, his faith was assailed, That whatever might happen, he was, nevertheless, well assured of his salvation in God.

PSALM 39

I said, "I will watch my ways." Since it was so hard a task for David to restrain his tongue, lest he should sin by giving way to complaints, let us learn from this example, whenever troubles molest us, to strive earnestly to moderate our affections, that no impious expression of dissatisfaction against God may slip from us.

My heart grew hot within me. The more strenuously anyone sets himself to obey God, and employs all his endeavours to attain the exercise of patience, the more vigorously is he assailed by temptation: for Satan, whilst he is not so troublesome to the indifferent and careless, and seldom looks near them, displays all his forces in hostile array against that individual. If, therefore, at any time we feel ardent emotions struggling and raising a commotion in our breasts, we should call to remembrance this conflict of David, that our courage may not fail us, or at least that our infirmity may not drive us headlong to despair.

Man is a mere phantom as he goes to and fro. There is nothing substantial in man. His life vanishes away before it can be known. David declares of every man individually what Paul extends to the whole world, when he says, 1 Corinthians 7:31, "The fashion of this world passes away." Thus he denies that there is anything abiding in men, because the appearance of strength which displays itself in them for a time soon passes away.

Save me from all my transgressions. In asking to be delivered from his transgressions, the Psalmist ascribes the praise of righteousness to God, while he charges upon himself the blame of all the misery which he endures; and he blames himself, not only on account of one sin, but acknowledges that he is justly chargeable with manifold transgressions. By this rule we must be guided, if we would wish to obtain an alleviation of our miseries; for, until the very source of them has been dried up, they will never cease to follow on another in rapid succession. If God should begin to deal with us according to the strict demands of the law, the consequence would be, that all would perish, and be utterly overwhelmed under his wrath. The only remedy by which men are cured of pride is when, alarmed with a sense of God's wrath, they begin not only to be dissatisfied with themselves, but also to humble themselves even to the dust.

PSALM 40:1-3

He put a new song in my mouth, a hymn of praise to our God. By this David denotes the consummation of his deliverance. In whatever way God is pleased to succour us, he asks nothing else from us in return but that we should be thankful for and remember it. As often, therefore, as he bestows benefits upon us, so often does he open our mouths to praise his name. Since God, by acting liberally towards us, encourages us to sing his praises, David with good reason reckons, that having been so wonderfully delivered, the matter of a new song had been furnished to him. He uses the word *new* in the sense of exquisite and not ordinary, even as the manner of his deliverance was singular and worthy of everlasting remembrance. It is true, that there is no benefit of God so small that it ought not to call forth his hand to help us, the more does it become us to stir up ourselves to fervent zeal in this holy exercise, so that our songs may correspond to the greatness of the favour which has been conferred upon us. Although God stands in no need of our praises, yet it is his will that this exercise for many reasons should prevail amongst us.

Many will see and fear and put their trust in the LORD. Here the Psalmist extends still further the fruit of the aid he had experienced, telling us, that it will prove the means of instruction common to all. And certainly it is the will of God that the benefits which he bestows upon any individual of the faithful should be proofs of the goodness which he constantly exercises towards all of them, so that the one, instructed by the example of the other, should not doubt that the same grace will be manifested towards himself. The terms *fear,* and *hope,* or *trust,* do not seem at first view to harmonise; but David has not improperly joined them together; for no man will ever entertain the hope of the favour of God but he whose mind is first imbued with the fear of God. This *fear* in general means the feeling of piety which is produced in us by the knowledge of the power, equity, and mercy of God. Now, whoever submits cordially to the will of God will of necessity join hope with fear; especially when there is presented to his view the evidence of the grace by which God commonly allures all men to himself.

PSALM 40:4-17

Sacrifice and offering you did not desire. God requires not mere ceremonies of those who serve him, but he is satisfied only with sincerity of heart, with faith and holiness of life: and he takes no pleasure merely in the visible sanctuary, the altar, the burning of incense, the killing of beasts, the lights, the costly apparel, and outward washings. From this David concludes that he ought to be guided by another principle, and to observe another rule in the service of God, than a mere attention to these: that he should yield himself wholly to God.

Then I said, "Here I am, I have come." However beautiful and splendid the works of men may appear, yet unless they spring from the living root of the heart, they are nothing better than a mere pretence; and, also, it is to no purpose that the feet, and hands, and eyes are framed for keeping the Law, unless obedience begin at the heart. Moreover, it appears from other places in Scripture, that it is the peculiar office of the Holy Spirit to engrave the Law of God on our hearts. God, it is true, does not perform his work in us as if we were stones or stocks, drawing us to himself, without the feeling or inward moving of our hearts towards him. But as there is in us naturally a will, which, however, is depraved by the corruption of our nature, so that it always inclines us to sin, God changes it for the better, and thus leads us cordially to seek after righteousness, to which our hearts were previously altogether averse. Hence arises the true freedom which we obtain when God frames our hearts, which before were in slavery to sin, unto obedience to himself.

It is written about me in the scroll. Although the literal doctrine of the Law belongs to all men in common, yet as of itself it is dead, and only beats the air. God teaches his own people after another manner; and that, as the inward and effectual teaching of the Spirit is a treasure which belongs peculiarly to them, it is written of them only in the secret book of God, that they should fulfil his will. The voice of God, indeed, resounds throughout the whole world, so that all who do not obey it are rendered inexcusable; but it penetrates into the hearts of the godly alone, for whose salvation it is ordained.

Blessed is he who has regard for the weak. David declares those to be blessed who form a wise and prudent judgment concerning the afflictions by which God chastises his servants. He had to contend in his own heart against the perverse judgments of foolish and wicked men, because, when affliction was pressing heavily upon him, many considered that he had fallen into a desperate condition, and was altogether beyond the hope of recovery. Doubtless, it happened to him as it did to the holy patriarch Job, whom his friends reckoned to be one of the most wicked of men, when they saw God treating him with great severity. And certainly, it is an error which is by far too common among men, to look upon those who are oppressed with afflictions as condemned and reprobate. The Scriptures in many places plainly and distinctly declare, that God, for various reasons, tries the faithful by adversities, at one time to train them to patience, at another to subdue the sinful affections of the flesh, at another to cleanse, and, as it were, purify them from the remaining desires of the flesh, which still dwell within them; sometimes to humble them, sometimes to make them an example to others, and at other times to stir them up to the contemplation of the divine life. For the most part, indeed, we often speak rashly and indiscriminately concerning others, and, so to speak, plunge even into the lowest abyss those who labour under affliction. To restrain such a rash and unbridled spirit, David says that they are blessed who do not suffer themselves, by speaking at random, to judge harshly of their neighbours; but, discerning aright the afflictions by which they are visited, mitigate, by the wisdom of the Spirit, the severe and unjust judgments to which we are naturally so prone.

The object which David had in view, when he saw himself, as it were, overwhelmed by the malicious and cruel judgments which were expressed concerning him, was to fortify himself by this as a ground of consolation, lest he should sink under the temptation. If, therefore, at any time Satan should endeavour to destroy the foundation of our faith, by the rash and presumptuous judgments of men, let us also learn to have recourse to this device of wisdom, lest unawares we fall into despair.

PSALM 42

As the deer pants for streams of water, so my soul pants for you, O God. David preferred to all the enjoyments, riches, pleasures, and honours of this world, the opportunity of access to the sanctuary, that in this way he might cherish and strengthen his faith and piety by the exercises prescribed in the Law. David, then, considering that the way of access was shut against him, cried to God, because he was excluded from the outward service of the sanctuary, which we cannot bear to miss by reason of our infirmity. The similitude which he takes from a hart is designed to express the extreme ardour of his desire. Being naturally of a hot and sanguine constitution, the hart suffers much from thirst in the Oriental regions. When in want of water, and unable to find it, it makes a mournful noise, and eagerly seeks the cooling river. And at certain seasons of the year, harts, with an almost incredible desire, and more intensely than could proceed from mere thirst, seek after water; which is probably what is referred to by the prophet here.

When can I go and meet with God? David does not simply speak here of the presence of God, but of the presence of God in connection with certain symbols; for he sets before himself the tabernacle, the altar, the sacrifices, and other ceremonies by which God had testified that he would be near his people; and that it behoved the faithful, in seeking to approach God, to begin by those things.

Why are you downcast, O my soul? Why so disturbed within me? Here there are two evils specified, which, however apparently different, yet assail our hearts at the same time; the one is discouragement, and the other disquietude. When we are quite downcast, we are not free of a feeling of disquietude, which leads us to murmur and complain. The remedy to both of them is here added, *hope in God,* which alone inspires our minds, in the first place, with confidence in the midst of the greatest troubles; and, secondly, by the exercise of patience, preserves them in peace. In what follows, David very well expresses the power and nature of hope by these words, *I shall yet praise him;* for it has the effect of elevating our thoughts to the contemplation of the grace of God, when it is hidden from our view.

PSALM 43

You are God my stronghold. Setting as a shield against temptation the fact, that he had experienced the power of God to be present with him, David complains that his life is spent in mourning, because he sees himself as it were abandoned to the will of his enemies. He considered it absolutely certain that his enemies had no power to do him harm except in so far as the Lord permitted them; and therefore he asks, as it were something altogether unaccountable, how it happened that his enemies prevailed against him whilst he was under the assured protection and guardianship of God. From this he gathers courage to pray, that God would be pleased again to manifest his favour, which he seemed to have hid from him for a time.

Send forth your light and your truth, let them guide me. In order to encourage himself in the hope of obtaining the grace of God, David rests with confidence in this, that God, who is true, and cannot deceive any, has promised to assist his servants. The knowledge of the divine favour, it is true, must be sought for in the Word of God; nor has faith any other foundation on which it can rest with security except his word; but when God stretches out his hand to help us, the experience of this is no small confirmation both of the word and of faith.

Let them guide me; let them bring me to your holy mountain. As the chief cause of his sorrow consisted in his being banished from the congregation of the godly, so David places the height of all his enjoyments in this, that he might be at liberty to take part in the exercise of religion, and to worship God in the sanctuary. Tacitly, indeed, David makes a vow of thanksgiving to God; but there can be no doubt, that by these words he intimates, that the end which he had in view in seeking deliverance from his afflictions was, that as formerly he might be at liberty to return to the sanctuary, from which he was driven by the tyranny of his enemies. And it deserves to be particularly noticed, that although he had been deprived of his wife, spoiled of his goods, his house, and all his other earthly comforts, yet he always felt such an ardent desire to come to the temple, that he forgot almost everything else. This holy desire of David ought to be imitated by all the faithful.

PSALM 44

For you loved them. The prophet does not suppose any worthiness in the person of Abraham, nor imagine any desert in his posterity, on account of which God dealt so bountifully with them, but ascribes all of it to the good pleasure of God. His words seem to be taken from the solemn declaration of Moses, "The Lord did not set his love upon you, nor choose you, because you were more in number than any people; (for you were the fewest of all people;) but because the Lord loved you" (Deut. 7:7–8). Certainly, the source and origin of the Church is the free love of God; and whatever benefits he bestows upon his Church, they all proceed from the same source. The reason, therefore, why we are gathered into the Church, and are nourished and defended by the hand of God, is only to be sought in God. Nor does the Psalmist here treat of the general benevolence of God, which extends to the whole human race; but he discourses of the difference which exists between the elect and the rest of the world; and the cause of this difference is here referred to as the mere good pleasure of God.

If we had forgotten the name of our God or spread out our hands to a foreign god, would not God have discovered it, since he knows the secrets of the heart? In order to show that they still continued stedfastly in the pure service of God, the Holy Fathers here affirm that they have not lifted up their hearts or their hands to any but to the God of Israel alone. It would not have been enough for them to have cherished some confused notion of the Deity: it was necessary that they should receive in its purity the true religion. Even those who murmur against God may be constrained to acknowledge some Divinity; but they frame for themselves a god after their own pleasure. And this is an artifice of the devil, who, because he cannot at once eradicate from our hearts all sense of religion, endeavours to overthrow our faith, by suggesting to our minds these devices—that we must seek another God; or that the God whom we have hitherto served must be appeased after another manner; or else that the assurance of his favour must be sought elsewhere than in the Law and the Gospel. Let us not cease to trust in the true God.

Listen, O daughter, consider and give ear: Forget your people and your father's house. The king is enthralled by your beauty; honor him, for he is your lord. This passage contains a remarkable prophecy in reference to the future calling of the Gentiles, by which the Son of God formed an alliance with strangers and those who were his enemies. There was between God and the uncircumcised nations a deadly quarrel, a wall of separation which divided them from the seed of Abraham, the chosen people (Eph. 2:14); for the covenant which God had made with Abraham shut out the Gentiles from the kingdom of heaven till the coming of Christ. Christ, therefore, of his free grace, desires to enter into a holy alliance of marriage with the whole world, in the same way as if a Jew in ancient times had taken to himself a wife from a foreign and heathen land. But in order to conduct into Christ's presence his bride, chaste and undefiled, the prophet exhorts the Church gathered from the Gentiles, to forget her former manner of living, and to devote herself wholly to her husband. As this change, by which the children of Adam begin to be the children of God, and are transformed into new men, is a thing so difficult, the prophet enforces the necessity of it the more earnestly. In enforcing his exhortation in this way by different terms, hearken, consider, incline your ear, he intimates, that the faithful do not deny themselves, and lay aside their former habits, without intense and painful effort; for such an exhortation would be superfluous, were men naturally and voluntarily disposed to it. And, indeed, experience shows how dull and slow we are to follow God.

By the word *daughter*, the prophet gently and sweetly soothes the new Church; and he also sets before her the promise of a bountiful reward, to induce her, for the sake of Christ willingly to despise and forsake whatever she made account of up to now. It is certainly no small consolation to know that the Son of God will delight in us, when we shall have put off our earthly nature. In the meantime, let us learn that to deny ourselves, is the beginning of that sacred union which ought to exist between us and Christ. By her father's house and her people is comprehended whatever men have belonging to themselves; for there is no part of our nature sound or free from corruption.

PSALM 46

The LORD Almighty is with us; the God of Jacob is our fortress. That our faith may rest truly and firmly in God, we must take into consideration at the same time these two parts of his character: his immeasurable power, by which he is able to subdue the whole world under him; and his fatherly love which he has manifested in his word. When these two things are joined together, there is nothing which can hinder our faith from defying all the enemies which may rise up against us, nor must we doubt that God will succour us, since he has promised to do it; and as to power, he is sufficiently able also to fulfil his promise, for he is the God of armies.

Come and see the works of the LORD, the desolations he has brought on the earth. The manifestations which God has given of his favour towards us in preserving us, ought to be kept continually before our eyes as a means of establishing in our hearts a persuasion of the stability of his promises. By this exhortation we have tacitly rebuked the indifference and stupidity of those who do not make so great account of the power of God as they ought to do; or rather, the whole world is charged with ingratitude, because there is scarcely one in a hundred who acknowledges that he has abundant help and security in God, so that they are all blinded to the works of God, or rather wilfully shut their eyes at that which would, nevertheless, prove the best means of strengthening their faith. We see how many ascribe to fortune that which ought to be traced to the providence of God. Others imagine that they obtain, by their own industry, whatever God had bestowed upon them, or ascribe to secondary causes what proceeds from him alone; while others are utterly lost to all sense.

Be still, and know that I am God. We have in the fourth psalm, at the fourth verse, a sentiment somewhat similar, "Stand in awe, and sin not: commune with your own heart upon your bed, and be still." In short, the Psalmist exhorts the world to subdue and restrain their turbulent affections, and to yield to the God of Israel the glory which he deserves; and he warns them, that if they proceed to act like madmen, his power is not enclosed within the narrow limits of Judea, and that it will be no difficult matter for him to stretch forth his arm afar to the Gentiles and heathen nations, that he may glorify himself in every land.

Day 125   MAY 4

How awesome is the LORD Most High, the great King over all the earth! Since no servitude is happy and desirable but that by which God subdues and brings under the standard and authority of Christ his Son those who before were rebels, it follows that this language is applicable only to the kingdom of Christ, who is called a high and terrible King, not that he makes the wretched beings over whom he reigns to tremble by the tyranny and violence of his sway, but because his majesty, which before had been held in contempt, will suffice to quell the rebellion of the whole world. It is to be observed, that the design of the Holy Spirit is here to teach, that as the Jews had been long contemptuously treated, oppressed with wrongs, and afflicted from time to time with divers calamities, the goodness and liberality of God towards them was now so much the more illustrious, when the kingdom of David had subdued the neighbouring nations on every side, and had attained to such a height of glory.

The nobles of the nations assemble as the people of the God of Abraham. When the doctrine of the gospel was manifested and shone forth, it did not remove the Jews from the covenant which God had long before made with them. As then the calling of the Gentiles was nothing else than the means by which they were grafted and incorporated into the family of Abraham, the prophet justly states, that strangers or aliens from every direction were gathered together to the chosen people, that by such an increase the kingdom of God might be extended through all the quarters of the globe. On this account Paul says (Eph. 3:6), that the Gentiles were made one body with the Jews, that they might be partakers of the ever-lasting inheritance. By the abolition of the ceremonies of the Mosaic economy, "the middle wall of partition," which made a separation between the Jews and the Gentiles, is now removed (Eph. 2:14), but it nevertheless remains true, that we are not accounted among the children of God unless we have been grafted into the stock of Abraham. We also learn from this that all who would be reckoned among the children of God ought to seek to have a place in the Church, and to join themselves to it, that they may maintain fraternal unity with all the godly.

PSALM 48

The joy of the whole earth . . . is Mount Zion. If the joy which men experience and cherish is without God, the issue of their joy at length will be destruction, and their laughter will be turned into gnashing of teeth. In the time of the prophet, the knowledge of the Gospel, it is true, had not yet reached foreign nations; but he makes use of this manner of expression with the highest propriety, to teach the Jews that true blessedness was to be sought for only from the gracious covenant of God, which was deposited in that holy place. At the same time also, he has foretold that which was at length fulfilled in the last time by the coming of Christ. From this we may learn, that to cause the hearts of the godly to rejoice, the favour of God alone abundantly suffices; as, on the contrary, when it is withdrawn, all men must inevitably be thrown into a state of wretchedness and sorrow.

God in the palaces of Zion is known for a defence.* By these words, the people of God are taught, that although they dwell in strongholds and palaces, they must, nevertheless, be carefully on their guard, that this magnificence or loftiness may not shroud or conceal from their view the power of God; and that they be not like worldly men, who, resting satisfied with riches and earthly means of help, set no value whatever upon having God for their guardian and protector. Worldly wealth, from our natural perverseness, tends to dazzle our eyes, and to make us forget God, and, therefore, we ought to meditate with special attention upon this doctrine, that whatever we possess, which seems worthy of being prized, must not be permitted to obscure the knowledge of the power and grace of God; but that, on the contrary, the glory of God ought always clearly to shine forth in all the gifts with which he may be pleased to bless and adorn us; so that we may account ourselves rich and happy in him, and nowhere else.

For this God is our God for ever and ever. We do not have an uncertain God, or a God of whom we have only a confused and an indistinct apprehension, but one of whom we have a true and solid knowledge. When the faithful here declare that God will continue unchangeably stedfast to his purpose in maintaining his Church, their object is to encourage and strengthen themselves to persevere in a continued course of faith.

Day 127 M A Y 6

PSALM 49

My mouth will speak words of wisdom; the utterance from my heart will give understanding. The Psalmist had no intention to vend fancies of his own, but to advance what he had learned in the school of God. This is the true method of instruction to be followed in the Church. The man who holds the office of teacher must apply himself to the reception of truth before he attempts to communicate it, and in this manner become the means of conveying to the hands of others that which God has committed to his own. Wisdom is not the growth of human genius. It must be sought from above. And it is impossible that anyone should speak with the propriety and knowledge necessary for the edification of the Church, who has not, in the first place, been taught at the feet of the Lord.

I will turn my ear to a proverb. The truths of revelation are so high as to exceed our comprehension; but, at the same time, the Holy Spirit has accommodated them so far to our capacity, as to render all Scripture profitable for instruction. None can plead ignorance; for the deepest and most difficult doctrines are made plain to the most simple and unlettered of mankind.

But God will redeem my life from the grave. We have here a convincing proof of that faith in which the saints under the Law lived and died. It is evident that their views were directed to another and a higher life, to which the present life was only preparatory. The promises of the Law were spiritual, and our fathers who embraced them were willing to confess themselves pilgrims upon earth, and sought an inheritance in heaven. The despairing fears which so many entertain when descending to the grave spring from the fact of their not commending their spirit to the preserving care of God. They do not consider it in the light of a precious deposit which will be safe in his protecting hands. Let our faith be established in the great truth, that our soul, though it appears to vanish upon its separation from the body, is in reality only gathered to the bosom of God, there to be kept until the day of the resurrection.

127 ❧ Daily Readings from Calvin on the Psalms

PSALM 50

I do not rebuke you for your sacrifices or your burnt offerings, which are ever before me. God now declares, that he attached no value whatsoever to sacrifices in themselves considered. Not that he asserts this rite of the Jews to have been in vain and useless, for in that case it never would have been instituted by God; but there is this difference between religious exercises and others, that they can only meet the approbation of God when performed in their true spirit and meaning. Mere outward ceremonies being therefore possessed of no value, God repudiates the idea that he had ever insisted upon them as the main thing in religion, or designed that they should be viewed in any other light than as helps to spiritual worship. The prophet Micah says (6:7), "Will the Lord be pleased with thousands of rams, or with ten thousands of rivers of oil? and what does the Lord require of you, but to do justly, and to love mercy?" "I desire mercy," he says in another place (Hosea 6:6), "and not sacrifice." Where a right use has been made of the institution, and they have been observed merely as ceremonies for the confirmation and increase of faith, then they are described as being essentially connected with true religion; but when offered without faith, or, what is still worse, under the impression of their meriting the favour of God for such as continue in their sins, they are reprobated as a mere profanation of divine worship.

I have no need of a bull from your stall or of goats from your pens. God is absolutely independent of human offerings. He here points at the wide distinction between himself and man, the latter being dependent for a frail subsistence upon food and drink, while he is the self-existent One, and communicates life to all beside. While the world had a beginning, he himself was from eternity. From this it follows, that, as he subsisted when there was nothing without him which could contribute to his fullness, he must have in himself a glorious all-sufficiency.

Sacrifice unto God praise.* Faith, self-denial, a holy life, and patient endurance of the cross, are all sacrifices which please God. But as prayer is the offspring of faith, and uniformly accompanied with patience and mortification of sin, while praise, where it is genuine, indicates holiness of heart, we need not wonder that these two points of worship should be here employed to represent the whole.

Day 129   M A Y   8

For I know my transgressions, and my sin is always before me. David declares that he is subjected by his sin to constant anguish of mind, and that it is this which imparts such an earnestness to his supplications. From his example we may learn who they are that can alone be said to seek reconciliation with God in a proper manner. They are such as have had their consciences wounded with a sense of sin, and who can find no rest until they have obtained assurance of his mercy. We will never seriously apply to God for pardon, until we have obtained such a view of our sins as inspires us with fear. The more easily satisfied we are under our sins, the more do we provoke God to punish them with severity, and if we really desire absolution from his hand, we must institute a rigid and formidable scrutiny into the character of our transgressions.

Against you, you only, have I sinned. David here intimates that though all the world should pardon him, he felt that God was the Judge with whom he had to do, that conscience hailed him to his bar, and that the voice of man could administer no relief to him, however much he might be disposed to forgive, or to excuse, or to flatter. His eyes and his whole soul were directed to God, regardless of what man might think or say concerning him.

The general doctrine which we are taught from the passage is, that whatever sins men may commit are chargeable entirely upon themselves, and never can implicate the righteousness of God. Men are ever ready to arraign his administration, when it does not correspond with the judgment of sense and human reason. But should God at any time raise persons from the depth of obscurity to the highest distinction, or, on the other hand, allow persons who occupied a most conspicuous station to be suddenly precipitated from it, we should learn from the example which is here set before us to judge of the divine procedure with sobriety, modesty, and reverence, and to rest satisfied that it is holy, and that the works of God, as well as his words, are characterised by unerring rectitude.

PSALM 51:5

Surely I was sinful at birth, sinful from the time my mother conceived me. We are cherished in sin from the first moment that we are in the womb. David is here brought, by reflecting on one particular transgression, to cast a retrospective glance upon his whole past life, and to discover nothing but sin in it.

The passage affords a striking testimony in proof of the original sin entailed by Adam upon the whole human family. It not only teaches the doctrine, but may assist us in forming a correct idea of it. The Bible, both in this and other places, clearly asserts that we are born in sin, and that it exists within us as a disease fixed in our nature. David does not charge it upon his parents, nor trace his crime to them, but sits himself before the Divine tribunal, confesses that he was formed in sin, and that he was a transgressor even before he saw the light of this world. It was therefore a gross error in Pelagius to deny that sin was hereditary, descending in the human family by contagion. We have no adequate idea of the dominion of sin, unless we conceive of it as extending to every part of the soul, and acknowledge that both the mind and heart of man have become utterly corrupt.

Here the question has been started, How sin is transmitted from the parents to the children? It is enough that we hold, that Adam, upon his fall, was despoiled of his original righteousness, his reason darkened, his will perverted, and that, being reduced to this state of corruption, he brought children into the world resembling himself in character. Should anyone object to it that generation is confined to bodies, and that souls can never derive anything in common from one another, the reply is, that Adam, when he was endued at his creation with the gifts of the Spirit, he did not sustain a private character, but represented all mankind, who may be considered as having been endued with these gifts in his person; and from this view it necessarily follows that when he fell, we all forfeited along with him our original integrity.

Day 131   M A Y   1 0

Surely you desire truth in the inner parts; you teach me wisdom in the inmost place. David asserts that, in order to meet the approval of God, it is not enough that our lives be conformed to the letter of his law, unless our heart be clean and purified from all guile. Are we conscious of having committed any one sin, let it be the means of recalling others to our recollection, until we are brought to prostrate ourselves before God in deep self-abasement. And if it has been our privilege to enjoy the special teaching of the Spirit of God, we ought to feel that our guilt is additionally heavy, having sinned in this case against light, and having trampled under foot the precious gifts with which we were instrusted.

Cleanse me with hyssop, and I will be clean; wash me, and I will be whiter than snow. The repetition of David's requests for pardon proves how earnestly he desired it. He speaks of *hyssop*, in allusion to the ceremonies of the law; and though he was far from putting his trust in the mere outward symbol of purification, he knew that, like every other legal rite, it was instituted for an important end. The sacrifices were seals of the grace of God. In them, therefore, he was anxious to find assurance of his reconciliation; and it is highly proper that, when our faith wavers, we should confirm it by improving such means of divine support. All which David here prays for is, that God would effectually accomplish, in his experience, what he had signified to his Church and people by these outward rites; and in this he has set us a good example for our imitation. It is no doubt to the blood of Christ alone that we must look for the atonement of our sins; but we are creatures of sense, who must see with our eyes, and handle with our hands; and it is only by improving the outward symbols of propitiation that we can arrive at a full and assured persuasion of it. It is the peculiar work of the Holy Spirit to sprinkle our consciences inwardly with the blood of Christ, and, by removing the sense of guilt, to secure our access into the presence of God.

Let me hear joy and gladness; let the bones you have crushed rejoice. The Psalmist prays, in general, for testimonies of the divine favour. When he speaks of his bones as having been broken, he alludes to the extreme grief and overwhelming distress to which he had been reduced. The joy of the Lord would reanimate his soul; and this joy he describes as to be obtained by hearing, for it is the word of God alone which can first and effectually cheer the heart of any sinner. There is no true or solid peace to be enjoyed in the world except in the way of reposing upon the promises of God. Those who do not resort to them may succeed for a time in hushing or evading the terror of conscience, but they must ever be strangers to true inward comfort. And, granting that they may attain to the peace of insensibility, this is not a state which could satisfy any man who has seriously felt the fear of the Lord. The joy which he desires is that which flows from hearing the word of God, in which he promises to pardon our guilt, and readmit us into his favour. It is this alone which supports the believer amidst all the fears, dangers, and distresses of his earthly pilgrimage; for the joy of the Spirit is inseparable from faith.

Hide your face from my sins and blot out all my iniquity. This represents our justification as consisting in a voluntary act of God, by which he condescends to forget all our iniquities; and it represents our cleansing to consist in the reception of a gratuitous pardon. David, in thus reiterating his one request for the mercy of God, evinces the depth of that anxiety which he felt for a favour which his conduct had rendered difficult of attainment. God's pardon is full and complete; but our faith cannot take in his overflowing goodness, and it is necessary that it should distil to us drop by drop. It is owing to this infirmity of our faith, that we are often found repeating and repeating again the same petition, not with the view surely of gradually softening the heart of God to compassion, but because we advance by slow and difficult steps to the requisite fullness of assurance.

Create in me a pure heart, O God, and renew a steadfast spirit within me. David now requests that the grace of the Spirit, which he had deserved to have forfeited, might be restored to him. By employing the term *create*, he expresses his persuasion that nothing less than a miracle could effect his reformation, and emphatically declares that repentance is the gift of God. He acknowledges that we are indebted entirely to the grace of God, both for our first regeneration, and, in the event of our falling, for subsequent restoration.

Do not cast me from your presence or take your Holy Spirit from me. If God reconcile us gratuitously to himself, it follows that he will guide us by the Spirit of adoption. It is only such as he loves, and has numbered among his own children, that he blesses with a share of his Spirit; and David shows that he was sensible of this when he prays for the continuance of the grace of adoption as indispensable to the continued possession of the Spirit. The elect, by falling into mortal sin, cannot lose the Spirit altogether, and be alienated from God. This is clearly declared by Peter, who tells us that the word by which we are born again is an incorruptible seed (1 Peter 1:23); and John is equally explicit in informing us that the elect are preserved from falling away altogether (1 John 3:9). However much they may appear to for a time to have been cast off by God, it is afterwards seen that grace must have been alive in their breast, even during that interval when it seemed to be extinct. It is natural that the saints, when they have fallen into sin, and have thus done what they could to expel the grace of God, should feel anxiety at this point; but it is their duty to hold fast the truth that grace is the incorruptible seed of God, which never can perish in any heart where it has been deposited.

I will teach transgressors your ways. The sanguine manner in which David expresses his expectation of converting others is not unworthy of our notice. We are too apt to conclude that our attempts at reclaiming the ungodly are vain and ineffectual, and forget that God is able to crown them with success.

PSALM 51:16-19

You do not delight in sacrifice, or I would bring it; you do not take pleasure in burnt offerings. By this language David expresses his confidence of obtaining pardon, although he brought nothing to God in the shape of compensation, but relied entirely upon the riches of Divine mercy. He confesses that he comes to God both poor and needy; but is persuaded that this will not prevent the success of his suit, because God attaches no importance to sacrifice. It is so that God had enjoined the observance of sacrifice, and David was far from neglecting it. He is not to be understood as asserting that the rite might warrantably be omitted, or that God would absolutely reject the sacrifices of his own institution, which, along with the other cere-monies of the Law, proved important helps, as we have already observed, both to David and the whole Church of God. He speaks of them as observed by the proud and the ignorant, under an impression of meriting the divine favour. Diligent as he was, therefore, in the practice of sacrifice, resting his whole dependence upon the satisfaction of Christ, who atoned for the sins of the world, he could yet honestly declare that he brought nothing to God in the shape of compensation, and that he trusted entirely to a gratuitous reconciliation.

The sacrifices of God are a broken spirit; a broken and contrite heart, O God, you will not despise. David now declares that he needed to bring nothing whatever to God but a contrite and humbled heart. The man of broken spirit is one who has been emptied of all vain-glorious confi-dence, and brought to acknowledge that he is nothing. The contrite heart abjures the idea of merit, and has no dealings with God upon the principle of exchange. Where the spirit has been broken and the heart has become contrite, through a felt sense of the anger of the Lord, a man is brought to genuine fear and self-loathing, with a deep conviction that of himself he can do or deserve nothing, and must be indebted uncondi-tionally for salvation to Divine mercy.

Then there will be righteous sacrifices. David had declared sacrifices to be of no value when considered in themselves, but now he acknowledges them to be acceptable to God when viewed as expressions or symbols of faith, penitence, and thanksgiving. He calls them distinctly sacrifices of righteousness, right, warrantable, and such as are offered in strict accor-dance with the commandment of God.

Day 135   M A Y   1 4

The righteous will see and fear. The Psalmist here adduces, as another reason why the ruin of the treacherous Doeg might be expected, that an important end would be obtained by it, in so far as it would promote religion in the heart of the Lord's people, and afford them a refreshing display of the Divine justice. Should it take place, it would be witnessed by the ungodly as well as by the righteous; but there are two reasons why the Psalmist represents it as being seen especially by the latter. The wicked are incapable of profiting by the judgments of God, being blind to the plainest manifestations which he has made of himself in his works, and it was only the righteous therefore who could see it. Besides, the great end which God has in view, when he prostrates the pride of the ungodly, is the comfort of his own people, that he may show to them the care with which he watches over their safety. It is they, therefore, whom David represents as witnessing this spectacle of Divine justice. And when he says that they would fear, it is not meant that they would tremble, or experience any slavish apprehension, but that their reverential regard for God would be increased by this proof of his care of their interests. When left exposed to the injurious treatment of their enemies, they are apt to be distressed with doubts as to the concern which he takes in the government of the world. But such illustrations to the contrary have the effect of quickening their discouraged zeal, and promoting that fear which is by no means inconsistent with the joy spoken of in the close of the verse. They are led to reverence him the more when they see that he is the avenger of cruelty and injustice: on the other hand, when they perceive that he appears in defence of their cause, and joins common battle with them against their adversaries, they are naturally filled with the most triumphant joy. The beautiful play upon the words see and fear, in the Hebrew, cannot be translated to our language; the form of the expression intimates that they would see and see effectually.

PSALM 52:8-9

But I am like an olive tree flourishing in the house of God; I trust in God's unfailing [goodness] for ever and ever. Let us engrave the useful lesson upon our hearts, that we should consider it the great end of our existence to be found numbered amongst the worshippers of God; and that we should avail ourselves of the inestimable privileges of the stated assemblies of the Church, which are necessary helps to our infirmity, and means of mutual excitement and encouragement. By these, and our common Sacraments, the Lord, who is one God, and who designed that we should be one in him, is training us up together in the hope of eternal life, and in the united celebration of his holy name. Let us learn with David to prefer a place in the house of God to all the lying vanities of this world. He adds the reason why he should be like the green olive-tree—because he hoped in the goodness of God. And in this he adverts to the contrast between him and his enemies. They might flourish for a time, spread their branches far and wide, and shoot themselves up to a gigantic stature, but would speedily wither away, because they had no root in the goodness of God; whereas he was certain to derive from this source ever renewed supplies of sap and vigour. As the term of his earthly trials might be protracted, and there was a danger that he might sink under their long continuance, unless his confidence should extend itself far into futurity, he declares expressly that he would not presume to prescribe times to God, and that his hopes were stretched into eternity. It followed that he surrendered himself entirely to God in all that regarded this life or his death. The passage puts us in possession of the grand distinction between the genuine children of God and those who are hypocrites. They are to be found together in the Church, as the wheat is mingled with the chaff on the same threshing-floor; but the one class abides forever in the stedfastness of a well-founded hope, while the other is driven away in the vanity of its false confidences.

Day 137   M A Y   1 6

Everyone has turned away, they have together become corrupt; there is no one who does good, not even one. David declares that all men are so carried away by their capricious lusts, that nothing is to be found either of purity or integrity in their whole life. He not only censures a portion of the people, but pronounces them all to be equally involved in the same condition. But it might be asked, how David makes no exception, how he declares that not a righteous person remains, not even one, when, nevertheless, he informs us a little after, that the poor and afflicted put their trust in God? Again, it might be asked, if all were wicked, who was that Israel whose future redemption he celebrates in the end of the psalm? No, as he himself was one of the body of that people, why does he not at least except himself? The answer is: It is against the carnal and degenerate body of the Israelitish nation that he here inveighs, and the small number constituting the seed which God had set apart for himself is not included among them. This is the reason why Paul, in his Epistle to the Romans, 3:10, extends this sentence to all mankind ("There is no one righteous, not even one.") David, it is true, deplores the disordered and desolate state of matters under the reign of Saul. At the same time, however, he doubtless makes a comparison between the children of God and all who have not been regenerated by the Spirit, but are carried away according to the inclinations of their flesh. The subject which Paul reasons upon is not, what is the character of the greater part of men, but what is the character of all who are led and governed by their own corrupt nature. It is, therefore, to be observed, that when David places himself and the small remnant of the godly on one side, and puts on the other side the body of the people, in general, this implies that there is a manifest difference between the children of God who are created anew by his Spirit, and all the posterity of Adam, in whom corruption and depravity exercise dominion. Only God can make us new creatures by his mysterious grace.

PSALM
54

Save me, O God, by your name; vindicate me by your might. By appealing to God as his judge, David asserts his uprightness. And it must strike us all, that in asking the divine protection it is indispensably prerequisite we should be convinced of the goodness of our cause, as it would argue the greatest profanity in any to expect that God should patronise iniquity. David was encouraged to pray for deliverance by the goodness of his cause and his consciousness of integrity; nor did he entertain a single doubt, that on representing this to God he would act the part of his defender, and punish the cruelty and treachery of his enemies.

Surely God is my help. Such language as this may show us that David did not direct his prayers at random into the air, but offered them in the exercise of a lively faith. He points, as it were, with the finger to that God who stood at his side to defend him; and was not this an amazing illustration of the power with which faith can surmount all obstacles, and glance, in a moment, from the depths of despair to the very throne of God?

I will freely sacrifice unto you: I will praise your name, O God! for it is good.* According to his usual custom, David engages, provided deliverance should be granted, to feel a grateful sense of it; and there can be no doubt that he here promises also to return thanks to God, in a formal manner, when he should enjoy an opportunity of doing so. Though God principally looks to the inward sentiment of the heart, that would not excuse the neglect of such rites as the Law had prescribed. He would testify his sense of the favour which he received, in the manner common to all the people of God, by sacrifices, and be thus the means of exciting others to their duty by his example. And he would sacrifice freely: by which he does not allude to the circumstance, that sacrifices of thanksgiving were at the option of worshippers, but to the alacrity and cheerfulness with which he would pay his vow when he had escaped his present dangers.

We are taught by the passage that, in coming into the presence of God, we cannot look for acceptance unless we bring to his service a willing mind.

Truly, it was not an enemy that cast disgrace upon me, for then I could have born it: . . . But it was you, a man of my own order, . . . and my close friend. We sweetly exchanged our most secret thoughts; we walked into the house of God in company.* We are taught by the experience of David, as here represented to us, that we must expect in this world to meet with the secret treachery of friends, as well as with sword and open war, but he has also raised up domestic enemies to injure it with the more secret weapons of stratagem and fraud. This is a species of foe which we can neither flee from nor put to flight. David was betrayed by one who had been his intimate associate, and to whom he had looked up as a leader, in matters not only secular but religious. We are taught by the Spirit to reverence all the natural ties which bind us together in society. Besides the common and universal tie of humanity, there are others of a more sacred kind, by which we should feel ourselves attached to men in proportion as they are more nearly connected with us than others by neighbourhood, relationship, or professional calling, the more as we know that such connections are not the result of chance, but of providential design and arrangement. The bond of religious fellowship is the most sacred of all.

I will call upon God, and Jehovah shall save me.* From the particular mention he makes of evening, morning, and noon, we are left to infer that these must have been the stated hours of prayer amongst the godly at that period. Sacrifices were offered daily in the temple morning and evening, and by this they were taught to engage privately in prayer within their own houses. At noon also it was the practice to offer additional sacrifices. As we are naturally indisposed for the duty of prayer, there is a danger that we may become remiss, and gradually omit it altogether, unless we restrict ourselves to a certain rule. In appointing particular fixed hours to be observed for his worship, there can be no doubt that God had respect to the infirmity of our nature, and the same principle should be applied to the secret as to the public services of devotion, as appears from the passage now before us, and from the example of Daniel (9:3).

PSALM 56

When I am afraid, I will trust in you. The true proof of faith consists in this, that when we feel the solicitations of natural fear, we can resist them, and prevent them from obtaining an undue ascendancy. Fear and hope may seem opposite and incompatible affections, yet it is proved by observation, that the latter never comes into full sway unless there exists some measure of the former. In a tranquil state of the mind, there is no scope for the exercise of hope. At such times it lies dormant, and its power is only displayed to advantage when we see it elevating the soul under dejection, calming its agitations, or soothing its distractions. This was the manner in which it manifested itself in David, who feared, and yet trusted, was sensible of the greatness of his danger, and yet quieted his mind with the confident hope of the divine deliverance.

Record my lament; list my tears on your scroll—are they not in your record? It was usual to preserve the wine and oil in bottles: so that the words amount to a request that God would not suffer his tears to fall to the ground, but keep them with care as a precious deposit. The prayers of David, as appears from the passage before us, proceeded upon faith in the providence of God, who watches our every step, and by whom (to use the expression of Christ) "the very hairs of our head are numbered" (Matt. 10:30). Unless persuaded in our mind that God takes special notice of each affliction which we endure, it is impossible that we can ever attain such confidence as to pray that God would put our tears into his bottle, with a view to regarding them, and being induced by them to interpose in our behalf. David animates his hope by the consideration that all his tears were written in the book of God, and would therefore be certainly remembered. And we may surely believe, that if God bestows such hon-our upon the tears of his saints, he must number every drop of their blood which is shed. Tyrants may burn their flesh and their bones, but the blood remains to cry aloud for vengeance; and intervening ages can never erase what has been written in the register of God's remembrance.

Day 141   M A Y   2 0

Have mercy on me, O God, have mercy on me, for in you my soul takes refuge. I will take refuge in the shadow of your wings until the disaster has passed. The repetition of the prayer proves that the grief, the anxiety, and the apprehension, with which David was filled at this time, must have been of no common description. It is noticeable, that this plea for mercy is, his having hoped in God. His soul trusted in him; and this is a form of expression, the force of which is not to be overlooked: for it implies that the trust which he exercised proceeded from his very innermost affections,—that it was of no volatile character, but deeply and strongly rooted. He declares the same truth in figurative terms, when he adds his persuasion that God would cover him with the shadow of his wings.

  David has committed himself, in short, entirely to the guardianship of God; and now experienced that blessed consciousness of dwelling in a place of safety, which he expresses in the beginning of the ninetieth psalm. The divine protection is compared to the shadow of wings, because God, the more familiarly to invite us to himself, is represented as stretching out his wings like a hen, or other birds, for the shelter of their young.

There are seasons when we are privileged to enjoy the calm sunshine of prosperity; but there is not a day of our lives in which we may not suddenly be overtaken by storms of affliction, and it is necessary we should be persuaded that God will cover us with his wings. To hope David adds prayer.

Be exalted, O God, above the heavens; let your glory be over all the earth. To perceive the appropriateness of this prayer, it is necessary that we reflect upon the height of audacity and pride to which the wicked proceed, when unrestrained by the providence of God, and upon the formidable nature of that conspiracy which was directed against David by Saul, and the nation in general, all which demanded a signal manifestation of divine power on his behalf. Nor is it a small comfort to consider that God, in appearing for the help of his people, at the same time advances his own glory. Against it, as well as against them, is the opposition of the wicked directed, and he will never suffer his glory to be obscured, or his holy name to be polluted with their blasphemies.

The righteous will be glad when they are avenged. It might appear at first sight that the feeling here attributed to the righteous is far from being consistent with the mercy which ought to characterise them; but we must remember that the affection which David means to impute to them is one of a pure and well-regulated kind; and in this case there is nothing absurd in supposing that believers, under the influence and guidance of the Holy Spirit, should rejoice in witnessing the execution of divine judgments. That cruel satisfaction which too many feel when they see their enemies destroyed, is the result of the unholy passions of hatred, anger, or impatience, inducing an inordinate desire of revenge. God is not prevented by his mercy from manifesting, upon fit occasions, the severity of the judge, when means have been tried in vain to bring the sinner to repentance, nor can such an exercise of severity be considered as impugning his clemency; and, in a similar way, the righteous would anxiously desire the conversion of their enemies, and evince much patience under injury, with a view to reclaim them to the way of salvation: but when wilful obstinacy has at last brought round the hour of retribution, it is only natural that they should rejoice to see it inflicted, as proving the interest which God feels in their personal safety.

Then men will say, "Surely the righteous still are rewarded; surely there is a God who judges the earth." Nothing tends more to promote godliness than an intimate and assured persuasion that the righteous shall never lose their reward. Hence the language of Isaiah, "Say to the righteous, that it shall be well with them; for they shall eat the fruit of their doings" (Isa. 3:10).

There is subjoined the reason why the righteous cannot fail to reap the reward of their piety, because God is the judge of the world; it being impossible, on the supposition of the world being ruled by the providence of God, that he should not, sooner or later, distinguish between the good and the evil. He is said more particularly to judge in the earth, because men have sometimes profanely alleged that the government of God is confined to heaven, and the affairs of this world abandoned to blind chance.

But do not kill them, O LORD, our shield, or my people will forget. In your might make them wander about, and bring them down. David very properly suggests this to his own mind, as a consideration which should produce patience. We are apt to think, when God has not annihilated our enemies at once, that they have escaped out of his hand altogether; and we look upon it as properly no punishment, that they should be gradually and slowly destroyed. It is true, that were not our eyes blinded, we would behold a more evident display of divine retribution in cases where the destruction of the ungodly is sudden; but these are apt to fade away from our remembrance, that he had good reason to express his desire that the spectacle might be one constantly renewed, and thus our knowledge of the judgments of God be more deeply graven upon our hearts. If the wicked were exterminated in a moment, the remembrance of the event might speedily be effaced. There is an indirect censure conveyed to the people of Israel for failing to improve the more striking judgments of God. But the sin is one too prevalent in the world even at this day. Those judgments which are so evident that none can miss to observe them without shutting his eyes, we sinfully allow to pass into oblivion; so that we need to be brought daily into that theatre where we are compelled to perceive the divine hand.

But I will sing of your strength, in the morning I will sing of your love; for you are my fortress, my refuge in times of trouble. David expresses still more explicitly the truth, that he owed his safety entirely to God. God has the strength of the wicked in his hands, to curb and to restrain it, and to show that any power of which they boast is vain and fallacious. His own people, on the other hand, he supports and secures, against the possibility of falling, by supplies of strength from himself. In the preceding part of the psalm, David had congratulated himself upon his safety, by reflecting that Saul was so completely under the secret restraint of God's providence as to be unable to move a finger without his permission. Now, weak as he was in himself, he maintains that he had good reason to engage in praise, as James the inspired apostle exhorts those who are merry to sing psalms (5:13).

PSALM 60

*Give us help from trouble, for vain is the help of man.** Again David reverts to the exercise of prayer, or rather is led to it naturally by the very confidence of hope, which we have seen that it entertained. He expresses his conviction, that should God extend his help, it would be sufficient of itself, although no assistance should be received from any other quarter. It is as if he had said, "O God, when pleased to put forth your might, you need no-one to help you; and when, therefore, once assured of an interest in your favour, there is no reason why we should desire the aid of man. All other resources of a worldly nature vanish before the brightness of your power."

Why is it almost universally the case with men that they are either staggered in their resolution, or buoy themselves up with confidences, vain, because not derived from God, but just because they have no apprehension of that salvation which he can extend, which is of itself sufficient, and without which, any earthly succour is entirely ineffectual? God, in accomplishing our preservation, may use the agency of man, but he reserves it to himself, as his peculiar prerogative, to deliver, and will not suffer them to rob him of his glory. The deliverance which comes to us in this manner through human agency must properly be ascribed to God. All that David meant to assert is, that such confidences as are not derived from God are worthless and in vain. And to confirm this position he declares in the last verse of the psalm, that as, on the one hand, we can do nothing without him, so, on the other, we can do all things by his help.

*Through God we shall do valiantly: for it is he that shall tread down our enemies.** If God withdraw his favour, any supposed strength which is in man will soon fail; but those whose sufficiency is derived from God only are armed with courage to overcome every difficulty. Even in our controversy with creatures like ourselves, we are not at liberty to share the honour of success with God; and must it not be accounted greater sacrilege still when men set free will in opposition to divine grace, and speak of their concurring equally with God in the matter of procuring eternal salvation? Those who arrogate the least fraction of strength to themselves apart from God, only ruin themselves through their own pride.

For you have heard my vows, O God; you have given me the heritage of those who fear your name. God never disappoints his servants, but crowns with everlasting happiness the struggles and the distresses which may have exercised their faith. They convey an implied censure of that unwarrantable confidence which is indulged in by the wicked, when favoured, through the Divine forbearance, with any interval of prosperity. The success which flatters them is merely imaginary, and speedily vanishes. But inheritance suggests that the people of God enjoy a species of prosperity more solid and enduring; their momentary and short-lived troubles having only the effect of promoting their eternal welfare. He praises God that those who fear his name are not left to the poor privilege of rejoicing for a few days, but secured in a permanent heritage of happiness. The truth is one which cannot be questioned. The wicked, having no possession by faith of the divine benefits which they may happen to share, live on from day to day, as it were, upon plunder. It is only such as fear the Lord who have the true and legitimate enjoyment of their blessings.

Increase the days of the king's life, his years for many generations. The series of years, and even ages, of which David speaks, extends prospectively to the coming of Christ, it being the very condition of the kingdom, that God maintained them as one people under one head, or, when scattered, united them again. The same succession still subsists in reference to ourselves. Christ must be viewed as living in his members to the end of the world. To this Isaiah alludes, when he says, "Who shall declare his generation or age?"—words in which he predicts that the Church would survive through all ages, notwithstanding the incessant danger of destruction to which it is exposed through the attacks of its enemies, and the many storms assailing it. So here David foretells the uninterrupted succession of the kingdom down to the time of Christ.

PSALM 62:1-10

My soul finds rest in God alone; my salvation comes from him. We know that the Lord's people cannot always reach such a measure of composure as to be wholly exempt from distraction. They would wish to receive the word of the Lord with submission, and to be dumb under his correcting hand; but inordinate affections will take possession of their minds, and break in upon that peace which they might otherwise attain to in the exercise of faith and resignation. David felt an inward struggle and opposition, which he found it necessary to check. Satan had raised a tumult in his affections, and wrought a degree of impatience in his mind, which he now curbs; and he expresses his resolution *to be silent.* The word implies a meek and submissive endurance of the cross. It expresses the opposite of that heat of spirit which would put us into a posture of resistance to God. The silence intended is, in short, that composed submission of the believer, in the exercise of which he acquiesces in the promises of God, gives place to word, bows to his sovereignty, and suppresses every inward murmur of dissatisfaction.

Trust in him at all times, O people; pour out your hearts to him, for God is our refuge. The expression, *at all times,* means both in prosperity and adversity, intimating the blameworthiness of those who waver and succumb under every variation in their outward circumstances. God tries his children with afflictions, but here they are taught by David to abide them with constancy and courage. We are bound to put honour upon his name by remembering, in our greatest extremities, that to him belong the issues of death. And as we are all too apt at such times to shut up our affliction in our breast—a circumstance which can only aggravate the trouble and embitter the mind against God, David could not have suggested a better expedient than that of disburdening our cares to him, and thus, as it were, pouring out our hearts before him. It is always found, that when the heart is pressed under a load of distress, there is no freedom in prayer. Under trying circumstances, we must comfort ourselves by reflecting that God will extend relief, provided we just freely roll them over upon his consideration.

Day 147   M A Y   2 6

One thing God has spoken, two things have I heard: that you, O God, are strong, and that you, O LORD, are loving. Usually they are swayed in different directions, or inclined at least to waver, just as they observe things changing in the world; but he brings under their notice a surer principle for the regulation of their conduct, when he recommends a deferential regard to God's Word. It is of great consequence that we be established in the belief of God's Word, and we are here directed to the unerring certainty which belongs to it. God acts consistently with himself, and can never swerve from what he has said. Every word which may have issued forth from God is to be received with implicit authority.

And that you, O LORD, are loving. It is essentially necessary, if we would fortify our minds against temptation, to have suitably exalted views of the power and mercy of God, since nothing will more effectually preserve us in a straight and undeviating course, than a firm persuasion that all events are in the hand of God, and that he is as merciful as he is mighty. The man who disciplines himself to the contemplation of these two attributes, which ought never to be dissociated in our minds from the idea of God, is certain to stand erect and immovable under the fiercest assaults of temptation; while, on the other hand, by losing sight of the all-sufficiency of God, (which we are too apt to do,) we lay ourselves open to be overwhelmed in the first encounter. The world's opinion of God is, that he sits in heaven an idle and unconcerned spectator of events which are passing. Need we wonder, that men tremble under every casualty, when they thus believe themselves to be the sport of blind chance? There can be no security felt unless we satisfy ourselves of the truth of a divine superintendence, and can commit our lives and all that we have to the hands of God. The first thing which we must look to is his power, that we may have a thorough conviction of his being a sure refuge to such as cast themselves upon his care. With this there must be conjoined confidence in his mercy, to prevent those anxious thoughts which might otherwise rise in our minds.

PSALM 62:12(b)

Surely you will reward each person according to what he has done. Here the Psalmist declares that the God who governs the world by his providence will judge it in righteousness. The expectation of this, duly cherished, will have a happy effect in composing our minds, allaying impatience, and checking any disposition to resent and retaliate under our injuries. In sitting himself and others before the great bar of God, he would both encourage his heart in the hope of that deliverance which was coming, and teach himself to despise the insolent persecution of his enemies, when he considered that every man's work was to come into judgment before him, who can no more cease to be Judge than deny himself. We can therefore rest assured, however severe our wrongs may be, though wicked men should account us the filth and the offscourings of all things, that God is witness to what we suffer, will interpose in due time, and will not disappoint our patient expectations. From this, and passages of a similar kind, the Papists have argued, in defence of their doctrine, that justification and salvation depend upon good works. No sooner is mention made of works, that they catch at the expression, as amounting to a statement that God rewards men upon the ground of merit. It is with a very different design than to encourage any such opinion, that the Spirit promises a reward to our works—it is to animate us in the ways of obedience, and not to inflame that impious self-confidence which cuts up salvation by the very roots. We know that there is none of our works which, in the sight of God, can be accounted perfect or pure, and without taint of sin. Any recompense they meet with must therefore be traced entirely to his goodness. Since the Scriptures promise a reward to the saints, with the sole intention of stimulating their minds, and encouraging them in the divine warfare, and not with the remotest design of derogating from the mercy of God, it is absurd in the Papists to allege that they, in any sense, merit what is bestowed upon them. As regards the wicked, none will dispute that the punishment awarded to them, as violaters of the law, is strictly deserved.

O God, you are my God, earnestly I seek you. It is apparent that David never allowed himself to be so far overcome by his trials, as to cease lifting up his prayer to heaven, and even resting, with a firm and constant faith, upon the divine promises. Apt as we are, when assaulted by the very slightest trials, to lose the comfort of any knowledge of God we may previously have possessed, it is necessary that we should notice this, and learn, by his example, to struggle to maintain our confidence under the worst troubles that can befall us. He does more than simply pray; he sets the Lord before him as his God, that he may throw all his cares unhesitatingly upon him, deserted as he was of man, and a poor outcast in the waste and howling wilderness. His faith, shown in this persuasion of the favour and help of God, had the effect of exciting him to constant and vehement prayer for the grace which he expected.

I have seen you in the sanctuary and beheld your power and your glory. It is apparent that God was always in the Psalmist's thoughts, though wandering in the wilderness under such circumstances of destitution. Even when so situated, in a wild and hideous solitude, where the very horrors of the place were enough to have distracted his meditations, he exercised himself in beholding the power and glory of God, just as if he had been in the sanctuary. It is noticeable of ignorant and superstitious persons, that they seem full of zeal and fervour so long as they come in contact with the ceremonies of religion, while their seriousness evaporates immediately upon these being withdrawn. David, on the contrary, when these were removed, continued to retain them in his recollection, and rise, through their assistance, to fervent aspirations after God. We may learn by this, when deprived at any time of the outward means of grace, to direct the eye of our faith to God in the worst circumstances, and not to forget him whenever the symbols of holy things are taken out of our sight. Or suppose that the Lord's Supper, and other means of advancing our spiritual welfare, were taken from us by an exercise of tyrannical power, it does not follow that our minds should ever cease to be occupied with the contemplation of God.

**PSALM
63:3-11**

Because your love is better than life, my lips will glorify you.
It is of no consequence how large a share men possess of prosperity, and of the means which are generally thought to make life secure, because the divine mercy is a better foundation of trust than any life fashioned out to ourselves, and than all other supports taken together. On this account the Lord's people, however severely they may suffer from poverty, or the violence of human wrongs, or the languor of desire, or hunger or thirst, or the many troubles and anxieties of life, may be happy notwithstanding; for it is well with them, in the best sense of the term, when God is their friend. Unbelievers, on the other hand, must be miserable, even when all the world smile upon them; for God is their enemy, and curse necessarily attaches to their lot.

My soul will be satisfied as with the richest of foods; with singing lips my mouth will praise you. If we would evidence a strong faith, we must anticipate the divine favour before it has been actually manifested, and when there is no present appearance of its forthcoming. From the instance here set before us, we must learn to be on our guard against despondency, in circumstances when we may see the wicked wallowing and rioting in the abundance of the things of this world, while we ourselves are left to pine under the want of them. David, in the present pressure to which he was exposed, might have given way to despair, but he knew that God was able to fill the hungry soul, and that he could lack nothing so long as he possessed an interest in his favour. It is God's will to try our patience in this life, by affliction of various kinds. Let us bear the wrongs which may be done to us with meekness, till the time come when all our desires shall be abundantly satisfied. It may be proper to observe, that David, when he speaks in figurative language of being filled with marrow and fatness, does not contemplate that intemperate and excessive indulgence to which ungodly men surrender themselves, and by which they brutify their minds. He looks forward to that moderate measure of enjoyment which would only quicken him to more alacrity in the praises of God.

PSALM
64

But God will shoot them with arrows; suddenly they will be struck down. The Psalmist now congratulates himself in the confident persuasion that his prayers have not been without effect, but already answered. Though there was no appearance of God's approaching judgment, he declares that it would suddenly be executed; and in this he affords a remarkable proof of his faith. He saw the wicked hardening themselves in their prosperity, and presuming upon impunity from the divine connivance and forbearance; but instead of yielding to discouragement, he was borne up by the belief that God, according to his usual mode of procedure with the wicked, would visit them at an unexpected moment, when they were flattering themselves with having escaped, and were indulging in extravagant confidence. It is a consideration which should comfort us, when subjected to long-continued trial, that God, in delaying to punish the ungodly, does so with the express design of afterwards inflicting judgments of a more condign description upon them, and when they shall say, "Peace and safety," he would overwhelm them with sudden destruction (Jer. 8:11).

He will turn their own tongues against them and bring them to ruin; all who see them will shake their heads in scorn. Pursuing the same subject, he remarks, that the poison concocted in their secret counsels, and which they revealed with their tongues, would prove to have a deadly effect upon themselves. The sentiment is the same with that expressed elsewhere by another figure, when they are said to be caught in their own snares, and to fall into the pit which they have digged themselves (Ps. 57:6). It is just that Heaven should make the mischiefs which they had devised against innocent and upright men to recoil upon their own heads. The judgment is one which we see repeatedly and daily exemplified before our eyes, and yet we find much difficulty in believing that it can take place. We should feel ourselves bound the more to impress the truth upon our hearts, that God is ever watching, as it were, his opportunity of converting the stratagems of the wicked into means just as completely effective of their destruction, as if they had intentionally employed them for that end. In the close of the verse, to point out the striking severity of their punishment, it is said that all who saw them should flee away. The knowledge of what God had so signally wrought would extend far and wide.

PSALM 65:1-3

Praise awaits you, O God. The meaning of the expression is, that God's goodness to his people is such as to afford constantly new matter of praise. It is diffused over the whole world, but specially shown to the Church. Besides, others who do not belong to the Church of God, however abundantly benefits may be showered upon them, see not whence they come, and riot in the blessings which they have received without any acknowledgement of them. Thanksgiving is due to the Lord for his goodness shown to his Church and people.

O you who hear prayer, to you all men will come. The title here given to God carries with it a truth of great importance, That the answer of our prayers is secured by the fact, that in rejecting them he would in a certain sense deny his own nature. The Psalmist does not say, that God has heard prayer in this or that instance, but gives him the name of the hearer of prayer, as what constitutes an abiding part of his glory, so that he might as soon deny himself as shut his ear to our petitions. Could we only impress this upon our minds, that it is something peculiar to God, and inseparable from him, to hear prayer, it would inspire us with unfailing confidence. The power of helping us he can never want, so that nothing can stand in the way of a successful issue of our supplications.

What follows in the verse is also well worthy of our attention, that *all flesh shall come* unto God. None could venture into his presence without a persuasion of his being open to entreaty; but when he anticipates our fears, and comes forward declaring that prayer is never offered to him in vain, the door is thrown wide for the admission of all. Before we can approach God acceptably in prayer, it is necessary that his promises should be made known to us, without which we can have no access to him, as is evident from the words of the apostle Paul (Eph. 3:12), where he tells us, that all who would come to God must first be endued with such a faith in Christ as may animate them with confidence. Invaluable is the privilege which we enjoy by the Gospel, of free access unto God. It is a prediction of Christ's future kingdom.

PSALM 65:4(a)

Blessed are those you choose. Having already acknowledged that the people had separated themselves from God by their sins, and forfeited all right to be heard, David now takes refuge in the free grace of God, which secures the remission of sin amongst other blessings. He thus casts an additional light upon what he had said on the point of guilt being purged away, by pointing to the cause of God's being favourable to poor sinners, which can only be found in his fatherly love leading him to welcome them into his presence, however undeserving. That pardon which we daily receive flows from our adoption, and on it also are all our prayers founded. How could the sinner venture into the sight of God, to obtain reconciliation with him, were he not persuaded of his being a Father? In the words before us, David does not speak of the grace of God as reaching to the Gentiles, but in terms which apply only to the times in which he wrote. The Church of God was confined to the Jews, and they only were admitted into the sanctuary; whereas now, when the distinction has been abolished, and other nations called to the same privilege, we are all at liberty to approach him with familiarity. Christ is our peace (Eph. 2:14), who has united in one those who were far off, and those who were near.

What has been now said may show at once the scope of the Psalmist. The Church and chosen people of God being in possession of the promise of the remission of sins, he calls those blessed whom God has included within that number, and introduced into the enjoyment of such a distinguished privilege. His language intimates, that the election did not at that time terminate upon all; for he insists upon it as the special prerogative of the Jews, that they had been chosen by God in preference to the other nations. Were it supposed that man could do anything to anticipate the grace of God, the election would cease to be with God himself, although the right and power of it are expressly ascribed to him. But the Jews had no excellency above others, except in the one point of having enjoyed the distinguishing favour of God. The middle wall of partition is now broken down, that the Gentiles might be called in.

PSALM 65:4(a)

Blessed are those you choose. It is evident that all are not alike called; and observation proves the ignorance of those who will assert that the grace of God is extended to all in common, without any choice exerted on his part. Can any reason be imagined why God should not call all alike, except it be that his sovereign election distinguishes some from others? Faith and prayer may be means for procuring us an interest in the grace of God; but the source whence it flows is not within but without us. There is a blessedness in exercising trust upon God, and embracing his promises—a blessedness experienced when, through faith in Christ the Mediator, we apprehend him as our Father, and direct our prayers to him in that character;—but before this faith and prayer can have any existence, it must be supposed that we who are estranged from God by nature have been brought near by an exercise of his favour. We are near him, not as having anticipated his grace, and come to him of ourselves, but because, in his condescension, he has stretched out his hand as far as hell itself to reach us. To speak more properly, he first elects us, and then testifies his love by calling us. It is noticeable, also, that though God separated the seed of Abraham to be a peculiar people, entitled as the circumcision to a place in his temple, there can be no question that David recognised a distinction even amongst those who were Jews, all not having been the subjects of God's effectual calling, nor yet properly entitled to a place in his temple. The Psalmist alludes, indeed, to the outward sanctuary, when he speaks of the Jews as chosen to approach God; but we must remember that all were not real members of the Church who trod the court of the temple, but that the great qualifications necessary were the pure heart and the clean hands. Accordingly, we must understand by those brought near to God, such as present themselves before him in the exercise of genuine faith, and not such as merely occupy a place in his temple as to outward appearance. But, again, the being chosen, and the being called to approach God, are two things mentioned here together, to correct any such vain idea as that the sheep of God's flock are allowed to wander at will for any length of time, and not brought into the fold.

PSALM
65:4(b)-13

And bring near to live in your courts! The Psalmist insists upon the fruit springing out of the blessed privilege of which he had spoken, when he adds, that believers would be satisfied with the fullness of his temple. We are not to understand that believers are fully replenished with the goodness of God at any one moment; it is conveyed to them gradually; but while the influences of the Spirit are thus imparted in successive measures, each of them is enriched with a present sufficiency, till all be in due time advanced to perfection. While it is true, as stated (Ps. 103:5), that "God satisfies our mouth with good things," at the same time it is necessary to remember what is said elsewhere, "Open your mouth, and I will fill it." By specifying particularly the goodness of the sanctuary, the Psalmist passes an implied commendation upon the outward helps which God has appointed for leading us into the enjoyment of heavenly blessings. In these former times God could have directly stretched out his hand from heaven to supply the wants of his worshippers, but saw fit to satisfy their souls by means of the doctrine of the law, sacrifices, and other rites and external aids to piety. Similar are the means which he employs in the Church still; and though we are not to rest in these, neither must we neglect them.

You care for the land and water it; you enrich it abundantly. While it is the kindness of God to his own people which is here more particularly celebrated as being better known, we are bound, in whatever part of the world we live, to acknowledge the riches of the Divine goodness seen in the earth's fertility and increase. It is not of itself that it brings forth such an inexhaustible variety of fruits, but only in so far as it has been fitted by God for producing the food of man. Accordingly, there is a propriety and force in the form of expression used by the Psalmist when he adds, that corn is provided for man, because the earth has been so prepared by God; which means, that the reason of that abundance with which the earth teems, is its having been expressly formed by God in his fatherly care of the great household of mankind, to supply the wants of his children.

PSALM
66:1-12

For you, O God, tested us; you refined us like silver. When visited with affliction, it is of great importance that we should consider it as coming from God, and as expressly intended for our good. It is in reference to this that the Psalmist speaks of their having been *tested and refined.* At the same time, while he adverts to God's trying his children with the view of purging away their sin, as dross is expelled from the silver by fire, he would intimate, also, that trial had been made of their patience. The figure implies that their probation had been severe; for silver is cast repeatedly into the furnace. They express themselves thankful to God, that, while proved with affliction, they had not been destroyed by it; but that their affliction was both varied and very severe, appears not only from the metaphor, but from the whole context, where they speak of having been cast into the net, being reduced to straits, men riding over their heads, and of being brought through shipwreck and conflagration.

We went through fire and water. It is noticeable, that the Psalmist speaks of all the cruelties which they had most unjustly suffered from the hands of enemies, as an infliction of Divine punishment; and would guard the Lord's people against imagining that God was ignorant of what they had endured, or distracted by other things from giving attention to it. In their condition, as here described, we have that of the Church generally represented to us; and this, that when subjected to vicissitudes, and cast out of the fire into the water, by a succession of trials, there may at last be felt to be nothing new or strange in the event to strike us with alarm.

But you brought us to a place of abundance. This is taken metaphorically for a condition of prosperity, the people of God being represented as brought into a pleasant and fertile place, where there is abundance of pasturage. The truth conveyed is, that God, although he visit his children with temporary chastisements of a severe description, will ultimately crown them with joy and prosperity.

PSALM
66:13-20

I will come to your temple with burnt offerings. We are taught that when God at any time succours us in our adversity, we do an injustice to his name if we forget to celebrate our deliverances with solemn acknowledgements. More is spoken of in this passage than thanksgiving. He speaks of vows having been contracted by him in his affliction, and these evidenced the constancy of his faith. The exhortation of the Apostle James (5:13) is worthy of our special notice: "Is any among you afflicted? let him pray. Is anyone merry? let him sing psalms of joy." How many are there who lavish their hypocritical praises upon God in the career of their good fortune, while they are no sooner reduced to straits than the fervour of their love is damped, or gives place to the violence of fretfulness and impatience. The best evidence of true piety is when we sigh to God under the pressure of our afflictions, and show, by our prayers, a holy perseverance in faith and patience; while afterwards we come forward with the expression of our gratitude.

I will sacrifice fat animals to you and an offering of rams; I will offer bulls and goats. However we might propose to ourselves to praise the name of God, we could only profane it with our impure lips, had not Christ once offered himself up a sacrifice, to sanctify both us and our services (Heb. 10:7). It is through him, as we learn from the apostle, that our praises are accepted. The Psalmist, by way of commendation of his burnt-offering, speaks of its incense or sweet savour; for although in themselves vile and loathsome, yet the rams and other victims, so far as they were figures of Christ, sent up a sweet savour unto God. Now that the shadows of the Law have been abolished, attention is called to the true spiritual service. What this consists in, is more clearly brought under our notice in the verse which follows, where the Psalmist tells us, that he would spread abroad the fame of the benefits which he had received from God. Such was the end designed, even in the outward ceremonies under the Law, apart from which they could only be considered as an empty show. It was this—the fact that they set forth the praises of the divine goodness—which formed the very season of the sacrifices, preserving them from insipidity.

PSALM 67

May God be gracious to us and bless us. The Psalmist begins by praying for the Divine blessing, particularly upon the Jews. Speaking, as the Psalmist does, of those who belonged to the Church of God, and not of those who were without, it is noticeable that yet he traces all the blessings they received to God's free favour; and from this we may learn, that so long as we are here, we owe our happiness, our success, and prosperity, entirely to the same cause. This being the case, how shall any think to anticipate his goodness by merits of their own?

May the peoples praise you, O God. Having spoken of all nations participating in the saving knowledge of God, the Psalmist next tells us that they would proclaim his goodness, and exhorts them to the exercise of gratitude. It is impossible that we can praise God aright, unless our minds be tranquil and cheerful; unless, as persons reconciled to God, we are animated with the hope of salvation, and "the peace of God, which passes all understanding," reign in our hearts (Phil. 4:7). The cause assigned for joy plainly in itself points to the event of the calling of the Gentiles. The reference is not to that government of God which is general in its nature, but to that special and spiritual jurisdiction which he exercises over the Church, in which he cannot properly be said to govern any but such as he has gathered under his sway by the doctrine of his law.

Then the land will yield its harvest. Mention having been made of the principal act of the Divine favour, notice is next taken of the temporal blessings which he confers upon his children, that they may have everything necessary to complete their happiness. And here it is to be remembered that every benefit which God bestowed upon his ancient people was, as it were, a light held out before the eyes of the world, to attract the attention of the nations to him. From this the Psalmist argues, that should God liberally supply the wants of his people, the consequence would be, to increase the fear of his name, since all ends of the earth would, by what they saw of his fatherly regard to his own, submit themselves with greater cheerfulness to his government.

But the righteous shall be glad; they shall rejoice before God, and leap for exultation.* It is here intimated by David, that when God shows himself formidable to the wicked, this is with the design of securing the deliverance of his Church. The wicked flee from the presence of God, as what inspires them with terror; the righteous again rejoice in it, because nothing delights them more than to think that God is near them. In Psalm 18:26 we saw why the Divine presence terrifies some and comforts others; for "with the pure he will show himself pure, and with the crooked He will show Himself shrewd." One expression is heaped by the Psalmist upon another, to show how great the joy of the Lord's people is, and how entirely it possesses and occupies their affections.

Sing to God, sing praise to his name, extol him who rides on the clouds. David now proceeds to call upon the Lord's people to praise God. And he begins by pointing out the grounds in general which they have for this exercise, because he comprehends the whole world under his power and government, adding, that he condescends to take the poorest and the most wretched of our family under his protection. His infinite power is commended, when it is said that he rides upon the clouds, or the heavens, for this proves that he sits superior over all things. The Holy Spirit may signify by the expression, that we should exclude from our minds everything gross and earthly in the conceptions we form of him; but he would, doubtless, impress us chiefly with an idea of his great power, to produce in us a due reverence, and make us feel how far short all our praises must come of his glory.

A father to the fatherless, a defender of widows, is God in his holy dwelling. David proceeds to insist upon God's transcendent goodness shown in condescending to the orphans and widows. The incomprehensible glory of God does not induce him to remove himself to a distance from us, or prevent him from stooping to us in our lowest depths of wretchedness. There can be no doubt that orphans and widows are named to indicate in general such as the world are disposed to overlook as unworthy of their regard. Generally we distribute our attentions where we expect some return. We give the preference to rank and splendour, and despise or neglect the poor. The poor are cheered to think that he is not far from them.

PSALM 68:7-27

When you went out before your people, O God. The Psalmist now proceeds to show that the Divine goodness is principally displayed in the Church, which God has selected as the great theatre where his fatherly care may be manifested. What follows is evidently added with the view of leading the posterity of Abraham, as the Lord's chosen people, to apply the observations which had been just made to themselves. The deliverance from Egypt having been the chief and lasting pledge of the Divine favour, which practically ratified their adoption under the patriarch, he briefly adverts to that event. He would intimate that in that remarkable exodus, proof had been given to all succeeding ages of the love which God entertained for his Church. Why were so many miracles wrought? why were heaven and earth put into commotion? why were the mountains made to tremble? but that all might recognise the power of God as allied with the deliverance of his people. He represents God as having been their leader in conducting them forth. And this not merely in reference to their passage of the Red Sea, but their journeys so long as they wandered in the wilderness.

The chariots of God are thousands of thousands of angels.* For the most part we are apt to undervalue the Divine presence, and therefore David presents us with a description fitted to exalt our thoughts of it. Owing to our unbelieving hearts, the least danger which occurs in the world weighs more with us than the power of God. We tremble under the slightest trials; for we forget or cherish low views of his omnipotence. To preserve us from this error, David directs us to the countless myriads of angels which are at God's command, a circumstance, the consideration of which may well enable us to defy the evils which beset us. Twenty thousand are spoken of; but it is a number designed to intimate to us that the armies of the living God, which he commissions for our help, are innumerable; and surely this should comfort us under the deadliest afflictions of this life.

The Lord says, "I will bring them from Bashan." The prophets are in the constant habit, as is well known, of illustrating the mercy of God by reference to the history of Israel's redemption, that the Lord's people, by looking back to their great original deliverance, might find an argument for expecting interpositions of a future kind. To make the deeper impression, God is introduced as speaking himself.

Day 161

Summon your power, O God; show us your strength, O God. Men are always disposed to arrogate to themselves the glory of what they may have done instead of tracing their success to God, and David reminds the people once more that they had not triumphed by their own strength, but by the power communicated from above. If they had acquitted themselves with energy on the field, he would have them consider that it was God who inspired them with this valour, and would guard them against the pride which overlooks and disparages the Divine goodness. As a consideration which might further tend to promote humility in their minds, he adverts to the dependence in which they stood of the future continuance of the same favour and protection; this being the great cause of presumptuous confidence, that we do not feel our own helplessness, and are not led under a sense of it to resort humbly to God for the supply of our want. Another lesson which the passage teaches us is, that more is required than that God should visit us at first with his preventing grace; that we stand constantly in need of his assistance throughout our whole lives. If this be true in the literal warfare, where our conflict is with flesh and blood, it must be still more so in matters of the soul. It is impossible that we could stand one moment in the contest with such enemies as Satan, sin, and the world, did we not receive from God the grace which secures our perseverance.

To him who rides the ancient skies above, who thunders with mighty voice. The heavens of ancient times is meant to intimate that the whole human family were under God's power from the very beginning. We have a signal proof of the glorious power of God in the fact, that, notwithstanding the immensity of the fabric of the heavens, the rapidity of their motion, and the conflicting revolutions which take place in them, the most perfect subordination and harmony are preserved; and that this fair and beautiful order has been uninterruptedly maintained for ages. It is apparent then how the ancientness of the heavens may commend to us the singular excellency of the handiwork of God.

PSALM 69:1-5

I am worn out calling for help; my throat is parched. My eyes fail, looking for my God. David, in seeking and calling upon God, when his affairs were in such a confused and desperate condition, exhibited an instance of rare and wonderful patience. He complains of having continued crying until he was exhausted and became hoarse, and all to no purpose. Although his bodily senses failed him, the vigour of his faith was by no means extinguished. While God spares us, we should meditate on this truth, and derive the aid which it is fitted to impart under calamity, That even in the most profound depths of adversity faith may hold us up, and, what is more, may elevate us to God; there being, as Paul testifies (Rom. 8:39), no height nor depth which can separate us from the infinite love of him who swallows up all depths, yes, even hell itself.

Those who hate me without reason outnumber the hairs of my head. David, as a means of preserving himself from succumbing under the perverse judgments of men, appeals to God as the judge of his cause; and possessing as he did the approving testimony of a good conscience, he regards in a great measure with indifference the unjust estimate which men might form of his character. It were indeed desirable that our integrity would also be acknowledged and approved of by men, and that not so much on our own account as for the edification of our brethren. But if, after we have done all in our power to make men form a favourable opinion respecting us, they misconstrue and pervert every good word which we utter, and every good action which we perform, we ought to maintain such greatness of mind as boldly to despise the world and all false accusers, resting contented with the judgment of God and with that alone; for those who are over anxious about maintaining their good name cannot but often experience fainting of heart. Let us be always ready to satisfy men; but if they refuse to listen to what we have to say in self-vindication, let us proceed in our course through evil report as well as good report, following the example of Paul in 1 Corinthians 4:5, where he fearlessly appeals to the judgment of God, "who will bring to light the hidden things of darkness."

I endure scorn for your sake. David here justly protests that it was not for any wickedness which he had committed, but because he had obeyed God, that men in general disapproved of and rashly condemned him. It is a source of great consolation to true believers when they can protest that they have the warrant and call of God for whatever they undertake or engage in. If we are hated by the world for making a public confession of the faith, a thing which we are to expect, it being evident from observation that the wicked ordinarily are never more fierce than when they assault the truth of God and the true religion, we have ground to entertain double confidence.

For zeal for your house consumes me. Forgetting himself, David burned with a holy zeal to maintain the Church, and at the same time the glory of God, with which it is inseparably connected. To make this the more obvious, let it be observed, that although all boast in words of allowing to God the glory which belongs to him; yet when the law, the rule of virtuous and holy living, presents its claims to them, men only mock him, and not only so, but they furiously rush against him by the opposition which they make to his word. They do this as if he willed to be honoured and served merely with the breath of the lip, and had not rather erected a throne among men, from which to govern them by laws. David, therefore, here places the Church in the place of God; not that it was his intention to transfer to the Church what is proper to God, but to show the vanity of the pretensions which men make of being the people of God, when they shake themselves loose from the control of God's holy law, of which the Church is the faithful guardian. Besides, David had to deal with a class of men who, although a hypocritical and bastard race, professed to be the people of God; for all who adhered to Saul boasted of having a place in the Church, and stigmatised David as an apostate or a rotten member. With this unworthy treatment David was so far from being discouraged, that he willingly sustained all assaults for the defence of the Church.

PSALM
69:6-21

PSALM 69:22-36

May the table set before them become a snare. It was not on his own account that David pleaded in this manner; but it was a holy zeal for the divine glory which impelled him to summon the wicked to God's judgment seat. It was also owing to this, that he was not carried away by violence of passion, like those who are actuated by a desire of taking revenge. Since, then, the Spirit of wisdom, uprightness, and moderation, put these imprecations into the mouth of David, his example cannot justly be pleaded in self-vindication by those who pour forth their wrath and spite upon every one that come their way, or who are carried away by a foolish impatience to take revenge; never allowing themselves to reflect for a moment what good purpose this can serve, nor making any efforts to keep their passion within due bounds. We need wisdom by which to distinguish between those who are wholly reprobate and those of whose amendment there is still some hope; we have also need of uprightness, that none may devote himself exclusively to his own private interests; and of moderation too, to dispose our minds to calm endurance. In short, if we would be true imitator of David, we must first clothe ourselves with the character of Christ, that he may not administer to us at the present day the same rebuke which he gave to two of his disciples of old, "You know not what manner of spirit you are of" (Luke 9:55).

May they be blotted out of the book of life. What is spoken by the Apostle John (1 John 2:19) remains true, that none who have been once really the children of God will ever finally fall away or be wholly cut off. But as hypocrites presumptuously boast that they are the chief members of the Church, the Holy Spirit well expresses their rejection, by the figure of their being blotted out of the book of life. Moreover, it is to be observed that all the elect of God are called the righteous; for, as Paul says in 1 Thessalonians 4:3, 4, 7, "This is the will of God, even our sanctification, that every one of us should know how to possess his vessel in sanctification and honour: for God has not called us unto uncleanness, but unto holiness." And the climax which the same Apostle uses in the eighth chapter of his Epistle to the Romans, at the 30th verse, is well known: "Those he predestined, he also called; those he called, he also justified; those he justified, he also glorified."

Day 165   J U N E   1 3

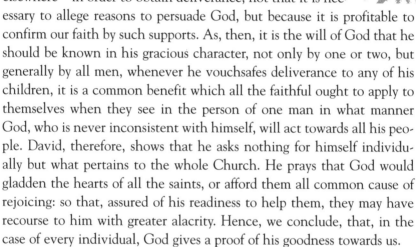

Hasten, O God, to save me. We are here taught that, when our enemies shall have persecuted us to the uttermost, a recompense is also prepared for them; and that God will turn back, and cause to fall upon their own heads, all the evil which they had devised against us; and this doctrine ought to act as a restraint upon us, that we may behave ourselves compassionately and kindly towards our neighbours.

But may all who seek you rejoice and be glad in you. David here uses another argument—one which he often adduces elsewhere—in order to obtain deliverance; not that it is necessary to allege reasons to persuade God, but because it is profitable to confirm our faith by such supports. As, then, it is the will of God that he should be known in his gracious character, not only by one or two, but generally by all men, whenever he vouchsafes deliverance to any of his children, it is a common benefit which all the faithful ought to apply to themselves when they see in the person of one man in what manner God, who is never inconsistent with himself, will act towards all his people. David, therefore, shows that he asks nothing for himself individually but what pertains to the whole Church. He prays that God would gladden the hearts of all the saints, or afford them all common cause of rejoicing: so that, assured of his readiness to help them, they may have recourse to him with greater alacrity. Hence, we conclude, that, in the case of every individual, God gives a proof of his goodness towards us.

May those who love your salvation always say, "Let God be exalted!" We may infer from this, that our faith is only proved to be genuine when we neither expect nor desire preservation otherwise than from God alone. Those who devise various ways and means of preservation for themselves in this world, despise and reject the salvation which God has taught us to expect from him alone. What had been said before, *those who seek you,* is to the same purpose. If any individual would depend wholly upon God, and desire to be saved by his grace, he must renounce every vain hope, and employ all his thoughts towards the reception of his strength.

PSALM 71

From birth I have relied on you. David not only celebrates the goodness of God which he had experienced from his childhood, but also those proofs of it which he had received previous to his birth. An almost similar confession is contained in Psalm 22:9 and 10 by which is magnified the wonderful power and inestimable goodness of God in the generation of men, the way and manner of which would be altogether incredible, were it not a fact with which we are quite familiar. We marvel at the fact that the infant, shut up in its mother's womb, can live in such a condition as would suffocate the strongest man in half an hour. But we thus see how little account we make of the miracles which God works, in consequence of our familiarity with them. The Spirit, therefore, justly rebukes this ingratitude, by commending to our consideration this memorable instance of the grace of God, which is exhibited in our birth and generation. When we are born into the world, although the mother do her office, and the midwife may be present with her, and many others may lend their help, yet if God did not, putting his hand, so to speak, under us, receive us into his bosom, what would become of us? and what hope would there be of the continuance of our life? Yea, rather, were it not for this, our very birth would be an entrance into a thousand deaths.

I will praise you more and more. The promises of God, and his truth in performing them, are inseparably joined together. Unless we depend upon the word of God, all the benefits which he confers upon us will be unsavoury or tasteless to us; nor will we ever be stirred up either to prayer or thanksgiving, if we are not previously illuminated by the Divine word. So much the more revolting, then, is the folly of that diabolical man, Servetus, who teaches that the rule of praying is perverted, if faith is fixed upon the promises; as if we could have any access into the presence of God, until he first invited us by his own voice to come to him.

Endow the king with your justice, O God; the royal son with your righteousness. This is a prayer that God would furnish the king whom he had chosen with the spirit of uprightness and wisdom. By the terms *righteousness* and *judgment*, the Psalmist means a due and well-regulated administration of government, which he opposes to the tyrannical and unbridled license of heathen kings, who, despising God, rule according to the dictates of their own will; and thus the holy king of Israel, who was anointed to his office by divine appointment, is distinguished from other earthly kings. From the words we learn by the way, that no government in the world can be rightly managed except under the conduct of God, and by the guidance of the Holy Spirit. If kings possessed in themselves resources sufficiently ample, it would have been to no purpose for David to have sought by prayer from another, that with which they were of themselves already provided. But in requesting that the righteousness and judgment of God may be given to kings, he reminds them that none are fit for occupying that exalted station, except in so far as they are formed for it by the hand of God. Accordingly, in the Proverbs of Solomon (8:15), "Wisdom proclaims that kings reign by her." Nor is this to be wondered at, when we consider that civil government is so excellent an institution, that God would have us to acknowledge him as its author, and claims to himself the whole praise of it. But it is proper for us to descend from the general to the particular; for since it is the peculiar work of God to set up and to maintain a rightful government in the world, it was much more necessary for him to communicate the special grace of his Spirit for the maintenance and preservation of that sacred kingdom which he had chosen in preference to all others.

He will defend the afflicted among the people. God is indeed no respecter of persons; but it is not without cause that God takes a more special care of the poor than of others, since they are most exposed to injuries and violence. Let laws and the administration of justice be taken away, and the consequence will be, that the more powerful a man is, he will be the more able to oppress his poor brethren. David, therefore, particularly mentions that the king will be the defender of those who can only be safe under the protection of the magistrate, and declares that he will be their avenger when they are made the victims of injustice and wrong.

PSALM 72.7-20

In his days the righteous will flourish. David prayed that the king might be adorned with righteousness and judgment, that the just might flourish and the people prosper. This prediction receives its highest fulfilment in Christ. It was, indeed, the duty of Solomon to maintain the righteous; but it is the proper office of Christ to make men righteous. He not only gives to every man his own, but also reforms their hearts through the agency of his Spirit. By this means he brings righteousness back, as it were, from exile, which otherwise would be altogether banished from the world. Upon the return of righteousness there succeeds the blessing of God, by which he causes all his children to rejoice in the way of making them to perceive that under their King, Christ, every provision is made for their enjoying all manner of prosperity and felicity.

May people ever pray for him and bless him all day long. When David speaks of the common prayers of the people, by which they will commend the prosperity of the king to the care of God, he intimates that so well-pleased will they be with being his subjects, that they will account nothing so desirable as to yield entire submission to his authority. Many, no doubt, reject his yoke, and hypocrites fret and murmur secretly in their hearts, and would gladly extinguish all remembrance of Christ, were it in their power; but the affectionate interest here predicted is what all true believers are careful to cultivate, not only because to pray for earthly kings is a duty enjoined upon them in the Word of God, but also because they ought to feel a special desire and solicitude for the enlargement of the boundaries of this kingdom, in which both the majesty of God shines forth, and their own welfare and happiness are included. Accordingly in Psalm 118:25, we will find a form of prayer dictated for the whole Church, That God would bless this king; not that Christ stands in need of our prayers, but because he justly requires from his servants this manifestation or proof of true piety; and by it they may also exercise themselves in praying for the coming of the kingdom of God. And although that kingdom often totters upon the earth when assailed with the furious hatred of the whole world, and battered by the most formidable engines of Satan, it is yet wonderfully upheld and sustained by God, that it may not altogether fail.

Day 169   J U N E   1 7

As for me, my feet had almost slipped; I had nearly lost my foothold. Experience shows how slight impression we have of the providence of God. We no doubt all agree in admitting that the world is governed by the hand of God; but were this truth deeply rooted in our hearts, our faith would be distinguished by far greater steadiness and perseverance in surmounting the temptations with which we are assailed in adversity. But when the smallest temptation which we meet with dislodges this doctrine from our minds, it is manifest that we have not yet been truly and in good earnest convinced of its truth.

Besides, Satan has numberless artifices by which he dazzles our eyes and bewilders the mind; and then the confusion of things which prevails in the world produces so thick a mist, as to render it difficult for us to see through it, and to come to the conclusion that God governs and extends his care to things here below.

When such is the state of affairs, where shall we find the person who is not sometimes tempted and importuned by the unholy suggestion, that the affairs of the world roll on at random, and as we say, are governed by chance? This unhallowed imagination has doubtless obtained complete possession of the minds of the unbelieving, who are not illuminated by the Spirit of God, and thereby led to elevate their thoughts to the contemplation of eternal life. Accordingly, we see the reason why Solomon declares, that since "all things come alike to all, and there is one event to the righteous and to the wicked," the hearts of the sons of men are full of impiety and contempt of God (Eccles. 9:2–3)—the reason is, because they do not consider that things apparently so disordered, are under the direction and government of God.

The children of God, before these perverse and detestable thoughts enter deep into their hearts, disburden themselves into the bosom of God, and their only desire is to acquiesce in his secret judgments, the reason of which is hidden from them.

If we would profit aright, when we address ourselves to the consideration of the works of God, we must first beseech him to open our eyes, (for those are sheer fools who would of themselves be clear-sighted, and of a penetrating judgment;) and, secondly, we must also give all due respect to his word, by assigning to it that authority to which it is entitled.

PSALM 73:18-24

As a dream when one awakes, so when you arise, O LORD, you will despise them as fantasies. This takes place not only when God restores to some measure of order matters which before were involved in confusion, but also when dispelling the darkness he gladdens our minds with a friendly light. We never, it is true, see things so well adjusted in the world as we would desire; for God, with the view of keeping us always in the exercise of hope, delays the perfection of our state to the final day of judgment. But whenever he stretches forth his hand against the wicked, he causes us to see as it were some rays of the break of day, that the darkness, thickening too much, may not lull us asleep, and affect us with dullness of understanding.

Yet I am always with you. Men are said to be with God in two ways; either, first, in respect of apprehension and thought, when they are persuaded that they live in his presence, are governed by his hand, and sustained by his power; or, secondly, when God, unperceived by them, puts upon them a bridle, by which, when they go astray, he secretly restrains them, and prevents them from totally apostatising from him. In short, God is always near his chosen ones; for although they sometimes turn their backs upon him, he nevertheless has always his fatherly eye turned towards them.

You hold me by my right hand. David ascribes it completely to the grace of God that he was enabled to restrain himself from breaking forth into open blasphemies, and from hardening himself in error, and that he was also brought to condemn himself of foolishness;—this he ascribes wholly to the grace of God, who stretched out his hand to hold him up, and prevent him from a fall which would have involved him in destruction. From this we see how precious our salvation is in the sight of God; for when we wander far from him, he yet continues to look upon us with a watchful eye, and to stretch forth his hand to bring us to himself. We must indeed beware of perverting this doctrine by making it a pretext for slothfulness; but experience nevertheless teaches us, that when we are sunk in drowsiness and insensibility, God exercises a care about us, and that even when we are fugitives and wanderers from him, he is still near us.

Whom have I in heaven but you? David declares that he desires nothing, either in heaven or on earth, except God alone, and that without God, all other objects which usually draw the hearts of men towards them were unattractive to him. And, undoubtedly, God then obtains from us the glory to which he is entitled, when, instead of being carried first to one object, and then to another, we hold exclusively by him, being satisfied with him alone. If we give the smallest portion of our affections to the creatures, we in so far defraud God of the honour which belongs to him. And yet nothing has been more common in all ages than this sacrilege, and it prevails too much at the present day. How small is the number of those who keep their affections fixed on God alone!

If, then, we would seek God aright, we must beware of going astray into various by-paths, and divested of all superstition and pride, must betake ourselves directly and exclusively to him. This is the only way of seeking him.

*And being with you, I desire nothing on earth.** This expression amounts to this: I know that of yourself, apart from every other object, you are sufficient, yes, more than sufficient for me, and therefore I do not let myself be carried away after a variety of desires, but rest in and am fully contented with you. In short, that we may be satisfied with God alone, it is of importance for us to know the plentitude of the blessings which he offers for our acceptance.

My flesh and my heart may fail, but God is the strength of my heart and my portion forever. We will seek nothing from God but what we are conscious of wanting in ourselves. Indeed, all men confess this, and the greater part think that all which is necessary is that God should aid our infirmities, or afford us succour when we have not the means of adequately relieving ourselves. But the confession of David is far more ample than this when he lays, so to speak, his own nothingness before God. He, therefore, very properly adds, that God is his portion. The portion of an individual is a figurative expression, employed in Scripture to denote the condition or lot with which every man is contented. Accordingly, the reason why God is represented as a portion is, because he alone is abundantly sufficient for us, and because in him the perfection of our happiness consists.

PSALM 74

Why have you rejected us forever, O God? Whenever we are visited with adversities, these are not the arrows of fortune thrown against us at venture, but the scourges or rods of God which, in his secret and mysterious providence, he prepares and makes use of for chastising our sins. When God executes his vengeance upon us, it is our duty seriously to reflect on what we have deserved, and to consider, that although he is not subject to the emotions of anger, yet it is not owing to us, who have grievously offended him by our sins, that his anger is not kindled against us. Moreover, his people, as a plea for obtaining mercy, flee to the remembrance of the covenant by which they were adopted to be his children.

We are given no miraculous signs; no prophets are left, and none of us knows how long this will be. Temporary punishments are the fatherly chastisements of God, and the consideration that they are temporary alleviates sorrow; but his continual displeasure causes poor and wretched sinners to sink into utter despair. If, therefore, we also would find matter for patience and consolation, when we are under the chastening hand of God, let us learn to fix our eyes on this moderation on the part of God, by which he encourages us to entertain good hope; and from it let us rest assured, that although he is angry, yet he ceases not to be a father. The correction which brings deliverance does not inflict unmitigated grief: the sadness which it produces is mingled with joy.

But you, O God, are my king from of old. We know how difficult it is to rise above all doubts, and boldly to persevere in a free and unrestrained course of prayer. Here, then, the faithful call to remembrance the proofs of God's mercy and working, by which he certified, through a continued series of ages, that he was the King and Protector of the people whom he had chosen. By this example we are taught, that as it is not enough to pray with the lips unless we also pray in faith, we ought always to remember the benefits by which God has given a confirmation of his fatherly love towards us, and should regard them as so many testimonies of his electing love.

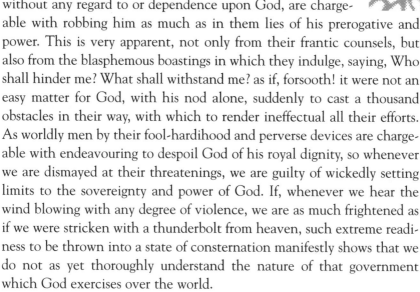

PSALM
75

But it is God who judges: He brings one down, he exalts another. To teach us, with all moderation and humility, to remain contented with our own condition, the Psalmist clearly defines in what the judgment of God, or the order which he observes in the government of the world, consists, telling us that it belongs to him alone to exalt or to abase those of mankind whom he pleases.

From this it follows that all those who, spreading the wings of their vanity, aspire after any kind of exaltation, without any regard to or dependence upon God, are chargeable with robbing him as much as in them lies of his prerogative and power. This is very apparent, not only from their frantic counsels, but also from the blasphemous boastings in which they indulge, saying, Who shall hinder me? What shall withstand me? as if, forsooth! it were not an easy matter for God, with his nod alone, suddenly to cast a thousand obstacles in their way, with which to render ineffectual all their efforts. As worldly men by their fool-hardihood and perverse devices are chargeable with endeavouring to despoil God of his royal dignity, so whenever we are dismayed at their threatenings, we are guilty of wickedly setting limits to the sovereignty and power of God. If, whenever we hear the wind blowing with any degree of violence, we are as much frightened as if we were stricken with a thunderbolt from heaven, such extreme readiness to be thrown into a state of consternation manifestly shows that we do not as yet thoroughly understand the nature of that government which God exercises over the world.

But the man who believes it to be an established principle that God disposes of all men as seems good in his sight, and shapes to every man his condition in this world, will not stop at earthly means: he will look above and beyond these things to God. The improvement which should be made of this doctrine is, that the godly should submit themselves wholly to God, and beware of being lifted up with vain confidence. When they see the impious waxing proud, let them not hesitate to despise their foolish and infatuated presumption. Again, although God has in his own hand sovereign power and authority, so that he can do whatever he pleases, yet he is styled judge, to teach us that he governs the affairs of mankind with the most perfect equity.

PSALM 76

And his tabernacle was in Salem, and his dwelling-place in Zion.* First, men had no ground to arrogate to themselves any share in the deliverance of the city here portrayed, God having strikingly showed that all the glory was his own, by displaying from heaven his power in the sight of all men; and, secondly, that he was induced to oppose his enemies from no other consideration but that of his free choice of the Jewish nation. God having, by this example, testified that his power is invincible for preserving his Church, it is a call and an encouragement to all the faithful to repose with confidence under his shadow. If his name is precious to himself, it is no ordinary pledge and security which he gives to our faith when he assures us that it is his will that the greatness of his power should be known in the preservation of his Church. Moreover, as the Church is a distinguished theatre on which the Divine glory is displayed, we must always take the greatest care not to shroud or bury in forgetfulness, by our ingratitude, the benefits which have been bestowed upon it, and especially those which ought to be held in remembrance in all ages. Further, although God is not now worshipped in the visible tabernacle, yet as by Christ he still dwells in the midst of us, yes even within us, we will doubtless experience, whenever we are exposed to danger, that under his protection we are in perfect safety.

Valiant men lie plundered. The enemies of the chosen people were deprived of that heroic courage of which they boasted, and which inspired them with such audacity; and, in consequence, neither mind, nor heart, nor hands, none either of their mental or bodily faculties, could perform their office. We are thus taught that all the gifts and power which men seem to possess are in the hand of God, so that he can, at any instant of time, deprive them of the wisdom which he has given them, make their hearts effeminate, render their hands unfit for war, and annihilate their whole strength. It is not without reason that both the courage and power of these enemies are magnified; the design of this being, that the faithful might be led, from the contrast, to extol the power and working of God.

PSALM 77

I will remember the deeds of the Lord. What the Psalmist here means is, that the wonderful power of God which he has always put forth for the preservation and salvation of his servants, provided we duly reflect upon it, is sufficient to enable us to overcome all sorrows. Let us learn from this, that, although sometimes the remembrance of the works of God may bring us less comfort than we would desire, and our circumstances would require, we must nevertheless strive, that the weariness produced by grief may not break our courage. This is deserving of our most careful attention. In the time of sorrow, we are always desirous of finding some remedy to mitigate its bitterness; but the only way by which this can be done is, to cast our cares upon God. It, however, often happens, that the nearer he approaches us, the more, to outward appearances, does he aggravate our sorrows. Many, therefore, when they derive no advantage from this course, imagine that they cannot do better than forget him. Thus they loathe his word, by the hearing of which their sorrow is rather embittered than mitigated, and what is worse, they desire that God, who thus aggravates and inflames their grief, would withdraw to a distance. Others, to bury the remembrance of him, devote themselves wholly to worldly business. It was far otherwise with the prophet. Although he did not immediately experience the benefit which he could have desired, yet he still continued to set God before his view, wisely supporting his faith by the reflection, that as God changes neither his love nor his nature, he cannot but show himself at length merciful to his servants. Let us also learn to open our eyes to behold the works of God; the excellence of which is of little account in our estimation, by reason of the dimness of our eyes, and our inadequate perception of them; but which, if examined attentively, will ravish us with admiration. The reason why so many examples of the grace of God contribute nothing to our profit, and fail in edifying our faith, is, that as soon as we have begun to make them the subjects of our consideration, our inconstancy draws us away to something else, and thus, at the very commencement, our minds soon lose sight of them.

PSALM 78

What we have heard and known. However high the majesty of the Word of God may be, this does not prevent the benefits or advantages of it from reaching even to the unlearned and to babes. The Holy Spirit does not in vain invite and encourage such to learn from it:—a truth which we ought carefully to mark. If God, accommodating himself to the limited capacity of men, speaks in an humble and lowly style, this manner of teaching is despised as too simple; but if he rise to a higher style, with the view of giving greater authority to his Word, men, to excuse their ignorance, will pretend that it is too obscure. As these two vices are very prevalent in the world, the Holy Spirit so tempers his style as that the sublimity of the truths which he teaches is not hidden even from those of the weakest capacity, provided they are of a submissive and teachable disposition, and bring with them an earnest desire to be instructed. It is the design of the prophet to remove from the mind all doubt respecting his sayings, and for this purpose, he determines to bring forward nothing new, but such subjects as had been long well known, and received without dispute in the Church.

What our fathers have told us. Many things are rashly spread abroad which have no foundation in truth; yes, nothing is more common than for the ears of men to be filled with fables. That is why the prophet says that the knowledge of these subjects had been communicated to the Jews by their *fathers.* This does not imply, that what is taught under the domestic roof is always faultless; but it is obvious, that there is afforded a more favourable opportunity of palming upon men forgeries for truth, when things are brought from a distant country. What is to be principally observed is, that all fathers are not here spoken of indiscriminately, but only those who were chosen to be God's peculiar people, and to whom the care of divine truth was instrusted. It was the will of God that these things should be published from age to age without interruption; so that being transmitted from father to child in each family, they might reach even the last family of man, so that they might celebrate the praises of Jehovah in the wonderful works which he has done.

PSALM
78:5-7

He decreed statutes for Jacob and established the law in Israel. As the reception or approbation of any doctrine by men would not be a sufficient reason for yielding a firm assent to its truth, the prophet proceeds further, and represents God as the author of what he brings forward. He declares, that the fathers were not led to instruct their children in these truths under the mere impulse of their own minds, but by the commandment of God. God not only acquired a right to the Jews as his people by his mighty power, but he also sealed up his grace, that the knowledge of it might never be obliterated. And, undoubtedly, it was then registered as it were in public records, when the covenant was ratified by the written law, in order to assure the posterity of Abraham that they had been separated from all other nations. It would have been a matter of very small importance to have been acquainted with, or to have remembered the bare history of what had been done, had their eyes not been, at the same time, directed to the free adoption and the fruit of it. The decree then is this, That the fathers being instructed in the doctrine of the law themselves, should recount, as it were, from the mouth of God, to their children, that they had been not only once delivered, but also gathered into one body as his Church, that throughout all ages they might yield a holy and pure obedience to him as their deliverer.

That they might set their hope in God.* The fathers, when they find that on the one hand they are the means of providing for the salvation of their children, should, by such a precious result of their labours, be the more powerfully stirred up to instruct their children. The children, on their part, being inflamed with greater zeal, should eagerly press forward in the acquisition of divine knowledge, and not suffer their minds to wander in vain speculations, but should aim at, or keep their eyes directed to, the right mark. It is unhappy and wretched toil to be "ever learning, and never able to come to the knowledge of the truth" (2 Tim. 3:7).

PSALM 78:8-37

And that they might not be as their fathers.* The experience of all ages shows that what Horace writes concerning his own nation is true everywhere:—

"The age that gave our fathers birth,
Saw them their noble sires disgrace:
We, baser still, shall leave on earth
The still increasing guilt of our degenerate race."

What then, would be the consequence, did not God succour the world which thus proceeds from evil to worse? As the prophet teaches the Jews from the wickedness and perverseness of their fathers, that they stood in need of a severe discipline to recall them from the imitation of bad examples, we learn from this, how great the folly of the world is, in persuading itself that the example of the fathers is to be regarded as equivalent to a law, which ought, in every case, to be followed. The fathers were not faithfully and stedfastly devoted to God, although they had solemnly sworn allegiance to him. The Papists make use of this passage as an argument to prove that man has the power of bending his own heart, and directing it either to good or evil as he pleases; but this is an inference from it which cannot stand examination for a single moment. Although the prophet justly blames those who have not directed their heart aright, his object is not expressly to speak of what men can do of themselves. It is the special work of God to turn to himself the hearts of men by the secret influence of his Holy Spirit. It does not however follow from this, that they will be exempted from blame, when their own lust and depravity draw them away from God. Moreover, from the sins which are here reproved, we should learn in what way he would have us to obey and serve him. In the first place, we must lay aside all obstinacy and take his yoke upon us; and, secondly, we must clothe ourselves with the spirit of meekness, bring the affections of the heart to the obedience of God, and follow after uprightness, and that not with the fervour of a mere transient impulse, but with unfeigned and unwavering stedfastness.

Yet he was merciful . . . and did not destroy them. The Israelites no doubt deserved to be involved in one common destruction; but it is declared that God mitigated his anger, that some seed of them might remain. That none might infer that God had proceeded to punish them with undue severity, we are told that the punishments inflicted upon them were moderate—yea, mild, when compared with the aggravated nature of their wickedness. God kept back his hand, not looking so much to what they had deserved, as desiring to give place to his mercy. We are not, however, to imagine that he is changeable, when at one time he chastises us with a degree of severity, and at another time gently draws and allures us to himself; for in the exercise of his matchless wisdom, he has recourse to different means by which to try whether there is really any hope of our recovery. But the guilt of men becomes more aggravated, when neither his severity can reform them nor his mercy melt them. It is to be observed, that the mercy of God, which is an essential attribute of his nature, is here assigned as the reason why he spared his people, to teach us that he was not induced by any other cause but this, to show himself so much inclined and ready to pardon.

He remembered that they were but flesh. Flesh and *spirit* are frequently contrasted in the Scriptures; not only when *flesh* means our depraved and sinful nature, and *spirit* the uprightness to which the children of God are born again; but also when men are called *flesh,* because there is nothing firm or stable in them. In this passage *flesh* means, that men are subject to corruption and putrefaction; and *spirit,* that they are only a breath or a fleeting shadow. As men are brought to death by a continual wasting and decay, the people are compared to a wind which passes away, and which, of its own accord, falls and does not return again. God, in the exercise of his mercy and goodness, bore with the Jews, not because they deserved this, but because their frail and transitory condition called forth his pity and induced him to pardon them.

PSALM 79:1-6

They have poured blood out like water . . . and there is no one to bury the dead. God, having intended that in the burial of men, there should be some testimony to the resurrection at the last day, it was a double indignity for the saints to be despoiled of this right after their death. But it may be asked, Since God often threatens the reprobate with this kind of punishment, why did he suffer his own people to be devoured of beasts? We must remember that the elect, as well as the reprobate, are subjected to the temporal punishments which pertain only to the flesh. The difference between the two cases lies solely in the issue; for God converts that which in itself is a token of his wrath into the means of the salvation of his own children. The same explanation, then, is to be given of their want of burial which is given of their death. The most eminent of the servants of God may be put to a cruel and ignominious death—a punishment which we know is often executed upon murderers, and other despisers of God; but still the death of the saints does not cease to be precious in his sight: and when he has suffered them to be unrighteously persecuted in the flesh, he shows, by taking vengeance on their enemies, how dear they were to him. In like manner, God, to stamp the marks of his wrath on the reprobate, even after their death, deprives them of burial; and, therefore, he threatens a wicked king, "He shall be buried with the burial of an ass, drawn and cast forth beyond the gates of Jerusalem" (Jer. 22:19). When he exposes his own children to the like indignity, he may seem for a time to have forsaken them; but afterwards converts it into the means of furthering their salvation; for their faith, being subjected to this trial, acquires a fresh triumph. When in ancient times the bodies of the dead were anointed, that ceremony was performed for the sake of the living whom they left behind them, when they saw the bodies of the dead carefully preserved, to cherish in their hearts the hope of a better life. The faithful, then, by being deprived of burial, suffer no loss, when they rise by faith above these inferior helps, that they may advance with speedy steps to a blessed immortality.

Pour out your wrath on the nations that do not acknowledge you, on the kingdoms that do not call on your name. Although it does not become us to prescribe to God the rule of his conduct, but rather patiently to submit to this ordination, "That judgment must begin at the house of God" (1 Peter 4:17); yet he permits his saints to take the liberty of pleading, that at least they may not be worse dealt with than unbelievers, and those who despise him.

PSALM 79:6-9

These two sentences, *that do not know you,* and *that do not call on your name,* are to be taken in the same sense. By these different forms of expression, it is intimated that it is impossible for any to call upon God without a previous knowledge of him, as the apostle Paul teaches, in Romans 10:14, "How, then, shall they call on him in whom they have not believed? and how shall they believe in him of whom they have not heard?" It belongs not to us to answer, "Thou art our God," till he has anticipated us by saying, "You are my people," (Hos. 2:23); but he opens our mouths to speak to him in this manner, when he invites us to himself. *Calling on the name of God* is often synonymous with prayer; but it is not here to be exclusively limited to that exercise. The amount is, that unless we are directed by the knowledge of God, it is impossible for us sincerely to profess the true religion. At that time the Gentiles everywhere boasted that they served God; but, being destitute of his word, and as they fabricated to themselves gods of their own corrupt imaginations, all their religious services were detestable; even as in our own day, the human invented religious observances of the blind and deluded votaries of the Man of Sin, who have no right knowledge of the God whom they profess to worship, and who inquire not at his mouth what he approves, are certainly rejected by him, because they set up idols in his place.

Do not hold against us the sins of the fathers. The godly Jews here confirm that they had justly deserved the chastisements which had been inflicted upon them. And they present this prayer, because they could only get relief from their calamities by obtaining reconciliation with God. This is the sovereign remedy for every kind of adversity; for so long as he is angry with us, even our prosperity turns out to be unproductive of advantage and happiness.

Why should the nations say, "Where is their God?" God extends his compassion towards us for his own name's sake; for, as he is merciful, and will have our mouths stopped, that he alone may be accounted righteous, he freely pardons our sins. But here, the faithful beseech him that he would not allow his sacred name to be exposed to the blasphemies and insults of the wicked. From this we are taught that we do not pray in a right manner, unless a concern about our own salvation, and zeal for the glory of God, are inseparably joined together in our exercise. Although God declares that he will execute vengeance upon our enemies, we are not warranted to thirst for revenge when we are injured. Let us remember that this form of prayer was not dictated for all men indiscriminately, that they might make use of it whenever impelled by their own passions, but that, under the guidance and instruction of the Holy Spirit, they might plead the cause of the whole Church, in common, against the wicked. If we would, therefore, offer up to God a prayer like this in a right manner, in the first place, our minds must be illuminated by the wisdom of the Holy Spirit; and, secondly, our zeal, which is often corrupted by the turbid affections of the flesh, must be pure and well-regulated; and then, with such a pure and well-tempered zeal, we may lawfully beseech God to show us, by evident examples, how precious in his sight, is the life of his servants whose blood he avenges. The faithful are not to be understood as expressing any desire to be glutted with the sight of the shedding of human blood, as if they longed greedily after it; they only desire that God would grant them some confirmation of their faith, in the exercise of his fatherly love which is manifested when he avenges the wrongs done to his own people.

It is further to be noticed that the name, *the servants of God,* is given to those who, nevertheless, were justly punished on account of their sins; for although he may chastise us, yet he does not forthwith cast us off, but, on the contrary, testifies thereby that our salvation is the object of his care.

PSALM 80:1-7

Hear us, O Shepherd of Israel . . . you who sit enthroned between the cherubim. The mercy-seat was a pledge of the presence of God, where he had promised to be near his people to hear their prayers. It was unlawful for men to change this divinely instituted form at their own pleasure. The Israelites, then, are admonished to return to their original state, if they would expect to find God gracious towards them. Besides, by the title which is here attributed to God, there is expressed his wonderful love towards men in humbling, and, so to speak, lowering himself in order to come down to them, and choose for himself a seat and habitation on the earth, that he might dwell in the midst of them. Properly speaking, God cannot be said to sit; nor is it to be supposed that it is possible for him, whom the heavens cannot contain, to be shut up in a certain place (1 Kings 8:27). But, in accommodation to the infirmity of men, he is represented as placed between the two Cherubim, that the faithful might not imagine him to be far from them; and, consequently, be perplexed with doubt and apprehension in approaching him. The Israelites are here furnished with a rule for enabling them to pray in a right manner, that they might be withdrawn from the worship of the god fabricated and set up by themselves at Dan and Bethel, and that, rejecting all superstitions, they might yield themselves to be guided by the true light of faith, and follow the Word of God.

Restore us, O God. The faithful, under the adversity with which they were afflicted, flee to God, whose peculiar work it is to restore life to the dead. They acknowledge, on the one hand, that all their miseries were to be traced to this as their cause, that God, being angry on account of their sins, hid his face from them; and, on the other hand, they expect to obtain complete salvation solely through the Divine favour. It will be to us, they say, a resurrection indeed, if once your countenance shine upon us. Their language implies, that provided God extended his mercy and favour to them, they would be happy, and all their affairs would prosper.

PSALM 80:8-9

You brought a vine out of Egypt. Under the figure of a vine, the singular grace which God was graciously pleased to exercise towards his people after he had redeemed them is celebrated; and this powerfully contributed to inspire them with the hope of being heard. For which of us can be so presumptuous as to dare to come into the presence of God until he himself has previously invited us? Now, he allures us to himself both by his benefits and by his word. The object in view in now presenting his liberality before him is, that he should not leave unfinished the work of his hands which he has commenced. It is indeed true that, without his word, the benefits which he has conferred upon us would make a faint impression upon our hearts; but when experience is added to the testimony of his word, it greatly encourages us. Now, the redemption of which mention is here made was inseparably connected with the covenant of God; for he had, even four hundred year before, entered into covenant with Abraham, in which he promised the deliverance of his seed. What is stated amounts in short to this, that it is unbecoming that God should now suffer the vine which he had planted and cultivated so carefully with his own hand to be wasted by wild beasts. God's covenant was not made to last only for a few days, or for a short time: when he adopted the children of Abraham, he took them under his keeping forever. By the word *vine*, is intimated the high place which this people held in the estimation of God, who not only was pleased to hold them as his own inheritance, but who also distinguished them by peculiar honour, even as a vine excels all other possessions. When it is said that the *land* or *ground was cleansed*, this is a repetition of what had been previously stated, that *the heathen were cast out* to make room for the chosen people. Perhaps, however, the allusion is to the continual digging which vines require, in order to their being kept clean lest they should degenerate; this allusion being made with the view of showing how God had performed the part of a good husbandman towards his people, since, after having planted them, he did not cease to employ every means to cherish and preserve them.

Why then have you broken down its walls? This is the application of the similitude; for nothing seems more inconsistent than that God should abandon the vine which he had planted with his own hand, to be rooted up by wild beasts. It is true that he often threatened and forewarned the people by his prophets that he would do this; but what constrained him to inflict upon them so strange and dreadful a species of punishment was, that he might render their ingratitude the more detestable. At the same time, it is not without reason that true believers are enjoined to take encouragement from such distinguished liberality on the part of God; that, even in the midst of this rooting up, they might at least hope that he, who never forsakes the work of his own hands, would graciously extend his care towards them (Ps. 138:8). The people were brought to desolation, on account of their own incurable obstinacy; but God did not fail to save a small number of shoots, by means of which he afterwards restored his vine. This form of supplicating pardon was, indeed, set forth for the use of the whole people, with the view of preventing a horrible destruction. But as very few sought to appease the wrath of God by truly humbling themselves before him, it was enough that these few were delivered from destruction, that from them a new vine might afterwards spring up and flourish.

Return to us, O God Almighty! Look down from heaven and see! Watch over this vine. We ought not to yield to temptation although God should hide his face from us for a time, yes even although to the eye of sense and reason he should seem to be alienated from us. For, provided he is sought in the confident expectation of his showing mercy, he will become reconciled, and receive into his favour those whom he seemed to have cast off. It was a distinguished honour for the seed of Abraham to be accounted the vineyard of God; but while the faithful adduce this consideration as an argument for obtaining the favour of God, instead of bringing forward any claims of their own, they only beseech him not to cease to exercise his accustomed liberality towards them.

PSALM 80:16-19

Your vine is cut down, it is burned with fire. The calamities of the people are now more clearly expressed. It had been said that the Lord's vine was abandoned to the wild beasts, that they might lay it waste. But it was a greater calamity for it to be consumed with fire, rooted up and utterly destroyed. The Israelites had perfidiously apostatised from the true religion; but they were still a part of the Church. We are accordingly warned by this melancholy example, of the severity of the punishment due to our ingratitude, especially when it is joined with obstinacy, which prevents the threatening and rebukes of God, however sharp and severe they may be, from being of any benefit to us. Let us also learn from the same example, when the Divine anger is blazing all around, and even when we are in the midst of its burning flames, to cast all our sorrows into the bosom of God, who, in a wonderful manner, raises up his Church from the gulf of destruction. He would assuredly be ready not only to exercise without interruption his favour towards us, but also to enrich us with his blessings more and more, did not our wickedness hinder him. As it is impossible for him not to be angry at the many offences which we have committed, it is an evidence of unparalleled mercy for him to extinguish the fire which we ourselves have kindled, and which has spread far and wide, and to save some portion or remnant of the Church, or, so to speak more properly, to raise up even from the very ashes a people to call upon his name. It is again repeated that the Church *perished* not by the strength and arms of her enemies, but at the rebuke of God's countenance. Never can we expect alleviation of our punishment, unless we are fully persuaded that we are justly chastised by the hand of God. It was a good sign of the repentance of these Israelites that, as is observed in Isaiah 9:12, "they looked to the hand of him who smote them."

PSALM
81:1-3

Sing for joy to God our strength. This psalm, it is probable, was appointed to be sung on the festival days on which
the Jews kept their solemn assemblies. In the exordium, there
is set forth the order of worship which God had enjoined.
They were not to stand deaf and dumb at the tabernacle; for
the service of God does not consist in indolence, nor in cold
and empty ceremonies; but they were, by such exercises as are
here prescribed, to cherish among themselves the unity of
faith; to make an open profession of their piety; to stir up
themselves to continual progress therein; to endeavour to
join, with one accord, in praising God; and, in short, to continue stedfast
in the sacred covenant by which God had adopted them to himself.

Such having been the use of festival days under the law, we may
conclude, that whenever true believers assemble together at the present
day, the end which they ought to have in view is to employ themselves
in the exercises of religion—to call to their remembrance the benefits
which they have received from God—to make progress in the knowledge
of his word—and to testify the oneness of their faith. Men only mock
God by presenting to him vain and unprofitable ceremonies, unless the
doctrine of faith go before, stirring them up to call upon God; and unless,
also, the remembrance of his benefits furnish matter of praise. Yes, rather
it is profanation of his name, when people quench the light of divine
truth, and satisfy themselves with performing mere outward service.
Accordingly, the faithful are here not only enjoined to come together to
the tabernacle, but are also taught the end for which they are to assemble there, which is, that the free and gracious covenant which God has
made with them may be brought anew to their remembrance, for increasing their faith and piety, that thus the benefits which they have received
from him may be celebrated, and their hearts thereby moved to thanksgiving.

PSALM 81:4-6

When he went out against Egypt, where we heard a language we did not understand. The people, having God for their conductor, passed freely and without obstruction through the land of Egypt, the inhabitants having been so discouraged and dismayed as not to dare to make any opposition to their passage. The prophet enhances the blessing of their deliverance, when, speaking in the name of the whole people, he affirms that he had been rescued from profound barbarism: *I heard a language which I did not understand.* Nothing is more disagreeable than to sojourn among a people with whom we can hold no communication by language, which is the chief bond of society. Language being, as it were, the image and mirror of the mind, those who cannot employ it in their mutual intercourse are no less strangers to one another than the wild beasts of the forest. When the prophet Isaiah (33:19) intends to denounce a very dreadful punishment, he says, "You will see those arrogant people, those people of an obscure speech, with their strange, incomprehensible tongue." Thus the people acknowledge that the benefit which God conferred was so much the more to be valued, because they were delivered from the Egyptians, with whose language they were unacquainted.

I removed the burden from their shoulders. Here God begins to recount the benefits which he had bestowed upon the Israelites, and the many ways in which he had laid them under obligations to him. The more galling the bondage was from which they had been delivered, the more desirable and precious was their liberty. As God has not only withdrawn our shoulders from a burden of brick, and not only removed us from the cruel and miserable tyranny of Satan, and drawn us from the depths of hell, the obligations under which we lie to him are of a much more strict and sacred kind than those under which he had brought his ancient people.

PSALM 81:7-9

In your distress you called and I rescued you. It sometimes happens that those who are reduced to extremity bewail their calamities with confused crying; but as this afflicted people still had in them some remains of godliness, and as they had not forgotten the promise made to their fathers, they directed their prayers to God. Even men without religion, who never think of calling upon God, when they are under the pressure of any great calamity, are moved by a secret instinct of nature to have recourse to him. This renders it the more probable that the promise was, as it were, a schoolmaster to the Israelites, leading them to look to God. As no man sincerely calls upon him but he who trusts in him for help; this crying ought the more effectually to have convinced them that it was their duty to ascribe to him alone the deliverance which was offered them.

I answered you out of a thundercloud. God was not seen by them face to face; but the thunder was an evident indication of his secret presence among them. To make them prize more highly this benefit, God upbraidingly tells them that they were unworthy of it, having given such a manifest proof *at the waters of Meribah,* that they were of wicked and perverse disposition, Exodus 17:7. Your wickedness, as if he had said, having at that time so openly shown itself, surely it must from this be incontrovertible that my favour to you did not proceed from any regard to your good desert. This rebuke is not less applicable to us than to the Israelites; for God not only heard our groanings when we were afflicted under the tyranny of Satan, but before we were born appointed his only begotten Son to be the price of our redemption; and afterwards, when we were his enemies, he called us to be partakers of his grace, illuminating our minds by his gospel and his Holy Spirit; while we, notwithstanding, continue to indulge in murmuring, yes, even proudly rebel against him.

PSALM
81:10

Open wide your mouth and I will fill it. By the expression *open wide*, the prophet tacitly condemns the contracted views and desires which obstruct the exercise of his beneficence. "If the people are in penury," we may suppose him to say, "the blame is to be entirely ascribed to themselves, because their capacity is not large enough to receive the blessings of which they stand in need; or rather, because by their unbelief they reject the blessings which would flow spontaneously upon them." He not only bids them open their mouth, but he magnifies the abundance of his grace still more highly, by intimating, that however enlarged our desires may be, there will be nothing wanting which is necessary to afford us full satisfaction. Whence it follows, that the reason why God's blessings drop upon us in a sparing and slender manner is, because our mouth is too narrow; and the reason why others are empty and famished is, because they keep their mouth completely shut. The majority of mankind, either from disgust, or pride, or madness, refuse all the blessings which are offered them from heaven. Others, although they do not altogether reject them, yet with difficulty take in only a few small drops, because their faith is so straitened as to prevent them from receiving an abundant supply. It is a very manifest proof of the depravity of mankind, when they have no desire to know God, in order that they may embrace him, and when they are equally disinclined to rest satisfied with him. He undoubtedly here requires to be worshipped by external service; but he sets no value upon the bare name of Deity—for his majesty does not consist in two or three syllables. He rather looks to what the name imports, and is solicitous that our hope may not be withdrawn from him to other objects, or that the praise of righteousness, salvation, and all blessings, may not be transferred from him to another.

PSALM 81:11-12

So I gave them over to their stubborn hearts to follow their own devices. By these words God testifies that he justly punished his people, when he deprived them of good and wholesome doctrine, and gave them over to a reprobate mind. As in governing us by means of his word, he restrains us, as it were, with a bridle, and thereby prevents us from going astray after our own perverse imaginations, so, by removing his prophets from the Jews, he gave loose reins to their forward and corrupt counsels, by which they were led into devious paths. It is assuredly the most dreadful kind of punishment which can be afflicted upon us, and an evidence of the utter hopelessness of our condition, when God, holding his peace, and conniving at our perverseness, applies no remedy for bringing us to repentance and amendment. So long as he administers reproof to us, alarms us with the dread of judgment, and summons us before his tribunal, he, at the same time, calls upon us to repent. But when he sees that it is altogether lost labour to reason any longer with us, and that his admonitions have no effect, he holds his peace, and by this teaches us that he has ceased to make our salvation the object of his care. Nothing, therefore, is more to be dreaded, than for men to be so set free from the Divine guidance, as recklessly to follow their own counsels, and to be dragged by Satan wherever he pleases. God, while he passed by all the rest of the world, was graciously pleased to bring the posterity of Abraham, by peculiar and exclusive privilege, into a special relation to himself. At the present day, this distinction has been abolished, and the message of the gospel, by which God reconciles the world to himself, is common to all men. Further, as this passage teaches us, that there is no plague more deadly than for men to be left to the guidance of their own counsels, the only thing which remains for us to do is to renounce the dictates of carnal wisdom, and to follow the guidance of the Holy Spirit.

PSALM 81:13-16

If my people would but listen to me, if Israel would follow my ways, how quickly would I subdue their enemies. Here God assumes the character of a father, and observing, after having tried every possible means for the recovery of his children, that their condition is utterly hopeless, he uses the language of one saddened, as it were, with sighing and groaning; not that he is subject to human passions, but because he cannot otherwise express the greatness of the love which he bears towards us.

God, in coming down to us by his word, and addressing his invitations to all men without exception, disappoints nobody. All who sincerely come to him are received, and find from actual experience that they were not called in vain. At the same time, we are to trace to the fountain of the secret electing purpose of God this difference, that the word enters into the heart of some, while others only hear the sound of it. And yet there is no inconsistency in his complaining, as it were, with tears, of our folly when we do not obey him. In the invitations which he addresses to us by the external word, he shows himself to be a father, and why may he not also by understood as still representing himself under the image of a father in using this form of complaint? In Ezekiel 18:32, he declares with the strictest regard to truth, "I have no pleasure in the death of him that dies," provided in the interpretation of the passage we candidly and dispassionately take into view the whole scope of it. God has no pleasure in the death of a sinner: How? because he would have all men turned to himself. But it is abundantly evident, that men by their own free-will cannot turn to God, until he first change their stony heart into hearts of flesh: yes, this renovation, as Augustine judiciously observes, is a work surpassing that of creation itself. Now what hinders God from bending and framing the hearts of all men equally in submission to him? Here modesty and sobriety must be observed, that instead of presuming to intrude into his incomprehensible decrees, we may rest contented with the revelation which he has made of his will in his word.

God presides in the great assembly; he gives judgment among the "gods": How long will you [judge unjustly]? It is unquestionably a very unbecoming thing for those whom God has been pleased to invest with the government of making for the common good, not to acknowledge the end for which they have been placed in so elevated a station; but instead of doing this, contemning every principle of equity, to rule just as their own unbridled passions dictate. So infatuated are they by their own splendour and magnificence, as to imagine that the whole world was made only for them. Besides, they think that it would derogate from their elevated rank were they to be governed by moderate counsels; and although their own folly is more than enough to urge them on in their reckless career, they, notwithstanding, seek for flatterers to soothe and applaud them in their vices. To correct this arrogance, the psalm opens by asserting, that although men occupy thrones and judgment-seats, God nevertheless continues to hold the office of supreme ruler. God has made even a heathen and licentious poet bear testimony to this truth in the following lines:—

> "Kings rule their subject flocks; great Jove
> O'er kings themselves his reign extends,
> Who hurl'd the rebel giants from above;
> At whose majestic nod all nature bends."
> *Horatii, Carm. Liber iii. Ode i.*
> *Boscawen's Translation*

That the potentates of this world may not arrogate to themselves more than belongs to them, the prophet here erects a throne for God, from which he judges them all, and represses their pride; a thing which is highly necessary. They may, indeed, admit that they owe their elevation to royal power to the favour of God, and they may worship him by outward ceremonies, but their greatness so infatuates them that they are chargeable with expelling and casting him to a distance from their assembly, by their vain imaginations; for they cannot bear to be subject to reason and laws. Thus the design of the prophet was to deride the madness by which the princes of this world are bewitched, in leaving God no place in their assembly.

PSALM 82:3-4

Defend the cause of the weak and fatherless. We are here briefly taught that a just and well-regulated government will be distinguished for maintaining the rights of the poor and afflicted. Rulers are appointed to be the defenders of the miserable and oppressed, both because such persons stand in need of the assistance of others, and because they can only obtain this where rulers are free from avarice, ambition, and other vices. The end, therefore, for which judges bear the sword is to restrain the wicked, and thus to prevent violence from prevailing among men, who are so much disposed to become disorderly and outrageous. According as men increase in strength, they become proportionally audacious in oppressing the weak; and hence it is that rich men seldom resort to magistrates for help, except when they happen to fall out among themselves. From these remarks, it is very obvious why the cause of the poor and needy is here chiefly commended to rulers; for those who are exposed an easy prey to the cruelty and wrongs of the rich have no less need of the assistance and protection of magistrates than the sick have of the aid of the physician. Were this truth deeply fixed in the minds of kings and other judges, that they are appointed to be the guardians of the poor, and that a special part of this duty lies in resisting the wrongs which are done to them, and in repressing all unrighteous violence, perfect righteousness would become triumphant through the whole world. Whoever thinks it not beneath himself to defend the poor, instead of allowing himself to be carried hither and thither by favour, will have a regard only to what is right. We may further learn from this passage, that although magistrates may not be solicited for succour, they are accounted guilty before God of negligence, if they do not, of their own accord, succour those who stand in need of their interference. When iniquity openly prevails, and when, on account of it, sighs and lamentations are everywhere heard, it is in vain for them to pretend that they cannot redress wrongs, unless complaints are addressed to them. Oppression utters a sufficiently loud cry of itself; and if the judge, sitting on a high watch-tower, seems to take no notice of it, he is here plainly warned, that such connivance shall not escape with impunity.

Day 195   J U L Y   1 3

They know nothing, they understand nothing. After having reminded princes of their duty, the Psalmist complains that his admonition from their infatuation is ineffectual, and that they refuse to receive wholesome instruction; yes, that although the whole world is shaken to its foundations, they, notwithstanding, continue thoughtless and secure in the neglect of their duty. He chiefly reprobates and condemns their madness as manifested in this, that although they see heaven and earth involved in confusion, they are no more affected at the sight than if the care of the interests of mankind did not belong to them, of which they are, notwithstanding, in a special manner the chosen and appointed conservators. What chiefly deprives them of understanding is, that, being dazzled with their own splendour, and perversely shaking off every yoke, no religious considerations have the effect of inclining them to moderation. All sound knowledge and wisdom must commence with yielding to God the honour which is his due, and submitting to be restrained and governed by his word.

I said, "You are 'gods'; you are all sons of the Most High." But you will die like mere men; you will fall like every other ruler. The government of the world has been committed to rulers upon the distinct understanding that they themselves also must one day appear at the judgment-seat of heaven to render up an account. The dignity, therefore, with which they are clothed is only temporary, and will pass away with the fashion of the world.

Rise up, O God, judge the earth, for all the nations are your inheritance. God has a rightful claim to the obedience of all nations, and tyrants are chargeable with wickedly and unjustly wresting from him his prerogative of bearing rule, when they set at nought his authority, and confound good and evil, right and wrong. We ought therefore to beseech him to restore to order the confusions of the world, and thus to recover the rightful dominion which he has over it.

PSALM 83:1-4

See how your enemies are astir. . . . With cunning they conspire against your people. This is one of the fruits of God's free and gracious covenant, in which he has promised to be an enemy to all our enemies,—a promise for which there is good cause, when it is considered that the welfare of his people, whom he has taken under his protection, cannot be assailed without an injury being, at the same time, done to his own majesty. Meanwhile, let us live at peace with all men, as much as in us lies, and let us endeavour to practise uprightness in our whole deportment, that we may be able confidently to appeal to God, that when we suffer at the hands of men, we suffer wrongfully. The pride and violent assaults of our enemies may be combined with craftiness. But when such is the case, it becomes us to yield to God the honour which belongs to him, by resting satisfied that he can succour us; for to break the proud who foam out their rage, and to take the crafty in their own craftiness, is work which he has been accustomed to perform in all ages. To keep us from thinking that we are abandoned to the snares and traps of our enemies, that prophet here seasonably sets before us a consideration calculated to administer the highest consolation and hope, when he calls us *God's people.* We are hidden under the shadow of God's wings; although to outward appearances we lie open, and are exposed to the will of the wicked and the proud, we are preserved by the hidden power of God. Accordingly it is said in another psalm (27:5), "For in the time of trouble he will keep me safe in his dwelling; he will hide me in the shelter of his tabernacle." However, none are hid under the keeping and protection of God but those who, renouncing all dependence on their own strength, flee with fear and trembling to him. We will best consult our own safety by taking shelter under the shadow of the Almighty, and, conscious of our own weakness, committing our salvation to him, casting it, so to speak, into his bosom.

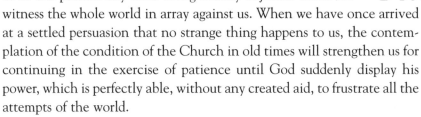

PSALM
83:5-18

With one mind they plot together. When the whole world may conspire together against us, we have as it were a wall of brass for the defence of Christ's kingdom in these words, "Why do the nations rage and the peoples plot in vain?" (Ps. 2:1).

It will be in no small degree profitable to us to contemplate this as an example in which we have represented to us, as in a mirror, what has been the lot of the Church of God from the beginning. This, if rightly reflected upon, will keep us at the present day from being unduly dejected when we witness the whole world in array against us. When we have once arrived at a settled persuasion that no strange thing happens to us, the contemplation of the condition of the Church in old times will strengthen us for continuing in the exercise of patience until God suddenly display his power, which is perfectly able, without any created aid, to frustrate all the attempts of the world.

To remove from the minds of the godly all misgivings as to whether help is ready to be imparted to them from heaven, the prophet distinctly affirms that those who molest the Church are chargeable with making war against God, who has taken her under his protection: "He that touches you, touches the apple of my eye" (Zech. 2:8). And, "Touch not my anointed ones, and do my prophets no harm" (Ps. 55:15). God will have the anointing with which he has anointed us to be, as it were, a buckler to keep us in perfect safety. The nations here enumerated did not avowedly make war against him; but as, when he sees his servants unrighteously assaulted, he interposes himself between them and their enemies to bear the blows aimed at them, they are here justly represented as *having formed an alliance against* God. God having declared that every injury which is done to us is an assault upon him, we may, as from a watchtower, behold in the distance by the eye of faith the approach of that destruction of which the votaries of Antichrist shall have at length the sad and melancholy experience.

PSALM 84:1-2

How lovely is your dwelling place, O LORD Almighty! David complains of his being deprived of liberty of access to the Church of God, there to make a profession of his faith, to improve in godliness, and to engage in the divine worship. David was debarred from the sanctuary. He knew that God had not in vain appointed the holy assemblies, and that the godly have need of such helps so long as they are sojourners in this world. He was also deeply sensible of his own infirmity; nor was he ignorant how far short he came of approaching the perfection of angels. He had therefore good ground to lament over his being deprived of those means, the utility of which is well known to all true believers. His attention was, no doubt, directed to the proper end for which the external ritual was appointed; for his character was widely different from that of hypocrites, who, while they frequent the solemn assemblies with great pomp, and seem to burn with ardent zeal in serving God, yet in all this, aim at nothing more than by an ostentatious display of piety to obtain the credit of having performed their duty towards him. David's mind was far from being occupied with this gross imagination. The end he had in view in desiring so earnestly to enjoy free access to the sanctuary was, that he might there worship God with sincerity of heart, and in a spiritual manner. Those are sadly deficient in understanding who carelessly neglect God's instituted worship, as if they were able to mount up to heaven by their own unaided efforts.

My heart and my flesh cry out for the living God. David declares this longing extended itself even to his body, that is, it manifested itself in the utterance of the mouth, the languor of the eyes, and the action of the hands. When we consider that the sluggishness of our flesh hinders us from elevating our minds to the height of the divine majesty, in vain would God call us to himself, did he not at the same time, on his part, come down to us; or, did he not at least, by the interposition of means, stretch out his hand to us, so to speak, in order to lift us to himself.

PSALM
84:3

Even the sparrow has found a home, and the swallow a nest for herself. David, with the view of aggravating the misery of his condition, compares himself with the sparrows and swallows, showing how hard a case it was for the children of Abraham to be driven out of the heritage which had been promised them, whilst the little birds found some place or other for building their nests. He might sometimes find a comfortable retreat, and might even dwell among unbelievers with some degree of honour and state; but so long as he was deprived of liberty of access to the sanctuary, he seemed to himself to be in a manner banished from the whole world. Undoubtedly, the proper end which we ought to propose to ourselves in living, is to be engaged in the service of God. The manner in which he requires us to serve him is spiritual; but still it is necessary for us to make use of those external aids which he has wisely appointed for our observance. This is the reason why David all at once breaks forth into the exclamation, O, *your altar! O Lord Almighty.* Some might be ready to say in reference to his present circumstances, that there were many retreats in the world, where he might live in safety and repose, yes, that there were many who would gladly receive him as a guest under their roof, and that therefore he had no cause to be so greatly distressed. To this he answers, that he would rather relinquish the whole world than continue in a state of exclusion from the holy tabernacle; that he felt no place delightful at a distance from God's altars; and, in short, that no dwelling-place was agreeable to him beyond the limits of the Holy Land. This he would intimate, by the appellations which he gives to God, *My King and my God.* In speaking thus, he gives us to understand that his life was uncomfortable and embittered, because he was banished from the kingdom of God. It is as if he had said, as you are my God, for what end do I live but to seek after you?

PSALM 84:4-5

Blessed are those who dwell in your house. Here the Psalmist expresses more distinctly the proper and legitimate use of the sanctuary; and thus he distinguishes himself from hypocrites, who are sedulously attentive to the observance of outward ceremonies, but destitute of genuine heart godliness. David, on the contrary, testifies, that the true worshipers of God offer to him the sacrifice of praise, which can never be dissociated from faith. Never will a man praise God from the heart, unless, relying upon his grace, he is a partaker of spiritual peace and joy.

Blessed are those whose strength is in you. David again informs us, that the purpose for which he desired liberty of access to the sanctuary was, not merely to gratify his eyes with what was to be seen there, but to make progress in faith. To lean with the whole heart upon God, is to attain to no ordinary degree of advancement: and this cannot be attained by any man, unless all his pride is laid prostrate in the dust, and his heart truly humbled. In proposing to himself this way of seeking God, David's object is to borrow from him by prayer the strength of which he feels himself to be destitute.

Who have set their hearts on pilgrimage. Those are happy who walk in the way which God has appointed; for nothing is more injurious to a man than to trust in his own understanding. It is not improperly said of the law, "This is the way, walk in it" (Isa. 30:21). Whenever then men turn aside, however little it may be, from the divine law, they go astray, and become entangled in errors. Also, those are happy whose highest ambition it is to have God as the guide of their life, and who therefore desire to draw near to him. God is not satisfied with mere outward ceremonies. What he desires is, to rule and keep in subjection to himself all whom he invites to his tabernacle. Whoever then has learned how great a blessedness it is to rely upon God, will put forth all the desires and faculties of his mind, that with all speed he may hasten to him.

As they pass through the valley of [weeping], they make it a place of springs. David intended this as an argument to prove the stedfastness of the godly, whom the scarcity of water, which often discourages travellers from prosecuting their journey, will not hinder from hastening to seek God, though their way should be through sandy and arid vales. In these words, reproof is administered to the slothfulness of those who will not submit to any inconvenience for the sake of being benefited by the service of God. They indulge themselves in their own ease and pleasures, and allow nothing to interfere with these. They will, therefore, provided they are not required to make any exertion or sacrifice, readily profess themselves to be the servants of God; but they would not give a hair of their head, to obtain the liberty of hearing the gospel preached, and of enjoying the sacraments. This slothful spirit, as is evident from daily observation, keeps multitudes fast bound to their nests, so that they cannot bear to forego in any degree their own ease and convenience. Yes, even in those places where they are summoned by the sound of the church-bell to public prayers, to hear the doctrine of salvation, or to partake of the holy mysteries, we see that some give themselves to sleep, some think only of gain, some are entangled with the affairs of the world, and others are engaged in their amusements. It is therefore not surprising, if those who live at a distance, and who cannot enjoy these religious services and means of salvation, without making some sacrifice of their worldly substance, remain lolling at home. That such may not live secure and self-satisfied in the enjoyment of outward prosperity, David declares, that those who have true heart religion, and who sincerely serve God, direct their steps to the sanctuary of God, not only when the way is easy and cheerful, under the shade and through delightful paths, but also when they must walk through rugged and barren deserts; and that they will rather make for themselves cisterns with immense toil, than be prevented from prosecuting their journey by reason of the drought of the country.

PSALM 84:7-10

They go from strength to strength. The saints are continually acquiring fresh strength from going up to mount Zion, and continue to prosecute their journey without weariness or fatigue, until they reach the wished-for-place, and behold the countenance of God. No visible image of God was there to be seen; but the ark of the covenant was a symbol of his presence, and genuine worshippers found from experience, that by this means they were greatly aided in approaching him.

Better is one day in your courts than a thousand elsewhere. Unlike the greater part of mankind, who desire to live without knowing why, wishing simply that their life may be prolonged, David here testifies, not only that the end which he proposed to himself in living was to serve God, but that in addition to this, he set a higher value on one day which he could spend in the divine service, than upon a long time passed among the men of the world, from whose society true religion is banished. It being lawful for none but the priests to enter into the inner and innermost courts of the temple, David expressly declares, that provided he were permitted to have a place at the porch, he would be contented with this humble station. The value which he set upon the sanctuary is presented in a very striking light by the comparison, that *he would prefer having a place at the very doors of the temple, to his having full possession of the tents of wickedness,* the plain import of which is, that he would rather be cast into a common and unhonoured place, provided he were among the people of God, than exalted to the highest rank of honour among unbelievers. A rare example of godliness indeed! Many are to be found who desire to occupy a place in the Church, but such is the sway which ambition has over the minds of men, that very few are content to continue among the number of the common and undistinguished class. Almost all are carried away with the frantic desire of rising to distinction, and can never think of being at ease until they have attained to some station of eminence.

Jehovah God is our sun and shield. * The idea conveyed by the comparison derived from the sun is, that as the sun by his light vivifies, nourishes, and rejoices the world, so the benign countenance of God fills with joy the hearts of his people, or rather, that they neither live nor breathe except in so far as he shines upon them. By the term *shield* is meant, that our salvation, which would otherwise be perilled by countless dangers, is in perfect safety under his protection. The favour of God in communicating life to us would be far from adequate to the exigencies of our condition, unless at the same time, in the midst of so many dangers, he interposed his power as a buckler to defend us.

The Lord bestows favor and honor; no good thing does he withhold from those whose walk is blameless. After God has once taken the faithful into his favour, he will advance them to high honour, and never cease to enrich them with his blessings. God's bounty can never be exhausted, but flows without intermission. We learn from these words, that whatever excellence may be in us proceeds solely from the grace of God. They contain, at the same time, this special mark, by which the genuine worshippers of God may be distinguished from others, That their life is framed and regulated according to the principles of strict integrity.

O Lord Almighty, blessed is the man who trusts in you. This exclamation with which David ends the psalm, seems to refer to the season of his banishment. He had previously described the blessedness of those who dwell in the courts of the Lord, and now he avows, that although he was for a time deprived of that privilege, he was far from being altogether miserable, because he was supported by the best of all consolations, that which arose from beholding from a distance the grace of God. So long as we are deprived of God's benefits, we must necessarily groan and be sad in heart. But that the sense of our distresses may not overwhelm us, we ought to impress it upon our minds, that even in the midst of our calamities we do not cease to be happy, when faith and patience are in exercise.

PSALM 85:1-8

I will listen to what God the LORD will say. The prophet, by his own example, here exhorts the whole body of the Church to quiet and calm endurance. The prophet enjoins silence, both upon himself and others, that they may patiently wait God's own time. He was persuaded that the care of God is exercised about his Church. Had he thought that fortune held the sovereignty of the world, and that mankind are whirled round by a blind impulse, he would not, as he does, have represented God as sustaining the function of governing. It is as if he had said, Being confident that the remedy for our present calamities is in the hand of God, I will remain quiet until the fit time for delivering the Church arrives. As then the unruliness of our passions murmur, and raise an uproar against God, so patience is a kind of silence by the godly keeps themselves in subjection to his authority.

He promises peace to his people, his saints—but let them not return to folly. After God has sufficiently chastised his church, he will at length show himself merciful to her, that the saints, taught by chastisements, may exercise a stricter vigilance over themselves in future. The cause is shown why God suspends and delays the communications of his grace. As the physician, although his patient may experience some alleviation of his disease, keeps him still under medicinal treatment, until he becomes fully convalescent, and until, the cause of his disease, being removed, his constitution become invigorated,—for to allow him all at once to use whatever diet he chose, would be highly injurious to him;—so God, perceiving that we are not completely recovered from our vices to spiritual health in one day, prolongs his chastisements: without which we would be in danger of a speedy relapse. Accordingly, the prophet, to assuage the grief with which the protracted duration of calamities would oppress the faithful, applies this remedy and solace, That God purposely continues his corrections for a longer period than they would wish, that they may be brought in good earnest to repent, and excited to be more on their guard in future.

PSALM
85:9-13

*Mercy and truth shall meet together, righteousness and peace embrace each other.** Mercy, truth, peace, and righteousness, will form the grand and ennobling distinction of the kingdom of Christ. The prophet does not proclaim the praises of men, but commends the grace which he had before hoped for, and supplicated from God only; thus teaching us to regard it as an undoubted truth, that all these blessings flow from God. By the figure synecdoche, some part being put for the whole, there is described in these four words all the ingredients of true happiness. When cruelty rages with impunity, when truth is extinguished, when righteousness is oppressed and trampled under foot, when all things are embroiled in confusion, were it not better that such a state of things should continue? Whence it follows, that nothing can contribute more effectually to the promotion of a happy life, than that these four virtues should flourish and rule supreme. The reign of Christ, in other parts of Scripture, is adorned with almost similar encomiums.

The LORD will indeed give what is good. God, while he bestows upon his people spiritual blessings, gives them, in addition to these, some taste of his fatherly love, in the outward benefits which relate to the life of the body; it being evident from the testimony of Paul, that "godliness is profitable unto all things, having promise of the life that now is, and of that which is to come" (1 Tim. 4:8). But let it be observed, that the faithful generally have only granted to them a limited portion of the comforts of this transitory life: that they may not be lulled asleep by the allurements of earth. Moreover, we are taught from this verse, that the power and capacity of the earth to produce fruit for the sustenance of our bodies was not given to it once for all,—as the heathen imagine God at the first creation to have adapted each element to its proper office, while he now sits in heaven in a state of indolence and repose;—but that the earth is from year to year rendered fruitful by the secret influence of God, who designs hereby to afford us a manifestation of his goodness.

PSALM 86:1-10

Guard my life, for I am devoted to you. Here the Psalmist adduces two other arguments by which to stir up God to grant them succour,—his own gentleness towards his neighbours, and the trust which he reposed in God. In the first clause he may seem at first sight to insinuate that by any merits of his own he had brought God under obligations to preserve him. But the particular mention he made of his *clemency* tends to exhibit in a more odious light the wickedness of his enemies, who had treated so shamefully, and with such inhumanity, a man against whom they could bring no wellfounded charge, and who had even endeavoured to the utmost of his power to please them. Since God then has avowed himself to be the defender both of good causes and of those who follow after righteousness, David, not without good reason, testifies that he had endeavoured to exercise kindness and gentleness; that from this it may appear that he was basely requited by his enemies, when they gratuitously acted with cruelty towards a merciful man. But as it would not be enough for our lives to be characterised by kindness and righteousness, an additional qualification is subjoined—that of *trust* or *confidence in God,* which is the mother of all true religion. Although we may have the testimony of an approving conscience, and although he may be the best witness of our innocence, yet if we are desirous of obtaining his assistance, it is necessary for us to commit our hopes and anxieties to him. If it is objected, that in this way the gate is shut against sinners, the answer is, that when God invites to himself those who are blameless and upright in their deportment, this does not imply that he forthwith repels all who are punished on account of their sins; for they have an opportunity given them, if they will improve it, for prayer and the acknowledgement of their guilt. But if those whom we have never offended unrighteously assail us, we have ground for double confidence before God.

Day 207

J U L Y   2 5

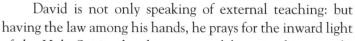

Teach me your way, O LORD, and I will walk in your truth. In submitting himself to God, and in imploring him to be his guide, David confesses that the only possible way by which we can be enabled to live a holy and upright life is, when God goes before us, while we follow after him; and, accordingly, that those who deviate, let it be ever so little, from the law through a proud conceit of their own wisdom, wander from the right path.

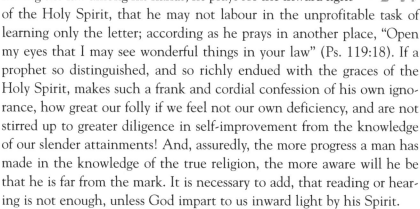

PSALM 86:11-17

David is not only speaking of external teaching: but having the law among his hands, he prays for the inward light of the Holy Spirit, that he may not labour in the unprofitable task of learning only the letter; according as he prays in another place, "Open my eyes that I may see wonderful things in your law" (Ps. 119:18). If a prophet so distinguished, and so richly endued with the graces of the Holy Spirit, makes such a frank and cordial confession of his own ignorance, how great our folly if we feel not our own deficiency, and are not stirred up to greater diligence in self-improvement from the knowledge of our slender attainments! And, assuredly, the more progress a man has made in the knowledge of the true religion, the more aware will he be that he is far from the mark. It is necessary to add, that reading or hearing is not enough, unless God impart to us inward light by his Spirit.

In addition to this, the Psalmist desires that his heart may be framed for yielding obedience to God, and that it may be firmly established therein; for as our understanding has need of light, so has our will of uprightness.

*Unite my heart to fear your name.** In the word *unite* there is very beautiful metaphor, conveying the idea, that the heart of man is full of tumult, drawn asunder, and, as it were, scattered about in fragments, until God has gathered it to himself, and holds it together in a state of stedfast and persevering obedience. From this also, it is manifest what free will is able to do of itself. Two powers are ascribed to it; but David confesses that he is destitute of both; setting the light of the Holy Spirit in opposition to the blindness of his own mind; and affirming that uprightness of heart is entirely the gift of God.

The LORD *loves the gates of Zion more than any of the dwellings of Jacob.* Here we are taught that all the excellence of the holy city depended on the free choice which God had made of it. If it is demanded why Jerusalem was so highly distinguished, let this short answer be deemed sufficient, *Because it so pleased God.* To this the divine love is to be traced as its source; but the end of such a choice was, that there might be some fixed place in which the true religion should be preserved, and the unity of the faith maintained, until the advent of Christ, and from which it might afterwards flow into all the regions of the earth. This, then, explains why the prophet celebrates Jerusalem as possessing the high distinction of having God for its master-builder, its founder and protector.

Indeed, of Zion it will be said, "This one and that one were born in her, and the Most High himself will establish her." The condition upon which Christ espouses the faithful to himself is, that they should forget their own people and their father's house (Ps. 45:10), and that, being formed into new creatures, and born again of incorruptible seed, they should begin to be the children of God as well as of the Church (Gal. 4:19). And the ministry of the Church and it alone, is undoubtedly the means by which we are born again to a heavenly life. We should remember the difference which the Apostle sets forth as subsisting between the earthly Jerusalem,—which, being herself a bondwoman, brings forth children also in bondage,—and the heavenly Jerusalem, which brings forth free children by the instrumentality of the Gospel.

The LORD *will write in the register of the peoples.* Those who are the bondslaves of Satan and of sin will assuredly never be able to obtain, by any efforts of their own, the right of citizenship in the heavenly Jerusalem. It is the Lord's peculiar work to divide people into their respective ranks, distinguishing one from another, as seems good to him, all men being on a level by nature. This passage is to be understood as referring to effectual calling. God, it is true, wrote the names of his children in the Book of Life before the creation of the world; but he enrols them in the catalogue of his saints, only when, having regenerated them by the Spirit of adoption, he impresses his own mark upon them.

Why, O Lord, do you reject me and hide your face from me? These lamentations at first sight would seem to indicate a state of mind in which sorrow without any consolation prevailed; but they contain in them tacit prayers. The Psalmist does not proudly enter into debate with God, but mournfully desires some remedy to his calamities. This kind of complaint justly deserves to be reckoned among the unutterable groanings of which Paul makes mention in Romans 8:26. Had the prophet thought himself rejected and abhorred by God, he certainly would not have persevered in prayer. But here he sets forth the judgment of the flesh, against which he strenuously and magnanimously struggled, that it might at length be manifest from the result that he had not prayed in vain. Although, therefore, this psalm does not end with thanksgiving, but with mournful complaint, as if there remained no place for mercy, yet it is so much the more useful as a means of keeping us in the duty of prayer. The prophet, in heaving these sighs, and discharging them, as it were, into the bosom of God, doubtless ceased not to hope for the salvation of which he could see no signs by the eye of sense. He did not call God, at the opening of the psalm, *the God of his salvation,* and then bid farewell to all hope of succour from him.

It is true, that when the heart is in perplexity and doubt, or rather is tossed hither and thither, faith seems to be swallowed up. But experience teaches us, that faith, while it fluctuates amidst these agitations, continues to rise again from time to time, so as not to be overwhelmed; and if at any time it is at the point of being stifled, it is nevertheless sheltered and cherished, for though the tempests may become ever so violent, it shields itself from them by reflecting that God continues faithful, and never disappoints or forsakes his own children.

PSALM 89:1-8

I will declare that your love stands firm forever. The Psalmist assigns the reason why he perseveres in singing the Divine praises in the midst of adversities; which is, that he does not despair of the manifestation of God's loving-kindness towards his people, although at present they were under severe chastisement. Never will a man freely open his mouth to praise God, unless he is fully persuaded that God, even when he is angry with his people, never lays aside his fatherly affection towards them. The words *I will declare,* imply that the truth which the inspired writer propounds was deeply fixed in his heart. Whatever, as if he had said, has hitherto happened, it has never had the effect of effacing from my heart the undoubted hope of experiencing the Divine favour as to the future, and I will always continue stedfastly to cherish the same feeling. It is to be observed, that it was not without a painful and arduous conflict that he succeeded in embracing by faith the goodness of God, which at that time had entirely vanished out of sight;—this we say is to be particularly noticed, in order that when God at any time withdraws from us all the tokens of his love, we may nevertheless learn to erect in our hearts this *love that stands firm forever,* which is here spoken of and by which is meant that the Divine mercy shall continue till it reach its end or consummation.

O LORD God Almighty, who is like you? This is repeated so that at least the fear of the Divine Majesty may teach us to beware of robbing him of the honour which belongs to him. That we may not, however, by too much fear, be prevented from approaching him, some portion of sweetness is intermingled with this description, when it is declared, that *his faithfulness surrounds him;* by which we are to understand, that God is always stedfast in his promises, and that whatever changes may happen, he nevertheless continues invariably true, both before and behind, on the right hand and on the left.

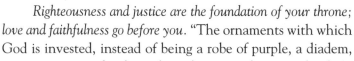

The land of Egypt was overthrown as a wounded man.* By these words the prophet magnifies the grace of God, which was displayed in the deliverance of the Church. He intended to set before his own mind and the minds of others, the paternal love of God, to encourage both himself and others to have recourse to him for succour, with the greater freedom and alacrity.

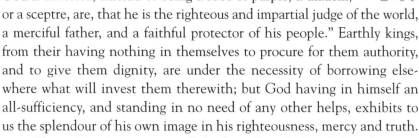

Righteousness and justice are the foundation of your throne; love and faithfulness go before you. "The ornaments with which God is invested, instead of being a robe of purple, a diadem, or a sceptre, are, that he is the righteous and impartial judge of the world, a merciful father, and a faithful protector of his people." Earthly kings, from their having nothing in themselves to procure for them authority, and to give them dignity, are under the necessity of borrowing elsewhere what will invest them therewith; but God having in himself an all-sufficiency, and standing in no need of any other helps, exhibits to us the splendour of his own image in his righteousness, mercy and truth.

They rejoice in your name all day long. It is declared that those are happy to whom it is given to rejoice in God; for although all men in common are sustained and nourished by his liberality, yet the feeling of his paternal goodness is far from being experienced by all men in such a manner as to enable them, from a certain persuasion that he is favourable to them, to congratulate themselves upon their happy condition. It is, therefore, a singular privilege which he confers upon his chosen ones, to make them taste of his goodness, that thereby they may be encouraged to be glad and rejoice. And, in fact, there is not a more miserable condition than that of believers, when by their brutish insensibility they trample under foot the Divine benefits which they greedily devour; for the more abundantly God pampers them, the fouler is their ingratitude. True happiness then consists in our apprehending the Divine goodness which, filling our hearts with joy, may stir us up to praise and thanksgiving.

If his [children] forsake my law and do not follow my statutes. The prophet declares that although the posterity of David should fall into sin, yet God had promised to show himself merciful towards them, and that he would not punish their transgressions to the full extent of their desert. Moreover, to give the promise the greater efficacy, he always introduces God speaking, as if he presented to him a request corresponding with the precise words and express articles of his covenant. It was very necessary that this should be added; for so easily do we slide into evil, and so prone are we to continual falls, that unless God, in the exercise of his infinite mercy, pardoned us, there would not be a single article of his covenant which would continue stedfast. God, therefore, seeing that it could not be otherwise, but that the posterity of David, in so far as it depended upon themselves, would frequently fall from the covenant, by their own fault, has provided a remedy for such cases, in his pardoning grace.

Further, as it is profitable for men to be subjected to divine correction, he does not promise that he will allow them to escape unpunished, which would be to encourage them in their sins; but he promises, that in his chastisements he will exercise a fatherly moderation, and will not execute vengeance upon them to the full extent which their sins deserve. It is also to be observed, that he promises pardon, not only for light offences, but also for great and aggravated sins.

If they violate my decrees and fail to keep my commands. When God adopts men into his family, they do not forthwith completely lay aside the flesh with its corruptions, as is held by some enthusiasts, who dream, that as soon as we are grafted into the body of Christ, all the corruption that is in us must be destroyed. Would to God that we could all of a sudden change our nature, and thus exhibit that angelic perfection which they require! But as it is quite apparent, that we are far from such an attainment, so long as we carry about with us this tabernacle of flesh, let us bid adieu to that devilish figment, and let us all betake ourselves to the sanctuary of forgiveness, which is at all times open for us.

I will punish their sin with the rod, their iniquity with flogging. Since God does not adopt us as his children to encourage us to take liberty to commit sin with the greater boldness, mention is here made at the same time of chastisement, by which he shows that he hates the sins of his children, and, warning them of what they have deserved in offending him, invites and exhorts them to repentance. This fatherly chastisement then, which operates as medicine, holds the medium between undue indulgence, which is an encouragement to sin, and extreme severity, which precipitates persons into destruction. God speaks of his chastising his people after the manner of men, either because the anger of a father in correcting his children proceeds from love,—for he sees that otherwise he would fail in promoting their good; or it contains a contrast between God and men, implying, that in the task of chastising he will with moderation and gentleness; for, were he to put forth his strength, he would immediately bring us to nothing, yes, he could do this simply by moving one of his fingers. Whenever God punishes the sins of true believers, he will observe a wholesome moderation; and it is therefore our duty to take all the punishments which he inflicts upon us, as so many medicines.

God has nothing else in view than to correct the vices of his children, in order that, after having thoroughly purged them, he may restore them anew to his favour and friendship; according to the words of Paul in 1 Corinthians 11:33, which affirm that the faithful "are chastened of the Lord, that they should not be condemned with the world." For this reason, lest they should be overwhelmed with the weight of chastisement, he restrains his hand, and makes considerate allowance for their infirmity. Thus the promise is fulfilled, That *he does not withdraw his loving-kindness from* his people, even when he is angry with them; for, while he is correcting them for their profit and salvation, he does not cease to love them. God then in this passage leads us further; promising that his covenant shall be stedfast and effectual, not only because he will be faithful on his part, but also because he will keep his people from falling away through their own inconstancy.

I will not violate my covenant or alter what my lips have uttered. As the true knowledge of God's mercy can only be obtained from his word, he enjoins us to keep our eyes intently fixed upon his covenant. The more excellent and invaluable a blessing it is, "Never to be rejected after having been once adopted by him," the more difficult it is for us to believe its truth. And we know how many thoughts from time to time present themselves to our minds, tempting us to call it in question. That the faithful, therefore, may not harass themselves beyond measure in debating in their own minds whether or not they are in favour with God, they are enjoined to look to the covenant, and to embrace the salvation which is offered to them in it. God here commends to us his own faithfulness, that we may account his promise sufficient, and that we may not seek the certainty of our salvation anywhere else.

*I will not suffer my faithfulness to fail.** God promises not only to be faithful on his side, but also that what he has promised shall take full effect, despite all the impediments which men may cast in the way; for he will strive against their sins, that by means of them the fruit of his goodness may not be prevented from reaching them. When the Jews, by their ingratitude and treachery, revolted from him, the covenant was not disannulled, because it was founded upon the perfect immutability of his nature. And still, at the present day, when our sins mount even to the heavens, the goodness of God fails not to rise above them, since it is far above the heavens.

Once for all, I have sworn by my holiness. God now confirms by an oath what he previously stated he had promised to David, from which it appears that it was not a matter of small importance; it being certain that God would not interpose his holy name in reference to what was of no consequence. It is a token of singular loving-kindness for him, upon seeing us prone to distrust, to provide a remedy for it so compassionately. We have, therefore, so much the less excuse if we do not embrace, with true and unwavering faith, his promise which is so strongly ratified, since in his deep interest about our salvation, he does not withhold his oath, that we may yield entire credence to his word.

PSALM 89: 36-45

His line will continue forever and his throne endure before me like the sun; it will be established forever like the moon. There now follows the promise that the right of sovereignty shall always remain with the posterity of David. These two things—his offspring and his throne, are conjoined; and by these words the everlasting duration of the kingdom is promised. The sun and the moon are produced as witnesses; for although they are creatures subject to corruption, they yet possess more stability than the earth or air; the elements, as we see, being subject to continual changes. As the whole of this lower world is subject to unceasing agitation and change, there is presented to us a more stedfast state of things in the sun and moon, that the kingdom of David might not be estimated according to the common order of nature. Since, however, this royal throne was shaken in the time of Rehoboam and afterwards broken down and overthrown, it follows that this prophecy cannot be limited to David. For although at length the outward majesty of this kingdom was put an end to without hope of being re-established, the sun ceased not to shine by day, nor the moon by night. Accordingly, until we come to Christ, God might seem to be unfaithful to his promises. But in the branch which sprung from the root of Jesse, these words were fulfilled in their fullest sense.

You have cut short the days of his youth. When the prophet complains that the issue does not correspond with the promise, or is not such as the promise led the chosen people to expect, he does not, on the account, charge God with falsehood, but brings forward this apparent discrepancy for another purpose—to encourage himself, from the consideration of the Divine promises, to come to the throne of grace with the greater confidence and boldness; and, while he urged this difficulty before God, he was fully persuaded that it was impossible for him not to show himself faithful to his word. As the majority of men drink up their sorrow and keep it to themselves, because they despair of deriving any benefit from prayer, so true believers, the more frankly and familiarly they appeal to God in reference to his promises, the more valiantly do they wrestle against their distrust, and encourage themselves in the hope of a favourable issue.

How long, O LORD? Will you hide yourself forever? Unbelievers in the agitation of trouble, may sometimes engage in prayer, yet whatever they ask proceeds from feigned lips. But the prophet, by connecting prayer with his complaints, bears testimony that he had never lost his confidence in the truth of the Divine promises.

Remember how fleeting is my life. After having confessed that the severe and deplorable afflictions which had befallen the Church were to be traced to her own sins as the procuring cause, the prophet, the more effectually to move God to commiseration, lays before him the brevity of human life, in which, if we receive no taste of the Divine goodness, it will seem that we have been created in vain. That we may understand the passage the more clearly, it will be better to begin with the consideration of the last member of the verse, *For what futility have you created all men!* The faithful, in putting this question, proceed upon an established first principle, That God has created men and placed them in the world, to show himself a father to them. And, indeed, as his goodness extends itself even to the cattle and lower animals of every kind, it cannot for a moment be supposed, that we, who hold a higher rank in the scale of being than the brute creation, should be wholly deprived of it. Upon the contrary supposition, it were better for us that we had never been born, than to languish away in continual sorrow. There is, moreover, set forth the brevity of the course of our life; which is so brief, that unless God make timely haste in giving us some taste of his benefits, the opportunity for doing this will be lost, since our life passes rapidly away. The drift of this verse is now very obvious, That the end for which men were created was, that they should enjoy God's bounty in the present world; and from this it is concluded that they are born in vain, unless he shows himself a father towards them. In the second place, as the course of this life is short, it is argued that if God does not make haste to bless them, the opportunity will no longer be afforded when their life shall have run out.

Remember how fleeting is my life. Here it may be said that the saints took too much upon themselves in prescribing to God a time in which to work; and, that although he afflict us with continual distresses, so long as we are in our state of earthly pilgrimage, yet there is no ground to conclude from this that we have been created in vain, since there is reserved for us a better life in heaven, to the hope of which we have been adopted; and that, therefore, it is not surprising though now our life is hidden from us on earth. The answer is, that it is by the permission of God that the saints take this liberty of urging him in their prayer to make haste; and that there is no impropriety in doing so, provided they, at the same time, keep themselves within the bounds of modesty, and, restraining the impetuosity of their afflictions, yield themselves wholly to his will. And, although we must continue to drag out our life amidst continual distresses, we have abundant consolation to aid us in bearing all our afflictions, provided we lift up our minds to heaven.

But still it is to be observed, in the first place, that it is certain, considering our great weakness, that no man will ever do this unless he has first tasted of the Divine goodness in this life; and, secondly, that the complaints of the people of God ought not to be judged of according to a perfect rule, because they proceed not from a settled and an undisturbed state of mind, but have always some excess arising from the impetuosity or vehemence of the affections at work in their minds. The man who measures the love of God from the state of things as presently existing, judges by a standard which must lead to a false conclusion; "because the Lord disciplines those whom he loves" (Heb. 12:6). But as God is never so severe towards his own people as not to furnish them with actual experimental evidence of his grace, it stands always true that life is profitless to men, if they do not feel, while they live, that he is their father.

PSALM 90:1-2

Lord, *you have been our dwelling place throughout all generations.* As the Israelites had always been pilgrims and wanderers, so God was to them instead of a dwelling-place. No doubt, the condition of all men is unstable upon earth; but we know that Abraham and his posterity were, above all others, sojourners, and as it were exiles. Since, then, they wandered in the land of Canaan till they were brought into Egypt, where they lived only by sufferance from day to day, it was necessary for them to seek for themselves a dwelling-place under the shadow of God, without which they could hardly be accounted inhabitants of the world, since they continued everywhere as strangers, and were afterwards led about through many windings and turnings. The grace which the Lord displayed in sustaining them in their wanderings, and shielding them with this hand when they sojourned among savage and cruel nations, and were exposed to injurious treatment at their hands—this grace is extolled by Moses in very striking terms, when he represents God as an abode or dwelling-place to these poor fugitives who were continually wandering from one place to another in quest of lodgings. This grace he magnifies from the length of time during which it had been exercised; for God ceased not to preserve and defend them for the space of more than four hundred years, during which time they dwelt under the wings of his protection.

Before the mountains were born or you brought forth the earth and the world, from everlasting to everlasting you are God. God is here contrasted with created beings, who, as all know, are subject to continual changes, so that there is nothing stable under heaven. As, in a particular manner, nothing is fuller of vicissitude than human life, that men may not judge of the nature of God by their own fluctuating condition, he is here placed in a state of settled and undisturbed tranquillity. Thus the everlastingness of which Moses speaks is to be referred not only to the essence of God, but also to his providence, by which he governs the world. Although he subjects the world to many alterations, he remains unmoved; and that not only in regard to himself, but also in regard to the faithful, who find from experience, that instead of being wavering, he is stedfast in his power, truth, righteousness, and goodness, even as he has been from the beginning.

PSALM 90:3

You turn men back to dust, saying, "Return to dust, O sons of men." Moses, in the first place, mentions how frail and transitory is the life of man, and bewails its miseries. This he does, not for the purpose of quarrelling with God, but as an argument to induce him the more readily to exercise his mercy, even as he is elsewhere said to pardon mortal men, when he considers of what they are made, and remembers that they are but dust and grass (Ps. 103:14). He compares the course of our life to a ring or circle, because God, placing us upon the earth, turns us about within a narrow circuit, and when we have reached the last point, draws us back to himself in a moment. We have here laid down a simple definition of our life, that it is, as it were, a short revolution in which we quickly complete our circle, the last point of which is the termination of our earthly course. This account of human life sets in a clearer light the gracious manner in which God deals with his servants, in adopting them to be his peculiar people, that he may at length gather them together into his everlasting inheritance. Although we are convinced from experience that men, when they have completed their circle, are forthwith taken out of the world, yet the knowledge of this frailty fails in making a deep impression upon our hearts, because we do not lift our eyes above the world. Whence proceeds the great stupidity of men, who, bound fast to the present state of existence, proceed in the affairs of life as if they were to live two thousand years, but because they do not elevate their conceptions above visible objects? Each man, when he compares himself with others, flatters himself that he will live to a great age. In short, men are so dull as to think that thirty years, or even a smaller number, are, as it were, an eternity; nor are they impressed with the brevity of their life so long as this world keeps possession of their thoughts. This is the reason why Moses awakens us by elevating our minds to the eternity of God, without the consideration of which we perceive not how speedily our life vanishes away. The imagination that we shall have long life, resembles a profound sleep in which we are all benumbed, until meditation upon the heavenly life swallow up this foolish fancy respecting the length of our continuance upon earth.

PSALM 90:4-10

For a thousand years in your sight are like a day that has just gone by, or like a watch in the night. This text is quoted by the Apostle Peter in a sense somewhat different. The design of Moses is to elevate the minds of men to heaven by withdrawing them from their own gross conceptions. And what is the object of Peter? As many, because Christ does not hasten his coming according to their desire, cast off the hope of the resurrection through the weariness of long delay, he corrects this preposterous impatience by a very suitable remedy. He perceives men's faith in the Divine promises fainting and failing, from their thinking that Christ delays his coming too long. Whence does this proceed, but because they grovel upon the earth? Peter therefore appropriately applies these words of Moses to cure this vice. As the indulgence in pleasures to which unbelievers yield themselves is to be traced to this, that having their hearts too much set upon the world, they do not taste the pleasures of a celestial eternity; so impatience proceeds from the same source. Hence we learn the true use of this doctrine. To what is it owing that we have so great anxiety about our life, that nothing suffices us, and that we are continually molesting ourselves, but because we foolishly imagine that we shall nestle in this world forever? Let us learn then not to judge according to the understanding of the flesh, but to depend upon the judgment of God; and let us elevate our minds by faith, even to his heavenly throne, from which he declares that this earthly life is nothing. Nor does Moses simply contrast a thousand years with one day, but he contrasts them with *yesterday,* which is already gone; for whatever is still before our eyes has a hold upon our minds, but we are less affected with the recollection of what is past.

With regard to the word *watch,* the ancients, as is well known, were accustomed to divide the night into four watches, consisting of three hours each. To express still more forcibly how inconsiderable that which appears to us a long period is in God's eyes, this similitude is added, That a thousand years in his sight differ nothing from three hours of the night, in which men scarcely know whether they are awake or asleep.

Who knows the power of your anger? For your wrath is as great as the fear that is due you. It is a holy awe of God, and that alone, which makes us truly and deeply feel his anger. We see that the reprobate, although they are severely punished, only chafe upon the bit, or kick against God, or become exasperated, or are stupefied, as if they were hardened against all calamities; so far are they from being subdued. And though they are full of trouble, and cry aloud, yet the Divine anger does not so penetrate their hearts as to abate their pride and fierceness. The minds of the godly alone are wounded with the wrath of God; nor do they wait for his thunderbolts, to which the reprobate hold out their hard and iron necks, but they tremble the very moment when God moves only his little finger. The prophet had said that the human mind could not sufficiently comprehend the dreadfulness of the Divine wrath. And we see how, although God shakes heaven and earth, many notwithstanding, like the giants of old, treat this with derision, and are actuated by such brutish arrogance, that they despise him when he brandishes his bolts. But as the Psalmist is treating of a doctrine which properly belongs to true believers, he affirms that they have a strongly sensitive feeling of the wrath of God which makes them quietly submit themselves to his authority. Although to the wicked their own conscience is a tormentor which does not suffer them to enjoy repose, yet so far is this secret dread from teaching them to humble themselves, that it excites them to clamour against God with increasing forwardness. In short, the faithful alone are sensible of God's wrath; and being subdued by it, they acknowledge that they are nothing, and with true humility devote themselves wholly to him. This is wisdom to which the reprobate cannot attain, because they cannot lay aside the pride with which they are inflated. They are not touched with the feeling of God's wrath, because they do not stand in awe of him.

PSALM 90:12

Teach us to number our days aright, that we may gain a heart of wisdom. As Moses perceived that what he had hitherto taught is not comprehended by the understandings of men until God shine upon them by his Spirit, he now sets himself to prayer. It indeed seems at first sight absurd to pray that we may know the number of our years. What? since even the strongest scarcely reach the age of eighty years, is there any difficulty in reckoning up so small a sum? Children learn numbers as soon as they begin to prattle; and we do not need a teacher in arithmetic to enable us to count the length of a hundred upon our fingers. So much the fouler and more shameful is our stupidity in never comprehending the short term of our life. Even he who is most skilful in arithmetic, and who can precisely and accurately understand and investigate millions of millions, is nevertheless unable to count eighty years in his own life. It is surely a monstrous thing that men can measure all distances without themselves, that they know how many feet the moon is distant from the centre of the earth, what space there is between the different planets; and, in short, that they can measure all the dimensions both of heaven and earth; while yet they cannot number seventy years in their own case. It is therefore evident that Moses had good reason to beseech God for ability to perform what requires a wisdom which is very rare among mankind. We then truly apply our hearts to wisdom when we comprehend the shortness of human life. What can be a greater proof of madness than to ramble about without proposing to oneself any end? True believers alone, who know the difference between this transitory state and a blessed eternity, for which they were created, know what ought to be the aim of their life. No man then can regulate his life with a settled mind, but he who, knowing the end of it, that is to say death itself, is led to consider the great purpose of man's existence in this world, that he may aspire after the prize of the heavenly calling.

Day 223 A U G U S T 1 0

Relent, O LORD! How long will it be? Have compassion on your servants. Moses prays that God, who had not ceased for a long time severely to punish his people, would at length be inclined to deal gently with them. Although God daily gave them in many ways some taste of his love, yet their banishment from the land of promise was a very grievous affliction; for it admonished them that they were unworthy of that blessed inheritance which he had appointed for his children. Moses, no doubt, combines that sore bondage which they had suffered in Egypt, with their wanderings in the wilderness; and therefore he justly bewails their protracted languishing in the words *how long.* As God is said to turn his back upon us, or to depart to a distance from us, when he withdraws the tokens of his favour, so by his return we are to understand the manifestation of his grace.

Establish the work of our hands for us. Moses intimates that we cannot undertake or attempt anything with the prospect of success, unless God become our guide and counsellor, and govern us by his Spirit. Whence it follows, that the reason why the enterprises and efforts of worldly men have a disastrous issue is, because, in not following God, they pervert all order and throw everything into confusion. Although God converts to good in the end whatever Satan and the reprobate plot and practise against him or his people; yet the Church, in which God rules with undisturbed sway, has in this respect a special privilege. By his providence, which to us is incomprehensible, he directs his work in regard to the reprobate externally; but he governs his believing people internally by his Holy Spirit; and therefore his is properly said to order or direct the work of their hands. The repetition shows that a continual course of perseverance in the grace of God is required. It would not be enough for us to be brought to the midst of our journey. He must enable us to complete the whole course.

PSALM 91:1-4

He who dwells in the shelter of the Most High will rest in the shadow of the Almighty. Those who dwell in the secret place of God are here said by the Psalmist to dwell under his shadow, in the sense that they experience to what a rich extent his protection reaches. Men generally seek out a great variety of hiding-places, having recourse to one or another, according as the calamities are different which threaten to overtake them; but here we are taught that the only safe and impregnable fortress to which we can flee is the protection of God. He contrasts the security of those who trust in God with the vanity of all other confidences by which we are apt to delude ourselves.

He will cover you with his feathers, and under his wings you will find refuge. This figure, which is employed in other parts of Scripture, is one which beautifully expresses the singularly tender care with which God watches over our safety. When we consider the majesty of God, there is nothing which would suggest a likeness such as is here drawn between him and the hen or other birds, who spread their wings over their young ones to cherish and protect them. But, in accommodation to our infirmity, he does not scruple to descend, as it were, from the heavenly glory which belongs to him, and to encourage us to approach him under so humble a similitude. Since he condescends in such a gracious manner to our weakness, surely there is nothing to prevent us from coming to him with the greatest freedom. By *the truth of God*, which, the Psalmist says, would be his *shield* and *buckler*, we must understand God's faithfulness, as never deserting his people in the time of their need; still we cannot doubt that he had in his eye the Divine promises, for it is only by looking to these that any can venture to cast themselves upon the protection of God. As, without the word, we cannot come to the enjoyment of that Divine mercy of which the Psalmist had already spoken, he now comes forward himself to bear witness on behalf of it. Formerly, under the comparison of a *fortress*, he had taught that by trusting in God we shall enjoy safety and security; now he compares God to a *shield*, intimating that he will come between us and all our enemies to preserve us from their attacks.

PSALM
91:5-7

You will not fear the terror of night, nor the arrow that flies by day. The Psalmist continues to insist upon the truth which we have just adverted to, that, if we confide with implicit reliance upon the protection of God, we will be secure from every temptation and assault of Satan. It is of importance to remember, that those whom God has taken under his care are in a state of the most absolute safety. Even those who have reached the most advanced experience find nothing more difficult than to rely upon Divine deliverance; and more especially when, overtaken by some of the many forms in which danger and death await us in this world, doubts will insinuate themselves into our hearts, giving rise to fear and disquietude. There was reason, therefore, why the Psalmist should enter upon a specification of different evils, encouraging the Lord's people to look for more than one mode of deliverance, and to bear up under various and accumulated calamities. Mention is made of *the fear of the night,* because men are naturally apprehensive in the dark, or because the night exposes us to dangers of different kinds, and our fears are apt at such a season to magnify any sound or disturbance. There is no kind of calamity which the shield of the Almighty cannot ward off and repel.

A thousand may fall at your side. The Psalmist proceeds to show that, though the state of all men may to appearance be alike, the believer has the special privilege of being exempted from evils of an imminent and impending nature; for it might be objected that he was but man, and, as such, exposed with others to death in its thousand different forms. To correct this mistake, the Psalmist does not hesitate to assert that, when universal ruin prevails around, we are privileged with a special exemption which secures our safety in the midst of dangers.

PSALM 91:7-11

A thousand may fall at your side, ten thousand at your right hand, but it will not come near you. There is much that is dark in the aspect of things in this world, yet the Psalmist hints that, amidst all the confusion which reigns, we may collect from what we see of God's judgments, that he does not disappoint the expectations of his believing people. He must be considered, however, as addressing those who have eyes to see, who are privileged with the true light of faith, who are fully awake to the consideration of the Divine judgments, and who wait patiently and quietly till the proper time arrive; for most men stagger and confuse their minds upon this subject, by starting to precipitate conclusions, and are prevented from discovering the providence of God by judging according to sense. It becomes us too to be satisfied with apprehending the judgments of God only in some imperfect measure while we remain upon earth, and leaving him to defer the fuller discovery of them to the day of complete revelation.

For he will command his angels concerning you to guard you in all your ways. When all these attempts to encourage us have been tried, and God finds that we still linger and hesitate to approach him, or cast ourselves upon his sole and exclusive protection, he next makes mention of the angels, and proffers them as guardians of our safety. As an additional illustration of his indulgent mercy, and compassion for our weakness, he represents those whom he has ready for our defence as being a numerous host; he does not assign one solitary angel to each saint, but commissions the whole armies of heaven to keep watch over every individual believer. It is the individual believer whom the Psalmist addresses, as we read also in Psalm 34:7—that "angels encamp round about them that fear him." We should rest satisfied of their being always intent upon their commission. We read elsewhere of their readiness to obey and execute the commands of God; and this must go to strengthen our faith, since their exertions are made use of by God for our defence.

Day 227 AUGUST 14

They will lift you up in their hands, so that you will not strike your foot against a stone. The Psalmist gives us a still higher idea of the guardianship of the angels, informing us, that they not only watch lest any evil should befall us, and are on the alert to extend assistance, but bear up our steps with their hands, so as to prevent us from stumbling in our course. Were we to judge indeed by mere appearances, the children of God are far from being thus borne up aloft in their career; often they labour and pant with exertion, occasionally they stagger and fall, and it is with a struggle that they  advance in their course; but as in the midst of all this weakness it is only by the singular help of God that they are preserved every moment from falling and from being destroyed, we need not wonder that the Psalmist should speak in such exalted terms of the assistance which they receive through the ministrations of angels. Never, besides, could we surmount the serious obstacles which Satan opposes to our prayers, unless God should bear us up in the manner here described. Let anyone combine together the two considerations which have been mentioned,—our own utter weakness on the one hand, and on the other the roughness, the difficulties, the thorns which beset our way, the stupidity besides which characterises our hearts, and the subtlety of the evil one in laying snares for our destruction,—and he will see that the language of the Psalmist is not that of hyperbole, that we could not proceed one step did not the angels bear us up in their hands in a manner beyond the ordinary course of nature. That we frequently stumble is owing to our own fault in departing from him who is our head and leader. And though God suffers us to stumble and fall in this manner that he may convince us how weak we are in ourselves, yet, inasmuch as he does not permit us to be crushed or altogether overwhelmed, it is virtually even then as if he put his hand under us and bore us up.

PSALM 91:12-13

PSALM 91:14-15

"Because he loves me," says the LORD, *"I will rescue him; I will protect him, for he acknowledges my name."* Here it is noticeable that God, in declaring from heaven that we shall be safe under the wings of his protection, speaks of nothing as necessary on the part of his people but hope or trust. We must rest with a sweet confidence in God, and rejoice in his favour. The language implies that we must be continually surrounded by death and destruction in this world, unless his hand is stretched out for our preservation. Occasionally he assists even unbelievers, but it is only to his believing people that his help is vouchsafed, in the sense of his being their Saviour to the end. Their *knowing the name* of God is spoken of in connection with their trust and expectation; and very properly, for why is it that men are found casting their eyes vainly round them to every quarter in the hour of danger, but because they are ignorant of the power of God? They cannot indeed be said to know God at all, but delude themselves with a vague apprehension of something which is not God, a mere idol substituted for him in their imaginations. As it is a true knowledge of God which begets confidence in him, and leads us to call upon him; and as none can seek him sincerely but those who have apprehended the promises, and put due honour upon his name, the Psalmist with great propriety and truth represents this knowledge as being the spring or fountain of trust.

He will call upon me, and I will answer him; I will be with him in trouble, I will deliver him and honor him. The Psalmist now shows more clearly what was meant by trusting in God, or placing our love and delight in him. For that affection and desire which is produced by faith, prompts us to call upon his name. This is another proof in support of the truth, which we had occasion to touch upon formerly, that prayer is properly grounded upon the word of God. We are not at liberty in this matter to follow the suggestions of our own mind or will, but must seek God only in so far as he has in the first place invited us to approach him. The context, too, may teach us, that faith is not idle or inoperative, and that one test, by which we ought to try those who look for Divine deliverances, is, whether they have recourse to God in a right manner.

With long life will I satisfy him and show him my salvation. **PSALM 91:16** Believers will never be exempt from troubles and embarrassments. God does not promise them a life of ease and luxury, but deliverance from their tribulations. Mention is here made of God glorifying believers, intimating that the deliverance which God extends, is not of a mere temporary nature, but will issue at last in their being advanced to perfect happiness. He puts much honour upon them in the world, and glorifies himself in them conspicuously, but it is not till the completion of their course that he affords them ground of triumph.

Wealth and other worldly comforts must be looked upon as affording some experience of the Divine favour or goodness, but it does not follow that the poor are objects of the Divine displeasure; soundness of body and good health are blessings from God, but we must not conceive on this account that he regards with disapprobation the weak and the infirm. Long life is to be classed among benefits of this kind, and would be bestowed by God upon all his children, were it not for their advantage that they should be taken early out of the world. They are more satisfied with the short period during which they live than the wicked, though their life should be extended for thousands of years. The expression cannot apply to the wicked, that they are *satisfied with length of days;* for however long they live, the thirst of their desires continues to be unquenched. It is life, and nothing more, which they riot in with such eagerness; nor can they be said to have had one moment's enjoyment of that Divine favour and goodness which alone can communicate true satisfaction. The Psalmist might therefore with propriety state it as a privilege peculiarly belonging to the Lord's people, that they are *satisfied with life.* The brief appointed term is reckoned by them to be sufficient, abundantly sufficient. Besides, longevity is never to be compared with eternity. The salvation of God extends far beyond the narrow boundary of earthly existence; and it is to this, whether we live or come to die, that we should principally look. It is with such a view that the Psalmist, after stating all the other benefits which God bestows, adds this as a last clause, that when he has followed them with his fatherly goodness throughout their lives, he at last shows them his salvation.

PSALM 92:1-3

*It is good to praise the L*ORD *and make music to your name, O Most High.* The reason why the Psalmist appropriated this psalm to the Sabbath is sufficiently obvious. That day is not to be holy, in the sense of it being devoted to idleness, as if this could be an acceptable worship to God, but in the sense of our separating ourselves from all other occupations, to engage in meditating upon the Divine works. As our minds are inconstant, we are apt, when exposed to various distractions, to wander from God. We need to be disentangled from all cares if we would seriously apply ourselves to the praises of God. The Psalmist then would teach us that the right observance of the Sabbath does not consist in idleness, as some absurdly imagine, but in the celebration of the Divine name. The argument which he adduces is drawn from the profitableness of the service, for nothing is more encouraging than to know that our labour is not in vain, and that what we engage in meets with the Divine approbation.

To proclaim your love in the morning and your faithfulness at night. Here the Psalmist adverts to the grounds which we have for praising God, that we may not imagine that God calls upon us to engage in this service without reason, or simply in consideration of his greatness and power, but in remembrance of his *goodness* and *faithfulness,* which should inflame our hearts to such exercise, if we had any proper sense and experience of them. He would have us consider, in mentioning these, that not only is God worthy of praise, but that we ourselves are chargeable with ingratitude and perversity should we refuse it. We are the proper objects of his faithfulness and goodness, and it would argue inexcusable indifference if they did not elicit our cordial praise.

Beginning to praise the Lord from earliest dawn, we should continue his praises to the latest hour of the night, this being no more than his goodness and faithfulness deserve. If we begin by celebrating his goodness, we must next take up the subject of his faithfulness. Both will occupy our continued praises, for they stand mutually and inseparably connected.

For you make me glad by your deeds, O LORD. What produces joy in our hearts is the exhibition which God gives of himself as a Father, and of his deep and watchful anxiety for our welfare. As the universe proclaims throughout that God is faithful and good, it becomes us to be diligently observant of these tokens, and to be excited by a holy joy to the celebration of his praise.

PSALM 92:4-15

But you, O LORD, are exalted forever. The Psalmist compares the stability of God's throne with the fluctuating and changeable character of this world, reminding us that we must not judge of him by what we see in the world, where there is nothing of a fixed and enduring nature. God looks down undisturbed from the altitude of heaven upon all the changes of this earthly scene, which neither affect nor have any relation to him. And this the Psalmist brings forward with another view than simply to teach us to distinguish God from his creatures, and put due honour upon his majesty; he would have us learn in our contemplations upon the wonderful and mysterious providence of God, to lift our conceptions above ourselves and this world, since it is only a dark and confused view which our earthly minds can take up. It is with the purpose of leading us into a proper discovery of the Divine judgments which are not seen in the world, that the Psalmist, in making mention of the majesty of God, would remind us, that he does not work according to our ideas, but in a manner corresponding to his own eternal Being. We, short-lived creatures as we are, often thwarted in our attempts, embarrassed and interrupted by many intervening difficulties, and too glad to embrace the first opportunity which offers, are accustomed to advance with precipitation; but we are taught here to lift our eyes unto that eternal and unchangeable throne on which God sits, and in wisdom defers the execution of his judgments. The words accordingly convey more than a simple commendation of the glorious being of God; they are meant to help our faith, and tell us that, although his people may sigh under many an anxious apprehension, God himself, the guardian of their safety, remains on high, and shields them with his everlasting power.

PSALM 93

The LORD reigns. We here see that in the power of God there is exhibited to us matter of confidence; for our not investing God with the power which belongs to him, as we ought to do, and thus wickedly despoiling him of his authority, is the source of that fear and trembling which we very often experience. This, it is true, we dare not do openly, but were we well persuaded of his invincible power, that would be to us an invincible support against all the assaults of temptation. The Psalmist proves that God will not neglect or abandon the world, from the fact that he created it. A simple survey of the world should of itself suffice to attest a Divine Providence. The heavens revolve daily, and, immense as is their fabric, and inconceivable the rapidity of their revolutions, we experience no concussion—no disturbance in the harmony of their motion. The sun, though varying its course every diurnal revolution, returns annually to the same point. The planets, in all their wanderings, maintain their respective positions. How could the earth hang suspended in the air were it not upheld by God's hand? By what means could it maintain itself unmoved, while the heavens above are in constant rapid motion, did not its Divine Maker fix and establish it?

Your statutes stand firm; holiness adorns your house for endless days, O LORD. As yet the Psalmist has insisted upon the excellency of God in the work of creation, and the providential government of the world. Now he speaks of his distinguishing goodness to his chosen people, in making known to them the doctrine which brings salvation. He begins by commending the absolute trustworthiness and truthfulness of the law of God. This being a treasure which was not extended to all nations promiscuously, he adds immediately that the house of God would be adorned with a glory which should last for ever. The Divine goodness is displayed in every part of the world, but the Psalmist justly considers it as of all others the most inestimable blessing, that God should have deposited in his Church the covenant of eternal life, and made his glory principally to shine out of it.

Day 233   A U G U S T   2 0

Blessed is the man you discipline, O LORD, the man you teach from your law. It is only in the Lord's school we can ever learn to maintain composure of mind, and a posture of patient expectation and trust under the pressure of distress. The Psalmist declares that the wisdom which would bear us onward to the end, with an inward peace and courage under long-continued trouble, is not natural to any of us, but must come from God. Accordingly he exclaims, that those are the truly blessed whom God has habituated through his word to the endurance of the cross, and prevented from sinking under adversity by the secret supports and consolations of his own Spirit. The word of God provides us with abundant ground of comfort, and none who rightly avails himself of it need ever count himself unhappy, or yield himself to hopelessness and despondency. One mark by which God distinguishes the true from the false disciple is, that of his being ready and prepared to bear the cross, and waiting quietly for the Divine deliverance, without giving way to fretfulness and impatience. A true patience does not consist in presenting an obstinate resistance to evils, or in that unyielding stubbornness which passed as a virtue with the Stoics, but in a cheerful submission to God, based upon confidence in his grace. The only consideration which will subdue our minds to a tractable submission is, that God, in subjecting us to persecutions, has in view our being ultimately brought into the enjoyment of a rest. Wherever there reigns this persuasion of a rest prepared for the people of God, and a refreshment provided under the heat and turmoil of their trouble, that they may not perish with the world around them,—this will prove enough, and more than enough, to alleviate any present bitterness of affliction. That man is blessed who has learned to be composed and tranquil under trials. The rest intended would then be that of an inward kind, enjoyed by the believer even during the storms of adversity; and the scope of the passage would be, that the truly happy man is he who has so far profited, by the word of God, as to sustain the assault of evils from without, with peace and composure.

PSALM 95

Come, let us bow down in worship . . . he is our God and we are the people of his pasture. While it is true that all men were created to praise God, there are reasons why the Church is specially said to have been formed for that end (Isa. 61:3). The Psalmist was entitled to require this service more particularly from the hands of his chosen people. This is the reason why he impresses upon the children of Abraham the invaluable privilege which God had conferred upon them in taking them under his protection. God may indeed be said in a sense to have done so much for all mankind. But when asserted to be the Shepherd of the Church, more is meant than that he favours her with the common nourishment, support, and government which he extends promiscuously to the whole human family; he is so called because he separates her from the rest of the world, and cherishes her with a peculiar and fatherly regard. His people are here spoken of accordingly as the *people of his pastures*, whom he watches over with peculiar care, and loads with blessings of every kind. The Psalmist wants to press upon the people a sense of the inestimable favour conferred upon them in their adoption, by virtue of which they were called to live under the faithful guardianship of God, and to the enjoyment of every species of blessings.

Today, if you hear his voice, do not harden your hearts. All men's hearts are naturally hard and stony; for Scripture does not speak of this as a disease peculiar to a few, but characteristic in general of all mankind (Ezek. 36:26). It is an inbred pravity; still it is voluntary; we are not insensible in the same manner that stones are, and the man who will not suffer himself to be ruled by God's word, makes that heart, which was hard before, harder still, and is convinced as to his own sense and feeling of obstinacy. The consequence by no means follows from this, that softness of heart—a heart flexible indifferently in either direction, is at our command. The will of man, through natural corruption, is wholly bent to evil; or, to speak more properly, is carried headlong into the commission of it. And yet every man, who disobeys God therein, hardens himself; for the blame of his wrong doing rests with none but himself.

Day 235　AUGUST　22

PSALM 96

For all the gods of the nations are idols, but the LORD *made the heavens.* Religion which meets with the approbation of the multitude is not necessarily the true religion, for then the judgment formed by the Psalmist must have fallen to the ground at once, if religion were a thing to be determined by the suffrages of men, and his worship depended upon the caprice. Be it then that ever so many agree in error, we shall insist after the Holy Ghost that they cannot take from God's glory; for man is vanity himself, and all that comes of him is to be mistrusted.

Say among the nations, "The LORD *reigns."* So far as the order of nature is concerned, we know that it has been Divinely established, and fixed from the beginning; that the same sun, moon, and stars, continue to shine in heaven; that the wicked and the unbelieving are sustained with food, and breathe the vital air, just as do the righteous. Still we are to remember that so long as ungodliness has possession of the minds of men, the world, plunged as it is in darkness, must be considered as thrown into a state of confusion, and of horrible disorder and misrule; for there can be no stability apart from God. The world is very properly here said therefore to be established, that it should not shake, when men are brought back into a state of subjection to God. Though all the creatures should be discharging their various offices, no order can be said to prevail in the world, until God erect his throne and reign amongst men. What more monstrous disorder can be conceived of, than exists where the Creator himself is not acknowledged? If God's method of governing men be to form and regulate their lives to righteousness, we may infer, that however easily men may be satisfied with themselves, all is necessarily wrong with them, till they have been made subject to Christ. All this righteousness of which the Psalmist speaks does not merely have reference to the outward actions. It comprehends a new heart, commencing as it does in the regeneration of the Spirit, by which we are formed again into the likeness of God.

PSALM
97:1-6

The LORD reigns, let the earth be glad; let the distant shores rejoice. God's throne is represented as founded in *justice* and *judgment*, to denote the benefit which we derive from it. The greatest misery which can be conceived of, is that of living without righteousness and judgment, and the Psalmist mentions it as matter of praise exclusively due to God, that when he reigns, righteousness revives in the world. He as evidently denies that we can have any righteousness, till God subjects us to the yoke of his word, by the gentle but powerful influences of his Spirit. A great proportion of men obstinately resist and reject the government of God. Hence the Psalmist was forced to exhibit God in his severer aspect, to teach the wicked that their perverse opposition will not pass unpunished. When God draws near to men in mercy, and they fail to welcome him with proper reverence and respect, this implies impiety of a very aggravated description. The Psalmist intimates that those who should despise God in the person of his only-begotten Son, will feel in due time and certainly the awful weight of his majesty.

The earth sees and trembles. So much is implied in this expression. For the wicked, when they find that their attempts are vain in fighting against God, resort to subterfuge and concealment. The Psalmist declares that they would not succeed by any such vain artifice in hiding themselves from God.

The heavens proclaim his righteousness. Here the Psalmist states that there would be such an illustrious display of the righteousness of God, that the heavens themselves would herald it. The spiritual righteousness of God should be so signally manifested under the reign of Christ as to fill both heaven and earth. The heavens are personified as if they were penetrated with a sense of the righteousness of God, and represented as speaking of it.

PSALM 97:7-9

All who worship images are put to shame. Prevented from coming to the true God by the slowness of their spiritual apprehension, men cannot fail to wander in vanities of their own; and it is the knowledge of the true God which dispels these, as the sun disperses the darkness. All have naturally a something of religion born with them, but owing to the blindness and stupidity, as well as the weakness of our minds, the apprehension which we conceive of God is immediately depraved. Religion is thus the beginning of all superstitions, not in its own nature, but through the darkness which has settled down upon the minds of men, and which prevents them from distinguishing between idols and the true God. The truth of God is effectual when revealed in dispelling and dissipating superstitions. Does the sun absorb the vapours which intervene in the air, and shall not the presence of God himself be effectual much more? We need not wonder then that the Psalmist, in predicting the Kingdom of God, triumphs over the ungodly nations, which boasted in graven images, as when Isaiah, speaking of the rise of the Gospel, adds, "Then all the idols of Egypt shall fall" (Isa. 19:1). Since the knowledge of God has been hid from the view of men, we are taught also that there is no reason to be surprised at the host of superstitions which have overspread the world. We have an exemplification of the same truth in our own day. The knowledge of the true doctrine is extinguished amongst the Turks, the Jews, and Papists, and, as a necessary consequence, the lie immersed in error; for they cannot possibly return to a sound mind, or repent of their errors, when they are ignorant of the true God. There are some who obstinately resist God, of which we have many examples in the Papacy; but we have every reason to believe that they are secretly prostrated by that which they affect to despise, and confounded notwithstanding their opposition.

PSALM 97:10-12

Let those who love the LORD hate evil, for he guards the lives of his faithful ones and delivers them from the hand of the wicked. Those that fear God are here enjoined to practise righteousness, as Paul says, "Everyone who confesses the name of the Lord must turn away from wickedness" (2 Tim. 2:19). He shows from the very nature of God, that we cannot be judged and acknowledged to be his servants unless we depart from sin, and practise holiness. God is in himself the foundation of righteousness, and he must necessarily hate all iniquity, unless we could suppose that he should deny himself; and we have fellowship with him only on the terms of separation from unrighteousness. As the persecution of the wicked is apt to provoke us to seek revenge, and unwarrantable methods of escape, the Psalmist guards us against this temptation, by asserting that God is the keeper and protector of his people. If persuaded of being under the Divine guardianship, we will not strive with the wicked, nor retaliate injury upon those who have wronged us, but commit our safety to him who will faithfully defend it. This gracious act of condescension, by which God takes us under his care, should serve as a check to any impatience we might feel in abstaining from what is evil, and preserving the course of integrity under provocation.

Light is shed upon the righteous and joy on the upright in heart. We have seen that the Lord's people are often treated with the utmost cruelty and injustice, and would seem to be abandoned to the fury of their enemies. The Psalmist reminds us for our encouragement that God, even when he does not immediately deliver his children, upholds them by his secret power. Righteousness does not consist in a mere outward appearance, but comprehends integrity of heart, more being required to constitute us righteous in God's sight than that we simply keep our tongue, hands, or feet, from wickedness. The Lord's people, looking upon God as their Redeemer, should lead a life corresponding to the mercy they have received, and rest contented under all the evils they encounter, with the consciousness that they enjoy his protection.

Day 239 AUGUST 26

Sing to the LORD a new song, for he has done marvelous things; his right hand and his holy arm have worked salvation for him. God had manifested his salvation in a singular and incredible manner. For having spoken of *marvellous things*, he represents this as the sum of all, that God had procured salvation *with his own right hand;* that is, not by human means, or in an ordinary way, but delivering his Church in an unprecedented manner. Isaiah enlarges upon this miracle of God's power: "The Lord looked if there were any to help, and wondered that there was no intercessor: therefore his own arm brought salvation, and his righteousness sustained him" (59:16).

He has remembered his love and his faithfulness to the house of Israel. God, having spoken of the general manifestation of his salvation, he now celebrates his goodness more particularly to his own chosen people. God exhibited himself as a Father to Gentiles as well as Jews; but to the Jews first, who were, so to speak, the first-born. The glory of the Gentiles lay in their being adopted and ingrafted into the holy family of Abraham, and the salvation of the whole world sprung from the promise made to Abraham. The Psalmist therefore very properly observes, that God in redeeming the world, *remembered his truth*, which he had given to Israel his people—which implies that he was influenced by no other motive than that of faithfully performing what he had himself promised. The more clearly to show that the promise was not grounded at all on the merit or righteousness of man, he mentions the *goodness* of God first, and afterwards his *faithfulness*, which stood connected with it. The cause, in short, was not to be found "out of God himself," but in his mere good pleasure, which had been testified long before to Abraham and his posterity. The word *remembered* is used in accommodation to man's apprehension; for what has been long suspended seems to have been forgotten. Upwards of two thousand years elapsed from the time of giving the promise to the appearance of Christ, and as the people of God were subjected to many afflictions and calamities, we need not wonder that they should have sighed, and given way to ominous fears regarding the fulfilment of this redemption.

PSALM 99

Exalt the LORD our God and worship at his footstool; he is holy. God desired to dwell in the midst of his people in such a manner, as not only to direct their thoughts to the outward temple and to the ark of the covenant, but rather to elevate them to things above. Hence the term house or dwelling-place tended to impart courage and confidence to them, that all the faithful might have boldness to draw near unto God freely, whom they beheld coming to meet them of his own accord.

But as the minds of men are prone to superstition, it was necessary to check this propensity, lest they should associate with their notions of God things fleshly and earthly, and their thoughts should be wholly engrossed by the outward forms of worship. The prophet, therefore, in calling the temple God's footstool, desires the godly to elevate their thoughts above it, for he fills heaven and earth with his infinite glory. Nevertheless, by these means he reminds us that true worship can be paid to God no where else than upon mount Zion. For he employs a style of writing such as is calculated to elevate the minds of the godly above the world, and, at the same time, does not in the least degree detract from the holiness of the temple, which alone of all places of the earth God had chosen as the place where he was to be worshipped.

The design of the prophet is to distinguish between legal worship, (which was the only worship that God sanctioned,) and the superstitious rites of the heathen, and thus he summons the children of Abraham to the temple to worship God there after a spiritual manner, because he dwells in celestial glory.

Now that the shadowy dispensation has passed away, God cannot otherwise be properly worshipped, than when we come to him directly through Christ, in whom all the fullness of the Godhead dwells. It were improper and absurd for any one to designate him a *footstool*. For the prophet merely spoke in this manner to show that God was not confined to the visible temple, but that he is to be sought for above all heavens, inasmuch as he is elevated above the whole world.

[Serve] the LORD with gladness; come before him with joyful songs. The prophet commands that God should be *served with gladness*, intimating that his kindness towards his own people is so great as to furnish them with abundant ground for rejoicing. This is better expressed in the third verse, in which he first reprehends the presumption of those men who had wickedly revolted from the true God, both in fashioning for themselves many gods, and in devising various forms of worshipping them. And as a multitude of gods destroys and suppresses the true knowledge of one God only, and tarnishes his glory, the prophet, with great propriety, calls upon all men to bethink themselves, and to cease from robbing God of the honour due to his name; and, at the same time, inveighs against their folly in that, not content with the one God, they became vain in their imaginations. For, however much they are constrained to confess with the mouth that there is a God, the maker of heaven and earth, yet they are ever and anon gradually despoiling him of his glory; and in this manner, the Godhead is, to the utmost extent of their power, reduced to a nonentity. As it is then a most difficult thing to retain men in the practice of the pure worship of God, the prophet, not without reason, recalls the world from its accustomed vanity, and commands them to recognise God as God. For we must attend to this short definition of the knowledge of him, namely, that his glory be preserved unimpaired, and that no deity be opposed to him that might obscure the glory of his name. True, indeed, in the Papacy, God still retains his name, but as his glory is not comprehended in the mere letters of his name, it is certain that there he is not recognised as God. Know, therefore, that the true worship of God cannot be preserved in all its integrity until the base profanation of his glory, which is the inseparable attendant of superstition, be completely reformed.

PSALM 100:3-5

Know that the LORD is God. It is he who has made us. To say *God made us* is a very generally acknowledged truth; but not to advert to the ingratitude so usual among men, that scarcely one among a hundred seriously acknowledges that he holds his existence from God, although, when hardly put to it, they do not deny that they were created out of nothing; yet every man makes a god of himself, and virtually worships himself, when he ascribes to his own power what God declares belongs to him alone. Moreover, it must be remembered that the prophet is not here speaking of creation in general, but of that spiritual regeneration by which he creates anew his image of his elect. Believers are the persons whom the prophet here declares to be God's workmanship, not that they were made men in their mother's womb, but in that sense in which Paul, in Ephesians 2:10, calls them *the workmanship* of God, because they are created unto good works which God has before ordained that they should walk in them; and in reality this agrees best with the subsequent context. For when he says, *We are his people, and the sheep of his pasture,* he evidently refers to that distinguishing grace which led God to set apart his children for his heritage, in order that he may, as it were, nourish them under his wings, which is a much greater privilege than that of merely being born men. Should any person be disposed to boast that he has of himself become a new man, who is there that would not hold in abhorrence such a base attempt to rob God of that which belongs to him? Nor must we attribute this spiritual birth to our earthly parents, as if by their own power they begot us; for what could a corrupt seed produce? Still the majority of men do not hesitate to claim for themselves all the praise of the spiritual life. Else what do the preachers mean by free-will, unless it be to tell us that by our own endeavours we have, from being sons of Adam, become the sons of God? In opposition to this, the prophet in calling us the *people of God,* informs us that it is of his own good will that we are spiritually regenerated. And by denominating us *the sheep of his pasture,* he gives us to know that through the same grace which has once been imparted to us, we continue safe and unimpaired to the end.

PSALM 101

My eyes will be on the faithful in the land, that they may dwell with me. David here lays down another virtue of a wise prince, when he affirms that it will be his care to make all *the faithful of the land* his intimate friends,—that he will avail himself of their good offices, and have as domestic servants such only as are distinguished for personal worth. He will exercise discretion and care, that, instead of taking persons into his service indiscriminately, he may wisely determine each man's character, so as to have those who live a life of strict integrity as his most intimate friends, and that he may intrust them with the offices of state. He speaks of the *faithful* in the first place, because, although a man may possess talents of a high order, yet if his servants and officers are not of a corresponding character, his subjects will experience hardly any advantage from his uncorrupted integrity. Servants are the hands of a prince, and whatever he determines for the good of his subjects they will wickedly overthrow it, provided they are avaricious, fraudulent, or rapacious. This has been more than sufficiently demonstrated by experience. Most kings, indeed, passing over the good and the upright, or, which is worse, driving them away from them, purposely seek to have as servants those who are like themselves, and who may prove to be fit tools for their tyranny; yes, even good and well disposed princes often manifest so much indolence and irresolution as to suffer themselves to be governed by the worst counsels, and inconsiderately prostitute the offices of state by conferring them on the unworthy.

No one who practices deceit will dwell in my house. It is impossible that he who does not maintain good order in his own house, can be a fit person for holding the government of a whole realm. The authority which cannot preserve its influence under the domestic roof is of little worth in state affairs.

**PSALM
102:1-3**

Hear my prayer, O LORD; let my cry for help come to you.
The Psalmist's earnestness shows that these words were not
dictated to be pronounced by the careless and light-hearted,
which could not have been done without grossly insulting
God. In speaking thus, the captive Jews bear testimony to
the severe and excruciating distress which they endured, and
therefore the ardent desire to obtain some alleviation with
which they were inflamed. No person could utter these words
with the mouth without profaning the name of God, unless
he were, at the same time, actuated by a sincere and earnest
affection of the heart. We ought particularly to attend to the circumstance already adverted to, that we are thus stirred up by the Holy Spirit
to the duty of prayer in behalf of the common welfare of the Church.
While each man takes sufficient care of his own individual interests,
there is scarcely one in a hundred affected as he ought to be with the
calamities of the Church. We have, therefore, the more need of incitements, even as we see the prophet here endeavouring, by an accumulation of words, to correct our coldness and sloth. The heart ought to move
and direct the tongue to prayer; but, as it often flags or performs its duty
in a slow and sluggish manner, it requires to be aided by the tongue. As
the heart, on the one hand, ought to go before the words, and frame
them, so the tongue, on the other, aids and remedies the coldness and
torpor of the heart. True believers may indeed often pray not only
earnestly but also fervently, while yet not a single word proceeds from the
mouth. There is, however, no doubt that by *crying* the prophet means the
vehemence into which grief constrains us to break forth.

*Make haste, answer me.** When God permits us to lay open before
him our infirmities without reserve, and patiently bears with our foolishness, he deals in a way of great tenderness towards us. To pour out our
complaints before him after the manner of little children would certainly
be to treat his Majesty with very little reverence, were it not that he has
been pleased to allow us such freedom.

PSALM 102:4-7

*My heart is smitten and withered like grass.** The Psalmist intends to express something more than that his heart was withered, and his bones reduced to a state of dryness. His language implies, that as the grass, when it is cut down, can no longer receive juice from the earth, nor retain the life and vigour which it derived from the root, so his heart being, as it were, torn and cut off from its root, was deprived of its natural nourishment.

*I have forgotten to eat my bread.** The meaning here is: My sorrow has been so great, that I have neglected my ordinary food. The Jews, it is true, during their captivity in Babylon, did eat their food; and it would have been an evidence of their having fallen into sinful despair, had they starved themselves to death. But what he means to say is, that he was so afflicted with sorrow as to refuse all delights, and to deprived himself even of food and drink. True believers may cease for a time to partake of their ordinary food, when, by voluntary fasting, they humbly beseech God to turn away his wrath, but the prophet does not here speak of that kind of abstinence from bodily sustenance. He speaks of such as is the effect of extreme mental distress, which is accompanied with a loathing of food, and a weariness of all things.

*I have become like a pelican in the wilderness.** In this verse there are pointed out certain melancholy birds, whose place of abode is in the holes of mountains and in deserts, and whose note, instead of being delightful and sweet to the ear, inspires those who hear it with terror. He says he is removed from the society of men, and has become almost like a wild beast of the forest. Although the people of God dwelt in a well cultivated and fertile region, yet the whole country of Chaldea and Assyria was to them like a wilderness, since their hearts were bound by the strongest ties of affection to the temple, and to their native country from which they had been expelled. The third similitude, which is taken from *the sparrow,* denotes such grief as produces the greatest uneasiness.

PSALM 102:8-9

All day long my enemies taunt me. The faithful, to excite the compassion of God towards them, tell him that they are not only objects of mockery to their enemies, but also that they swore by them. The indignity complained of is, that the ungodly so shamefully triumphed over God's chosen people, as even to borrow from their calamities a form of swearing and imprecation. When the ungodly give themselves loose reins in pouring forth against us contumelious language, let us learn to fortify ourselves with this armour, by which such kind of temptation, however sharp, may be overcome. The Holy Spirit, in dictating to the faithful this form of prayer, meant to testify that God is moved by such revilings to succour his people; even as we find it stated in Isaiah 37:23, "Who is it you have insulted and blasphemed? Against whom have you raised your voice, and lifted your eyes in pride? Against the Holy One of Israel!" It is surely an inestimable comfort that the more insolent our enemies are against us, the more is God incited to gird himself to aid us.

Because of your great anger and your wrath.* The prophet now declares that the greatness of his grief proceeded not only from outward troubles and calamities, but from a sense that these were a punishment inflicted upon him by God. And surely there is nothing which ought to wound our hearts more deeply, than when we feel that God is angry with us. The meaning then amounts to this—O Lord!, I do not confine my attention to those things which would engage the mind of worldly men; but I rather turn my thoughts to your wrath; for were it not that you are angry with us, we would have been still enjoying the inheritance given us by you, from which we have justly been expelled by your displeasure. When God then strikes us with his hand, we should not merely groan under the strokes inflicted upon us, as foolish men usually do, but should chiefly look to the cause that we may be truly humbled. This is a lesson which it would be of great advantage to us to learn.

PSALM
102:10

For you have taken me up and thrown me aside. It is as if the Psalmist said, Lord, you have crushed me more severely by throwing me down headlong from on high, than if I had merely fallen from the station which I occupied. But this seems to be another amplification of his grief. Nothing being more bitter to an individual than to be reduced from a happy condition to extreme misery, the prophet mournfully complains that the chosen people were deprived of the distinguished advantages which God had conferred upon them in time past, so that the very remembrance of his former goodness, which should have afforded consolation to them, embittered their sorrow. Nor was it the effect of ingratitude to turn the consideration of the divine benefits, which they had formerly received, into matter of sadness; since they acknowledged that their being reduced to such a state of wretchedness and degradation was through their own sins. God has no delight in changing, as if, after having given us some taste of his goodness, he intended forthwith to deprive us of it. As his goodness is inexhaustible, so his blessing would flow upon us without intermission, were it not for our sins which break off the course of it. Although, then, the remembrance of God's benefits ought to assuage our sorrows, yet still it is a great aggravation of our calamity to have fallen from an elevated position, and to find that we have so provoked his anger, as to make him withdraw from us his benignant and bountiful hand. Thus when we consider that the image of God, which distinguished Adam, was the brightness of the celestial glory; and when, on the contrary, we now see the ignominy and degradation to which God has subjected us in token of his wrath, this contrast cannot surely fail of making us feel more deeply the wretchedness of our condition. Whenever, therefore, God, after having stripped us of the blessing which he had conferred upon us, gives us up to reproach, let us learn that we have so much the greater cause to lament, because through our own fault, we have turned light into darkness.

PSALM 102:11

My days are like the evening shadow that declines.* When the sun is directly over our heads, that is to say, at mid-day, we do not observe such sudden changes of the shadows which his light produces; but when he begins to decline towards the west the shadows vary almost every moment. What the Psalmist here attributes to the afflicted Church seems indeed to be equally applicable to all men; but he had a special reason for employing this comparison to illustrate the condition of the Church when subjected to the calamity of exile. It is true, that as soon as we advance towards old age, we speedily fall into decay. But the complaint here is, that this befell the people of God in the very flower of their age. By the term *days* is to be understood the whole course of their life; and the meaning is, that the captivity was to the godly as the setting of the sun, because they quickly failed. In the end of the verse the similitude of *withered grass*, used a little before, is repeated, to intimate that their life during the captivity was involved in many sorrows which dried up in them the very sap of life. Nor is this wonderful, since to live in that condition would have been worse than a hundred deaths had they not been sustained by the hope of future deliverance. But although they were not altogether overwhelmed by temptation, they must have been in great distress, because they saw themselves abandoned by God.

But you, O LORD, sit enthroned forever. The prophet, for his own encouragement, sets before himself the eternity of God. This knowledge of the blessed repose enjoyed by God enables us the better to perceive that our life is a mere illusion. But the inspired writer, calling to remembrance the promises by which God had declared that he would make the Church the object of his special care, and trusting to that sacred and indissoluble bond, has no hesitation in representing all the godly languishing, though they were in a state of suffering and wretchedness, as partakers of this celestial glory in which God dwells.

Your renown endures through all generations. What advantage would we derive from this eternity and immutability of God's being, unless we had in our hearts the knowledge of him, which, produced by his gracious covenant, begets in us the confidence arising from a mutual relationship between him and us? The meaning then is, "We are like withered grass, we are decaying every moment, we are not far from death, yes rather, we are, as it were, already dwelling in the grave; but since you, O God! has made a covenant with us, by which you have promised to protect and defend your own people, and have brought yourself into a gracious relationship to us, giving us the fullest assurance that you will always dwell in the midst of us, instead of desponding, we must be of good courage; and although we may see only ground for despair if we depend upon ourselves, we ought nevertheless to lift up our minds to the heavenly throne, from which you will at length stretch forth your hand to help us." Whoever is in a moderate degree acquainted with the sacred writings, will readily acknowledge that whenever we are besieged with death, in a variety of forms, we should reason thus: As God continues unchangeably the same—"without variableness of shadow of turning"—nothing can hinder him from aiding us; and this he will do, because we have his word, by which he has laid himself under obligation to us, and because he has deposited with us his own memorial, which contains in it a sacred and indissoluble bond of fellowship.

You will arise and have compassion on Zion. We have here the conclusion drawn from the truth stated in the preceding verse: God is eternal, and therefore he will have compassion upon Zion. God's eternity is to be considered as impressed upon the memorial, or word, by which he has brought himself under obligation to maintain our welfare. Besides, as he is not destitute of the power, and as it is impossible for him to deny himself, we ought not to entertain any apprehension of his failing to accomplish, in his own time, what he has promised.

PSALM
102:13-15

For it is time to show favor to her; the appointed time has come. When the prophet treats of the restoration of the Church, he sets forth the divine mercy as its cause. He represents this mercy under a twofold aspect, and therefore employs different words. In the first place, as in the matter under consideration, the good deserts of men are entirely out of the question, and as God cannot be led from any cause external to himself to build up his Church, the prophet traces the cause of it solely to the free goodness of God. In the second place, he contemplates this mercy as connected with the Divine promises. In magnifying the Divine mercy, his design was to teach true believers that their safety depended on it alone.

That the faithful might not sink into despondency, through the long continuance of their calamities, they needed to be supported by the hope that an end to their captivity had been appointed by God, and that it would not extend beyond seventy years. Daniel was employed in meditating on this very topic, when he "turned to the Lord God and pleaded with him in prayer and petition, in fasting, and in sackcloth and ashes" for the re-establishment of the Church (9:20). In like manner, the object now aimed at by the prophet was to encourage both himself and others to confidence in prayer, putting God in mind of this remarkable prophecy, as an argument to induce him to bring to a termination their melancholy captivity. And surely if, in our prayers, we do not continually remember the Divine promises, we only cast forth our desires into the air like smoke. It is, however, to be observed, that although the time of the promised deliverance was approaching, or had already arrived, yet the prophet does not cease from the exercise of prayer, to which God stirs us up by means of his word. And although the time was fixed, yet he calls upon God, for the performance of his covenant, in such a manner, as that he is still betaking himself to his free goodness alone; for the promises by which God brings himself under obligation to us do not, in any degree, obscure his grace.

For the LORD will . . . appear in his glory. This verse refers to the manifestation which God made of himself when he brought forth his Church from the darkness of death. In like manner, by again gathering to himself his people who were dispersed, and in raising his Church, as it were, from death to life, he appeared in his glory. It is surely no ordinary consolation to know that the love of God towards us is so great, that he will have his glory to shine forth in our salvation.

PSALM 102:16-24

He will respond to the prayer of the destitute; he will not despise their plea. It is worthy of notice, that the deliverance of the chosen tribes is ascribed to the prayers of the faithful. God's mercy was indeed the sole cause which led him to deliver his Church, according as he had graciously promised this blessing to her; but to stir up true believers to greater earnestness in prayer, he promises that what he has purposed to do of his own good pleasure, he will grant in answer to their requests. Nor is there any inconsistency between these two truths, that God preserves the Church in the exercise of his free mercy, and that he preserves her in answer to the prayers of his people; for as their prayers are connected with the free promises, the effect of the former depends entirely upon the latter.

The more effectually to induce God to listen to his prayer, he calls upon all the godly, who were then in the world, to join with him in the same request. It unquestionably, very much contributes to increase the confidence of success, when supplications are made by all the people of God together, as if in the person of one man, according to what the Apostle Paul declares (2 Cor. 1:11), "Then many will give thanks on our behalf for the gracious favour granted us in answer to the prayers of many."

PSALM 102:25-28

In the beginning you laid the foundations of the earth, and the heavens are the work of your hands. Two subjects are here brought under our consideration. The first is, that since the heavens themselves are in the sight of God almost as evanescent as smoke, the frailty of the whole human race is such as may well excite his compassion; and the second is, that although there is no stability in the heavens and the earth, yet the Church shall continue stedfast for ever, because she is upheld by the eternal truth of God. By the first of these positions, true believers are taught to consider with all humility, when they come into the divine presence, how frail and transitory their condition is, that they may bring nothing with them but their own emptiness. Such self-abasement is the first step to our obtaining favour in the sight of God, even as he also affirms that he is moved by the sight of our miseries to be merciful to us. The comparison taken from the heavens is a very happy illustration; for how long have they continued to exist, when contrasted with the brief span of human life, which passes or rather flies away so swiftly? How many generations of men have passed away since the creation, while the heavens still continue as they were amidst this continual fluctuation? Again, so beautiful is their arrangement, and so excellent their frame-work, that the whole fabric proclaims itself to be the product of *God's hands.* And yet neither the long period during which the heavens have existed, nor their fair embellishment, will exempt them from perishing. What then shall become of us poor mortals, who die when we are as yet scarcely born? for there is no part of our life which does not rapidly hasten to death.

The heavens will perish,* but you remain. Two things are to be here attended to; first, that the heavens are actually subject to corruption in consequence of the fall of man; and, secondly, that they shall be so renewed as to warrant the prophet to say that *they shall perish;* for this renovation will be so complete that they shall not be the same heavens but other heavens. The amount is, that to whatever quarter we turn our eyes, we will see everywhere nothing but ground for despair till we come to God. What is there in us but rottenness and corruption? and what else are we but a mirror of death? Again, what are the changes which the whole world undergoes but a kind of presage, yes a prelude of destruction? If the whole frame-work of the world is hastening to its end, what will become of the human race? If all nations are doomed to perish, what stability will there be in men individually considered? We ought therefore to seek stability nowhere else but in God.

PSALM 103:1-3

Praise the LORD, O my soul; all my inmost being, praise his holy name. The prophet, by stirring himself to gratitude, gives by his own example a lesson to every man of the duty incumbent upon him. And doubtless our slothfulness in this matter has need of continual incitement. If even the prophet, who was inflamed with a more intense and fervent zeal than other men, was not free from this malady, of which his earnestness in stimulating himself is a plain confession, how much more necessary is it for us, who have abundant experience of our own torpor, to apply the same means for our quickening? The Holy Spirit, by his mouth, indirectly upbraids us on account of our not being more diligent in praising God, and at the same time points out the remedy, that every man many descend into himself and correct his own sluggishness. Not content with calling his *soul* (by which he unquestionably means the seat of the understanding and affections) to bless God, the prophet expressly adds his *inward parts*, addressing as it were his own mind and heart, and all the faculties of both. When he thus speaks to himself, it is as if, removed from the presence of men, he examined himself before God.

And forget not all his benefits. Here he instructs us that God is not deficient on his part in furnishing us with abundant matter for praising him. It is our own ingratitude which hinders us from engaging in this exercise. In the first place, he teaches us that the reason why God deals with such liberality towards us is, that we may be led to celebrate his praise; but at the same time he condemns our inconstancy, which hurries us away to any other object rather than God. How is it that we are so listless and drowsy in the performance of this the chief exercise of true religion, if it is not because our shameful and wicked forgetfulness buries in our hearts the innumerable benefits of God, which are openly manifest to heaven and earth? Did we only retain the remembrance of them, the prophet assures us that we would be sufficiently inclined to perform our duty, since the sole prohibition which he lays upon us is, *not to forget them.*

PSALM 103:4-7

He redeems my life from the pit and crowns me with love and compassions.* The Psalmist expresses more plainly what our condition is previous to God's curing our maladies—that we are dead and adjudged to the grave. The consideration that the mercy of God delivers us from death and destruction ought, therefore, to lead us to prize it the more highly. If the resurrection of the soul from the grave is the first step of spiritual life, what room for self-glorification is left to man? The prophet next teaches us that the incomparable grace of God shines forth in the very commencement of our salvation, as well as in its whole progress; and the more to enhance the commendation of this grace, he adds the word *compassions* in the plural number. He asserts that we are *surrounded* with them; as if he had said, Before, behind, on all sides, above and beneath, the grace of God presents itself to us in immeasurable abundance; so that there is no place devoid of it. The same truth he afterwards amplifies in these words, *your mouth is satisfied,* by which metaphor he alludes to the free indulgence of the palate, to which we surrender ourselves when we have a well-furnished table; for those who have scanty fare dare scarcely eat till they are half satisfied. Not that he approves of gluttony in greedily devouring God's benefits, as men give loose reins to intemperance whenever they have great abundance; but he borrowed this phraseology from the common custom of men, to teach us that whatever good things our hearts can wish flow to us from God's bounty, even to perfect satisfaction. The Psalmist next adds, that God was constantly infusing into him new vigour, so that his strength continued unimpaired, even as the prophet Isaiah (65:20), in discoursing on the restoration of the Church, says that a man of a hundred years old shall be like a child. By this mode of expression, he intimates that God, along with a very abundant supply of all good things, communicates to him also inward vigour, that he may enjoy them; and thus his strength was as it were continually renewed.

PSALM 103:7-8

He made known his ways to Moses, his deeds to the people of Israel. We must understand in general, that the true knowledge of God corresponds to what faith discovers in the written Word; for it is not his will that we should search into his secret essence, except in so far as he makes himself known to us, a point worthy of our special notice. We see that whenever God is mentioned, the minds of men are perversely carried away to cold speculations, and fix their attention on things which meet our eyes, and which afford a vivid reflection of his character. To whatever subjects men apply their minds, there is none from which they will derive greater advantage than from continual meditation on his wisdom, goodness, righteousness, and mercy; and especially the knowledge of his goodness is fitted both to build up our faith, and to illustrate his praises. Accordingly Paul, in Ephesians 3:18, declares that our height, length, breadth, and depth, consists in knowing the unspeakable riches of grace, which have been manifested to us in Christ. This also is the reason why David, copying from Moses, magnifies by a variety of terms the mercy of God. In the first place, as we have no worse fault than that devilish arrogance which robs God of his due praise, and which yet is so deeply rooted in us, that it cannot be easily eradicated; God rises up, and that he may bring to nought the heaven-daring presumption of the flesh, asserts in lofty terms his own mercy, by which alone we stand. Again, when we ought to rely upon the grace of God, our minds tremble or waver, and there is nothing in which we find greater difficulty than to acknowledge that he is merciful to us. David, to meet and overcome this doubting state of mind, after the example of Moses, employs these synonymous terms: first, that God is merciful; secondly, that he is gracious; thirdly, that he patiently and compassionately bears with the sins of men; and, lastly, that he is abundant in mercy and goodness.

PSALM 103:9-13

He will not always chide, nor will he harbour his anger for-ever.* David, from the attributes ascribed to God in the pre-ceding verse, draws the conclusion, that when God has been offended, he will not be irreconcilable, since, from his nature, he is always inclined to forgive. It was necessary to add this statement; for our sins would be continually shutting the gate against his goodness were there not some way of appeasing his anger. David tacitly intimates that God insti-tutes an action against sinners to lay them low under a true sense of their guilt; and that yet he recedes from it whenever he sees them subdued and humbled. God speaks in a different manner in Genesis 6:3, where he says, "My Spirit shall no longer strive with man," because the wickedness of men being fully proved, it was then time to condemn them. But here David maintains that God will not always chide, because so easy is he to be reconciled, and so ready to pardon, that he does not rigidly exact from us what strict justice might demand.

As far as the east is from the west, so far has he removed our transgres-sions from us. The Psalmist confirms that he does not treat in general of what God is towards the whole world, but of the character in which he manifests himself towards the faithful. Whence also it is evident that he does not here speak of that mercy by which God reconciles us to himself at the first, but of that with which he continually follows those whom he has embraced with his fatherly love. There is one kind of mercy by which he restores us from death to life, while as yet we are strangers to him, and another by which he sustains this restored life; for that blessing would forthwith be lost did he not confirm it in us by daily pardoning our sins. Whence also we gather how egregiously the Papists trifle in imagining that the free remission of sins is bestowed only once, and that afterwards righteousness is acquired or retained by the merit of good works, and that whatever guilt we contract is removed by satisfactions. Here David does not limit to a moment of time the mercy by which God reconciles us to himself in not imputing to us our sins, but extends it even to the close of life.

PSALM
103:14-16

For he knows how we are formed, he remembers that we are dust. David here annihilates all the worth which men would arrogate to themselves, and asserts that it is the consideration of our misery, and that alone, which moves God to exercise patience towards us. This again we ought carefully to mark, not only for the purpose of subduing the pride of our flesh, but also that a sense of our unworthiness may not prevent us from trusting in God. The more wretched and despicable our condition is, the more inclined is God to show mercy, for the remembrance that we are clay and dust is enough to incite him to do us good.

As for man, his days are like grass . . . the wind blows over it and it is gone, and its place remembers it no more. All the excellency of man withers away like a fading flower at the first blast of the wind. Although, as long as we live in this world, we are adorned with natural gifts, and "live, and move, and have our being in God" (Acts 17:28); yet as we have nothing except what is dependent on the will of another, and which may be taken from us every hour, our life is only a show or phantom that passes away. The subject here treated, is properly the brevity of life, to which God has a regard in so mercifully pardoning us, as it is said in another psalm:—"He remembered that they were but flesh, a wind that passes away, and comes not again" (Ps. 78:39). If it is asked why David, making no mention of the soul, which yet is the principal part of man, declares us to be dust and clay, the answer is, that it is enough to induce God mercifully to sustain us, when he sees that nothing surpasses our life in frailty. And although the soul, after it has departed from the prison of the body, remains alive, yet its doing so does not arise from any inherent power of its own. Were God to withdraw his grace, the soul would be nothing more than a puff or blast, even as the body is dust; and thus there would doubtless be found in the whole man nothing but mere vanity.

PSALM
103:17

From everlasting to everlasting the LORD'S *love is with those who fear him, and his righteousness with their children's children.* The Psalmist leaves nothing to men to rely upon but the mercy of God; for it would be egregious folly to seek a ground of confidence in themselves. After having shown the utter emptiness of men, he adds the seasonable consolation, that, although they have no intrinsic excellence, which does not vanish into smoke, yet God is an inexhaustible fountain of life, to supply their wants. This contrast is to be particularly observed; for whom does he thus divest of all excellence? The faithful who are regenerated by the Spirit of God, and who worship him with true devotion, these are the persons whom he leaves nothing on which their hope may rest but the mere goodness of God. As the Divine goodness is everlasting, the weakness and frailty of the faithful does not prevent them from boasting of eternal salvation to the close of life, and even in death itself. David does not confine their hope within the limits of time: he views it as commensurate in the duration with the grace on which it is founded. To *goodness* is subjoined *righteousness,* denoting the protection by which God defends and preserves his own people. He is then called righteous, not because he rewards every man according to his desert, but because he deals faithfully with his saints, in spreading the hand of his protection over them. The prophet has properly placed this righteousness after goodness, as being the effect of goodness. He also asserts that it extends to the children and children's children, according to these words in Deuteronomy 7:9, "God keeps his covenant of love to a thousand generations." It is a singular proof of his love that he not only receives each of us individually into his favour, but also herein associates with us our offspring, as it were by hereditary right, that they may be partakers of the same adoption. How shall he cast us off, who, in receiving our children and children's children into his protection, shows to us in their persons how precious our salvation is in his sight?

PSALM 103:18

[The LORD'S love is] with those who keep his covenant and remember to obey his precepts. As nothing is more easy than for hypocrites to flatter themselves under false pretext, that they are in favour with God, or for degenerate children groundlessly to apply to themselves the promises made to their fathers, it is again stated, by way of exception, in the 18th verse, that God is merciful only to *those who,* on their part, *keep his covenant,* which the unbelieving make of none effect by their wickedness. The *keeping,* or *observing of the covenant,* which is here put instead of the *fear of God,* is worthy of notice; for thus David intimates that none are the true worshippers of God but those who reverently obey his Word. Very far from this are the Papists, who, thinking themselves equal to the angels in holiness, nevertheless shake off the yoke of God, like wild beasts, by trampling under foot his Holy Word. David, therefore, rightly judges of men's godliness, by their submitting themselves to the Word of God, and following the rule which he has prescribed to them. As the covenant begins with a solemn article containing the promise of grace, faith and prayer are required, above all things, to the proper keeping of it.

[Who] remember to obey his precepts. Although God is continually putting us in mind of them, yet we soon slide away to worldly cares—are confused by a multiplicity of avocations, and are lulled asleep by many allurements. Thus forgetfulness extinguishes the light of truth, unless the faithful stir up themselves from time to time. David tells us that this remembrance of God's statutes has an invigorating effect when men employ themselves in doing them. Many are sufficiently forward to discourse upon them with their tongues whose feet are very slow, and whose hands are well nigh dead, in regard to active service.

PSALM 103:19-22

The LORD *has established his throne in heaven, and his kingdom rules over all.* David, having recounted the benefits by which God lays each of us in particular, and also the whole Church, under obligation to him, now extols in general his infinite glory. The amount is, that whenever God is mentioned, men should learn to ascend in their contemplations above the whole world, because his majesty transcends the heavens; and they should further learn not to measure his power by that of man, since it has under its control all kingdoms and dominions.

Praise the LORD, *you his angels, you mighty ones who do his bidding, who obey his word.* That none may think that earthly creatures only are here put in subjection to God, the Psalmist chiefly addresses the angels. In calling upon them to join in praising God, he teaches both himself and all the godly, that there is not a better nor a more desirable exercise than to praise God, he teaches both himself and all the godly that there is not a better nor a more desirable exercise than to praise God, since there is not a more excellent service in which even the angels are employed. The angels are doubtless too willing and prompt in the discharge of this duty, to stand in need of incitement from us. With what face then, it may be said, can we, whose slothfulness is so great, take it upon us to exhort them? But although these exalted beings run swiftly before us, and we with difficulty come lagging after them, yet David enjoins them to sing God's praises for our sake, that by their example he may awaken us from our drowsiness. The object he has in view, is to be noted, which is, by addressing his discourse to the angels to teach us, that the highest end which they propose to themselves is to advance the divine glory. Accordingly, while in one sentence he clothes them with *strength,* in the immediately following, he describes them as hanging on God's word, waiting for his orders,—*You who obey his word.* However great the power, as if he had said, with which you are endued, you reckon nothing more honourable than to obey God. And it is not only said that they execute God's commandments, but to express more distinctly the promptitude of their obedience, it is asserted, that they are always ready to perform whatever he commands them.

*He wraps himself in light as with a garment, he spreads out the heavens as a curtain.** If men attempt to reach the infinite height to which God is exalted, although they fly above the clouds, they must fail in the midst of their course. Those who seek to see him in his naked majesty are certainly very foolish. That we may enjoy the sight of him, he must come forth to view with his clothing; that is to say, we must cast our eyes upon the very beautiful fabric of the world in which he wishes to be seen by us, and not be too curious and rash in searching into his secret essence. Now, since God presents himself to us clothed with light, those who are seeking pretexts for their living without the knowledge of him, cannot allege in excuse of their slothfulness, that he is hidden in profound darkness. When it is said that *the heavens are a curtain*, it is not meant that under them God hides himself, but that by them his majesty and glory are displayed; being, as it were, his royal pavilion.

He . . . rides on the wings of the wind. The winds do not blow by chance, nor the lightnings flash by a fortuitous impulse, but that God, in the exercise of his sovereign power, rules and controls all the agitations and disturbances of the atmosphere. From this doctrine a twofold advantage may be reaped. In the first place, if at any time noxious winds arise, if the south wind corrupt the air, or if the north wind scorch the corn, and not only tear up trees by the root, but overthrow houses, and if other winds destroy the fruits of the earth, we ought to tremble under these scourges of Providence. In the second place, if on the other hand, God moderate the excessive heat by a gentle cooling breeze, if he purify the polluted atmosphere by the north wind, or if he moisten the parched ground by the south winds; in this we ought to contemplate his goodness.

PSALM 104:5-26

He set the earth on its foundations; it can never be moved. Nothing in the world is stable except in as far as it is sustained by the hand of God. The world did not originate from itself, consequently, the whole order of nature depends on nothing else than his appointment, by which each element has its own peculiar property. Nor is the language of the prophet to be viewed merely as an exhortation to give thanks to God; it is also intended to strengthen our confidence in regard to the future, that we may not live in the world in a state of constant fear and anxiety, as we must have done had not God testified that he has given the earth for a habitation to men. It is a singular blessing, which he bestows upon us, in his causing us to dwell upon the earth with undisturbed minds, by giving us the assurance that he has established it upon everlasting pillars. Although cities often perish by earthquakes, yet the body of the earth itself remains. Yes, all the agitations which befall it more fully confirm to us the truth, that the earth would be swallowed up every moment were it not preserved by the secret power of God.

Wine that gladdens the heart of man. In these words we are taught, that God not only provides for men's necessity, and bestows upon them as much as is sufficient for the ordinary purposes of life, but that in his goodness he deals still more bountifully with them by cheering their hearts with wine and oil. Nature would certainly be satisfied with water to drink; and therefore the addition of wine is owning to God's superabundant liberality. The proper rule with respect to the use of bodily sustenance, is to partake of it that it may sustain, but not oppress us. As the prophet in this account of the divine goodness in providence makes no reference to the excesses of men, we gather from his words that it is lawful to use wine not only in cases of necessity, but also thereby to make us merry. This mirth must however be tempered with sobriety, first, that men may not forget themselves, drown their senses, and destroy their strength, but rejoice before their God, according to the injunction of Moses (Lev. 23:40); and, secondly, that they may exhilarate their minds under a sense of gratitude, so as to be rendered more active in the service of God.

PSALM 104:27-28

These all look to you to give them their food at the proper time. The prophet here again describes God as acting the part of the master of a household, and a foster-father towards all sorts of living creatures, by providing liberally for them. He had said before, that God made food to grow on the mountains for the support of cattle, and that sustenance is ministered to the very lions by the hand of the same God, although they live upon prey. Now he amplifies this wonder of the divine beneficence by an additional circumstance. While the different species of living creatures are almost innumerable, and the number in each species is so great, there is yet not one of them which does not stand in need of daily food. They could not continue in existence even for a few days, unless God were to supply their daily need, and to nourish each of them in particular. We thus see why there is so great a diversity of fruits; for God assigns and appoints to each species of living creatures the food suitable and proper for them. The brute beasts are not indeed endued with reason and judgment to seek the supply of their wants from God, but stooping towards the earth, they seek to fill themselves with food; still the prophet speaks with propriety, when he represents them as waiting upon God; for their hunger must be relieved by his bounty, else they would soon die. Nor is the specification of *the season* when God furnishes them with food superfluous, since God lays up in store for them, that they may have the means of sustenance during the whole course of the year. As the earth in winter shuts up her bowels, what would become of them if he did not provide them with food for a long time? The miracle, then, is the greater from the circumstance, that God, by making the earth fruitful as stated seasons, extends in this way his blessing to the rest of the year which threatens us with hunger and famine. Now if he supply wild and brute beasts with sustenance in due season, by which they are fed to the full, his blessing will doubtless be to us an inexhaustible source of plenty, provided we ourselves do not hinder it from flowing to us by our unbelief.

PSALM 104:29-32

When you hide your face, they are terrified; when you take away their breath, they die and return to the dust. In these words, the Psalmist declares, that we stand or fall according to the will of God. We continue to live, as long as he sustains us by his power; but no sooner does he withdraw his life-giving spirit than we die. Even Plato knew this, who so often teaches that, properly speaking, there is but one God, and that all things subsist, or have their being only in him. Nor do I doubt, that it was the will of God, by means of that heathen writer, to awaken all men to the knowledge, that they derive their life from another source than from themselves. In the first place, the Psalmist asserts, that *if God hide his face they are afraid;* and, secondly, that *if he take away their spirit they die, and return to their dust;* by which words he points out, that when God vouchsafes to look upon us, that look gives us life, and that as long as his serene countenance shines, it inspires all the creatures with life. Our blindness then is doubly inexcusable, if we do not on our part cast our eyes upon that goodness which gives life to the whole world. The prophet describes step by step the destruction of living creatures, upon God's withdrawing from them his secret energy, that from the contrast he may the better commend that continued inspiration, by which all things are maintained in life and vigour. He could have gone further, and have asserted, that all things, unless upheld in being by God, would return to nothing; but he was content with affirming in general and popular language, that whatever is not cherished by him falls into corruption.

When we see the world daily decaying, and daily renewed, the life-giving power of God is reflected to us herein as in a mirror. All the deaths which take place among living creatures, are just so many examples of our nothingness, so to speak; and when others are produced and grow up in their place, we have in that presented to us a renewal of the world. Since then the world daily dies, and is daily renewed in its various parts, the manifest conclusion is, that it subsists only by a secret virtue derived from God.

PSALM
104:33-35

I will sing to the LORD all my life; I will sing praise to my God as long as I live. Here the Psalmist points out to others their duty by his own example, declaring, that throughout the whole course of his life he will proclaim the praise of God without ever growing weary of that exercise. The only boundary which he fixes to the celebration of God's praises is death; not that the saints, when they pass from this world into another state of existence, desist from this religious duty, but because the end for which we are created is, that the divine name may be celebrated by us on the earth. Conscious of his unworthiness of offer to God so precious a sacrifice, he humbly prays, *that the praises which he will sing to God may be acceptable to him,* although they proceed from polluted lips. It is true, that there is nothing more acceptable to God, nor anything of which he more approves, than the publication of his praises, even as there is no service which he more peculiarly requires us to perform. But as our uncleanness defiles that which in its own nature is most holy, the prophet with good reason betakes himself to the goodness of God, and on this ground alone pleads that he would accept of his song of praise. Accordingly, the Apostle, in Hebrews 13:15, teaches that our sacrifices of thanksgiving are well pleasing to God, when they are offered to him through Christ. It being however the case, that while all men indiscriminately enjoy the benefits of God, there are yet very few who look to the author of them, the prophet subjoins the clause, *I will rejoice in the Lord;* intimating, that this is a rare virtue; for nothing is more difficult than to call home the mind from those wild and erratic joys, which disperse themselves through heaven and earth in which they vanish, that it may keep itself fixed on God alone.

But may sinners vanish from the earth and the wicked be no more. Let us then take care so to weigh the providence of God, as that being wholly devoted to obeying him, we may rightly and purely use the benefits which he sanctifies for our enjoying them. Further, let us be grieved, that such precious treasures are wickedly squandered away, and let us regard it as monstrous and detestable, that men not only forget their Maker, but also, as it were, purposely turn to a perverse and an unworthy end, whatever good things he has bestowed upon them.

PSALM
105:1-3

Give thanks to the LORD, *call on his name; make known among the nations what he has done.* The object of these words simply is, that the offspring of Abraham should place all their blessedness in the free adoption of God. It was indeed a blessing not to be despised that they had been created men, that they had been cherished in the world by God's fatherly care, and that they had received sustenance at his hand; but it was a far more distinguished privilege to have been chosen to be his peculiar people. While the whole human race are condemned in Adam, the condition of the Israelites was so different from all other nations, as to give them ground to boast, that they were consecrated to God. This is the reason why the prophet heaps together so many words in commendation of this grace. He does not treat of the government of the whole world as he did in the preceding psalm, but he celebrates the fatherly favour which God has manifested towards the children of Israel. He indeed names in general *his works*, and *his wonders*, but he limits both to that spiritual covenant by which God made choice of a church, which might lead on earth a heavenly life. He does not intend to include as among these wonders, that the sun, moon and stars, daily rise to give light to the world, that the earth produces its fruit in its seasons, that every living creature is supplied with abundance of all good things for its food, and that the human family are liberally provided with so many conveniences; but he celebrates the sovereign grace of God, by which he chose for himself from amongst the lost race of Adam a small portion to whom he might show himself to be a father. Accordingly, he enjoins them *to rejoice in the name of God,* and *to call upon him;* a privilege by which the Church alone is distinguished. Whence it follows, that this language is addressed to none but true believers, whom God would have to glory in his name, since he has taken them under his special protection.

Look to the LORD and his strength; seek his face always. Although he had in the preceding verse characterised the faithful by the honourable designation, *those who seek God,* yet the Psalmist again exhorts them to earnestness in seeking him, which is not an unnecessary exhortation. Seeking God, it is true, is the mark by which all genuine saints are particularly distinguished from the men of the world; but they come far short of seeking him with due ardour; and, accordingly, they have always need of incitements, to urge them on to this exercise, although they run of their own accord. Those whom the prophet here stirs up to seek God are not fickle persons, nor such as are altogether indolent, and who cleave to the impurities of earth, but those who with a prompt and ready mind already aim at doing this; and he thus stimulates them, because he perceives that they are obstructed by many impediments from advancing in their course with sufficient rapidity. However willing then we may be, we have notwithstanding need of such incitement to correct our slowness. *The strength* and *face of God,* doubtless refer to that kind of manifestation by which God, accommodating himself to the rudeness of the times, drew at that time true believers to himself. The ark of the covenant is in many other places called both *the strength* and *the face of God,* because by that symbol the people were reminded, that he was near them, and also really experienced his power. The more familiarly then God showed himself to them, with the more promptitude and alacrity would the prophet have them to apply their hearts in seeking him; and the aid by which God relieves our weakness should prove an additional stimulus to our zeal. Modesty also is recommended to us, that, mindful of our slowness in seeking God, we may keep the way which he has prescribed to us, and may not despise the rudiments through which he by little and little conducts us to himself. It is added *continually,* that no person may grow weary in this exercise, or, inflated with a foolish opinion of having reached perfection, may neglect the external aids of piety, as is done by many, who, after having advanced a few degrees in the knowledge of God, exempt themselves from the common rank of others, as if they were elevated above the angels.

PSALM 105:6-10

O descendants of Abraham his servant, O sons of Jacob, his chosen ones. The Psalmist addresses himself by name to his own countrymen, whom, as has been stated, God had bound to himself by a special adoption. Before they were born children of Abraham, they were already heirs of the covenant, because they derived their origin from the holy fathers, and the fathers themselves had not acquired this prerogative by their own merit or worth, but had been freely chosen; for this is the reason why Jacob is called *God's chosen.* From this covenant the Psalmist infers that although the government of God extends through the whole world, and although he executes his judgment in all places, he was nevertheless especially the God of that one people, (verse 7) according to the statement in the song of Moses (Deut. 32:8–9), "When the Most High divided to the nations their inheritance, when he separated the sons of Adam, he set the bounds of the people, according to the number of the children of Israel: For the Lord's portion is his people; Jacob is the lot of his inheritance." The prophet again intended to show that the reason why the children of Israel excelled others was not because they were better than others, but because such was the good pleasure of God. If the divine judgments are extended through all the regions of the globe, the condition of all nations is in this respect equal. Whence it follows that the difference referred to proceeded from the love of God,—that the source of the superiority of the Israelites to other nations was his free favour. Although, then, he is the rightful proprietor of the whole earth, it is declared that he chose one people over whom he might reign. This is a doctrine which applies to us also at the present day. If we duly ponder our calling, we will undoubtedly find that God has not been induced from anything out of himself to prefer us to others, but that he was pleased to do so purely from his own free grace.

PSALM 105:11-25

"To you I will give the land of Canaan as the portion you will inherit." The prophet shows that a part of what God had promised to the fathers had received its complete accomplishment. His drift is to intimate that they did not possess the land of Canaan by any other right than because it was the legitimate inheritance of Abraham according to the covenant which God had made with him. If man exhibit the promised earnest of a contract, he does not violate the contract. When, therefore, the prophet proves by a visible symbol that God did not make a covenant with his servants in vain, and that he did not disappoint their hope, he does not take away or abolish the other blessings included in it. No, rather, when the Israelites heard that they possessed the land of Canaan by right of inheritance, because they were the chosen people of God, it became them to look beyond this, and to take a comprehensive view of all the privileges by which he had vouchsafed to distinguish them. Hence it is to be noted, that when he in part fulfils his promises towards us, we are base and ungrateful if this experience does not conduce to the confirmation of our faith. Whenever he shows himself to be a father towards us, he undoubtedly really seals on our hearts the power and efficacy of his word. But if the land of Canaan ought to have led the children of Israel in their contemplations to heaven, since they knew that they had been brought into it on account of the covenant which God had made with them, the consideration that he has given to us his Christ "in whom all the promises are yes and amen" (2 Cor. 1:20), ought to have much greater weight with us.

And he sent a man before them—Joseph, sold as a slave. God so governs human affairs by his secret controlling influence, and overrules men's wicked devices to a right end, as that his judgments are notwithstanding uncontaminated by the depravity of men. The brethren of Joseph wickedly conspire his death; they also wrongfully sell him: the fault is in themselves. Contemplate now how God directs and controls all. By the hand of these brethren he provides for the good both of themselves and of their father Jacob, yes for that of the whole Church.

PSALM 105:26-30

He sent Moses his servant, and Aaron, whom he had chosen. Moses is called *the servant of the Lord*, to teach us that he was not self-elected to his office, and that he attempted nothing by his own authority, but, had been intrusted. The same thing is expressed still more plainly with respect to Aaron, when he is said *to have been chosen.* What is attributed to each of these eminent men in particular, applies equally to both, and therefore the sentence ought to be explained thus: God sent Moses and Aaron, his servants, not because of their own intrinsic fitness, or because they spontaneously offered to him their service, but because he chose them. This passage teaches us, that those who are engaged in active and useful service for the Church, are not prepared exclusively by their own exertions, or framed to it by their own talents, but are stirred up thereto by God. Moses was a man of heroic virtue: but, considered merely in himself, he was nothing. Accordingly, the prophet would have all that is accounted worthy of remembrance in Moses, as well as in Aaron, to be ascribed to God alone. Thus it appears that whatever men do for the welfare of the Church, they owe the power of doing it to God, who, of his free goodness, has been pleased thus to honour them.

Their land teemed with frogs, which went up into the bedrooms of their rulers. In this verse we learn how easily, and as it were by a kind of mockery, God humbles those who pride themselves in the flesh. He did not gather together an army to fight against the Egyptians, nor did he forthwith arm his angels, or thunder out of heaven, but brought forth frogs, which contemptuously trampled upon the pride of that haughty nation, who held in contempt the whole world beside. It would have been no disgrace for them to have been conquered by powerful enemies; but how dishonourable was it to be vanquished by frogs? God thus intended to show that he has no need of powerful hosts to destroy the wicked; for he can do this, as it were in sport, whenever he pleases.

He spoke, and there came swarms of flies, and gnats throughout their country. By the word *spoke*, the Psalmist intimates that *the flies* and *lice* came not forth by chance. The command, we know, was uttered by the mouth of Moses; for although God could have given the command himself, he interposed Moses as his herald. God, however, gave no less efficacy to his word, when he commanded it to be uttered by a man, than if he himself had thundered from heaven. When the minister executes his commission faithfully, by speaking only what God puts into his mouth, the inward power of the Holy Spirit is joined with his outward voice.

*And he brought them forth with silver and gold.** The prophet celebrates the grace of God which preserved the chosen people untouched and safe from all these plagues. If both parties had been indiscriminately afflicted with them, the hand of God would not have been so signally manifest. But now when the Israelites, amidst so many calamities, experienced an entire exemption from harm, this difference exhibits to us, as in a picture, God's fatherly care about his own people.

For he remembered his holy promise. The Psalmist again mentions the cause why God dealt so graciously with that people, and sustained them so tenderly, namely, that he might fulfil his promise; for he had entered into a covenant with Abraham, engaging to be the God of his seed. Nor did the prophets without cause teach so carefully as we find them doing, that the free covenant is the fountain whence the deliverance, and the continual welfare of the people flowed. Thereby the grace of God became better known, since what took place, so far from happening upon the sudden, and without anticipation, was only the fulfilment of what he had promised four hundred years before. God then, for ages previous to this, gave the light of his word of promise, that his grace and truth might be brought the more distinctly into view. God had spoken it to Abraham; but the force of the covenant did not die with him. God continued to show himself faithful towards the posterity of the patriarch.

PSALM 106:1-13

Then they believed his promises and sang his praise. In stating that they believed God's word, and sang his praise, the prophet does not say this to their commendation, but rather to increase, in a twofold manner, their guilt; because, being convinced by such indubitable testimony, they yet instantly resumed their wonted disposition of mind, and began to rebel against God, as if they had never beheld his wonderful works. How very inexcusable was that impiety which in a moment could forget the remarkable benefits which they had been constrained to admit! Overpowered by the grandeur of God's works, they were, he says, in spite of themselves, compelled to believe in God, and give glory to him, and thus the criminality of their rebellion was increased; because, although their stubbornness was overcome, yet they immediately relapsed into their former state of unbelief. A question, however, arises, seeing that true faith always corresponds with the nature of the word, and as the word is an incorruptible seed, so though it may happen to almost, it never can be totally destroyed. But there is a temporary faith, as Mark calls it (4:17), which is not so much the fruit of the Spirit of regeneration, as of a certain mutable affection, and so it soon passes away. It is not a voluntary faith which is here extolled by the prophet, but rather that which is the result of compulsion, namely, because men, whether they will or not, by a sense which they have of the power of God, are constrained to show some reverence for him. This passage ought to be well considered, that men, when once they have yielded submission to God, may not deceive themselves, but may know that the touchstone of faith is when they spontaneously receive the word of God, and constantly continue firm in their obedience to it.

We must here observe what we have seen elsewhere, that the only cause why men are so ungrateful towards God, is their despising of his benefits. Were the remembrance of these to take fast hold of our hearts, it would serve as a bridle to keep us in his fear.

PSALM 106:14-18

In the desert they gave in to their craving; in the wasteland they put God to the test. Should anyone inquire in what way they did not attend to God's counsel, he answers, because they had indulged in the gratification of their lusts; for the only way of acting with proper moderation is, when God rules and presides over our affections. It is therefore the more necessary to bridle that strong tendency to fleshly lusts which naturally rage within us. For whoever allows himself to desire more than is needful, openly sets himself in direct opposition to God, inasmuch as all fleshly lusts are directly opposed to him.

To tempt God is not to acquiesce in his will, but to desire more than he is willing to grant. And since there are a variety of modes of tempting God, the prophet here adverts to one mode of doing so, namely, that the people had been so presumptuous as to limit God to means of their own devising; and thus, in rejecting the way which they ought to have followed, they ascribed to God a property altogether novel, as much as to say, If God do not feed us with flesh we will not regard him as God. He gave them the food which ought to have satisfied them. And though God is not limited by any means whatsoever, yet it is his will that our minds be rendered subservient to the means which he has appointed. For instance, although he can nourish us without bread, nevertheless it is his will that our life be sustained by such provision; and if we neglect it, and wish to point out to him another way of nourishing us, we tempt his power.

The earth opened up and swallowed Dathan. The heinousness of their sin may be seen in the magnitude of the punishment by which it was visited. But the design of the prophet was to accuse and reprove publicly the obstinacy of the people, who, so far from being bettered by their corrections (although the vengeance of God was so terrible as almost to move the very stones,) conducted themselves the more perversely.

PSALM 106:19-20

At Horeb they made a calf and worshiped an idol cast from metal. Here he represents their rebellion as exceedingly base, in that they abandoned the true worship of God, and made to themselves a calf. From this the prophet infers, that God had been robbed of his honour, and that all his glory had been tarnished. And surely it is so; for although the idolaters feign to serve God with great zeal, yet when, at the same time, they represent to themselves a God visible, they abandon the true God, and impiously make for themselves an idol. But he reproaches them with being guilty of still greater impiety, when he says, *after the likeness of an ox that eats grass;* and contrasts with it *their honour* or *glory*. For seeing that God had clothed them with his own glory, what madness was it to substitute in place of him not only an ox, but the inanimate form of an ox, as if there were any resemblance between God who creates all kinds of foods, and that stupid animal which feeds upon grass?

It is necessary, however, to observe the design of the prophet, which is to point out the blindness of men as more base and abominable, because not contenting themselves with any common form of superstition, but casting off all shame, they give themselves up to the most shocking forms of worshipping God. Had the people formed for themselves a likeness of God under the likeness of a man, even that would have been impiously robbing God of his due; how much more shameful was their conduct when they assimilated God to an ox? When men preserve their life by eating and drinking, they acknowledge how frail they are, because they derive from dead creatures the means of its continuation. How much greater is the dishonour done to God when he is compared to the brutal tribes? Moreover, the comparison referred to increases the enormity of their guilt. For what credit was it for a holy people to worship the inanimate likeness of an ox instead of the true God? But God had condescended to spread out the overshadowing wings of his glory upon the children of Abraham, that he might put on them the highest honour. Therefore, in denuding themselves of this honour, they had exposed their own baseness to the derision of all the nations of the earth.

PSALM 106:21-34

They forgot the God who saved them, who had done great things in Egypt. The prophet again repeats that the people had sinned not simply through ignorance, but also wilfully, inasmuch as God had already given a very palpable manifestation of his power and glory. And as he makes himself known in the creation of the heavens and of the earth, the blindness of men is totally inexcusable. But far more aggravating is the sin of the children of Israel, who, after God had made himself known to them, in the most condescending manner, cast him off altogether, and gave themselves up to the practice of brutish idolatry. And God having from heaven put forth his Almighty power for their salvation, there must surely be no little importance attached to such displays of his power as proclaim the praise and honour of his great name. Had he merely given an ordinary token of his power, even that ought to have attracted so much consideration as should have kept the people in the fear and worship of God.

So he said he would destroy them. To represent how highly God was offended, the prophet says that he had purposed to destroy the transgressors: not that God is subject to human passions, to be very angry for a little, and then immediately afterwards, on being appeased, changes his purpose; for God, in his secret counsel, had resolved upon their forgiveness, even as he actually pardoned them. But the prophet makes mention of another purpose, by which God designed to strike the people with terror, that coming to know and acknowledge the greatness of their sin, they might be humbled on account of it. This is that repentance so frequently referred to in the Scriptures. Not that God is mutable in himself; but he speaks after the manner of men, that we may be affected with a more feeling sense of his wrath: like a king who had resolved to pardon an offender, yet sitted him before his judgment-seat, the more effectually to impress him with the magnitude of the kindness done to him. God, therefore, while he keeps to himself his secret purpose, declared openly to the people that they had committed a trespass which deserved to be punished with eternal death.

PSALM 106:35-36

But they mingled with the nations and adopted their customs. He describes what was the result of this foolish humanity; namely, that they were defiled with the pollutions of the nations whom they had spared. Had they exclusively inhabited the land of Canaan, they would have more easily retained the pure worship of God. Allured by the influence of such neighbours, it is not wonderful that they soon degenerated from the footsteps of their fathers, for we are more inclined to follow the example of the bad than of the good. And now he speaks of the descendants of those who had so frequently provoked God's anger in the wilderness, and declares, that as the same unbelief, rebellion, and ingratitude, were rampant in the succeeding race, they were no better than their fathers.

In mingling with the heathens they openly rejected the distinguishing loving-kindness of God, who adopted them as his children, under the express condition that they should be separated from these profane nations. Therefore, in associating with them indiscriminately, they render this holy covenant of no effect. When he adds, *that they learned their works,* he warns us, that nothing is more dangerous than associating with the ungodly; because, being more prone to follow the vice than virtue, it cannot but be, that the more conversant we are with corruption, the more widely will it spread. In such circumstances, the utmost care and caution are requisite, lest the wicked, with whom we come into contact, infect us by their vitiated morals; and particularly where there is danger of relapsing into idolatry, to which we are all naturally prone. What, then, will be the effect produced upon us when instigated by others to commit sin, but to add sin to sin? The prophet, therefore, declares that the Jews are already so much under the tuition of the heathen as to abandon themselves to the practice of their idolatrous rites. He adds that this *issued in their overthrow,* in order that their obstinate attachment to their follies, and their despising the chastisements of God, may more palpably appear.

They sacrificed their sons and their daughters to demons. The prophet here mentions one species of superstition which demonstrates the awful blindness of the people; their not hesitating to sacrifice their sons and daughters to devils. In applying such an abominable designation to the sin of the people, he means to exhibit it in more hateful colours. From this we learn that inconsiderate zeal is a flimsy pretext in favour of any act of devotion. For by how much the Jews were under the influence of burning zeal, by so much does the prophet convict them with being guilty of greater wickedness; because their madness carried them away to such a pitch of enthusiasm, that they did not spare even their own offspring. Were good intentions meritorious, as idolaters suppose, then indeed the laying aside of all natural affection in sacrificing their own children was a deed deserving of the highest praise. But when men act under the impulse of their own capricious humour, the more they occupy themselves with acts of external worship, the more do they increase their guilt.

They shed innocent blood. Should anyone object that Abraham is praised, because he did not withhold his only son, the answer is plain, That he did it in obedience to God's command, so that every vestige of inhumanity was effaced by means of the purity of faith. For if obedience is better than sacrifice (1 Sam. 15:22), it is the best rule both for morality and religion. It is an awful manifestation of God's vindictive wrath, when the superstitious heathens, left to their own inventions, become hardened in deeds of horrid cruelty. As often as the martyrs put their life in jeopardy in defence of the truth, the incense of such a sacrifice is pleasing to God. But when the two Romans, by name Decii, in an execrable manner devoted themselves unto death, that was an act of atrocious impiety. It is not without just cause, therefore, that the prophet enhances the guilt of the people by this consideration, that to the perverse mode of worshipping God, they had added excessive cruelty.

PSALM
106:43-48

Many times he delivered them, but they were bent on rebellion and they wasted away in their sin. As the wicked perversity of the people was manifested in that God's severe chastisements failed to produce their reformation, so now, on the other hand, the prophet deduces the detestable hardness of their hearts from the fact, that all the benefits which they had received from God could not bend them into obedience. They did, indeed, in the time of their afflictions, groan under the burden of them; but when God not only mitigated their punishment, but also granted them wonderful deliverances, can their subsequent backsliding be excused? It becomes us to bear in mind, that there, as in a mirror, we have a picture of the nature of all mankind; for let God but adopt those very means which he employed in relation to the Israelites, in order to reclaim the majority of the sons of men, how comparatively few are there who will not be found continuing in the very same state as they were? and if he either humble us by the severity of his rod, or melt us by his kindness, the effect is only temporary; because, though he visit us with correction upon correction, and heap kindness upon kindness, yet we very soon relapse into our wonted vicious practices. As for the Jews, their insensate stupidity was insufferable, in that, notwithstanding the many and magnificent deliverances which God wrought out for them, they did not cease from their backslidings.

Moreover, he informs us, that though they were most deserving of all their afflictions, yet their groanings were heard; whence they learn, that God, in his unwearied kindness, did not cease to strive with them on account of their perverseness of spirit.

For what pity was this, to hear the cry of those who turned a deaf ear to his wise instructions, and were regardless of all his warnings and threatenings? And yet after all this forbearance and long-suffering, their exceedingly depraved hearts remained unchanged.

Then they cried to the LORD in their trouble, and he saved them from their distress. Those who are wandering in desert places are often pinched with hunger and thirst in consequence of finding no place in which to lodge; and who, when all hope of deliverance fails them, then cry unto God. There may be not a few whose hope does not centre on God, who, nevertheless, are constrained, by some invisible disposition of mind, to come to him, when under the pressure of dire necessity. And this is the plan which God sometimes pursues, in order to extort from such persons the acknowledgement that deliverance is to be sought for from no other quarter than from himself alone; and even the ungodly, who, while living voluptuously, scoff at him, he constrains, in spite of themselves, to invoke his name. It has been customary in all ages for heathens, who look upon religion as a fable, when compelled by stern necessity, to call upon God for help. Did they do so in jest? By no means; it was by a secret natural instinct that they were led to reverence God's name, which formerly they held in derision. The Spirit of God, therefore, here narrates what frequently takes place, namely, that persons destitute of piety and faith, and who have no desire to have anything to do with God, if placed in perilous circumstances, are constrained by natural instinct, and without any proper conception of what they are doing, to call on the name of God. Since it is only in dubious and desperate cases that they betake themselves to God, this acknowledgement which they make of their helplessnesss is a palpable proof of their stupidity, that in the season of peace and tranquillity they neglect him, so much are they then under the intoxicating influence of their own prosperity; and notwithstanding that the germ of piety is planted in their hearts, they nevertheless never dream of learning wisdom, unless when driven by the dint of adversity; meaning, to learn the wisdom of acknowledging that there is a God in heaven who directs every event.

PSALM 107:20-41

He sent forth his word and healed them; he rescued them from the grave. In saying that they are delivered from destruction, the prophet shows that he is here alluding to those diseases which, in the opinion of men, are incurable, and from which few are delivered. Besides, he contrasts God's assistance with all the remedies which are in the power of man to apply; as if he should say, that their disease having baffled the skill of earthly physicians, their recovery has been entirely owing to the exertion of God's power. It is proper also to notice the manner in which their recovery is effected; God has but to will it, or to speak the word, and instantly all diseases, and even death itself, are expelled. I do not regard this as exclusively referring to the faithful, as many expositors do. Indeed, it is of comparatively little consequence to us to be the subjects of bodily care, if our souls still remain unsanctified by the word of God; and hence it is the intention of the prophet that we consider the mercy of God as extending to the evil and unthankful. The meaning of the passage, therefore, is, that diseases neither come upon us by chance, nor are to be ascribed to natural causes alone, but are to be viewed as God's messengers executing his commands; so that we must believe that the same person that sent them can easily remove them, and for this purpose he has only to speak the word. And since we now perceive the drift of the passage, we ought to attend to the very appropriate analogy contained in it. Corporeal maladies are not removed except by the word or command of God, much less are men's souls restored to the enjoyment of spiritual life, except this word be apprehended by faith.

He turned the parched grounds into flowing springs.* Here is an account of changes which it would be the height of folly to attribute to chance. Fruitful lands become unfruitful, and barren lands assume the new aspect of freshness and fruitfulness. It is, however, not sufficient merely to observe, that these wonderful revolutions of the surface of the earth are the result of God's overruling purpose, unless we also observe, in the second place, what the prophet does not omit, that the earth is cursed by him on account of the iniquity of its inhabitants, who prove themselves to be undeserving of being so amply sustained by his bountiful hand.

The upright see and rejoice. In whatever manner the wicked may be constrained to recognise God as the supreme ruler of the universe, nevertheless, in seeing they see not, and derive nothing from the sight, except that their conduct is rendered the more inexcusable. But the righteous are not only able to form a good and sound judgment of these events, they also spontaneously open their eyes to contemplate the equity, goodness, and wisdom of God, the sight and knowledge of which are refreshing to them. For the joy which they experience in this exercise is a pledge that their thus observing these things was the spontaneous effusion of their hearts.

Whoever is wise, let him heed these things and consider the great love of the LORD. We are now informed that men begin to be wise when they turn their whole attention to the contemplation of the works of God, and that all others beside are fools. For however much they may pique themselves upon their superior acuteness and subtlety, all this is of no avail so long as they shut their eyes against the light which is presented to them. In employing this interrogatory form of address, he indirectly adverts to that false persuasion which prevails in the world, at the very time when the most daring heaven-despiser esteems himself to be the wisest of men; as if he should say, that all those who do not properly observe the providence of God, will be found to be nothing but fools. This caution is the more necessary, since we find that some of the greatest of philosophers were so mischievous as to devote their talents to obscure and conceal the providence of God, and, entirely overlooking his agency, ascribed all to secondary causes.

By the term, *observe,* he informs us, that the bare apprehension of the works of God is not enough,—they must be carefully considered in order that the knowledge of them may be deliberately and maturely digested. And, therefore, that it may be engraven upon our hearts, we must make these works the theme of our attentive and constant meditation.

PSALM 108

God has spoken in his holiness. Hitherto David has adverted to the proofs which had come under the observation of the whole nation, and from which they might easily see that God had manifested his favour in a manner new, and for many years unprecedented. He had raised the nation from a state of deep distress to prosperity, and had changed the aspect of affairs so far, that one victory was following another in rapid succession. But now he calls their attention to a point of still greater importance, the divine promise—the fact that God had previously declared all this with his own mouth. However numerous and striking may be the practical demonstrations we receive of the favour of God, we can never recognise them, except in connection with this previously revealed promise. David says that God had spoken *in his holiness,* as he adverts to the fact of the truth of the oracle having been confirmed, and the constancy and efficacy of the promise having been placed beyond all doubt by numerous proofs of a practical kind. It might be true that he had gained many victories, and that these had tended to encourage his heart; but he intimates, that no testimony which he had received of this kind gave him so much satisfaction as the word. This accords with the general experience of the Lord's people. Cheered, as they unquestionably are, by every expression of the divine goodness, still faith must ever be considered as holding the highest place—as being that which dissipates their worst sorrows, and quickens them even when dead to a happiness which is not of this world. Nor does David mean that he merely rejoiced himself. He includes, in general, all who feared the Lord in that kingdom. And now he proceeds to give the sum of the oracle, which it is observable that he does in such a way as to show, in the very narration of it, how firmly he believed in its truth: for he speaks of it as something which admitted of no doubt whatsoever, and boasts that he would do what God had promised.

Day 283 OCTOBER 9

May the iniquity of his fathers be remembered before the LORD; *may the sin of his mother never be blotted out.* As the destruction which the prophet denounces against the houses and families of the wicked is so extensive, that God punishes them in the person of their posterity, so he desires that *God may remember the iniquities of their fathers and mothers,* in order that their condemnation may be complete; and this is a principle in perfect accordance with the commonly received doctrine of Scripture. God, out of regard to his covenant, which is in force to a thousand generations, extends and continues his mercy towards posterity; but he also punishes iniquity unto the third and fourth generation. In doing this he does not involve the guiltless with the wicked indiscriminately, but by withholding from the reprobate the grace and illumination of his Spirit, he prepares the vessels of wrath for destruction, even before they are born (Rom. 9:21). To the common sense of mankind, the thought of such severity is horrifying: but then we must recollect, that if we attempt to measure the secret and inscrutable judgments of God by our finite minds, we do him wrong. Struck with horror at the severity of this threatening, let us improve it as the means of filling us with reverence and godly fear. In reference to the language of Ezekiel 18:20, "The son shall not bear the iniquity of the father, but the soul that sins, it shall die"; we know that in these words he disproves the groundless complaints of the people, who, boasting that they were guiltless, imagined that they were punished wrongfully. When, however, God continues his vengeance from the father to the children, he leaves them no room for palliation or complaint, because they are all equally guilty. Vengeance commences when God in withdrawing his Spirit, both from the children and the fathers, delivers them over to Satan. It is the design of David that the vengeance of God may be so manifest, that the whole world may acquiesce in his equity as a judge.

PSALM 109:21-26

But you, O Sovereign LORD, deal well with me for your name's sake. After having fled to God as his guardian and deliverer, the Psalmist appears to take occasion, from this circumstance, to encourage himself in prayer; even as all the pious reflections by which the faithful exercise and strengthen their faith, stimulate them to call on the name of God. All our prayers will vanish in smoke, unless they are grounded upon the mercy of God. The case of Christ was indeed a peculiar one, inasmuch as it was by his own righteousness that he appeased the wrath of his Father towards us. As, however, his human nature was entirely dependant on the good pleasure of God, so it was his will, by his own example, to direct us to the same source. What can we do, seeing that the most upright among us is constrained to acknowledge that he is chargeable with the commission of much sin; surely we never can make God our debtor? It follows, therefore, that God, on account of the benignity of his nature, takes us under his protection; and that, because of the goodness of his mercy, he desires his grace may shine forth in us. In coming to God, we must always remember that we must possess the testimony of a good conscience, and must beware of harbouring the thought that we have any inherent righteousness which would render God our debtor, or that we deserve any recompense at his hands. For if, in the preservation of this short and frail life, God manifests the glory of his name and of his goodness, how much more ought all confidence in good works to be laid aside, when the subject-matter referred to is life heavenly and eternal? If, in the prolonging of my life for a short time on earth, his name is thereby glorified, by manifesting of his own accord towards me his benignity and liberality; when, therefore, having delivered me from the tyranny of Satan, he adopts me into his family, washes away my impurity in the blood of Christ, regenerates me by his Holy Spirit, unites me to his Son, and conducts me to the life of heaven,—then, assuredly, the more bountifully he treats me, the less should I be disposed to arrogate to myself any portion of the praise.

Let them know that it is your hand, that you, O LORD, have done it. These words may be viewed as referring both to David's deliverance from his enemies, and to his affliction; his desire being to attribute his deliverance mainly to the grace of God; because, in opposing the hand of God to fortune and to all human means of deliverance, it is plainly his intention that God should be recognised as the only author of it. This deserves to be carefully considered by us, for however anxious we are to be delivered by the hand of God, yet there is scarcely one among a hundred who makes the manifestation of God's glory his chief end; that glory for which we ought to have a greater regard than for our own safety, because it is far more excellent. Whosoever then is desirous that the ungodly may be constrained to acknowledge the power of God, ought the more carefully to take heed to the help of God which in his own case he experiences; for it would be most absurd to point out the hand of God to others, if our minds have not recognised it.

With my mouth I will greatly extol the LORD. David declares that he will acknowledge the goodness of God, not only in some obscure corner, but also in the great assembly of the people, and among governors and those of noble rank. In the celebration of God's praises, there can be no question that these must issue from the heart before they are uttered by the lips; at the same time, it would be an indication of great coldness, and of lack of fervour, did not the tongue unite with the heart in this exercise. The reason why David makes mention of the tongue only is, that he takes it for granted that, unless there be a pouring out of the heart before God, those praises which reach no further than the ear are vain and frivolous; and, therefore, from the very bottom of his soul, he pours forth his heart-felt gratitude in fervent strains of praise; and this he does, from the same motives which ought to influence all the faithful—the desire of mutual edification; for to act otherwise would be to rob God of the honour which belongs to him.

PSALM 110:1-3

The LORD said to my Lord: "Sit at my right hand." Earthly kings may indeed be said to sit at God's right hand, inasmuch as they reign by his authority; here, however, something more lofty is expressed, in that one king is chosen in a peculiar manner, and elevated to the rank of power and dignity next to God, of which dignity the twilight only appeared in David, while in Christ it shone forth in meridian splendour. And as God's right hand is elevated far above all angels, it follows that he who is seated there is exalted above all creatures. The simile is borrowed from what is customary among earthly kings, that the person who is seated at his right hand is said to be next to him, and hence the Son, by whom the Father governs the world, is by this session represented as metaphorically invested with supreme dominion.

Until I make your enemies a footstool for your feet. By these words the prophet affirms that Christ would subdue all the opposition which his enemies in their tumultuous rage might employ for the subversion of his kingdom. At the same time, he intimates that the kingdom of Christ would never enjoy tranquillity until he had conquered his numerous and formidable enemies. And even should the whole world direct their machinations to the overthrow of Christ's royal throne, David here declares that it would remain unmoved and unmoveable, while all they who rise up against it shall be ruined. From this let us learn that, however numerous those enemies may be who conspire against the Son of God, and attempt the subversion of his kingdom, all will be unavailing, for they shall never prevail against God's immutable purpose, but, on the contrary, they shall, by the greatness of his power, be laid prostrate at Christ's feet. And as this prediction will not be accomplished before the last day, it must be that the kingdom of Christ will be assailed by many enemies from time to time until the end of the world; and thus by-and-bye it is said, *you will rule in the midst of your enemies.*

PSALM
110:4-7

"You are a priest forever, in the order of Melchizedek." This verse is satisfactory proof that the person here spoken of is none other than Christ. The Holy Ghost here refers to something specific and peculiar, as distinguishing and separating this king from all other kings. This, too, is the well known title with which Melchizedek was honoured by Moses (Gen. 14:18). Anciently among heathen nations kings were wont to exercise the priestly office; but Melchizedek is called "the priest of the most high God." The priesthood of Christ is invested with great importance, seeing that it is ratified by the oath of God. And, in fact, it is the very turning point upon which our salvation depends; because, but for our reliance on Christ our Mediator, we would be all debarred from entering into God's presence. In prayer, too, nothing is more needful for us than sure confidence in God, and therefore he not only invites us to come to him, but also by an oath has appointed an advocate for the purpose of obtaining acceptance for us in his sight. As for those who shut the door against themselves, they subject themselves to the guilt of impeaching him with being a God of untruth and of perjury. It is in this way that the Apostle argues the disannulling of the Levitical priesthood; because, while that remained entire, God would not have sworn that there should be a new order or priesthood unless some change had been contemplated. What is more, when he promises a new priest, it is certain that he would be one who would be superior to all others, and would also abolish the then existing order.

He will drink from a brook beside the way. David figuratively attributes military prowess to Christ, declaring that he would not take time to refresh himself, but would hastily drink of the river which might come in his way. This is designed to strike his enemies with terror, intimating to them the rapid approach of impending destruction.

PSALM 111:1-4

Great are the works of the LORD. In consequence to so few applying themselves to the study of the works of God, the prophet teaches us that that is the reason why so many are blind amidst a flood of light; for, when he says that the excellency of the works of God is known to all who desire it, he means that none are ignorant of it, except such as are wilfully blind, or rather, malignantly and contemptuously quench the light which is offered to them. We must, however, attend to the means which we possess for arriving at the knowledge of these works, because we know, that as long as the faithful are on earth, their understandings are dull and weak, so that they cannot penetrate the mysteries, or comprehend the height of the works of God. But incomprehensible as is the immensity of the wisdom, equity, justice, power, and mercy of God, in his works, the faithful nevertheless acquire as much knowledge of these as becomes them for manifesting the glory of God; only it becomes us to begin the study of his works with reverence, that we may take delight in them, contemptible though they be in the estimation of the reprobate, who treat them with impious scorn.

*His work is beautiful.** It is not the design of God to furnish us with such a display of his power and sovereignty in his works, as might only fill our minds with terror, but he also gives us a display of his justice in a manner so inviting as to captivate our hearts. This commendation of the works and ways of God is introduced in opposition to the clamour and calumny of the ungodly, by which they impiously endeavour, to the utmost extent of their power, to disfigure and deface the glory of the works of God.

He has caused his wonders to be remembered, is equivalent to the doing of works worthy of being remembered, or the renown of which shall continue for ever. And having above called upon us to contemplate his justice, now, in like manner, and almost in like terms, he celebrates the grace and mercy of God, principally in relation to his works, because that justice which he displays in the preservation and protection of his people, issues from the source of his unmerited favour which he bears towards them.

He provides food for those who fear him. The Church being a mirror of the grace and justice of God, what the prophet said respecting them is here expressly applied to her; not that he designs to treat of the justice of God, in general, but only of that which he peculiarly displays towards his own people. Hence he adds, that God's care of his people is such as to lead him to make ample provision for the supply of all their wants. God had given his people all that was needful, and that, considered as a portion, it was large and liberal; for we know that the people of Israel were enriched, not in consequence of their own industry, but by the blessing of God, who, like the father of a family, bestows upon his household everything necessary for their subsistence. In the following clause of the verse, he assigns as the reason for his care and kindness, his desire of effectually demonstrating that his covenant was not null and void. And here it must be carefully observed, that if, in former times, and from a respect to his gracious covenant, he manifested so great kindness towards the people of Israel, in like manner, the goodness which we receive from him is the result of our adoption into his family; and because God is never weary in showing kindness to his people, he says that the remembrance of his covenant shall never be effaced. Moreover, as he daily and constantly loads us with his benefits, so our faith must, in some measure, correspond with it: it must not fail, but must rise above life and death.

God, in bestowing upon his people the heritage of the heathen, had manifested to them the power of his works. Possession of the Holy Land was not acquired by mere human power, but it was given to them by Divine power, and through the working of many miracles; and thus God, as it were, openly testified to the descendants of Abraham with what incomparable power he is invested. It is on this account that he sets up the people of Israel as a match for so many other nations, who would assuredly never have vanquished so many enemies, unless they had been sustained from on high.

PSALM 111:10

The fear of the LORD is the beginning of wisdom. Having treated of the kindness of God, and paid a well-merited tribute to the law, the prophet goes on to exhort the faithful to reverence God, and be zealous in the keeping of the law. In calling the *fear of God, the beginning* or *source of wisdom*, he charges with folly those who do not render implicit obedience unto God. As if he should say, They who fear not God, and do not regulate their lives according to his law, are brute beasts, and are ignorant of the first elements of true wisdom. To this we must carefully attend; for although mankind generally wish to be accounted wise, almost all the world lightly esteem God, and take pleasure in their own wicked craftiness. And as the very worst of men are reputed to be superior to all others in point of wisdom; and, puffed up with this confidence, harden themselves against God, the prophet declares all the wisdom of the world, without the fear of God, to be vanity or an empty shadow. And, indeed, all who are ignorant of the purpose for which they live are fools and madmen. But to serve God is the purpose for which we have been born, and for which we are preserved in life. There is, therefore, no worse blindness, no insensibility so grovelling, as when we contemn God, and place our affections elsewhere. For whatever ingenuity the wicked may possess, they are destitute of the main thing, genuine piety.

Though all men, without exception, boast that they fear God, yet nothing is more common than for them to live in the neglect of his law. Hence the prophet very properly inculcates upon us the voluntary assumption of his yoke, and submission to the regulations of his word, as the most satisfactory evidence of our living in the fear of God. In this passage *fear* is not to be understood as referring to the first or elementary principles of piety, as in 1 John 4:18, but is comprehensive of all true godliness, or the worship of God. The conclusion of the psalm requires no explanation; it being the object of the prophet simply to inculcate upon the faithful, that nothing is more profitable for them, than to spend their lives in the celebration of the praises of God.

PSALM 112:1-4

Blessed is the man . . . who finds great delight in his commands. The prophet makes a distinction between a willing and prompt endeavour to keep the law, and that which consists in mere servile and constrained obedience. We must, therefore, cheerfully embrace the law of God, and that, too, in such a manner, that the love of it, with all its sweetness, may overcome all the allurements of the flesh, otherwise, mere attention to it will be unavailing. Hence a man cannot be regarded as a genuine observer of the law, until he has attained to this—that the delight which he takes in the law of God renders obedience agreeable to him. The prophet, in affirming that the worshippers of God *are happy*, guards us against the very dangerous deception which the ungodly practise upon themselves, in imagining that they can reap a sort of happiness, who knows what, from doing evil.

The generation of the upright will be blessed. As not a few are disposed to pervert this doctrine, by applying it as the standard according to which God dispenses his temporal favours, it is therefore proper to bear in mind what is said in Psalm 37:25, that these are bestowed according to the manner, and in the same measure, which God pleases. Sometimes it happens that a good man is childless; and barrenness itself is considered a curse of God. Again, many of God's servants are oppressed with poverty and want, are borne down under the weight of sickness, and harassed and perplexed with various calamities. It is therefore necessary to keep this general principle in view, That God sometimes bestows his bounty more profusely, and, at other times, more sparingly, upon his children, according as he sees it to be most for their good; and, moreover, he sometimes conceals the tokens of his kindness, apparently as if he had no regard for his people at all. Still, amid this perplexity, it constantly appears that these words were not uttered in vain, *the righteous and their offspring are blessed.*

PSALM 112:5-8

Good will come to him who is generous and lends freely, who conducts his affairs with justice. It shall be well with those who are gracious and communicative; because this is more in accordance with the purport of the prophet's language. It is his intention to show how greatly the ungodly are deceived, when they aspire after happiness by nefarious and unlawful practices; seeing that the favour of God is the source and cause of all good things. Hence it becomes necessary to supply the relative *who.* He proceeds, therefore, to put us on our guard as to the deception which those practise upon themselves, who hasten to enrich themselves by sordid parsimony and oppressive extortion; inasmuch as the faithful, by their clemency and kindness, open up a channel, through which the favour of God flows to them. It is the truly liberal, who from compassion, and not with the design of ensnaring the poor, grant relief to them, that God makes prosperous. The righteous will manage their affairs with prudence and discernment; so that, in their domestic affairs, they will neither be too lavish nor sordidly parsimonious; but, in everything they will study to combine frugality with economy, without giving way to luxury. And, in all their mercantile transactions, they will always be guided by the principles of equity and morality.

He will have no fear of bad news; his heart is steadfast, trusting in the LORD. Genuine stability is that which the prophet here describes, and which consists in reposing with unshaken confidence in God. A sense of calamities, while it alarms and disconcerts the faithful, does not make them faint-hearted, because it does not shake their faith, by which they are rendered bold and steadfast. In a word, they are not insensible to their trials, but the confidence which they place in God enables them to rise above all the cares of the present life. Thus they preserve calmness and composedness of mind, and wait patiently till the fit season arrives for taking vengeance upon the reprobate.

PSALM 112:9-10

He has scattered abroad his gifts to the poor. The righteous never lose the fruit and the reward of their liberality. They do not give sparingly and grudgingly, as some do who imagine that they discharge their duty to the poor when they dole out a small pittance to them, but that they give liberally as necessity requires and their means allow; for it may happen that the liberal heart does not possess a large portion of the wealth of this world. The praise which belongs to liberality does not consist in distributing our goods without any regard to the objects upon whom they are conferred, and the purposes to which they are applied, but in relieving the wants of the really necessitous, and in the money being expended on things proper and lawful. God by his benefits preserves the glory of that righteousness which is due to their liberality, and does not disappoint them of their reward, in that he exalts their horn more and more, that is, their power or their prosperous condition.

The wicked man will see and be vexed. Though the wicked may cast off all regard to piety, and banish from their minds all thoughts of human affairs being under the superintending providence of God, they shall yet be made to feel, whether they will or not, that the righteous, in compliance with God's command, do not vainly devote themselves to the cultivation of charity and mercy. Let them harden themselves as they choose, yet he declares that the honour, which God confers upon his children, shall be exhibited to them, the sight of which shall make them gnash with their teeth, and shall excite an envy that shall consume them by inches.

In conclusion he adds that *the wicked shall be disappointed of their desires.* They are never content, but are continually thirsting after something, and their confidence is as presumptuous as their avarice is unbounded. And hence, in their foolish expectations, they do not hesitate at grasping at the whole world. But the prophet tells them that God will snatch from them what they imagined was already in their possession, so that they shall always depart destitute and famishing.

**PSALM
113:1-4**

From the rising of the sun to the place where it sets, the name of the LORD is to be praised. The prophet confirms that the praises of God must be continued throughout the whole course of our life. If his name is to be continually praised, it ought, at least, to be our earnest endeavour, during our brief pilgrimage here, that the rememberance of it may flourish after we are dead. He also extends the glory of God's name to all parts of the earth; wherefore our apathy will be totally inexcusable, if we do not make its praises resound among ourselves. Under the law, God could not be praised aright, excepting in Judea by his own people, to whom the knowledge of him was confined. His works, however, which are visible to all nations, are worthy of the admiration of the whole world. To the same effect is the following clause respecting the loftiness of God's glory; for can there be anything more base, than for us to magnify it but seldom and tardily, considering it ought to fill our thoughts with enrapturing admiration? In extolling the name of God so highly, the prophet intends to show us that there is no ground for indifference; that silence would savour of impiety were we not to exert ourselves to the utmost of our ability to celebrate his praises, in order that our affections may, as it were, rise above the heavens. When he adds, that *God is high above all nations,* there is an implied reproach, by which he fastens upon the chosen people the charge of apathy in the exercise of praise. For can there be anything more preposterous, than for those who are eye-witnesses of God's glory, which shines forth even among the blind, to refrain from making it the theme of their praises? At the very time when God conferred upon the Jews the exclusive honour of being the depositories of the knowledge of his heavenly doctrine, he was nevertheless, according to Paul, not without a witness (Acts 14:17; Rom. 1:20). After the promulgation of the Gospel, his exaltation above the nations was more evident, for then the whole world was placed under his sway.

Who is like the LORD our God, the One who sits enthroned on high, who stoops down to look on the heavens and the earth? The prophet strengthens his position for the celebration of God's praises, by contrasting the height of his glory and power with his unbounded goodness. Not that his goodness can be separated from his glory; but this distinction is made out of regard to men, who would not be able to endure his majesty, were he not kindly to humble himself, and gently and kindly draw us towards him. The amount is, that God's dwelling above the heavens, at such a distance from us, does not prevent him from showing himself to be near at hand, and plainly providing for our welfare; and, in saying that God is exalted above the heavens, he magnifies his mercy towards men, whose condition is mean and despicable, and informs us that he might righteously hold even angels in contempt, were it not that, moved by paternal regard, he condescends to take them under his care. If in regard to angels he humble himself, what is to be said in regard to men, who, grovelling upon the earth, are altogether filthy? The answer is obvious. The words of the prophet simply mean, that God may trample the noblest of his creatures under his feet, or rather that, by reason of their infinite distance, he may entirely disregard them. In short, we must conclude that it is not from our proximity to him, but from his own free choice, that he condescends to make us the objects of his peculiar care.

As a happy mother of children. The meaning is, that the woman who was formerly barren is blessed with fruitfulness, and fills the house with children. He attributes joy to mothers, because, though the hearts of all are prone to aspire after wealth, or honour, or pleasures, or any other advantages, yet is progeny preferred to every thing else. Wherefore, since God superintends the ordinary course of nature, alters the current of events, elevates those of abject condition and ignoble extraction, and makes the barren woman fruitful, our insensibility is very culpable, if we do not attentively contemplate the works of his hand.

PSALM 113:5-9

PSALM 114

The sea looked and fled, the Jordan turned back. He does not enumerate in succession all the miracles which were wrought at that time, but briefly alludes to the sea, which, though a lifeless and senseless element, is yet struck with terror at the power of God. Jordan did the same, and the very mountains shook. It is in a poetical strain that the Psalmist describes the receding of the sea and of the Jordan. The description, however, does not exceed the facts of the case. The sea, in rendering such obedience to its Creator, sanctified his name; and Jordan, by its submission, put honour upon his power; and the mountains, by their quaking, proclaimed how they were overawed at the presence of his dreadful majesty. By these examples it is not meant to celebrate God's power more than the fatherly care and desire which he manifests for the preservation of the Church; and, accordingly, Israel is very properly distinguished from the sea, the Jordan, and the mountains—there being a very marked difference between the chosen people and the insensate elements.

Why was it, O sea, that you fled? The prophet interrogates the sea, Jordan, and the mountains, in a familiar and poetical strain, as lately he ascribed to them a sense and reverence for God's power. And, by these similitudes, he very sharply reproves the insensibility of those persons, who do not employ the intelligence which God has given them in the contemplation of his works. The appearance which he tells us the sea assumed, is more than sufficient to condemn their blindness. It could not be dried up, the river Jordan could not roll back its waters, had not God, by his invisible agency, constrained them to render obedience to his command. The words are indeed directed to the sea, the Jordan, and the mountains, but they are more immediately addressed to us, that every one of us, on self-reflection, may carefully and attentively weigh this matter. And, therefore, as often as we meet with these words, let each of us reiterate the sentiment,—"Such a change cannot be attributed to nature, and to subordinate causes, but the hand of God is manifest here."

Not to us, O Lord, not to us but to your name be the glory, because of your love and faithfulness. The faithful betake themselves to God, in circumstances of extreme distress. In their distress they desire to obtain consolation and support; but, finding nothing in themselves meritorious of God's favour, they call upon him to grant their requests, that his glory may be maintained. This is a point to which we ought carefully to attend, that, altogether unworthy as we are of God's regard, we may cherish the hope of being saved by him, from the respect that he has for the glory of his name, and from his having adopted us on condition of never forsaking us. It must also be noticed, that their humility and modesty prevent them from openly complaining of their distresses, and that they do not begin with a request for their own deliverance, but for the glory of God. Suffused with shame by reason of their calamity, which, in itself, amounts to a kind of rejection, they durst not openly crave, at God's hand, what they wished, but made their appeal indirectly, that, from a regard to his own glory, he would prove a father to sinners, who had no claim upon him whatever. And, as this formulary of prayer has once been delivered to the Church, let us also, in all our approaches unto God, remember to lay aside all self-righteousness, and to place our hopes entirely on his free favour. Moreover, when we pray for help, we ought to have the glory of God in view, in the deliverance which we obtain. And it is most likely they adopted this form of prayer, being led to do so by the promise. For, during the captivity, God had said, "Not for your sake, but for mine own sake will I do this," Isaiah 48:11. When all other hopes fail, they acknowledge this to be their only refuge. The repetition of it is an evidence how conscious they were of their own demerit, so that, if their prayers should happen to be rejected a hundred times, they could not, in their own name, prefer any charge against him.

PSALM 115:3(a)

Our God is in heaven. The faithful, when they place God in heaven, do not confine him to a certain locality, nor sets limits to his infinite essence, but they deny the limitation of his power, its being shut up to human instrumentality only, or its being subject to fate or fortune. In short, they put the universe under his control; and, being superior to every obstruction, he does freely everything that may seem good to him. This truth is still more plainly asserted in the subsequent clause, *he does whatever pleases him.* God, then, may be said to dwell in heaven, as the world is subject to his will, and nothing can prevent him from accomplishing his purpose.

That God can do whatsoever he pleases is a doctrine of great importance, provided it be truly and legitimately applied. If we would derive advantage from this doctrine, we must attend to the import of God's doing whatsoever he pleases in heaven and on the earth. And, first, God has all power for the preservation of his Church, and for providing for her welfare; and, secondly, all creatures are under his control, and therefore nothing can prevent him from accomplishing all his purposes. However much, then, the faithful may find themselves cut off from all means of subsistence and safety, they ought nevertheless to take courage from the fact, that God is not only superior to all impediments, but that he can render them subservient to the advancement of his own designs. This, too, must also be borne in mind, that all events are the result of God's appointment alone, and that nothing happens by chance. This much it was proper to premise respecting the use of this doctrine, that we may be prevented from forming unworthy conceptions of the glory of God, as men of wild imaginations are wont to do. Adopting this principle, we ought not to be ashamed frankly to acknowledge that God, by his eternal counsel, manages all things in such a manner, that nothing can be done but by his will and appointment.

PSALM 115:3(b)

He does whatever pleases him. From this passage Augustine very properly and ingeniously shows, that those events which appear to us unreasonable not only occur simply by the permission of God, but also by his will and decree. For if our God does whatsoever pleases him, why should he permit that to be done which he does not wish? Why does he not restrain the devil and all the wicked who set themselves in opposition to him? If he be regarded as occupying an intermediate position between doing and suffering, so as to tolerate what he does not wish, then, according to the fancy of the Epicureans, he will remain unconcerned in the heavens. But if we admit that God is invested with prescience, that he superintends and governs the world which he has made, and that he does not overlook any part of it, it must follow that every thing which takes place is done according to his will. And yet it is not his will that any evil should be done. For however incomprehensible his counsel may be to us, still it is always based upon the best of reasons.

It is deserving of notice, that if God does whatsoever he pleases, then it is not his pleasure to do that which is not done. The knowledge of this truth is of great importance, because it frequently happens, when God winks and holds his peace at the afflictions of the Church, that we ask why he permits her to languish, since it is in his power to render her assistance. Avarice, fraud, perfidy, cruelty, ambition, pride, sensuality, drunkenness, and, in short, every species of corruption in these times is rampant in the world, all which would instantly cease did it seem good to God to apply the remedy. Wherefore, if he at any time appears to us to be asleep, or has not the means of succouring us, let this tend to make us wait patiently, and to teach us that it is not his pleasure to act too speedily the part of our deliverer, because he knows that delay and procrastination are profitable to us; it being his will to wink at and tolerate for a while what assuredly, were it his pleasure, he could instantly rectify.

PSALM 115:4-7

But their idols. This contrast is introduced for the purpose of confirming the faith of the godly, by which they repose upon God alone; because, excepting him, all that the minds of men imagine of divinity is the invention of folly and delusion. To know the error and the madness of the world certainly contributes in so small degree to the confirmation of true godliness; while, on the other hand, a God is presented to us, who we know assuredly to be the maker of heaven and earth, and whom we are to worship, not without reason or at random. The prophet reminds us that nothing is more unbecoming than for men to say that they can impart either essence, or form or honour to a god, since they themselves are dependant upon another for that life which will soon disappear. From this it follows, that the heathen vainly boast of receiving help from gods of their own devising. Whence does idolatry take its origin but from the imaginations of men?

The prophet satirically adds, that while the heathen fashion members for their idols, they cannot enable them to move or use them. It is on this account that the faithful experience their privilege to be the more valuable, in that the only true God is on their side, and because they are well assured that all the heathen vainly boast of the aid which they expect from their idols, which are nothing but shadows.

From this doctrine we learn, generally, that it is foolish to seek God under outward images, which have no resemblance or relation to his celestial glory. To this principle we must still adhere, otherwise it would be easy for the heathen to complain that they were unjustly condemned, because, though they make for themselves idols upon earth, they yet were persuaded that God is in heaven.

Why do we betake ourselves to God, but from the conviction that we are dependant upon him for life; that our safety is in him, and that the abundance of good, and the power to help us, are with him? As these images are senseless and motionless, what can be more absurd than to ask from them that of which they themselves are destitute?

PSALM
115:8-11

Those who make them will be like them, and so will all who trust in them. The reason why God holds images so much in abhorrence appears very plainly from this, that he cannot endure that the worship due to himself should be taken from him and given to them. That the world should acknowledge him to be the sole author of salvation, and should ask for and expect from him alone all that is needed, is an honour which peculiarly belongs to him. If a man carve an image of marble, wood, or brass, or if he cast one of gold or silver, this of itself would not be so detestable a thing; but when men attempt to attach to God their inventions, and to make him, as it were, descend from heaven, then a pure fiction is substituted in his place. It is very true that God's glory is instantly counterfeited when it is invested with a corruptible form; nevertheless, he is doubly injured when his truth, and grace, and power, are imagined to be concentrated in idols. To make idols, and then to confide in them, are things which are almost inseparable. Else whence is it that the world so strongly desires gods of stone, or of wood, or of clay, or of any earthly material, were it not that they believe that God is far from them, until they hold him fixed to them by some bond? Averse to seek God in a spiritual manner, they therefore pull him down from his throne, and place him under inanimate things. Thus it comes to pass, that they address their supplications to images, because they imagine that in them God's ears, and also his eyes and hands, are near to them. These two vices can hardly be severed: those who, in forging idols, change the truth of God into a lie, must also ascribe something of divinity to them. When the prophet says that unbelievers put their trust in idols, his design was to condemn this as the chief and most detestable piece of profanity.

The LORD remembers us and will bless us. It is as if it is said here: "We have already, from long experience, been taught how valuable the favour of our God is, because from this source alone have flowed our prosperity, our abundance, and our stability." The prophet assumes the principle, that we neither enjoy prosperity nor happiness further than it pleases God to bless us. As there is no acceptance of persons before God, our low and abject condition ought to be no obstruction to our drawing near to him, since he so kindly invites to approach him those who appear to be held in no reputation. God's liberality is an inexhaustible fountain, which will never cease to flow so long as its progress is not impeded by the ingratitude of men. And hence it will be continued to their posterity, because God manifests the grace and the fruit of his adoption even to a thousand generations.

The highest heavens belong to the LORD, but the earth he has given to man. Here the prophet extols the bounty of God, and his paternal regard for the human race, in that, though he stood in need of nothing himself, he yet created the world, with all its fullness, for their use. How comes it to pass that the earth is every where covered with such a great variety of good things, meeting our eye in all directions, unless that God, as a provident father of a family, had designed to make provision for our wants? In proportion, therefore, to the comforts which we here enjoy, are the tokens of his fatherly care. The amount is, that God, satisfied with his own glory, has enriched the earth with abundance of good things, that mankind may not lack any thing. At the same time he demonstrates, that, as God has his dwelling-place in the heavens, he must be independent of all worldly riches; for, assuredly, neither wine, nor corn, nor anything requisite for the support of the present life, is produced there. Consequently, God has every resource in himself.

PSALM 116:1-11

I love the LORD, *for he heard my voice.* We know that our hearts will be always wandering after fruitless pleasures, and harassed with care, until God knit them to himself. This distemper David affirms was removed from him, because he felt that God was indeed propitious towards him. And, having found by experience that, in general, they who call upon God are happy, he declares that no allurements shall draw him away from God. When therefore, he says, *I have loved,* it imports that, without God, nothing would be pleasant or agreeable to him. From this we are instructed that those who have been heard by God, but do not place themselves entirely under his guidance and guardianship, have derived little advantages from the experience of his grace.

With the design of magnifying God's glory according to its desert, he says that there was no way of his escaping from death, for he was like one among enemies, bound with fetters and chains, from whom all hope of deliverance was cut off. He acknowledges, therefore, that he was subjected to death, that he was overtaken and seized, so that escape was impossible. And as he declares that he was *bound by the cords of death,* so he, at the same time, adds, that *he fell into tribulation and sorrow.* And here he confirms what he said formerly, that when he seemed to be most forsaken of God, that was the proper time, and the right season for him to give himself to prayer.

Be at rest once more, O my soul, for the LORD *has been good to you.* If the faithful regain their peace of mind only when God manifests himself as their deliverer, what room is there for the exercise of faith, and what power will the promises possess? For, assuredly, to wait calmly and silently for those indications of God's favour, which he conceals from us, is the undoubted evidence of faith. And strong faith quiets the conscience, and composes the spirit; so that, according to Paul, "the peace of God, which passes all understanding," reigns supremely there (Phil. 4:7).

How can I repay the LORD for all his goodness to me? After confessing his having nothing to offer to God as a sufficient compensation for his benefits, David at the same time adds in confirmation of it, that he was laid under such obligations, not by one series of benefits only, but by a variety of innumerable benefits. "There is no benefit on account of which God has not made me a debtor to him, how should I have means of repaying him for them?" All recompense failing him, he has recourse to an expression of thanksgiving as the only return which he knows will be acceptable to God. David's example in this instance teaches us not to treat God's benefits lightly or carelessly, for if we estimate them according to their value, the very thought of them ought to fill us with admiration. There is not one of us who has not God's benefits heaped upon us. But our pride, which carries us away into extravagant theories, causes us to forget this very doctrine, which ought nevertheless to engage our unremitting attention. And God's bounty towards us merits the more praise, that he expects no recompense from us, nor can receive any, for he stands in need of nothing, and we are poor and destitute of all things.

Precious in the sight of the LORD is the death of his saints. When we are in danger, and God apparently overlooks us, we then consider ourselves to be contemned as poor slaves, and that our life is regarded as a thing of nought. And we are aware that when the wicked perceive that we have no protection, they wax the more bold against us, as if God took no notice either of our life or death. In opposition to their erroneous doctrine, David introduces this sentiment, that God does not hold his servants in so little estimation as to expose them to death casually. We may indeed for a time be subjected to all the vicissitudes of fortune and of the world; we will nevertheless always have this consolation, that God will, eventually, openly manifest how dear our souls are to him.

Day 305   O C T O B E R   3 1

Praise the LORD, *all you nations.* The Holy Spirit having, by the mouth of the prophet, exhorted all nations to celebrate the praises of God's mercy and faithfulness, Paul, in his Epistle to the Romans, very justly considers this as a prediction respecting the calling of the whole world (15:11). How can unbelievers be qualified for praising God, who, though not entirely destitute of his mercy, yet are insensible of it, and are ignorant of his truth? It would therefore serve no purpose for the prophet to address the heathen nations, unless they were to be gathered together in the unity of the faith with the children of Abraham.

God's mercy and truth* furnish materials for celebrating his praises. Besides, the prophet does not mean that God shall be praised everywhere by the Gentiles, because the knowledge of his character is confined to a small portion of the land of Judea, but because it was to be spread over the whole world. First, he enjoins God to be praised, *because his goodness is increased,* or *strengthened,* for the Hebrew terms admits of both meanings. Secondly, *because his truth remains stedfast for ever.* How, then, are those qualified to celebrate his praises, who, with brutal insensibility, pass over his goodness, and shut their ears against his heavenly doctrine?

The *truth* of God, in this passage, is properly introduced as an attestation of his grace. For he can be true even when he menaces the whole world with perdition and ruin. The prophet, however, has placed his *mercy* first in order, that his faithfulness and truth, comprising an assurance of his paternal kindness, might encourage the hearts of the godly. His power and justice are equally praiseworthy; but as men will never cordially praise God until they are drawn by a foretaste of his goodness, the prophet very justly selects God's mercy and truth, which alone open the mouths of those who are mute to engage in this exercise.

PSALM
118:1-17

It is better to trust in the Lord.* When God and men come into comparison, he must be viewed as infinitely exalted above them, and therefore it is best to trust in him for the aid which he has promised to his own people. Many acknowledge this, and yet there is scarcely one among a hundred who is fully persuaded that God alone can afford him sufficient help. That man has attained a high rank among the faithful, who, resting satisfied in God, never ceases to entertain a lively hope, even when he finds no help upon earth. The comparison, however, is improper, inasmuch as we are not allowed to transfer to men even the smallest portion of our confidence, which must be placed in God alone. The meaning is by no means ambiguous; the Psalmist is ridiculing the illusory hopes of men by which they are tossed here and there; and declares, that when the world smiles upon them they wax proud, and either forsake God or despise him.

In the ninth verse, in which he substitutes *princes* for *men*, there is an extension of the idea. "Not only those who put their confidence in men of low degree act foolishly, but also those who confide even in the greatest potentates; for the trust that is put in flesh shall at last be accursed, but the enjoyment of God's favour will convert even death into life."

I will not die but live, and will proclaim what the Lord *has done.* We, whose life is hid with Christ in God, ought to meditate upon this song all our days (Col. 3:3). If we occasionally enjoy some relaxation, we are bound to unite with David in saying, that we who were surrounded with death are risen to newness of life.

The LORD has chastened me severely, but he has not given me over to death. In these words David owns that his enemies assailed him unjustly, that they were employed by God to correct him, that this was fatherly chastisement, God not inflicting a deadly wound, but correcting him in measure and in mercy. He seems to anticipate the perverse decisions of perverse men which grievously pressed upon him, as if all the ills which he had endured were so many evidences of his being cast off by God. These calumnies which the reprobate cast upon him he applies very differently, by declaring that his correction was mild and paternal. The main thing in adversity is to know that we are laid low by the hand of God, and that this is the way which he takes to prove our allegiance, to arouse us from our torpidity, to crucify our old man, to purge us from our filthiness, to bring us into submission and subjection to God, and to excite us to meditate on the heavenly life.

If these things were recollected by us, there is not one of us who would not shudder at the thought of fretting against God, but would much rather yield submission to him with a mild and meek spirit. Our champing the bit, and rushing forward impatiently, certainly proceeds from the majority of men not looking upon their afflictions as God's rods, and from others not participating in his paternal care. The last clause of the verse, therefore, merits particular attention, That God always deals mercifully with his own people, so that his correction proves their cure. Not that his paternal regard is always visible, but that in the end it will be shown that his chastisements, so far from being deadly, serve the purpose of a medicine, which, though it produce a temporary debility, rids us of our malady, and renders us healthy and vigorous.

PSALM 118:22-29

The stone the builders rejected has become the capstone. David proceeds to repeat that it is erroneous to estimate the kingdom of Christ by the sentiments and opinions of men, because, in spite of the opposition of the world, it is erected in an astonishing manner by the invisible power of God. In the meantime, we ought to remember, that all that was accomplished in the person of Christ extends to the gradual development of his kingdom, even until the end of the world. When Christ dwelt on the earth, he was despised by the chief priests; and now, those who call themselves the successors of Peter and Paul, but who are truly Ananiases and Caiaphases, giant-like wage war against the Gospel and the Holy Ghost. Not that this furious rebellion ought to give us any uneasiness: let us rather humbly adore that wonderful power of God which reverses the perverse decisions of the world. If our limited understandings could comprehend the course which God follows for the protection and preservation of his Church, there would be no mention made of a miracle. From this we conclude, that his mode of working is incomprehensible, baffling the understandings of men.

If we can call to mind this prophecy, our faith will not fail, but will be more and more confirmed; because, from these things it will the better appear that the kingdom of Christ does not depend upon the favour of men, and that it does not derive its strength from earthly supports, even as he has not attained it by the suffrages of men. If, however, the master-builders build well, the perverseness of those who will not permit themselves to be appropriated to the sacred edifice will be so much the less excusable. Moreover, as often as we shall, by the species of temptation, be put to the trial, let us not forget that it is unreasonable to expect that the Church must be governed according to our understanding of matters, but that we are ignorant of the government of it, inasmuch as that which is miraculous surpasses our comprehension.

PSALM 119:1-8

Blessed are they whose ways are blameless. In these words the prophet sets forth the same paradox which we met with in the commencement of the Book of Psalms. All men naturally aspire after happiness, but instead of searching for it in the right path, they resignedly prefer wandering up and down through endless by-paths, to their ruin and destruction. The Holy Spirit deservedly condemns this apathy and blindness. And but for man's cupidity, which, with brutish impetuosity, hurries him in the opposite direction, the meaning of the words would appear quite plain to him. And the further a man wanders from God, the happier does he imagine himself to be; and hence all treat, as a fable, what the Holy Spirit declares about true piety and the service of God. This is a doctrine which scarcely one among a hundred receives.

The term *way*, is here put for the manner, or course and way of life: and hence he calls those upright in their way, whose sincere and uniform desire it is to practise righteousness, and to devote their life to this purpose. In the next clause of the verse, he specifies more clearly, that a godly and righteous life consists *in walking in the law of God*. If a person follow his own humour and caprice, he is certain to go astray; and even should he enjoy the applause of the whole world, he will only weary himself with every vanity. But it may be asked, whether the prophet excludes from the hope of happiness all who do not worship God perfectly? Were this his meaning, it would follow, that none except angels alone would be happy, seeing that the perfect observance of the law is to be found in no part of the earth. The answer is easy: When uprightness is demanded of the children of God, they do not lose the gracious remission of their sins, in which their salvation alone consists. While, then, the servants of God are happy, and this is fulfilled that which is declared in Psalm 32:2, "Blessed are they to whom God imputes no sins."

PSALM 119:9-10

How can a young man keep his way pure? By living according to your word. However much men may pique themselves upon their own works, there is nothing pure in their life until they have made a complete surrender of themselves to the word of the Lord. The more effectually to excite them to this, he produces, in a special manner, the example of children or youths. In mentioning these, he by no means gives an unbridled license to those who have arrived at mature years, or who are aged, as if their own prudence served as a law to them; but because youth puts men where two ways meet, and renders it imperative for them to select the course of life which they mean to follow, he declares that, when a person sets about the regulation of his life, no advice will prove of any advantage, unless he adopts the law of God as his rule and guide. In this way the prophet stimulates men to an early and seasonable regulation of their manners, and not to delay doing so any longer, agreeably to the words of Solomon, "Remember your Creator in your youth, before the days of trouble come, and the years which shall be grief to you" (Eccles. 12:1).

We may reason from the greater to the less; for if the law of God possess the power of restraining the impetuosity of youth, so as to preserve pure and upright all who take it for their guide, then, assuredly, when they come to maturity, and their irregular desires are considerably abated, it will prove the best antidote for correcting their vices. The reason, therefore, of so much evil prevailing in the world, arises from men wallowing in their own inclination than to heavenly instruction. The only sure protection is, to regulate ourselves according to God's word. Some, wise in their own conceit, throw themselves into the snares of Satan; others, from listlessness and languor, live a vile and wicked life.

PSALM
119:11-16

I have hidden your word in my heart that I might not sin against you. This psalm not being composed for the personal and peculiar use of the author only, we may therefore understand, that as frequently as David sets before us his own example, under this model he points out the course we ought to pursue. Here we are informed that we are well fortified against the stratagems of Satan when God's law is deeply seated in our hearts. For unless it have a fast and firm hold there, we will readily fall into sin. Among scholars, those whose knowledge is confined to books, if they have not the book always before them, readily discover their ignorance; in like manner, if we do not imbibe the doctrine of God, and are well acquainted with it, Satan will easily surprise and entangle us in his meshes. Our true safeguard, then, lies not in a slender knowledge of his law, or in a careless perusal of it, but in hiding it deeply in our hearts. Here we are reminded, that however men may be convinced of their own wisdom, they are yet destitute of all right judgment, except as far as they have God as their teacher.

Teach me your decrees. This passage informs us generally, that if God do not enlighten us with the spirit of discernment, we are not competent to behold the light which shines forth from this law, though it be constantly before us. And thus it happens, that not a few are blind even when surrounded with the clear revelation of this doctrine, because, confident in their own perspicacity, they contemn the internal illumination of the Holy Spirit. Further, let us learn from this that none are possessed of such superiority of intellect as not to admit of constant increase. If the prophet, upon whom God had conferred so honourable an office as a teacher of the Church, confesses himself to be only a disciple or scholar, what madness is it for those who are greatly behind him in point of attainments not to strain every nerve to rise to higher excellence? Nor does he depend upon his own merits for obtaining his request; he beseeches God to grant them from a regard to his own glory.

PSALM 119:17-29

Open my eyes that I may see wonderful things in your law. The prophet here describes the main object of our existence. He declares it to be owing to the peculiar grace of the Holy Spirit, that any person keeps the law of God. Had he imagined that the preparing of himself for the observance of his law depended on his own free will, then this prayer would have been nothing else than downright hypocrisy. Having acknowledged that power to keep the law is imparted to men by God, he, at the same time, adds, that every man is blind, until he also enlighten the eyes of his understanding. Admitting that God gives light to us by his word, the prophet here means that we are blind amid the clearest light, until he remove the veil from our eyes. When he confesses that his eyes are veiled and shut, rendering him unable to discern the light of the heavenly doctrine, until God, by the invisible grace of his Spirit, open them, he speaks as if he were deploring his own blindness, and that of the whole human race. But, while God claims this power for himself, he tells us that the remedy is at hand, provided we do not, by trusting to our own wisdom, reject the gracious illumination offered to us. Let us learn, too, that we do not receive the illumination of the Spirit of God to make us contemn the external word, and take pleasure only in secret inspirations, like many fanatics, who do not regard themselves spiritual, except they reject the word of God, and substitute in its place their own wild speculations. Very different is the prophet's aim which is to inform us that our illumination is to enable us to discern the light of life, that God manifests by his word. Not only the ten commandments are included in the term law, but also the covenant of eternal salvation, with all its provisions, which God has made. And knowing, as we do, that Christ, "in whom are hid all the treasure of knowledge and wisdom," " is the end of the law," we need not be surprised at the prophet commending it, in consequence of the sublime mysteries which it contains (Col. 2:3; Rom. 10:4).

PSALM 119:30-32

I have chosen the way of truth. In this and the following verse the prophet affirms that he was so disposed as to desire nothing more than to follow righteousness and truth. It is, therefore, with great propriety he employs the terms *to choose.* The old adage, that man's life is as it were at the point where two ways meet, refers not simply to the general tenor of human life, but to every particular action of it. For no sooner do we undertake anything, no matter how small, than we are grievously perplexed, and as if hurried off by a tempest, are confounded by conflicting counsels. Hence the prophet declares, that in order constantly to pursue the right path, he had resolved and fully determined not to relinquish the truth. And thus he intimates that he was not entirely exempted from temptations, yet that he had surmounted them by giving himself up to the conscientious observance of the law.

I run in the path of your commands, for you have set my heart free. The meaning of the prophet is, that when God shall inspire him with love for his law, he will be vigorous and ready, no, even steady, so as not to faint in the middle of his course. His words contain an implied admission of the supineness and inability of men to make any advancement in well-doing, until God enlarge their hearts. No sooner does God expand their hearts, than they are fitted not only for walking, but also for running in the way of his commandments. He reminds us that the proper observance of the law consists not merely in external works,—that it demands willing obedience, so that the heart must, to some extent, and in some way, enlarge itself. Not that it has the self-determining power of doing this, but when once its hardness and obstinacy are subdued, it moves freely without being any longer contracted by its own narrowness. Finally, this passage tells us, when God has once enlarged our hearts, there will be no lack of power, because, along with proper affection, he will furnish ability, so that our feet will be ready to run.

PSALM 119.33-46

[Renew] my life according to your word. It is as if the prophet is saying here, "Lord, as the whole life of mankind is accursed, as long as they employ their powers in committing sin, grant that the power which I possess may aspire after nothing except the righteousness which you appoint to us." The better to manifest this, we must lay it down as a first principle, that seeing, hearing, walking, and feeling, are God's precious gifts; that our understandings and will, with which we are furnished, are a still more valuable gift; and, after all, there is no look of the eyes, no motion of the senses, no thought of the mind, unmingled with vice and depravity. Such being the case, the prophet, with good reason, surrenders himself entirely to God, for the mortification of the flesh, that he may begin to live anew.

I will always obey your law. This verse teaches us that, if any man yield implicit obedience to God, he will receive this as his reward, that he shall walk with a calm and composed mind; and should he encounter difficulties, he will find the means to overcome them. The faithful, however readily and submissively they give themselves up to God, may happen to find themselves involved in perplexity; nevertheless, the end contemplated by Paul is accomplished, that though they be in trouble and toil, yet they do not continue in irremediable distress, because it is the duty (so to speak) of God to point out a way for them where there seems to be no way (2 Cor. 4:8). Moreover, when grievously oppressed, even then they walk at ease, for they commit the doubtful issue of events to God in such a manner, that, having him for their guide, they have no doubt they will come out boldly from the depths of distress.

I will speak of your statutes before kings and will not be put to shame. These words inform us that we have profited well and truly by God's word, when our hearts are so completely fortified against the fear of man, that we do not dread the presence of kings, even though all the world attempt to fill us with dejection and dismay. It is most unbecoming that God's glory should be obscured by their empty splendour.

Remember your word to your servant. The Psalmist prays that God would really perform what he promised; for the event proves that he does not forget his word. That he is speaking of the promises we infer from the end of the verse, in which he declared that cause was given to him to hope, for which there could be no place unless grace had been presented to him. In the second verse he asserts, that though God still kept him in suspense, yet he reposed with confidence in his word. At the same time he informs us, that during his troubles and anxieties, he did not search after vain consolation as the world is wont to do, who look around them in all quarters to find something to mitigate their miseries; and if any allurements tickle their fancy, they make use of these as a remedy for alleviating their sorrows. On the contrary, the prophet says he was satisfied with the word of God itself; and that when all other refuges failed him, there he found life full and perfect; nevertheless, he covertly confesses, that if he does not acquire courage from the word of God, he will become a dead man. The ungodly may sometimes experience elevation of spirit during their miseries, but they are totally destitute of this inward strength of mind. The prophet, then, had good reason for stating, that in the time of affliction the faithful experience animation and vigour solely from the *word of God inspiring them with life.* Hence, if we meditate carefully on his word, we shall live even in the midst of death, nor will we meet with any sorrow so heavy for which it will not furnish us with a remedy. And if we are bereft of consolation and succour in our adversities, the blame must rest with ourselves; because, despising or overlooking the word of God, we purposely deceive ourselves with vain consolation.

I remember your ancient laws, O LORD. The faithful learn, that after the wicked have revelled in licentiousness for a season, they shall at length be sifted before the judgment-seat of God; but they themselves, after having patiently combated under such a guardian of their welfare, can be in no doubt about their preservation.

PSALM 119:54-61

Your decrees are the theme of my song wherever I lodge. The Psalmist says that the law of God was his sole or special delight during all his life. Singing is an indication of joy. The saints are pilgrims in this world, and must be regarded as God's children and heirs of heaven, from the fact that they are sojourners on earth. By *lodge* or *house of their pilgrimage,* then, may be understood their journey through life. One circumstance merits particular notice, that David, during his exile from his native country, ceased not to draw consolation, amid all the sadness which his banishment occasioned him. It was a noble specimen of rare virtue, that when he was denied a sight of the temple, could not draw near the sacrifices, and was deprived of the ordinances of religion, he yet never departed from his God. *Lodge* or *house of his pilgrimage* is employed, therefore, to enhance the conduct of David, who, when banished from his country, still retained the law of God deeply engraven on his heart, and who, amid the severity of that exile, which was calculated to deject his spirits, cheered himself by meditating upon the law of God.

You are my portion, O LORD. Here David seems to be saying, "I am fully persuaded that my best portion consists in keeping God's law";—and this accords with the saying of Paul, "Godliness is the best gain" (1 Tim. 6:6). David here draws a comparison between the keeping of the law, and the imaginary good which captivates the ambition of mankind: "Let everyone covet what seems to him good, and revel in his own pleasures; I have no ground to envy them, provided I retain this as my portion, the complete surrender of myself to the word of God."

I have considered my ways and have turned my steps to your statutes. When a person is inclined in good earnest to frame the course of his life well, there is nothing better than for him to follow the direction which the Lord points out. In fact, were not men infatuated, they would universally and unanimously make choice of God to be the guide of their life.

PSALM
119:62-63

At midnight I rise to give you thanks. In this verse David shows not only that he approved and embraced with his whole heart whatever the divine law contains, but that he also gave evidence of his gratitude to God for having made him partaker of so great a blessing. It seems to be quite a common thing professedly to assent to God when he teaches us by his law; for who would dare lift up his voice against him? But still the world is very far from acknowledging that the truth which he has revealed is in all respects reasonable. In the first place, such is the rebellion of our corrupt nature, that every man would have somewhat either altered or taken away. Again, if men had their choice, they would rather be governed by their own will than by the word of God. In short, human reason, as well as human passions, is widely at variance with the Divine law. He then has profited not a little, who both obediently embraces revealed truth, and, taking sweet delight in it, gives thanks to God for it. The prophet, however, does not simply declare that he magnifies God's righteous judgments; he also affirms that *he rose at midnight* to do so, by which he expresses the earnestness of his desire; for the studies and cares which break our sleep necessarily imply great earnestness of soul. David also, at the same time intimates, that in bearing his testimony in behalf of the Divine law, he was far from being influenced by ostentation, since in his secret retirement, when no human eye was upon him, he pronounced the highest encomiums on God's righteous judgments.

I am a friend to all who fear you. David does not simply speak of the brotherly love and concord which true believers cultivate amongst themselves, but intimates that, whenever he met with any individual who feared God, he gave him his hand in token of fellowship, and that he was not only of the number of God's servants, but also their helper. Such concord is no doubt required in all the godly, that they may contribute to each other's advancement in the fear of God.

PSALM 119:73-97

Your hands have made and fashioned me. * The avowal of the prophet, that he had been created by the hand of God, greatly contributed to inspiring him with the hope of obtaining the favour which he supplicates. As we are the creatures and the workmanship of God, and as he has not only bestowed upon us vital motion, in common with the lower animals, but has, in addition thereto, given us the light of understanding and reason,—this encourages us to pray that he would direct us to the obedience of his law. And yet the prophet does not call upon God, as if he were under any obligations to him; but, knowing that God never forsakes the work which he has begun, he simply asks for new grace, by which God may carry on to perfection what he has commenced. We have need of assistance of the *law*, since all that is sound in our understandings is corrupted; so that we cannot perceive what is right, unless we are taught from some other source. But our blindness and stupidity are still more strikingly manifest, from the fact that teaching will avail us nothing, until our souls are renewed by Divine grace. What I have previously said must be borne in mind, That whenever the prophet prays for understanding being imparted to him, in order to his learning the Divine commandments, he condemns both himself and all mankind as in a state of blindness; for which the only remedy is the illumination of the Holy Spirit.

The Psalmist puts *the fear*, or *the reverence of God*, in the first place; but he immediately joins it to the *knowledge of Divine truth*, to teach us that these two things are inseparably connected. The superstitious, indeed, exhibit a fear of God of a certain kind, but it is a mere show, which quickly vanishes. Besides, they weary themselves in their own inventions to no purpose; for God will take no account of any other services, but those which are performed in obedience to his commandments. True religion, then, and the worship of God, have their origin in faith—in the faith of what he has enjoined; so that no person can serve God aright, but he who has been taught in his school.

May my heart be blameless toward your decrees. Having, a little before, desired to be endued with a sound understanding, he now prays, in a similar manner, for sincere affection of heart. The understanding and affections, as is well known, are the two principal faculties of the human soul, both of which he clearly shows to be depraved and perverse, when he requests that his understanding may be illuminated, and, at the same time, that his heart may be framed to the obedience of the law. This plainly refutes all that the Papists babble about free will. The prophet not only here prays that God would help him, because his will was weak; but he testifies, without qualification, that uprightness of heart is a gift of the Holy Spirit. We are, moreover, taught by these words, in what the true keeping of the law consists. A great part of mankind, after having carelessly framed their lives according to the Divine law, by outward obedience, think that they want nothing. But the Holy Spirit here declares that no service is acceptable to God, except that which proceeds from integrity of heart.

Though I am like a wineskin in the smoke, I do not forget your decrees. The obvious design of the Psalmist is to teach us, that, although he had been proved by severe trials, and wounded to the quick, he yet had not been withdrawn from the fear of God. In comparing himself to a *wineskin*, he intimates that he was, as it were, parched by the continual heat of the adversities. Whence we learn, that that sorrow must have been intense which reduced him to such a state of wretchedness and emaciation, that like a shrivelled bottle he was almost dried up. It, however, appears that he wants to point out, not only the severity of his affliction, but also its lingering nature—that he was tormented, as it were, at a slow fire; even as the smoke which proceeds from heat dries bladders by slow degrees. The prophet experienced a long series of griefs, which might have consumed him a hundred times, and that, by their protracted and lingering nature, had he not been sustained by the word of God. In short, it is a genuine evidence of true godliness, when, although plunged into the deepest afflictions, we yet cease not to submit ourselves to God.

PSALM 119:89-90

Your word, O LORD, [endures forever]. As we see nothing constant or of long continuance upon earth, the prophet elevates our minds to heaven, that they may fix their anchor there. David, no doubt, might have said, as he had done in many other places, that the whole order of the world bears testimony to the stedfastness of God's word—that word which is most true. But as there is reason to fear that the minds of the godly would hang in uncertainty if they rested the proof of God's truth upon the state of the world, in which such manifold disorders prevail; by placing God's truth in the heavens, he allots it to a habitation subject to no changes. That no person then may estimate God's word from the various vicissitudes which meet his eye in this world, heaven is tacitly set in opposition to the earth. Our salvation, as if it had been said, being shut up in God's word, is not subject to change, as all earthly things are, but is anchored in a safe and peaceful haven. The same truth the prophet Isaiah teaches in somewhat different words: "All flesh is grass, and goodliness thereof is as the flower of the field" (Isa. 40:6), he means, according to the apostle Peter's exposition (1 Peter 1:24), that the certainty of salvation is to be sought in the word, and, therefore, that they do wrong who settle their minds upon the world; for the stedfastness of God's word far transcends the stability of the world.

The prophet, on the one hand, exhorts us to rise above the whole world by faith, so that the word of God may be found by experience to be adequate, as it really is adequate, to sustain our faith; and, on the other hand, he warns us that we have no excuse, if, by the very sight of the earth, we do not discover the truth of God, since legible traces of it are to be found at our feet. In the first clause, men are called back from the vanity of their own understanding; and, in the other, their weakness is relieved, that they may have a foretaste upon earth of what is to be found more fully in heaven.

PSALM 119.91-95

Your laws endure to this day, for all things serve you. Men are very perverse, when, by their unbelief, they do what they can to shake and impair the faithfulness of God, upon which all creatures repose; and, moreover, when by their rebellion they impeach his righteousness, and deny the authority of his commands, upon which the stability of the whole world depends. It is a harsh manner of expression to say, that *all the elements are God's servants;* but it expresses more than if it had been said, that all things are ready to yield obedience to him. How can we account for it, that the air, which is so thin, does not consume itself by blowing incessantly? How can we account for it, that the waters do not waste away by flowing, but on the principle that these elements obey the secret command of God? By faith, it is true, we perceive that the continued existence of the world is owing to the fiat of God; but all who have the smallest pretensions to understanding are led to the same conclusion, from the manifest and undoubted proofs of this truth, which every where meet their eye. Let it then be thoroughly impressed upon our minds, that all things are so governed and maintained by the secret operation of God, as that their continuing in the same state is owing to their obeying his commandment or word. We must always remember the point that the prophet aims at; which is, that God's faithfulness, which shines forth in his external works, may gradually conduct us higher, until we attain such a persuasion of the truth of the heavenly doctrine as is entirely free from doubt. He here unquestionably commends the very same word, which he had but now said dwelt in heaven. Though it resound on earth, enter into our ears, and settle in our hearts, yet it still retains its celestial nature; for it descends to us in such a manner, as that it is not subject to the changes of the world. The prophet declares that he was grievously oppressed by a weight of afflictions enough to overwhelm him; but that the consolation which he derived from the Divine Law, in such desperate circumstances, was as life to him.

PSALM 119:96-104

To all perfection I see a limit; but your commands are boundless. The word of God is not subject to change, because it is elevated far above the perishable elements of this world. He here asserts, that there is nothing under heaven so perfect and stable, or so complete, in all respects, as not to have an end; and that the Divine word alone possesses such amplitude as to surpass all boundaries and limits.

Your word . . . [is] sweeter than honey to my mouth! David was so powerful attracted by the sweetness of the Divine Law, as to have no desire after any other delight. It is possible that a man may be affected with reverence towards the Law of God; but no one will cheerfully follow it, save he who has tasted this sweetness. God requires from us no slavish service: he will have us come to him cheerfully, and this is the very reason why the prophet commends the sweetness of God's word so often in this psalm. If it is demanded in what sense he declares that he took such sweet delight in God's Law, which, according to the testimony of Paul (1 Cor. 3:9), does nothing else but strike fear into men, the solution is easy: The prophet does not speak of the dead letter which kills those who read it, but he comprehends the whole doctrine of the Law, the chief part of which is the free covenant of salvation. When Paul contrasts the Law with the Gospel, he speaks only of the commandments and threatenings. Now if God were only to command, and to denounce the curse, the whole of his communication would, undoubtedly, be deadly. But the prophet is not here opposing the Law to the Gospel; and, therefore, he could affirm that the grace of adoption, which is offered in the Law, was sweeter to him than honey; that is to say, that no delight was to him equal to this. The Law of God will be unsavoury to us, or, at least, it will never be so sweet to us, as to withdraw us from the pleasures of the flesh, until we have struggled manfully against our own nature, in order to subdue the carnal affections which prevail within us.

Your word is a lamp to my feet and a light for my path. In this verse the Psalmist testifies that the Divine Law was his schoolmaster and guide in leading a holy life. He thus, by his own example, prescribes the same rule to us all; and it is highly necessary to observe this rule; for while each of us follows what seems good in his own estimation, we become entangled in inextricable and frightful mazes. The more distinctly to understand his intention, it is to be noted, that the word of God is set in opposition to all human counsels. What the world judges right is often crooked and perverse in the judgment of God, who approves of no other manner of living, than that which is framed according to the rule of his law. It is also to be observed, that David could not have been guided by God's word, unless he had first renounced the wisdom of the flesh, for it is only when we are brought to do this, that we begin to be of a teachable disposition. But the metaphor which he uses implies something more; namely, that unless the word of God enlighten men's path, the whole of their life is enveloped in darkness and obscurity, so that they cannot do anything else than miserably wander from the right way; and again, that when we submit ourselves with docility to the teaching of God's law, we are in no danger of going astray. Let us, then, be assured that an unerring light is to be found there, provided we open our eyes to behold it. The Apostle Peter (2 Peter 1:19) has more plainly expressed the same sentiment, when he commends the faithful for taking heed to the word of prophecy, "as a light that shines in a dark place."

Your statutes are my heritage forever; they are the joy of my heart. The prophet, to stir us up by his own example, asserts, that he took such pleasure in God's ceremonies as to esteem nothing more precious. It is love only which leads us to set a value on any object; and therefore, it is requisite, in order to our observing the Divine law with the reverence due to it, that we begin with this delight in it. God's testimonies convey to our minds a joy, which, causing us to reject and despise all other things, holds our affections fast bound to them.

Away from me, you evildoers, that I may keep the commands of my God! As David saw how great a hindrance the ungodly are to us, he banishes them to a distance from him; or rather, he testifies that he will beware of entangling himself in their society. If we would hold on in the way of the Lord without stumbling, we must endeavour, above all things, to keep at a greatest possible distance from worldly and wicked men, not in regard to distance of place, but in respect of intercourse and conversation. Provided we contract an intimate acquaintance with them, it is scarcely possible for us to avoid being speedily corrupted by the contagion of their example. The dangerous influence of fellowship with wicked men is but too evident from observation; and to this it is owing, that few continue in their integrity to the close of life, the world being fraught with corruptions. From the extreme infirmity of our nature, it is the easiest thing in the world to catch infection, and to contract pollution from the slightest touch. The prophet, then, with good reason, bids the wicked depart from him, that he may advance in the fear of God without obstruction. Whoever entangles himself in their companionship will, in process of time, proceed the length of abandoning himself to a contempt of God, and of leading a dissolute life. With this statement agrees the admonition of Paul, in 2 Corinthians 6:14, "Be not unequally yoked together with unbelievers." It was, indeed, beyond the prophet's power to chase the wicked to a distance from him; but by these words he intimates, that from henceforth he will have no intercourse with them. He emphatically designates God as *his God*, to testify that he makes more account of him alone than of all mankind. Finding extreme wickedness universally prevailing on the earth, he separated himself from men, that he might join himself wholly to God. At the present day, that bad examples may not carry us away to evil, it greatly concerns us to put God on our side, and to abide constantly in him, because he is ours.

And because I consider all your precepts right, I hate every wrong path. The prophet, waiting patiently for God's judgments, and also earnestly calling for their infliction, had subscribed to the law of God in every particular, and embraced it without a single exception—and moreover, he hated every false way. There is nothing to which we are naturally more inclined than to despise or reject whatever in God's law is not agreeable to us. Every man, according as he is tainted with this or that particular vice, would desire that the commandment which forbids it were razed out of the law. But we cannot lawfully make any addition to it, or take away anything from it; and since God has joined his commandments together by a sacred and inviolable bond, to separate any one of them from the rest is altogether unwarrantable. We perceive then how the prophet, inspired with a holy jealousy for the law, contended against the wicked rebellion of those who despised it. And assuredly, when we see that the ungodly mock God with such effrontery, at one time audaciously rising up against him, and at another perverting every part of the law, it becomes us to be more inflamed with zeal, and to be the more courageous in maintaining the truth of God. The extreme impiety of our age especially demands of all the faithful that they should exercise themselves in this holy zeal. Profane men strive to outdo one another in scornfully aspersing the doctrine of salvation, and endeavour to bring God's sacred Word into contempt by their derisive jeers. Others pour forth their blasphemies without intermission. We cannot, therefore, avoid being chargeable with the crime of treacherous indifference, if our hearts are not warmed with zeal, and unless we burn with a holy jealousy. The prophet not merely says, that he approved of God's law wholly and without exception, but he adds, *that he hated every way of lying,* or *every false way.* And, undoubtedly, no one subscribes in good earnest to the law of God, but he who rejects all the slanders by which the wicked taint or obscure the purity of sound doctrine.

PSALM
119:128

Your statutes are wonderful; therefore I obey them. It is impossible for any man to keep the law of God from the heart, unless he contemplates it with feelings of reverence, for reverence is the beginning of pure and right subjection. Accordingly, many despise God's Word, because they think it inferior to the acuteness of their own understandings. Yes, many are led to break forth more audaciously into this heaven-daring contempt, from the vanity of showing their own ingenuity. But, although worldly men may flatter themselves in that proud disdain of divine law, yet the commendation which the prophet pronounces upon it still holds true, that it comprehends mysteries which far transcend all the conceptions of the human mind.

The unfolding of your words gives light; it gives understanding to the simple. By *the simple* the Psalmist denotes such as neither excel in ingenuity nor are endued with wisdom, but rather are unskilled in letters, and unrefined by education. Of such he affirms that, as soon as they have learned the first principles of the law of God, they will be endued with understanding. It ought to have a most powerful influence in exciting in us an earnest desire to become acquainted with the law of God, when we are told that even those who, in the estimation of the world, are fools, and contemptible simpletons, provided they apply their minds to the subject, acquire from it wisdom sufficient to lead them to eternal salvation. Although it is not given to all men to attain to the highest degree in this wisdom, yet it is common to all the godly so far as to know the certain and unerring rule by which to regulate their life. Thus no man who surrenders himself to the teaching of God, will loose his labour in his school, for from his first entrance he will reap inestimable fruit. Meanwhile we are warned, that all who follow their own understanding, wander in darkness. By affirming that *it gives understanding to the simple*, David intimates, that it is only when men, divested of all self-confidence, submit themselves with humble and docile minds to God, that they are in a proper state for becoming proficient scholars in the study of the divine law.

Streams of tears flow from my eyes, for your law is not obeyed. Here David affirms that he was inflamed with no ordinary zeal for the glory of God, inasmuch as he wholly dissolved into tears on account of the contempt put upon the divine law. He speaks hyperbolically; but still he truly and plainly expresses the disposition of mind with which he was endued; and it corresponds with what he says in another place, "The zeal of your house has eaten me up ["consumes me"—NIV]" (Ps. 69:9). Wherever the Spirit of God reigns, he excites this ardent zeal, which burns the heart of the godly when they see the commandment of the Most High God accounted as thing of nought. It is not enough that each of us endeavour to please God; we must also desire that his law may be held in estimation by all men. In this way holy Lot, as the Apostle Peter testifies, vexed his soul when he beheld Sodom a sink of all kinds of wickedness (2 Peter 2:8). If, in former times, the ungodliness of the world extorted from the children of God such bitter grief, so great is the corruption into which we at this day are fallen, that those who can look upon the present state of things unconcerned and without tears, are thrice, yes four times, insensible. How great in our day is the frenzy of the world in despising God and neglecting his doctrine? A few, no doubt, are to be found who with the mouth profess their willingness to receive it, but scarcely one in ten proves the sincerity of his profession by his life. Meanwhile countless multitudes are hurried away to the impostures of Satan and to the Pope; others are as thoughtless and indifferent about their salvation as the lower animals; and many Epicureans openly mock all religion. If there is, then, the smallest portion of piety remaining in us, full rivers of tears, and not merely small drops, will flow from our eyes. But if we would give evidence of pure and uncorrupted zeal, let our grief begin at ourselves—at our seeing that we are yet far from having attained to a perfect observance from the law; yes, that the depraved lusts of our carnal nature are often rising up against the righteousness of God.

PSALM 119:136-58

**PSALM
119:159-70**

*See how I love your precepts; preserve my life, O LORD,
according to your love.* When the saints speak of their own
piety before God they are not chargeable with obtruding
their own merits as the ground of their own confidence; but
they regard this as a settled principle, that God, who distinguishes his servants from the profane and wicked, will be
merciful to them because they seek him with their whole
heart. Besides, an unfeigned love of God's law is an undoubted evidence of adoption, since this love is the work of
the Holy Spirit. The prophet, therefore, although he arro-
gates nothing to himself, very properly adduces his own piety for the purpose of encouraging himself to entertain the more ensured hope of
obtaining his request, through the grace of God which he had experienced. At the same time we are taught that there can be no true keeping
of the law but what springs from free and spontaneous love. God
demands voluntary sacrifices, and the commencement of a good life is to
love him, as Moses declares (Deut. 10:12), "And now, O Israel! what
does the Lord require of you, but to love him." The same thing is also
repeated in the summary of the law (Deut. 6:5), "You shall love the Lord
your God." For this reason David has previously stated, that the law of
God was not only precious but also delightful to him. Now as in keeping
the law it behoves us to begin with voluntary obedience, so that nothing
may delight us more than the righteousness of God, so on the other hand,
it must not be forgotten that a sense of the free goodness of God and of
his fatherly love is indispensably necessary in order to our hearts being
inclined to this affection. So far are the bare commandments from win-
ning men to obey them, that they rather frighten them away. Hence it is
evident, that it is only when a man shall have tasted the goodness of God
from the teaching of the law, that he will apply his heart to love it in
return. The frequency with which the prophet repeats the prayer, *that
God would quicken him,* teaches us that he knew well the frailty of his own
life, so that in his estimation men live only in so far as God every
moment breathes life into them.

May my lips overflow with praise, for you teach me your decrees. David again confirms the doctrine, That the way by which we become truly wise is, first by submitting ourselves to the Word of God, and not following our own imaginations; and, secondly, by God's opening our understanding and subduing it to the obedience of his will. He here joins together both these truths—namely, that when God has set before us his law, from which we are to learn whatever is profitable to our welfare, he, at the same time, teaches us inwardly. It were not enough to have ours stricken with the outward sound, did not God illuminate our minds by the Spirit of understanding, and correct our obduracy by the Spirit of docility. As the labours of teachers is to no purpose until virtue and efficacy has been given to it, so it is also to be noticed that such as are truly taught of God, are not led away from the law and the Scriptures by secret revelations, like some fanatics, who think that they linger still at their A B C, unless disdainfully trampling under foot the Word of God, they fly away after their own foolish fancies.

*Let my soul live and let it praise you.** This sentence may be expounded thus: Lord, when you shall have bestowed life upon me, I will endeavour, by celebrating your praises, to show that I am not ungrateful. The prophet, depending upon the divine promises, confidently proclaims, that his life will continue in safety. Certainly, although our life is hidden under the shadow of death, we may, nevertheless, boast that it is safe, because God is its faithful guardian; and this assured confidence proceeds from his quickening grace, which is offered to us in his word.

PSALM 120

Too long have I lived among those who hate peace. I am a man of peace. The Psalmist now shows, without figure, and, so to speak, points with the finger to those whom he had before indirectly marked out by the terms *Mesech* and *Kedar*, namely, the perfidious Israelites, who had degenerated from the holy fathers, and who rather wore the mask of Israelites than were the true seed of Israel. He calls them *haters of peace*, because they wilfully, and with deliberate malice, set themselves to make war upon the good and unoffending. To the same purpose he adds immediately after, that his heart was strongly inclined to seek after peace, or rather, that he was wholly devoted to it, and had tried every means in order to win their favour, but that the implacable cruelty of their disposition invariably impelled them to do him mischief.

I am a man of peace. This is an expression implying that he had not done them any injury or wrong which could give occasion for their hatred: there having been always peace on his part. He even proceeds further, asserting, that when he saw them inflamed with resentment against him, he endeavoured to pacify them, and to bring them to a good understanding; for *to speak,* is here equivalent to offering conditions of peace in an amicable spirit, or to treating of reconciliation. From this it is still more apparent, how savage and brutal was the pride of David's enemies, since they disdained even to speak with him—to speak with a man who had deserved well at their hands, and who had never in any respect injured them. We are taught by his example, that it is not enough for the faithful to abstain from hurting others: they must, moreover, study to allure them by gentleness, and to bend them to good will. Should their moderation and kindness be rejected, let them wait in patience, until God at length show himself from heaven as their protector. Let us, however, remember, that if God does not immediately stretch forth his hand on our behalf, it is our duty to bear the wearisomeness occasioned by delay, like David, whom we find in this psalm giving thanks to God for his deliverance, while, at the same time, as if worn out by the weariness of waiting for it, he bewails the long oppression to which he had been subjected by his enemies.

PSALM
121:1-2

I will lift up my eyes to the hills—where does my help come from? What then is the meaning of this unsettled looking of the prophet, who casts his eyes now on this side and now on that, as if faith directed him not to God? The thoughts of the godly are never so stayed upon the word of God as not to be carried away at the first impulse to some allurements and especially when dangers disquiet us, or when we are assailed with sore temptations, it is scarcely possible for us, from our so being inclined to the earth, not to be moved by the entice-ments presented to us, until our minds put a bridle upon themselves, and turn them back to God. Whatever we may think, would the prophet say, all the hopes which draw us away from God are vain and delusive. The Psalmist declares that those lose their pains who, disre-garding God, gaze to a distance all around them, and make long and devi-ous circuits in quest of remedies to their troubles. It is indeed certain, that in thus speaking of himself, he exhibits to us a malady with which all mankind are inflicted; but still, it will not be unsuitable to suppose, that he was prompted to speak in this manner from his own experience; for such is the inconstancy natural to us, that so soon as we are smitten with any fear, we turn our eyes in every direction, until faith, drawing us back from all these erratic wanderings, direct us exclusively to God. All the difference between believers and unbelievers in this respect is, that although all are prone to be deceived, and easily cheated by impostures, yet Satan bewitches unbelievers by his enchantments; whereas, in regard to believers, God corrects the vice of their nature, and does not permit them to persevere in going astray. The meaning of the prophet is abun-dantly obvious, which is, that although all the helps of the world, even the mightiest, should offer themselves to us, yet we ought not to seek safety anywhere but in God, yes, rather, that when men shall have long wearied themselves in hunting after remedies, now in one quarter and now in another, they will at length find from experience, that there is no assured help but in God alone.

PSALM 121:3-8

He will not let your foot slip—he who watches over you will not slumber. Here the prophet, in order to recall the faithful to the right path, and to defeat the influence of all the allurements which are wont to distract their minds, affirms that whatever advantages worldly men are accustomed to desire or hope for from the world, true believers will find abundantly and at hand in God alone. He not only attributes power to God, but also teaches that he is so affectioned towards us, that he will preserve us in all respects in perfect safety. As often as the power of God is extolled, there are many who immediately reply, It is very true that he can do such and such things if he is inclined, but we do not certainly know what is his intention. In this passage, therefore, God is exhibited to the faithful as their guardian, that they may rest assured with assured confidence on his providence. As the Epicureans, in imagining that God has no care whatever about the world, extinguish all piety, so those who think that the world is governed by God only in a general and confused manner, and believe not that he cherishes with special care each of his believing people, leave men's minds in suspense, and are themselves kept in a state of constant fluctuation and anxiety. In short, never will the hearts of men be led in good earnest to call upon God, until a persuasion of the truth of this guardianship is firmly fixed in their minds. The Hebrew word which is here used, signifies both *a sliding* or *falling,* and *a trembling* or *staggering.* Now, although it often happens that the faithful stagger, yes, are even ready to fall altogether, yet as God sustains them by his power, they are said to stand upright. And as amidst the dangers which every moment threaten us, it is difficult for us to get rid of all anxiety and fear, the prophet at the same time testifies, that God keeps watch unceasingly over our safety.

The prophet repeats, *Jehovah is your keeper,* so that no person might hesitate to apply to himself that which belonged to whole community of Israel. Besides, God is called *a defence at the right hand,* to teach us that it is not necessary for us to go far in seeking him, but that he is at hand, or rather stands at our side to defend us.

There the thrones for judgment stand. The prophet means, that the throne of the kingdom was fixed or established at Jerusalem, or that there it had its permanent seat. Among that people some order of judgments had always existed: these, however, had formerly been in an unsettled state, and frequently changed, but God at length ordained, in the person of David, a new government which should flow in a continual course; for it was his will that the children of David should succeed their father in this royal dignity from age to age until the coming of Christ. The prophet has a little before spoken of the Temple and the priesthood; and now he affirms, that this kingdom, which God had erected, will be firm and stable; in order to distinguish it from all the other kingdoms of the world, which are not only temporary, but also frail and subject to a variety of changes. This everlastingness of the kingdom has been expressly confirmed by other prophets in various parts of their writings, and not without cause; for the object was, to teach the faithful that God would be the guardian of their welfare only upon the supposition of their remaining under the protection and defence of David, and that, therefore, if they desired to continue in safety and to prosper, they should not make for themselves new kings at their own pleasure, but should live quietly under that kind of government which God had set up among them.

For the sake of the house of the LORD *our God, I will seek your prosperity.* If the salvation of our brothers is regarded by us as an object of importance, if religion is with us a matter of heart-work, we ought, at the same time, as much as in us lies, to take an interest in the prosperity of the Church. Whence it follows, that such as are indifferent about her condition, are no less cruel than impious; for if she is "the pillar and foundation of truth," the inevitable consequence of her destruction must be the extinction of true piety. If the body is destroyed, how can each of the members fail to be involved in destruction? Further, this passage teaches us, that the Church is not an empty title, but must be sought for where the true religion prevails.

PSALM 123

As the eyes of slaves look to the hand of their master, as the eyes of a maid look to the hand of her mistress, so our eyes look to the LORD our God, till he shows us his mercy. This similitude is very similar to the present case. It implies that without the protection of God true believers have no comfort, are completely disarmed and exposed to all manner of wrongs, have neither strength nor courage to resist; in short, that their safety depends entirely upon aid derived from another. We know how shamefully servants were treated in ancient times, and what reproaches might be cast upon them, whilst yet they dared not move a finger to repel the outrage. Being therefore deprived of all means of defending themselves, the only thing which remained for them to do was, what is here stated, to crave the protection of their masters. The same explanation is equally applicable to the case of *handmaids*. Their condition was indeed shameful and degrading; but there is no reason why we should be ashamed of, or offended at, being compared to slaves, provided God is our defender, and takes our life under his guardianship; God, I say, who purposely disarms us and strips us of all worldly aid, that we may learn to rely upon his grace, and to be contented with it alone. It having been anciently a capital crime for bondmen to carry a sword or any other weapon about them, and as they were exposed to injuries of every description, their masters were wont to defend them with so much the more spirit, when any one causelessly did them violence. Nor can it be doubted that God, when he sees us placing an exclusive dependence upon his protection, and renouncing all confidence in our own resources, will as our defender encounter, and shield us from all the molestation that shall be offered to us. It is, however, certain that we have here properly the description of a period in which the people of God were reduced to a state of extreme necessity, and brought even to the brink of despair. The word "hand" here is used for "help."

PSALM 124

Our help is in the name of the LORD, the Maker of heaven and earth. David extends to the state of the Church in all ages that which the faithful had already experienced. As I interpret the verse, he not only gives thanks to God for one benefit, but affirms that the Church cannot continue safe except in so far as she is protected by the hand of God. His object is to animate the children of God with the assured hope, that their life is in perfect safety under the divine guardianship. The contrast between the help of God, and other resources in which the world vainly confides, as we have seen in Psalm 20:7, "Some trust in chariots, and some in horses, but we will remember the name of the Lord our God," is to be noticed, that the faithful, purged from all false confidence, may betake themselves exclusively to his succour, and depending upon it, may fearlessly despise whatever Satan and the world may plot against them.

The *name of God* is nothing else than God himself; yet it tacitly conveys a significant idea, implying that as he has disclosed to us his grace by his word, we have ready access to him, so that in seeking him we need not go a distance, or follow long circuitous paths. Nor is it without cause that the Psalmist again honours God with the title of Creator. We know with what disquietude our minds are agitated till they have raised the power of God to its appropriate elevation, that, the whole world being put under, it alone may be pre-eminent; which cannot be the case unless we are persuaded that all things are subject to his will. He did not show once and in a moment his power in the creation of the world and then withdraw it, but he continually demonstrates it in the government of the world. Moreover, although all men freely and loudly confess that God is the Creator of heaven and earth, so that even the most wicked are ashamed to withhold from him the honour of his title, yet no sooner does any terror present itself to us than we are convicted of unbelief in hardly setting any value whatever upon the help which he has to bestow.

PSALM 125

The scepter of the wicked will not remain over the land allotted to the righteous, for then the righteous might use their hands to do evil. This is, as it were, a correction of the preceding sentence. The Psalmist has said that the hand of God was extended on all sides to defend his Church. But as we are disposed to draw the divine promises to our own advantage, in the way of interpreting them as securing our exemption from all trouble, we are here warned that the guardianship of God does not secure us from being sometimes exercised with the cross and afflictions, and that therefore the faithful ought not to promise themselves a delicate and easy life in this world, it being enough for them not be abandoned of God when they stand in need of his help. Their heavenly father, it is true, loves them most tenderly, but he will have them awakened by the cross, lest they should give themselves too much to the pleasures of the flesh. If, therefore, we embrace this doctrine, although we may happen to be oppressed by the tyranny of the wicked, we will wait patiently till God either break their sceptre, or shake it out of their hands. It is a sore temptation to see the wicked exercising cruelty in the heritage of the Lord, and the faithful lying extended beneath their feet; but as God does not without just reason thus humble his people, they should comfort themselves from the consideration suggested in the text.

God, from his willingness to bear with our weakness, moderates our adversities. Although, then, we may not possess in ourselves a sufficient amount of fortitude and constancy to enable us to persevere in our duty for a single moment, yet let this sentiment be present to our minds, That God will take care that, broken as we may be by afflictions, we shall not forsake his service.

The Lord seasonably sets limits to our temptations, because he knows that we are too feeble to withstand them.

However vigorous, then, the fear of God may be in our hearts, let us remember that we are not endowed with adequate strength for enduring to the end, unless the Lord have a regard to our infirmity.

PSALM 126

Restore our fortunes, O LORD. This verse contains a prayer that God would gather together the residue of the captives. All the Jews, no doubt, had a door opened to them, and perfect liberty granted them, to come out of the land of their captivity, but the number of those who partook of this benefit was small when compared with the vast multitude of the people. Some were kept from returning by fear, and others by sloth and want of courage, on seeing such perils at hand as they apprehended they had not power to overcome, choosing rather to lie torpid in their own filthiness, than to undertake the hardship of the journey. It is probable also that many of them preferred their present ease and comfort to eternal salvation. What the prophet Isaiah had foretold was no doubt fulfilled (10:22) that although the people were in number as the sand of the sea, yet only a remnant of them should be saved. Since, then, many openly refused the benefit when it was offered them, and as there were many difficulties and impediments to be encountered by those who availed themselves of this liberty granted them by the good pleasure of the king, so that it was only a few of sounder judgment and of a more intrepid heart, who dared to move a foot—and even they with reluctance,—it is no wonder that the prophet requires the Church still to make supplication to God for the bringing back of the captivity. Along with this, the state of those who had already returned is also to be noted; for their land being in the possession of strangers, who were all their inveterate and sworn enemies, they were no less captives in their own country than among the Babylonians. It was therefore necessary, on a twofold account, that the church should earnestly beseech God to gather together such as were dispersed; first, that he would give courage to the timid, awaken the torpid, cause the besotted to forget their pleasures, and stretch forth his hand to be a guide to all; and, secondly, that he would settle the body of the people who had returned in liberty and ease.

PSALM 127:1

Unless the LORD builds the house, its builders labor in vain. In affirming that God governs the world and the life of man, Solomon does so for two reasons: First, whatever prosperous event may fall out to men, their ingratitude is instantly manifested by their ascribing it wholly to themselves; and thus God is defrauded of the honour which is his due. Solomon, to correct such a perverse error, declares, that nothing happens prosperously to us except in so far as God blesses our proceedings. Secondly, his purpose was to beat down the foolish presumption of men, who, setting God aside, are not afraid to undertake to do anything, whatever it may be, in exclusive reliance upon their own wisdom and strength. Stripping them, therefore, of that which they groundlessly arrogate to themselves, he exhorts them to modesty and the invocation of God. He does not, however, reject either the labour, the enterprises, or the counsels of men; for it is a praiseworthy virtue diligently to discharge the duties of our office. It is not the will of the Lord that we should be like blocks of wood, or that we should keep our arms folded without doing anything; but that we should apply to use all the talents and advantages which he has conferred upon us. Solomon, therefore, does not condemn watchfulness, a thing which God approves; nor yet men's labour, by which when they undertake it willingly, according to the commandment of God, they offer to him an acceptable sacrifice; but lest, blinded by presumption, they should forcibly appropriate to themselves that which belongs to God, he admonishes them that their being busily occupied will profit them nothing, except in so far as God blesses their exertions.

There is a synecdoche in the words *builder* and *keeper;* for he intends to say in general that whatever labour, foresight, and skill men may employ in maintaining a family, or in preserving a city, will be to no purpose unless God grant from heaven a prosperous issue to the whole.

In vain you rise early and stay up late, toiling for food to eat.
Solomon now expresses more clearly that men in vain wear
themselves out with toiling, and waste themselves by fasting
to acquire riches, since these also are a benefit bestowed only
by God. The more effectually to move them, he addresses
himself to every man in particular. *It is,* says he, *in vain for
you.* He particularises two means which are thought to contribute in an eminent degree to the amassing of riches. It is
not surprising to find those growing rich in a short time sparing no exertion, but consume night and day in plying their
occupations, and allow themselves only scanty fare from the product of
their labour. Solomon, however, affirms that neither living at a small
expense, nor diligence in business will by themselves profit anything at
all. Not that he forbids us to practise temperance in our diet and to rise
early to engage in our worldly business; but to stir us up to prayer, and to
calling upon God, and also to recommend gratitude for the divine blessings, he brings to nought whatever would obscure the grace of God.
Consequently, we shall then enter upon our worldly avocations in a right
way when our hope depends exclusively upon God, and our success in
that case will correspond to our wishes. But if a man, taking no account
of God, eagerly makes haste, he will bring ruin upon himself by his too
precipitate course. It is not, therefore, the design of the prophet to
encourage men to give way to sloth, so that they should think upon
nothing all their life long, but fall asleep and abandon themselves to idleness: his meaning rather is, that, in executing what God has enjoined
upon them, they should always begin with prayer and calling upon his
name, offering to him their labours that he may bless them.

For he grants sleep to those he loves. God will give his children those
things which unbelievers labour to acquire by their own industry.

The faithful, although they lead a laborious life, they yet follow
their vocations with composed and tranquil minds. Thus their hands are
not idle, but their minds repose in the stillness of faith, as if they were
asleep.

PSALM 127:3-5

Sons are a heritage from the LORD, children a reward from him. Children are not the fruit of chance, but God, as it seems good to him, distributes to every man his share of them. Moreover, as the prophet repeats the same thing twice, *heritage* and *reward* are to be understood as equivalent; for both these terms are set in opposition to fortune, or the strength of men. The stronger a man is he seems so much the better fit for procreation. Solomon declares on the contrary, that those become fathers to whom God vouchsafes that honour.

As the majority of children are not always a source of joy to their parents, a second favour of God is added, which is his forming the minds of children, and adorning them with an excellent disposition, and all kinds of virtues. The similitude introduced for this purpose is, that as an archer is armed with a well-furnished bow, so men are defended by their children, as it were with a bow and an arrow. Those who are without children are in a manner unarmed; for what else is it to be childless but to be solitary? It is no small gift of God for a man to be renewed in his posterity; for God then gives him new strength, that he who otherwise would straightaway decay, may begin as it were to live a second time.

The knowledge of this doctrine is highly useful. The fruitfulness even of the lower animals is expressly ascribed to God alone; and if he would have it to be accounted his benefit that kine, and sheep, and mares conceive, how inexcusable will be the impiety of men, if when he adorns them with the honourable title of fathers, they account this favour as nothing. It is also to be added, that unless men regard their children as the gift of God, they are careless and reluctant in providing for their support, just as on the other hand this knowledge contributes in a very eminent degree to encourage them in bringing up their offspring. Further, he who thus reflects upon the goodness of God in giving him children, will readily and with a settled mind look for the continuance of God's grace; and although he may have but a small inheritance to leave them, he will not be unduly careful on that account.

You will eat the fruit of your labor; blessings and prosperity will be yours. Here the prophet teaches us that we ought to form a different estimate of what happiness consists in, from that formed by the world, which makes a happy life to consist in ease, honours, and great wealth. He recalls God's servants to the practice of moderation, which almost all men refuse to exercise. How few are to be found who, were it left to their own choice, would desire to live by their own labour; yes, who would account it a single benefit to do so! No sooner is the name of happiness pronounced, than instantly every man breaks forth into the most extravagant ideas of what is necessary to it, so insatiable a gulf is the covetousness of the human heart. The prophet therefore bids the fearers of God be content with this one thing—with having the assurance that having God for their foster-father, they shall be suitably maintained by the labour of their own hands; just as it is said in Psalm 34:10, "The young lions do lack, and suffer hunger, but they that seek the Lord shall not lack any good thing." We must remember that the prophet does not speak of the highest blessedness, which consists not in meat and drink, nor is confined within the narrow bounds of this transitory life; but he assures God's believing people that even in this pilgrimage or earthly place of sojourn they shall enjoy a happy life, until he has at last brought us to eternal glory (1 Tim. 4:8).

The prophet, therefore, very properly reminds the faithful that they already receive some fruit of their integrity, when God gives them their food, makes them happy in their wives and children, and condescends to take care of their life. But his design in commending the present goodness of God is to animate them to hasten forward with alacrity on the path which leads to their eternal inheritance.

PSALM 129

But the LORD is righteous; he has cut me free from the cords of the wicked. Although God may seem to dissemble for a time, yet he never forgets his righteousness, so as to withhold relief from his afflicted people. Paul in like manner adduces the same reason why God will not always suffer them to be persecuted (2 Thess. 1:6–7)—"Seeing it is a righteous thing with God to recompense tribulation to them that trouble you; and to you who are troubled rest with us." ["God is just: he will pay back trouble to those who trouble you and give relief to you who are troubled, and to us as well."] It is a point worthy of special notice, that the welfare of the Church is inseparably connected with the righteousness of God. The prophet, also, wisely teaches us that the reason why the enemies of the Church did not prevail, was because God brought to nothing their enterprises, and did not suffer them to go beyond what he had determined in his own mind.

As the Psalmist has borrowed this illustration of his doctrine from the affairs of ordinary life, we are taught that whenever there is a hopeful prospect of a good harvest, we ought to beseech God, whose peculiar province it is to impart fertility to the earth, that he would give full effect to his blessing. And considering that the fruits of the earth are exposed to so many hazards, it is certainly strange that we are not stirred up to engage in the exercise of prayer from the absolute necessity of these to man and beast. Nor does the Psalmist, in speaking of passers-by blessing the reapers, speak exclusively of the children of God, who are truly taught by his word that the fruitfulness of the earth is owing to his goodness; but he also comprehends worldly men in whom the same knowledge is implanted naturally. In conclusion, provided we not only dwell in the Church of the Lord, but also labour to have a place among the number of her genuine citizens, we will be able to despise all the might of our enemies fearlessly; for although they may flourish and have a great outward show for a time, yet they are but barren grass, on which the curse of heaven rests.

PSALM 130

But with you there is forgiveness; therefore you are feared. It is, indeed, a matter which comes under our daily observation, that those who proceed not beyond the step of thinking themselves deserving of endless death, rush, like frenzied men, with great impetuosity against God. The better, therefore, to confirm himself and others, the prophet declares that God's mercy cannot be separated or torn away from himself. "As soon as I think upon you," he says in amount, "your clemency also presents itself to my mind, so that I have no doubt that you will be merciful to me, it being impossible for you to divest yourself of your own nature: the very fact that you are God is to me a sure guarantee that you will be merciful." At the same time let it be understood, that he does not here speak of a confused knowledge of it as enables the sinner to conclude with certainty, that as soon as he seeks God he shall find him ready to be reconciled towards him. It therefore not surprising that among the Papists there is no steady calling upon God, when we consider that, in consequence of their mingling their own merits, satisfactions, and worthy preparation—as they term it—with the grace of God, they continue always in suspense and doubt respecting their reconciliation with God. Thus it comes to pass, that by praying they only augment their own sorrows and torments, just as if a man should lay wood upon a fire already kindled. Whoever would reap profit from the exercise of prayer, must necessarily begin with free remission of sins. It is also proper to mark the final cause—as we say—for which God is inclined to forgive, and never comes forward without showing himself easy to be pacified towards those who serve him; which is the absolute necessity of this hope of obtaining forgiveness, to the existence of piety, and the worship of God in the world.

PSALM
131

My heart is not proud, O LORD. Here David teaches us a very useful lesson, and one by which we should be ruled in life: to be contented with the lot which God has marked out for us, to consider what he calls us to, and not to aim at fashioning our own lot; to be moderate in our desires, to avoid entering upon rash undertakings, and to confine ourselves cheerfully within our own sphere, instead of attempting great things. He denies that *his heart is proud,* for this is the true cause of all unwarranted rashness and presumption in conduct. Is it not pride that leads men, under the instigation of their passions, to dare such presumptuous flights, to hurry on recklessly in their course, and throw the whole world into confusion? Were this loftiness of spirit checked, the consequence would be, that all men would study moderation of conduct.

We see how God confounds the proud and boasted enterprises of the children of this world. They run the full course of their wild career, they turn the earth upside down at their pleasure, and put forth their hand in every direction; they are filled with complacency at the thought of their own talents and industry, and, in a moment, when all their plans have been fully formed, they are entirely overthrown, because there is no solidity in them. There are two different forms which the presumption of those takes who will not submit to the humble followers of God, but must needs run before him. Some rush forward with a reckless precipitancy, and seem as if they would build to the skies; others do not so openly exhibit the inordinateness of their desires, are slower in their movements, and cautiously calculate upon the future, and yet their presumption appears no less from the very fact, that, with a total oversight of God, as if heaven and earth were subject to them, they pass their decree as to what shall be done by them some ten or twenty years from now. These build, as it were, in the deep sea. But never shall it come to the surface, however extended may be the term of their lives; while those who, like David, submit themselves to God, keeping in their own sphere, moderate in their desires, will enjoy a life of tranquillity and assurance.

PSALM
132:1-11

He swore an oath to the LORD and made a vow to the Mighty One of Jacob. Until informed of the place of the Ark's destined residence, David was full of concern and anxiety, dwelling in his house, or when he lay upon his bed. As to the vow itself, this and other passages afford no ground for supposing, with the Papists, that God approves of whatever vows they may utter, without regard to the nature of them. To vow unto God that which he has himself declared to be agreeable to him, is a commendable practice; but it is too much presumption on our part to say that we will rush upon such vows as suit our carnal inclination. The great thing is that we consider what is agreeable to his will, otherwise we may be found depriving him of that wherein indeed his principal right lies, for with him "to obey is better than sacrifice" (1 Sam. 15:22).

Let us go to his dwelling place; let us worship at his footstool. On the one hand, it is a mere superstition to suppose God confined to the temple, and on the other hand, the external symbols are not without their use in the Church. In short, we should improve these as helps to our faith, but not rest in them. While God dwells in heaven, and is above all heavens, we must avail ourselves of helps in rising to the knowledge of him; and in giving us symbols of his presence, he sets, as it were, his feet upon the earth, and suffers us to touch them. It is thus that the Holy Spirit condescends for our profit, and in accommodation to our infirmity, raising our thoughts to heavenly and divine things by these worldly elements.

May your priests be clothed with righteousness. God is said to clothe us with his righteousness when he appears as our Saviour and help, defends us by his power, and shows in his government of us that we are the objects of his care. The *rejoicing* which is spoken of has reference to a life of happiness. The saints of God are called *merciful ones* because mercy and beneficence is that grace which assimilates us most to God.

PSALM 132:12-18

If your sons keep my covenant. We must remember, in the first place, that the covenant was perfectly gratuitous, so far as related to God's promise of sending a Saviour and Redeemer, because this stood connected with the original adoption of those to whom the promise was made, which was itself free. Indeed the treachery and rebellion of the nation did not prevent God from sending forth his Son, and this was a public proof that he was not influenced by the consideration of their good conduct. Hence Paul says (Rom. 3:3), "What if some did not believe? is therefore the truth of God of no effect?" intimating that God had not withdrawn his favour from the Jews, having chosen them freely of his grace. We know too, that notwithstanding their efforts, as if it had been of set purpose, to destroy the promises, God met their malicious opposition with displays of his marvellous love, made his truth and faithfulness to emerge in a most triumphant manner, and showed that he stood firm to his own purpose, independently of any merit of theirs. This may serve to show in what sense the covenant was not conditional; but as there were other things which were accessories to the covenant, a condition was appended, to the effect that God would bless them if they obeyed his commandments. The Jews, for declining from this obedience, were removed into exile.

God, on the one hand, took vengeance upon the people for their ingratitude, so as to show that the terms of the covenant did not run conditionally to no purpose; while on the other, at the coming of Christ there was a free performance of what had been freely promised, the crown being set upon Christ's head. The obedience which God demands is particularly stated to be the obedience of his covenant, to teach us that we must not serve him by human inventions, but confine ourselves within the prescription of his word.

How good it is when brothers live together in peace.* We have here clear proof that David holds all true union among brothers to take its rise from God, and to have this for its legitimate object: that all may be brought to worship God in purity, and call upon his name with one consent. Would the similitude have been borrowed from holy ointment if it had not been to denote that religion must always hold the first place? Any concord, it is thus insinuated, which may prevail amongst men, is insipid, if not pervaded by a sweet savour of God's worship. We maintain, therefore, that men are to be united amongst themselves in mutual affection, with this as the great end, that they may be placed together under the government of God.

It is as if the dew of Hermon were falling on Mount Zion. A holy unity has not only a sweet savour before God, but is productive of good effects, as the dew moistens the earth and supplies it with sap and freshness. Moses, we know, said of Judea, that it was not like Egypt, fertilised by the overflowing of its river, but such as drank daily of the rain of heaven (Deut. 11:11). David suggests, that the life of man would be sapless, unprofitable, and wretched, unless sustained by brotherly harmony.

For there the LORD bestows his blessing, even life forevermore. David adds in the close, that God commands his blessing where peace is culti-vated; by which is meant, that he testifies how much he is pleased with concord amongst men, by showering down blessing upon them. The same sentiment is expressed by Paul in other words (2 Cor. 13:11; Phil. 4:9), "Live in peace, and the God of peace shall be with you." Let us then, as much as lies in us, study to walk in brotherly love, that we may secure the divine blessing. Let us even stretch out our arms to those who differ from us, desiring to bid them welcome if they will but return to the unity of the faith. Do they refuse? Then let them go. The only brother-hood that can be recognised, is that amongst the children of God.

PSALM 134

Bless the Lord, all the servants of the LORD, *who stand at night in the house of the Lord.** Many of the Levites, through the tendency which there is in all men to abuse ceremonies, considered that nothing more was necessary than standing idly in the Temple, and thus overlooked the principal part of their duty. The Psalmist would show that merely to keep nightly watch over the Temple: kindle the lamps, and superintend the sacrifices, was of no importance, unless they served God spiritually, and referred all outward ceremonies to that which must be considered the main sacrifice: the celebration of God's praises. You may think it a very laborious service, as if he had said, to stand at watch in the Temple, while others sleep in their own houses; but the worship which God requires is something more excellent than this, and demands of you to sing his praises before all the people.

May the LORD, *the Maker of heaven and earth, bless you from Zion.* Express mention is intentionally made of two things, which are in themselves distinct, when the God who blessed them out of Zion is said to be also the Creator of heaven and earth. Mention is made of his title as *Creator* to set forth his power, and convince believers there is nothing that may not be hoped from God. For what is the world but a mirror in which we see his boundless power? And those must be senseless persons indeed, that are not satisfied with the favour of him who is recognised by them as having all dominion and all riches in his hand. Since many, however, are inclined, when they hear God spoken of as Creator, to conceive of him as standing at a distance from them, and doubt their access to him, the Psalmist makes mention also of that which was a symbol of God's nearness to his people—and this that they might be encouraged to approach him with the freedom and unrestrained confidence of persons who are invited to come to the bosom of a Father. By looking to the heavens then, they were to discover the power of God—by looking to Zion, his dwelling-place, they were to recognise his fatherly love.

*I know that the LORD is great, and our God above all gods.** We have here a general description of the power of God, to show the Israelites that the God they worshipped was the same who made the world, and rules over all according to his will, neither is there any other besides him. He would not exclude others when he speaks of having known himself the greatness of God, but is rather to be considered as taking occasion from his own experience to stir up men generally to attend to this subject, and awake to the recognition of what lies abundantly open to observation. The immensity of God is what none can comprehend; still his glory, so far as was seen fit, has been sufficiently manifested, to leave all the world without excuse for ignorance. How can one who has enjoyed a sight of the heavens and of the earth shut his eyes so as to overlook the Author of them without sin of the deepest dye? It is with the view, then, of stirring us up more effectually,—that the Psalmist makes reference to himself in inviting us to the knowledge of God's glory; or rather he reprehends our carelessness in not being alive enough to the consideration of it.

Your name, O LORD, endures forever. The displeasure of God towards his people is but temporary, and, in taking vengeance upon their sins, he remembers mercy in the midst of wrath, as Habakkuk says (3:2). Thus God is spoken of as man, manifesting a father's affection, and restoring his children, who deserved to have been cast off, because he cannot bear that the fruit of his own body should be torn from him. Such is the sense of the passage—that God has a compassion for his people because they are his children, that he would not willingly be bereaved of them, and left childless, that he is placable towards them, as being dear to him, and that having recognised them as his offspring, he cherishes them with a tender love.

PSALM
136

*Praise God, for he is good, for his mercy endures forever.** Men may not deny the divine goodness to be the source and fountain of all their blessings, but the graciousness of his bounty is far from being fully and sincerely recognised, though the greatest stress is laid upon it in Scripture. Paul in speaking of it (Rom. 3:23), calls it emphatically by the general terms of the glory of God, intimating, that while God should be praised for all his works, it is his mercy principally that we should glorify. It is evident from what we read in sacred history, that it was customary for the Levites, according to the regulation laid down by David for conducting the praises of God, to sing by response, "for his mercy endures forever."

Who remembered us in our low estate. The Psalmist represents every age as affording displays of the same goodness as had been shown to their fathers, since God had never failed to help his people by a continued succession of deliverances. It was a more notable proof of his mercy to interpose for the nation at a time when it was nearly overwhelmed by calamities, than to preserve it in its entire state and under a more even course of affairs, there being something in the emergency to awaken attention and arrest the view. Besides, in all the deliverances which God grants his people, there is an accompanying remission of their sins.

In the close he speaks of the paternal providence of God as extending not only to all mankind, but to every living creature, suggesting that we have no reason to feel surprise at his sustaining the character of a kind and provident father to his own people, when he condescends to care for the cattle, and the asses of the field, and the crow, and the sparrow. Men are much the better than brute beasts, and there is a great difference between some men and others, though not in merit, yet as regards the privilege of the divine adoption, and the Psalmist is to be considered as reasoning from the less to the greater, and enhancing the incomparably superior mercy which God shows to his own children.

How shall we sing the LORD's song in a foreign land?* The Babylonians abstained from their songs, as from their legal sacrifices, because the land where they now were, was polluted. The Chaldeans thought the Jews were bound down permanently to this place of their exile. The Psalmist, when he calls it a *foreign land*, suggests that it was but the place of their temporary stay. In our own day under the Papacy, great as the danger may be to which the faithful expose themselves by not conforming to the example around them, the Holy Spirit makes use of such a barrier as this to separate them from sinful compliances. To those, whether Frenchmen, Englishmen, or Italians, who love and practise the true religion, even their native country is a foreign clime when they live under that tyranny. And yet there is a distinction between us and God's ancient people, for at that time the worship of God was confined to one place, but now he has his Temple wherever two or three are met together in Christ's name, if they separate themselves from all idolatrous profession, and maintain purity of divine worship. The Psalmist by the language which he employs would by no means put down every attempt on their part to celebrate God's praises. He rather exhorts them under their affliction to wait with patience till the liberty of publicly worshipping God was restored, saying upon the matter: We have been bereft of our Temple and sacrifices, we wander as exiles in a polluted land, and what remains but that in remembrance of our outcast state we should sigh and groan for the promised deliverance.

If the divine promises inspire us with hope and confidence, and God's Spirit attemper our afflictions to the rule of his own uprightness, we shall lift up our heads in the lowest depths of affliction to which we may be cast down, and glory in the fact that it is well with us in our worst distresses, and that our enemies are devoted to destruction.

PSALM 138

The LORD will fulfill his purpose for me; your love, O LORD, endures forever—do not abandon the works of your hands. Having once been delivered by an act of Divine mercy, David concludes that what had been done would be perfected, as God's nature is unchangeable, and he cannot divest himself of that goodness which belongs to him. There can be no doubt that the way to maintain good hope in danger is to fix our eyes upon the Divine goodness on which our deliverance rests. God is under no obligation on his part, but when, of his mere good pleasure, he promises to interest himself in our behalf. Men may leave off a work for very slight reasons which they foolishly undertook from the first, and from which they may have been diverted through their inconstancy, or they may be forced to give up through inability what they enterprised above their strength; but nothing of this kind can happen with God, and, therefore, we have no occasion to apprehend that our hopes will be disappointed in their course towards fulfilment. Nothing but sin and ingratitude on our part interrupts the continued and unvarying tenor of the Divine goodness. What we firmly apprehend by our faith, God will never take from us, or allow to pass out of our hands. When he declares that God perfects the salvation of his people, David would not encourage sloth, but strengthen his faith and quicken himself to the exercise of prayer. What is the cause of that anxiety and fear which are felt by the godly, but the consciousness for their own weakness and entire dependence upon God? At the same time they rely with full certainty upon the grace of God, "being confident," as Paul writes to the Philippians, "that he who has begun the good work will perform it till the end" (Phil. 1:6). The use to be made of the doctrine is, to remember, when we fall or are disposed to waver in our minds, that since God has wrought the beginning of our salvation in us, he will carry it forward to its termination. Accordingly, we should betake ourselves to prayer, that we may not, through our own indolence, bar our access to that continuous stream of the divine goodness which flows from a fountain that is enexhaustible.

PSALM 139:1-10

Before a word is on my tongue you know it completely, O LORD. The words admit a double meaning. They imply that God knows what we are about to say before the words are formed on our tongue; and also, that though we speak not a word, and try by silence to conceal our secret intentions, we cannot elude his notice. The idea meant to be conveyed is, that while the tongue is the index of thought to man, being the great medium of communication, God, who knows the heart, is independent of words. The innermost recesses of our spirit stand present to his view.

Such knowledge is too wonderful for me, too lofty for me to attain. It is foolish to measure God's knowledge by our own, when his knowledge rises prodigiously above us. Many when they hear God spoken of, conceive of him as like unto themselves, and such presumption is most condemnable. Very commonly they will not allow his knowledge to be greater than what comes up to their own apprehensions of things. David, on the contrary, confesses it to be beyond his comprehension, virtually declaring that words could not express this truth of the absoluteness with which all things stand patent to the eye of God, this being a knowledge having neither bound nor measure, so that he could only contemplate the extent of it with conscious imbecility.

Where can I go from your Spirit? Where can I flee from your presence? By the *Spirit of God* we are not here, as in several other parts of Scripture, to conceive of his power merely, but his understanding and knowledge. In man the spirit is the seat of intelligence, and so it is here in reference of God. David means in short that he could not change from one place to another without God seeing him, and following him with his eyes as he moved.

Even there your hand will guide me, your right hand will hold me fast. Though one should fly with the speed of light, he could find no recess where he would be beyond the reach of divine power. For by *hand* we are to understand power, and the assertion is to the effect that should man attempt to withdraw from the observation of God, it were easy for him to arrest and draw back the fugitive.

PSALM 139:11-16

If I say, "Surely the darkness will hide me and the light become night around me," even the darkness will not be dark to you; the night will shine like the day, for darkness is as light to you. If anyone should think it a very unnecessary observation to say that as respects God there is no difference between light and darkness, it is enough to remind him that all observation proves with what reluctance and extreme difficulty men are brought to come forward openly and unreservedly into God's presence. In words we all grant that God is omniscient; meanwhile what none would ever think of controverting we secretly make no account of whatsoever, in so far as we make no scruple of mocking God, and lack even that reverence of him which we extend to one of our fellow-creatures. We are ashamed to let men know and witness our delinquincies; but we are as indifferent to what God may think of us, as if our sins were covered and veiled from his inspection. This infatuation, if not sharply reproved, will soon change light, so far as we are concerned, into darkness, and therefore David insists upon the subject at length in order to refute our false apprehensions.

For you created my inmost being; you knit me together in my mother's womb. David represents God as sitting king in the very reins of man, as the centre of his jurisdiction, and shows it ought to be no ground of wonder that all the windings and recesses of our hearts are known to him who, when we were inclosed in our mother's womb, saw us as clearly and perfectly as if we had stood before him in the light of midday.

My frame was not hidden from you when I was made in the secret place. David no doubt means figuratively to express the inconceivable skill which appears in the formation of the human body. When we examine it, even to the nails of our fingers, there is nothing which could be altered, without felt inconveniency, as at something disjointed or put out of place; and what, then, if we should make the individual parts the subject of enumeration? Where is the embroiderer who, with all his industry and ingenuity, could execute the hundredth part of this complicated and diversified structure? We need not then wonder if God, who formed man so perfectly in the womb, should have an exact knowledge of him after he is ushered into the world.

When I awake, I am still with you. We are here put in possession of the true meaning of David, to the effect that God's providential government of the world is such that nothing can escape him, not even the profoundest thoughts. And although many precipitate themselves in an infatuated manner into all excess of crime, under the idea that God will never discover them, it is in vain that they resort to hiding-places, from which, however reluctantly, they must be dragged to light. The truth is one which we would do well to consider more than we do, for while we may cast a glance at our hands and our feet, and occasionally survey the elegance of our shape with complacency, there is scarcely one in a hundred who thinks of his Maker. Or if any recognise their life as coming from God, there is none at least who rises to the great truth that he who formed the ear, and the eye, and the understanding heart, himself hears, and sees and knows everything.

Search me, O God, and know my heart; test me and know my anxious thoughts. See if there is any offensive way in me, and lead me in the way ever-lasting. David insists upon this as being the only cause why he opposed the despisers of God, that he himself was a genuine worshipper of God, and desired others to possess the same character. It indicates no common confidence that he should submit himself so boldly to the judgment of God. But being fully conscious of sincerity in his religion, it was not without due consideration that he placed himself so confidently before God's bar; neither must we think that he claims to be free from all sin, for he groaned under the felt burden of his transgressions. The saints in all that they say of their integrity still depend only upon free grace. Yet persuaded as they are that their godliness is approved before God, notwithstanding their falls and infirmities, we need not wonder that they feel themselves at freedom to draw a distinction between themselves and the wicked. While he denies that his heart was double or insincere, he does not profess exemption from all sin, but only that he was not de-voted to wickedness.

PSALM 140

O LORD, I say to you, "You are my God." Hear, O LORD, my cry for mercy. In these words David shows that his prayers were not merely those of the lips, as hypocrites will make loud appeals to God for mere appearance sake, but that he prayed with earnestness, and from a hidden principle of faith. Till we have a persuasion of being saved through the grace of God there can be no sincere prayer. We have here an exellent illustration of the nature of faith, in the Psalmist's turning himself away from man's view, that he may address God apart, hypocrisy being excluded in this internal exercise of the heart. This is true prayer—not the mere idle lifting up of the voice, but the presentation of our petitions from an inward principle of faith. To beget in himself persuasion of his obtaining his present requests from God, he recalls to his mind what deliverances God had already extended to him. He speaks of his having been to him as a shield in every time of danger. Some read the words in the future tense: "who will shield my head in the day of battle." But it is evident that David speaks of protection formerly experienced from the hand of God, and from this derives comfort to his faith. He comes forth, not as a raw and undisciplined recruit, but as a soldier well tried in previous engagements.

I know that the LORD secures justice for the poor and upholds the cause of the needy. There can be no question that David here seals or corroborates his prayer by turning his thoughts and discourse to the providential judgments of God, for doubtful prayer is no prayer at all. He declares it to be a thing known and ascertained that God cannot but deliver the afflicted. As he may connive for a time, however, and suffer good and upright persons to be grievously tried, David suggests as a consideration which may meet this temptation, that God does so advisedly, that he may relieve those who are in affliction, and recover those who are oppressed.

Set a guard over my mouth, O LORD; keep watch over the door of my lips. Even persons of the most self-possessed temper, if unwarrantably injured, will sometimes proceed to make retaliation, through their resenting the unbecoming conduct of their enemies. In committing himself to the guidance of God, both as to thoughts and words, David acknowledges the need of the influence of the Spirit for the regulation of his tongue and of his mind, particularly when tempted to be exasperated by the insolence of opposition. If, on the one hand, the tongue be liable to slip and too fast of utterance, unless continually watched and guarded by God; on the other, there are disorderly affections of an inward kind which require to be restrained. What a busy workshop is the heart of man, and what a host of devices is there manufactured every moment! If God do not watch over our heart and tongue, there will confessedly be no bounds to words and thoughts of a sinful kind,—so rare a gift of the Spirit is moderation in language, while Satan is ever making suggestions which will be readily and easily complied with, unless God prevent. It need not seem absurd to speak of God inclining our hearts to evil, since these are in his hand, to turn them wheresoever he wills at his pleasure. Not that he himself prompts them to evil desires, but as according to his secret judgments he surrenders and effectually gives over the wicked to Satan's tyranny, he is properly said to blind and harden them. The blame of their sins rests with men themselves, and the lust which is in them; and, as they are carried out to good or evil by a natural desire, it is not from any external impulse that they incline to what is evil, but spontaneously and of their own corruption.

PSALM 142

I cry aloud to the LORD. . . . *before him I tell my trouble.* While David did not give way before men to loud and sense-less lamentations, neither did he suffer himself to be tor-mented with inward and suppressed cares, but made known his griefs with unsuspecting confidence to the Lord.

When my spirit grows faint within me, it is you who know my way. Though he owns here that he felt anxiety, yet he confirms what he had said as to the constancy of his faith. The figure which he uses of his spirit being *faint,* aptly repre-sents the state of the mind in alternating between various resolutions when there was no apparent outgate from danger, and increasing its distress by resorting to all kinds of devices. He adds, that though there was no apparent way of safety, God knew from the begin-ning in what way his deliverance should be effected. We are taught that when we have tried every remedy and know not what to do, to rest sat-isfied with the conviction that God is acquainted with our afflictions, and condesends to care for us, as Abraham said: "The Lord will provide" (Gen. 22:8).

Look to my right and see; no one is concerned for me. I have no refuge; no one cares for my life. David shows that there was good cause for the dreadful sufferings he experienced, since no human aid or comfort was to be expected, and destruction seemed inevitable. When he speaks of hav-ing looked and yet not perceived a friend amongst men, he does not mean that he had turned his thoughts to earthly helps in forgetfulness of God, but that he had made such inquiry as was warrantable after one on the earth who might assist him. Had any person of the kind presented himself, he would no doubt have recognised him as an instrument in the hand of God's mercy, but it was God's purpose that he should be aban-doned of all assistance from man, and that his deliverance from destruc-tion should thus appear more extraordinary.

Do not bring your servant into judgment, for no one living is righteous before you. David here declares that there is none amongst men who could be just before God were he called to plead his cause. The passage is one fraught with much instruction, teaching us that God can only show favour to us in our approaches by throwing aside the character of a judge, and reconciling us to himself in a gratuitous remission of our sins. All human righteousness, accordingly, go for nothing, when we come to his tribunal. In order to obtain a proper view of the whole matter, we are first to note what is meant by being justified. The passage before us clearly proves that the man who is justified, is he who is judged and reckoned just before God, and can only be absolved in the way of acknowledging they might justly be condemned. Had perfection been a thing to be found in the world, he certainly of all others was the man who might justly have boasted of it; and the righteousness of Abraham and the holy fathers was not unknown to him; but he spares neither them nor himself, but lays it down as the one universal rule of conciliating God, that we must cast ourselves upon his mercy.

There is nothing intermediate between these two things, which are represented in Scripture as opposites: being justified by faith and justified by works. It is absurd for the Papists to invent a third species of righteousness, which is partly wrought out by works of their own, and partly imputed to them by God in his mercy. Without all doubt, when he affirmed that no man could stand before God were his works brought to judgment, David had no idea of this complex or twofold righteousness, but would shut us up at once to the conclusion that God is only favourable upon the ground of his mercy, since any reputed righteousness of man has no significancy before him.

PSALM 144

To the One who gives victory to kings. While God preserves all men without exception, his care is peculiarly extended to the maintenance of political order, which is the foundation of the common safety of all. It is in effect as if he called him the guardian and defender of kingdoms; for as the very mention of government is an odious thing, and none willingly obeys another, and nothing is more contrary to natural inclination than servitude, men would seek to throw off the yoke, and subvert the thrones of kings, were these not hedged round by a hidden divine presidency. David, however, distinguishes himself from other kings, as elsewhere he is called "the first-born of kings" (Ps. 90:27); at least he speaks of the goodness of God as having been pre-eminently shown to him, representing himself as holding the highest place, on account of the holy anointing which had been more eminently bestowed upon him. As a title of distinction, he claims the special name of *God's servant;* for although all kings are God's servants, and Cyrus has the name applied to him by Isaiah emphatically (45:1), yet as no heathen prince ever recognised himself as called of God, and David alone of all others in the world was invested with legitimate authority, and had a warrant to reign which faith could rest upon with certainty, it was not without reason that this mark of distinction is applied to him.

Blessed are the people whose God is the LORD. The kind providence of God in not suffering us to want any of the means of life is surely a striking illustration of his wonderful love. What more desirable than to be the objects of God's care, especially if we have sufficient understanding to conclude from the liberality with which he supports us that he is our Father? For everything is to be viewed with a reference to this point. Better it were at once to perish for want than have a mere brute satisfaction, and forget the main thing of all, that they only are happy whom God has chosen for his people.

Day 361 DECEMBER 26

The LORD is gracious and compassionate, slow to anger and rich in love. The closer a person feels himself drawn to God, the more has he advanced in the knowledge of him. If it be true that God is not only willing to befriend us, but is spoken of as touched with sympathy for our miseries, so as to be all the kinder to us the more that we are miserable, what folly were it not to flee to him without delay? But as we drive God's goodness away from us by our sins, and block up the way of access, unless his goodness overcome this obstacle, it would be in vain that the prophets spoke of his grace and mercy.

The LORD is good to all; he has compassion on all he has made. Not only does God, with fatherly indulgence and clemency, forgive sin, but is good to all without discrimination, as he makes his sun to rise upon the good and upon the wicked (Matt. 5:45). Forgiveness of sin is a treasure from which the wicked are excluded, but their sin and depravity do not prevent God from showering down his goodness upon them, which they appropriate without being at all sensible of it. Meanwhile believers, and they only, know what it is to enjoy a reconciled God, as elsewhere it is said: "Those who look to him are radiant; their faces are never covered with shame. Taste and see that the Lord is good" (Ps. 34:5, 8).

The eyes of all look to you, and you give them their food at the proper time. The food David notices as given in its season; for here also we are to notice the admirable arrangements of divine providence, that there is a certain time appointed for harvest, vintage, and hay crop, and that the year is so divided into intervals, that the cattle are fed at one time upon grass, at another on hay, or straw, or acorns, or other products of the earth. Were the whole supply poured forth at one and the same moment, it could not be gathered together so conveniently; and we have no small reason to admire the seasonableness with which the different kinds of fruit and aliment are yearly produced.

PSALM 146

Do not put your trust in princes, in mortal men, who cannot save. When their spirit departs, they return to the ground. This he explains more fully in the verse which follows, where he tells us how short and fleeting the life of man is. Though God throw loose the reins, and suffer princes even to invade heaven in the wildest enterprises, the passing of the spirit, like a breath, suddenly overthrows all their counsels and plans. The body being the dwelling-place of the soul, what is here said may very well be so understood; for at death God recalls the spirit. We may understand it more simply, however, of the vital breath; and this will answer better with the context, that as soon as man has ceased to breathe, his corpse is subject to putrefaction. It follows, that those who put their trust in men, depend upon a fleeting breath.

On that very day their plans come to nothing. Under this expression David censures the madness of princes in setting no bounds to their hopes and desires, and sealing the very heavens in their ambition, like the insane Alexander of Macedon, who, upon hearing that there were other worlds, wept that he had not yet conquered one, although soon after the funeral urn sufficed him. Observation itself proves that the schemes of princes are deep and complicated. That we may not fall, therefore, into the error of connecting our hopes with them, David says that the life of princes also passes away swiftly and in a moment, and that with it all their plans vanish.

Blessed is he whose help is the God of Jacob. David does not restrict the happiness of believers to present sense, as if they were only happy when God openly and in outward acts appeared as their helper, but he places their happiness in this, that they are truly persuaded of its being entirely by the grace of God they stand. He calls him *the God of Jacob,* to distinguish him from the multitude of false gods in which unbelievers gloried at that time; and there was good reason for this; for while all purpose to themselves to seek God, few take the right way.

PSALM 147

The LORD builds up Jerusalem. It was not the Psalmist's object directly to celebrate the free mercy of God in the first institution of the Church, but to argue from its original, that God would not suffer his Church altogether to fall, having once founded it with the design of preserving it forever; for he forsakes not the work of his own hands. This comfort ought to be improved by ourselves at the present period, when we see the Church on every side so miserably rent asunder, leading us to hope that all the elect who have been adjoined to Christ's body, will be gathered unto the unity of the faith, although now scattered like members torn from one another, and that the mutilated body of the Church, which is daily distracted, will be restored to its entireness, for God will not suffer his work to fail.

He sends his command to the earth; his word runs swiftly. When once God has intimated his will, all things concur to carry it into effect. That man has little discernment who, in the sudden snows and hoar-frosts, does not perceive how quickly the word of God runs. If we would avoid a senseless natural philosophy, we must always start with this principle, that everything in nature depends upon the will of God, and that the whole course of nature is only the prompt carrying into effect of his orders. When the waters congeal, when the hail spreads through the air, and hoar-frosts darken the sky, surely we have proof how effectual his word is. But if all these wonders produce no effect upon most men, at least the piercing cold which benumbs our bodies, should force us to recognise the power of God. When the heat of the sun scorches us in summer, and again, upon the succession of winter, all things are bound up, such a change as this, which must have appeared incredible, had we not been accustomed to it, cries out loudly that there is a being who reigns above.

PSALM 148

Let them praise the name of the LORD, for his name alone is exalted; his splendor is above the earth and the heavens. He has raised up for his people a horn, the praise of all his saints, of Israel, the people close to his heart. Praise the LORD. As we saw in the former psalm, that the perfections of God are to be seen more conspicuously in the Church than in the constitution of the world at large, the Psalmist has added this sentence, as to the Church being protected by the divine hand, and armed with a power against all enemies which secures its safety in every danger. By *the horn* is meant strength and dignity. Accordingly the Psalmist means that God's blessing is apparent in his Church and among his chosen people, inasmuch as it only flourishes and is powerful through his strength. There is a tacit comparison implied between the Church of God and other hostile powers, for it needs divine guardianship as being exposed on all sides to attack.

*Praise is to all the merciful ones of God,** for they have ground given them in the singular goodness of his condescension both for self-congratulation and praise. In calling the children of Israel *a people near unto God,* he reminds them of the gracious covenant which God made with Abraham. For how came the nearness, except in the way of God's preferring an unknown despised stranger to all nations? Nor are we to seek the cause of the distinction elsewhere than in the mere love of God. Though all the world equally belongs to God, he graciously discovered himself to the children of Israel, and brought them near to him, strangers as they were from God, even as are the whole race of Adam. Hence the words of Moses: "When the Most High divided to the nations their inheritance, and distributed the peoples, he stretched forth his line to Jacob" (Deut. 32:8). He is to be considered, therefore, as pointing out the cause why God has extended such signal blessings to a single people, and a people poor and despised: his adoption of them to himself.

Day 365 D E C E M B E R 3 0

May the praise of God be in their mouths and a double-edged sword in their hands, to inflict vengeance on the nations and punishment on the peoples. God's children may not execute vengeance but when called to it, there being an end of all moderation when men yield themselves up to the impulse of their own spirits. The doctrine laid down in the passage admits of being rightly applied to our practice, in this way, that what is here said of the two-edged sword, applies more especially to the Jews, and not properly to us, who have not a power of this kind permitted; except, indeed, that rulers and magistrates are vested by God with the sword to punish all manner of violence; but this is something peculiar to their office. As to the Church collective, the sword now put into our hand is of another kind, that of the word and spirit, that we may slay for a sacrifice to God those who formerly were enemies, or again deliver them over to everlasting destruction unless they repent (Eph. 6:17). For what Isaiah predicted of Christ extends to all who are his members: "He shall smite the wicked with the word of his mouth, and shall slay them with the breath of his lips" (Isa. 11:4). If believers quietly confine themselves within these limits of their calling, they will find that the promise of vengeance upon their enemies has not been given them in vain. For when God calls us to judgment written, he puts a restraint both upon our spirits and actions, so as that we must not attempt what he has not commanded.

This is the glory of all his saints. Here the Psalmist not only exhorts to the practice of piety, but gives us a support for our encouragement, lest we should think that we might be losers by exercising mercy and patience, as most men give vent to fury and rage, under the idea that the only way to defend their life is by showing the savageness of wolves. Although God's people, therefore, having nothing of the strength of the giant, and will not move a finger without divine permission, and have a calm spirit, the Psalmist declares, that they have an honourable and splendid issue out of all their troubles.

PSALM 150

Praise him with the sounding of the trumpet. It will not be insisted upon of the words in the Hebrew signifying the musical instruments; only let the reader remember that sundry different kinds are here mentioned, which were in use under the legal economy, the more forcibly to teach the children of God that they cannot apply themselves too diligently to the praises of God—as if he would enjoin them strenuously to bring to this service all their powers, and devote themselves wholly to it. Nor was it without reason that God under the law, enjoined this multiplicity of songs, that he might lead men away from those vain and corrupt pleasures to which they are excessively addicted, to a holy and profitable joy. Our corrupt nature indulges in extraordinary liberties, many devising methods of gratification which are preposterous, while their highest satisfaction lies in suppressing all thoughts of God. This perverse disposition could only be corrected in the way of God's retaining a weak and ignorant people under many restraints, and constant exercises. The Psalmist, therefore, in exhorting believers to pour forth all their joy in the praises of God, enumerates, one upon another, all the musical instruments which were then in use, and reminds them that they ought all to be consecratated to the worship of God.

Let everything that has breath praise the LORD. We may very well suppose that the words have reference here to men, who, although they have vital breath in common with the brute creation, obtain by way of distinction the name of breathing, as of living creatures. As yet the Psalmist has addressed himself in his exhortations to the people who were conversant with the ceremonies under the law, now he turns to men in general, tacitly intimating that a time was coming when the same songs, which were then only heard in Judea, would resound in every quarter of the globe. And in this prediction we have been joined in the same symphony with the Jews, that we may worship God with constant sacrifices of praise, until being gathered into the kingdom of heaven, we sing with elect angels an eternal hallelujah.